THE INTIMATE OTHER

The Intimate Other
Love Divine in Indic Religions

Edited by
ANNA S. KING
JOHN BROCKINGTON

Orient Longman

ORIENT LONGMAN PRIVATE LIMITED

Registered Office
3-6-752 Himayatnagar, Hyderabad 500 029 (A.P.), India
e-mail: hyd2_orlongco@sancharnet.in

Other Offices
Bangalore, Bhopal, Bhubaneshwar, Chennai, Ernakulam,
Guwahati, Hyderabad, Kolkata, Lucknow, Mumbai,
New Delhi, Patna, Pune

© Orient Longman Private Limited 2005
First Published 2005

ISBN 81 250 2801 3

Typeset in 11/14 pt. Adobe Garamond

Typeset by
Scribe Consultants
New Delhi

Printed in India at
Chaman Enterprises
New Delhi

Published by
Orient Longman Private Limited
1/24 Asaf Ali Road
New Delhi 110 002
e-mail: olldel@del6.vsnl.net.in

Julia Leslie
1948–2004

We offer this book as a celebration of the life and work of Dr. Julia Leslie, Reader in Hindu Studies, founder and chair of the Centre for Gender and Religions Research at SOAS, brilliant Sanskritist, inspirational teacher, colleague and friend.

Tamal Krishna Goswami
1946–2002

We also lovingly dedicate The Intimate Other to the joyful memory of Tamal Krishna Goswami, guru, scholar and devotee, who not only lived a life in bhakti and for bhakti but died in bhakti.

Contents

CHAPTER ONE

Introduction

ANNA S. KING

This book arises from the sixth international conference of the Dharam Hinduja Institute of Indic Religions (DHIIR), University of Cambridge, which was established on 1 January 1995. The aim of the Institute is to study Indic traditions in an interdisciplinary context. Perhaps the most characteristic feature of the DHIIR is that it requires research to be of contemporary practical relevance and to be open and accessible to the public. Its conferences have offered spaces where professional Indologists encounter and engage each other, but perhaps more importantly where the audience talks and academics listen. 'Devotion in the Indian Tradition' held in 2000 at the Divinity Faculty of University of Cambridge proved to be one of the most popular DHIIR conferences. It was crowded with international academics, research students and interested participants from many countries, all major Indic religious traditions and all walks of life. Debates and workshops were sometimes lyrical, often impassioned and illuminatingly disputatious.

The organisers of this conference were drawn from the Ritual and Devotion Research Group chaired by the convenor, Professor John Brockington of Edinburgh University, and supported particularly by Dr Elizabeth de Michaelis, Professor Gavin Flood and Dr Anna King. They agreed after much discussion that the category 'Indic traditions' should be interpreted inclusively and that contributions on the arts, particularly devotional poetry and music, would be welcome. The conference topic of devotion was regarded as an opportunity to explore the dominating spiritual path of Indians today, both in India and among diasporic communities. The organisers also wanted to bring together those with personal devotion to particular gods, *gurus* or sacred texts, and those whose religious traditions have historically qualified, disclaimed or even contested such devotion. The dialogic nature of the workshops enabled participants to engage across boundaries of religion, country and community, and gave devotees voices within an academic setting. The agenda was often set by practitioners. The decision to publish some of the papers followed, and the editors in keeping with the mission statement of the DHIIR agreed that the publication should be multidisciplinary and directed at a much wider readership than would be usual in academic contexts. It was extraordinarily difficult to choose from among wide-ranging topics. However, we hope that this publication as it now stands, embraces many of the themes and questions opened up in debate.

Devotion is the dominant form of Hinduism today. It is one of the three paths or disciplines (*margas* or *yogas*) which lead to spiritual fulfilment or eternal bliss. Some Hindus consider that each path requires exclusive concentration and is sufficient for liberation in itself. There are also religious schools and texts which proclaim one path to be superior to another. However, many Hindu teachers have taught a *yoga* of synthesis, arguing that the disciplines are essentially linked and non-different, and that liberating knowledge may be obtained through all. We find, for example, that contemporary *gurus* often identify passionate love of God with the active expression of that love in the world.[1]

Bhakti enables human beings to obtain liberation whilst still living in the world. While the renouncer conquers or suppresses ego and egotistical desire by breaking away from society and its multiple bonds, the *bhakta* seeks to overcome self by losing himself or herself in the love and imitation of God. For many Hindu Bhakti theologians existence in the world has positive value, and *moksha* may be perceived less as an escape from the world than as the bliss experienced here and now in all-consuming and passionate service to a personal Lord. God is worshipped as alive, present and embodied on earth.

Deities like Krishna, Shiva, Vishnu and Rama, and various forms of Devi manifest in the world, respond to devotion with saving grace and are worshipped in various relational modes: as a servant, as a friend, as a mother, as a child, or in the passionate desire of a beloved for her lover. The lovers Krishna and Radha serve as divine models for the mutual love of God and devotee. Theirs is a love which shows itself in extremity of emotion, in ecstasy and intense longing, in despair and desperation at separation (*viraha*). Direct experience of Krishna is understood as ultimate bliss. Hardy points out that Krishna and Radha, as eternal lovers, are both separate and one. In the same way human beings are separated from the divine:

> Built into the world is a sense of yearning, of longing. But this is where man's religious chance lies. If he opens himself, like a sensitive 'connoisseur', to this sense of yearning and 'separation' and cultivates it within his heart, *rasa* is triggered off within him. But it is more than merely an 'aesthetic' experience: it is religious ecstasy (thus called *bhakti-rasa*). (1994: 518)

This kind of ecstasy and love-in-separation has infused much of Hindu and indeed Indian culture with a culturally sophisticated understanding of erotic love. Powerful deities like Shiva and Kali may demand a different kind of trust, an acceptance of divine destructiveness as well as of divine creativity, but even then devotees claim to find bliss and fulfilment in their love.

Divine presence and playfulness in the world thus releases vast human energies and creativity. Streams of literature and poetry, music and song, flow from its devotional impulse. In this sense *bhakti* seems unarguably dualistic, but it also exists within monistic systems as the path leading to realisation and the insight of non-dualism. *Bhakti* has a place in Shankara's Vedanta. In the non-dualistic Shaivism of Kashmir, devotion to Shiva leads to the understanding that subject and object are coterminous and that *bhakti* is liberation which is knowledge of the non-dual Shiva. If *bhakti* in a monistic context appears paradoxical, scholars have equally pointed to the paradox of conceptualising the divine anthropomorphically. God is the intimate other. There are creative tensions between the God's immanence and his or her transcendence and between the devotee's feelings of intimacy and otherness. These provide major themes that weave throughout Indian devotional literature.

Devotees who follow the path of *bhakti* often claim that while *jnana* (knowledge) is a hard path, accessible only to a religious elite, *bhakti marga* in contrast is open to all without distinction of race, sex or caste. Scholars have on the whole operated with more suspicion, observing that while *bhakti* and Bhakti movements have brought with them a liberating release from caste or gender constraints for religious practice; they have often continued in practice to uphold the institution of *varnashrama dharma* and to elevate *stri dharma* (see Sherma 2000: 29). The Bhagavad Gita's appropriation of *bhakti* for example can be turned into a justification of the brahminic social order and any liberating message is then too easily lost. Yet as Lele (1981: 10–13) points out, love for God may be joyful precisely because it negates an oppressive social order. It may create a community with which the actuality of daily social relations is contrasted, a community of saints characterised by compassion, kindness, mercy and truth. For women poets like Mahadevi Akka or Mirabai, devotion may symbolise the overcoming of the alien and inauthentic manifestation of duty, and the affirmation of inherent duty as duty which is authentic and pleasurable, erotic and joyful (ibid.: 13). Passionate devotion to a divine consort has provided emotional freedom and solace for many women devotees in an otherwise painful life, and some have refused to be drawn into socially defined roles and ordinary marriage.

While *bhakti* may imply a critique of an oppressive social order, it is seldom a root-and-branch critique of the whole order of society.

It need not even presuppose a commitment to social issues. It is not a charter for egalitarianism or human rights. Dalit intellectuals and activists are therefore often deeply suspicious of Hindu *bhakti* which is interpreted not as an enabling force, but as an instrument of oppression.[2] Zelliot and Gokhale-Turner who examine *bhakti* in terms of providing models for emulation, show why Dalits reject *bhakti* as irrelevant. Yet, as Gokhale-Turner (1981: 29) points out, it is well known that the Bhakti tradition has included the Mahar saints Chokhamela, Karmamela, Banka and Nirmala, the courtesan Kanhopatra, as well as the non-Brahmin Namdev (tailor), Gora (potter), Sawata (gardener), Sena (barber) and Tukaram (Kunbhi). She observes that many of the religious poems of these poet-saints (and especially those of the Untouchables) express in poignant terms the inequalities and injustices suffered by the lower castes. And in its own time the poet-saint movement was revolutionary in that the saints rebelled against the *varna* order. However, the message of the poet-saints can be read today as meaning that the Untouchables must accept their fate with faith. Untouchability is part of a divine plan. Chokhamela indeed seems to believe that the merging of oneself with the divine through *bhakti* is the only solution to social oppression (cf. ibid.: 31). Chokha writes:

I am your Mahar's Mahar
I am hungry
For your leftovers
I am hopeful
I am the servant of your slaves
For your leavings
I've brought my basket. (Gokhale-Turner: 32)

The legacy of the Bhakti tradition has been identified by some with the acceptance of the *varna* order and the place of the Untouchables within it. Thus, modern Dalit views of Chokhamela and the Bhakti tradition are described as 'ambivalent at best, and condemnatory at worst' (ibid.: 32). Gokhale-Turner comments that worldwide movements for justice and equality, and Buddhism (understood as the original religion of the Mahars) now provide the frames of reference for many Dalit poets. Buddhism for many becomes the conceptual basis of a new society, inspiring attitudes of self-respect, autonomy and freedom. However, it is evident that *bhakti* can be employed to both legitimate, and also to contest and subvert the social order. Dalits have used *bhakti* symbols, images and metaphors to overthrow an oppressive and unjust tradition, and to create a new culture. Thus the Buddha is worshipped not as a monk teaching about individual salvation, but as a social reformer profoundly engaged with the lives of the poor and broken. Ambedkar, deified as a *bodhisattva* or Buddha-to-be, is worshipped with as much fervour and piety as Vitthala was by Chokhamela. The relationship between Ambedkar and the Dalit people mirrors that between deity and devotee in the Bhakti tradition. Thus fresh transmutations of *bhakti* are occurring, and we can see from the example of many contemporary groups that *bhakti* retains the emotional and psychological power to inspire new visions of society.

We now turn to consider why and how, within Hindu religious traditions, devotion has come to be identified with what is termed the Bhakti movement. Even so, the term *bhakti* covers a wider field than religious devotion, since, according to one interpretation, the word comes from a root meaning 'to share' and in origin denoted primarily loyalty to a master (and the master's obligations to a servant). Studies of *bhakti* have to consider whether devotion exists even when the term *bhakti* is absent or used in the texts in a way which is far from the later meaning of devotion to a personal god. In the Rig Veda for example *bhakti* usually means 'portion' or 'share'. Miller comments that *bhakti* is not usually considered as playing any decisive role in the Vedas, let alone in the Rig Veda, yet she affirms that *bhakti* is present in the Vedic hymns as in the later Bhakti literature. There can be no doubt that the attitude of deep devotion of the *rishis* to their gods exists:

Shelter, dependence, friendship, graciousness, fatherliness, motherliness, are all expressions of the relationship between god and man, characteristic of *bhakti*. (1993: 31)

The drift towards belief in a single supreme God with whom human beings could enter into relationships, a drift already manifested in the Vedic hymns, becomes more evident in some of the Upanishads. In the period following the Upanishads there was a great development of devotional religion. This was most strikingly expressed in the most popular of all Hindu scriptures, the Bhagavad Gita. Indeed the Bhagavad Gita contains the earliest significant use of the term *bhakti*, where it retains much of the earlier sense of sharing. Typical of the Bhagavad Gita's use of the term is the way that Krishna's self-revelation produces in Arjuna a spirit of humble adoration, but a hint of later developments can be seen in Krishna's declaration at the end of the poem of his attachment (*bhakti*) to Arjuna and his promise that he can be attained and entered into through his grace. Thus the Bhagavad Gita emphasises the importance of devotion and reveals God's reciprocal love for the devotee who calls upon him. Among its most important passages is Krishna's revelation of his awesome and terrifying universal form to Arjuna in Chapter 11. But this *bhakti* is more formal than later *bhakti*, for its characteristics are sacrifice and discipline, with little spontaneity, but rather a stress on one's duty (*dharma*)—specifically one's caste duties. Nor is there much suggestion of intimacy, except as part of the goal, and the devotee's attitude should be like Arjuna's —of subservience and awe. However, the way of *bhakti*, available to all, is placed above the ways of knowledge (*jnana*) and action (*karma*). The Mahabharata and Ramayana, and the Puranas further developed this emotional *bhakti* emphasis.

A more intense meaning was given to the term *bhakti* by the emergence around the seventh century CE in Tamil Nadu of what is usually known simply as the Bhakti movement. This was characterised by an intense personal relationship between the deity and the devotee in which worship became a response of total commitment through the experiencing of divine grace. The intensity of this emotion left no room for any other deity and it focussed exclusively on Vishnu or Shiva, or rather on one or other of the local deities identified with or related to them. The Tamil poets of this movement delighted in praising the deity of a particular locality and yet were fully aware of his transcendence; this apparently paradoxical blending of particularity and universality arose from the intensity of the poets' experience of the deity, here and now, in their own particular situation, including the shrine at which each worshipped.

Whether Vaishnava or Shaiva, these mystical poets emphasise the same recurrent themes. The religious life is no longer a question of contemplating a transcendent and impersonal absolute, but rather consists of rapturous response to a very personal deity in all his immanence. This results in a deep sense of the worshipper's own inadequacy and so an appeal to the deity's forgiveness and grace, accompanied by a total surrender to him. This divine love should find expression in concern for one's fellows and cannot be limited by the bounds of caste and sex.

The collecting together of these Bhakti poets' works in the tenth century began the process of systematising these essentially individual perceptions—a process which led to the Shrivaishnava and Shaiva Siddhanta movements. As the movement spread beyond the Tamil-speaking area, first into other parts of South India and then into North India, a series of other movements emerged. Thus, there developed in Karnataka the Virashaiva movement (popularly known as the Lingayat movement) from the social ideas of Basava (c. 1105–67) and the Vaishnava movement founded by Madhva. In Maharashtra the cult of Vitthala (identified with Krishna) which is usually called the Varkari Panth – the pilgrims' path – became ever more popular. In North India a mass of often only half distinct groups arose, among which two of the most important have been those centred on two contemporary leaders, Chaitanya (1486–1533) and Vallabha (1479–1531). The blending of Vaishnava Bhakti with certain other strands of Hindu thought led to the widely spread but rather poorly defined movement generally called the Sant tradition.

Each of these naturally have their distinctive emphases but there are also certain common themes. The deity's loving involvement with his or her worshipper is clearly the most basic but this leads to a cluster of others, including commonly, a social concern for others (especially but not exclusively fellow devotees), stress on total surrender to the deity and reliance on his grace, and a tendency to see the goal not so much as release, *moksha*, but more as union with the deity both now and hereafter. Meykandar and other theologians of the Shaiva Siddhanta school emphasise that *bhakti* produces in the individual the necessary attitude for receiving Shiva's grace in order to love him properly, making use of four types or stages of *bhakti*. Whereas the *Bhagavata Purana*, which is closely related to the corresponding Vaishnava Bhakti movement, recognises a nine-fold classification of *bhakti* that has been adopted by many later authors and schools. For Ramanuja, the most important figure in the Shrivaishnava movement, *bhakti* is the best means of salvation, and consists of intense devotion and submission to Narayana (the name for the deity whom Ramanuja prefers). Surrender (*prapatti*) to him as one's sole refuge is both the start and the continuing of devotion to the deity, and it demands that the devotee submit entirely to the deity. Though inaccessible in the fullness of his majesty, Vishnu is full of grace and love for his creation. Within two centuries of Ramanuja's death the Shrivaishnava community had divided into the northern school, the Vadagalai, and the southern school, the Tengalai, on the issue of the relationship of surrender to divine grace. The northern school affirms that the devotee needs to make some effort to win the grace of the deity, whereas the southern school declares that Vishnu's grace alone confers salvation, each appealing to Ramanuja's writings in support of their own position. Both, however, continue to stress the commitment to the deity, who totally directs and fills the lives of his true devotees.

In the spread of the Bhakti movement northwards, a key role was played by Maharashtra (geographically part of the south but linguistically and so culturally part of the north). Typical of the Bhakti movement there is the emphasis on devotion to the deity even by the lowest castes and at the same time on the direct relationship between deity and devotee. The earliest figure in the Varkari Panth, Jnandev, is best known for his Marathi commentary on the Bhagavad Gita, while his younger contemporary Namdev centres his poetry around the theme of Vitthala's accessibility to everyone, so that religious practices open only to the higher castes and even renunciation are unnecessary, since the one necessity is to love the deity and sing his name. In Namdev's own life the irrelevance of caste among devotees is illustrated by his friendship with the Mahar, Chokhamela (d. 1338), and his willingness to seek out his body and give it a proper funeral, after Chokhamela was killed while carrying out forced labour for the village. Not surprisingly, Chokhamela's own poetry often expresses the tension between his love for Vitthala and the difficulties in showing it because of his polluted state as an Untouchable.

In North India itself, a significant role seems to have been played by the rather shadowy figure of Ramananda, an apparently liberal figure, particularly in his attitude towards caste and other restrictions; however, his main significance lies in the individuals whom he inspired, such as Kabir and Tulsidas. The complexity of Kabir's background (flourishing in the first half of the fifteenth century, he was born into a Muslim weaver community but was most familiar with the tantric *yoga* traditions of the Naths) accounts for some of the harshness of his poetry, in which he castigates all pretence in religion, as well as much of the outward forms of both Hindu and Muslim traditions of his time. His particular importance lies in putting forward the view of the deity as an absolute being without earthly incarnation or personal form, in contrast to the understanding of the Vaishnava Bhakti traditions, and so inaugurating what has been termed the Sant tradition (or *nirguna bhakti*), which stresses both direct worship of the supreme deity and the demanding nature of the path of spiritual progress. Nevertheless, his approach to this unqualified (*nirguna*), absolute deity is full of the love and devotion of the Bhakti tradition, while also emphasising the inner search – the seeking of the soul for the hidden deity who is yet deep within one's own heart (and not in temples or images) – and presenting the goal of the mystical quest as the merging of the individual with the One, in which all duality is abolished.

Whereas Kabir represents the monistic strand which emerges in parts of the Bhakti movement, his contemporaries Chaitanya and Vallabha show very clearly the strongly emotional aspect which is its most characteristic feature. Although there had been a tradition of Vaishnava devotional songs in Bengal before the time of Chaitanya, he was the first to establish a distinct community. After a dramatic conversion experience at the pilgrimage centre of Gaya, he became the centre of a group singing devotional songs to Krishna every night, out of which developed the various *kirtans* so characteristic of Bengali Vaishnavism (as the movement founded by Chaitanya is commonly called) and its contemporary offshoot, the International Society for Krishna Consciousness, established by Swami Bhaktivedanta Prabhupada. Over time, and probably even within his own lifetime, Chaitanya came to be seen by his followers as an incarnation of Krishna and indeed of Radha and Krishna together in one body. It is this experience of the bliss of that union, the paradigm of the ecstatic union between the devotee and the deity, which is the goal for Chaitanya and his followers.

For Vallabha, service to the deity tended to focus more on the elaboration of ritual worship of the deity, through the images which are regarded as his actual embodiments (*svaroopa*), but also had a strong devotional element, seen for example in the way that the great Hindi poet of Krishna Bhakti, Surdas (c. 1478–1564), is

claimed by Vallabha's community, the Pushti Marg, as belonging
to it.

The best-known Bhakti poet in Hindi, however, even surpassing
the fame of Surdas, is Tulsidas, among whose numerous works is
the adaptation of the Ramayana into any of the modern languages
of India. In this work, the *Ramcharitmanas*, there are indications
that Tulsidas was a follower of Ramananda but his great strength
is that he draws on and draws together many different strands
within the whole Bhakti movement and beyond, uniting the
nirguna emphasis on an absolute with the Vaishnava *saguna*
devotion to a personal deity by elevating Rama to the status of
Brahman and by emphasising the saving power of the name of
Rama (a designation for the deity shared by many of these poets,
from Kabir onwards). His concern is to give his message as wide
an appeal as possible and in this context he even states that the
name surpasses Rama himself, since Rama as an incarnation, *avatar*,
saved only a few, whereas his name continues to bring salvation.

One of the recurring themes of this book is an insistence that
devotion extends through the various religions of Asia. When we
come to the Jaina and Buddhist traditions however we find that the
existence of *bhakti* has been doubted or denied (Werner 1993: xv).
The characteristics of devotional Hinduism – ecstatic rapture and
surrender, desire for divine union, dependence on grace, etc. – seem
absent. Jaina philosophy indeed has often been interpreted as
antithetical to devotion. The name Jain points to the dominating
religious concern of the Jain community, Jaina monks must fight an
ascetic battle to conquer the senses and *karma*, seeking to attain a
purity of soul that liberates them from all bondage. Those who have
succeeded in this quest are Jinas, conquerors, and their disciples are
Jains. Progress towards liberation is achieved only with difficulty
and culminates in the ascetic life of the monk or nun. And while
the omniscient Jina is worthy of respect and veneration, and images
of the *tirthankaras* came to be venerated, the holy ones are beyond
the possibility of affecting or being affected by what goes on in the

rest of the cosmos. In what sense then do the *tirthankaras* function as the gods of popular religion, as recipients of devotion?

In fact, Jains soon developed forms of devotional practice directed towards the *tirthankaras* and other worthy figures. Most prominent among these rituals is *devapuja*, in which followers worship the Jinas physically represented by statues depicting them in poses of deepest meditation. Worshippers approach and bow before the image, chant the Jina's names, circumambulate, bathe the image, make a series of physical offerings to it, and wave lamps before it. Orthodox Jains do not regard the Jinas as actually present in their images, nor do they suppose that the offerings have any effect on the Jina, but rather view *devapuja* as a meditational discipline intended to remind worshippers of the ideal state achieved by the Jina and to inspire them to seek that state for themselves. However, Jaina devotional hymns indicate that most Jains have looked to the *tirthankara* for direct benefits, and have believed the Jina to inhabit the images they honoured. Jains also incorporated into their temple liturgy the worship of goddesses and other guardian deities, lesser beings who may intervene in worldly affairs on behalf of the votary. Jaina goddesses like Chakra could grant practical rewards such as wealth and release from earthly prison, as well as helping their devotees on the way to escaping the prison of *karma*.

The development of loving devotion to a superior being also appears to contrast with the inwardly directed discipline of serene meditation that has been so inspirational in Buddhism. Some Buddhist scholars have denied that the element of *bhakti* exists in Buddhism or have assumed that devotional cults were essentially for the laity and for the less spiritually advanced monks (Embree 1988: 94). For them devotion is inconsistent with Buddhist teachings that affirm that *nibbana* is the abandonment of individuality and that the Buddha no longer exists as an individual. Core Buddhist values of wisdom (*panna*) and compassion (*karuna*) seem to lead to the cultivation of morality (*sila*) rather than devotion. However, much depends upon the interpretative approach and assumptions brought to the study of Buddhist texts and practices. Many contemporary writers agree that there can be no doubt that deep devotion or *bhakti/bhatti* does exist in Buddhism and that it had its beginnings in the earliest days (e.g. Werner 1993: 45). They point to a range of supportive evidence. The Buddha himself taught that he was a Buddha, a being far above gods (ibid.: 38). Early followers considered the Buddha to be a superhuman figure, a perfected human being or a representative of the ultimate transcendental reality of *nibbana*. He and his successors were conceived of as truly compassionate and accessible beings who were concerned for the suffering of all beings and intent on guiding them towards the final goal of *nirvana*.

Devotion was an integral aspect of this quest. Buddhists preserved the bodily charisma of the Buddha by placing his ashes and relics in burial mounds (*stupas*) which became centres of Buddhist devotion. Taking refuge (*sarana*) in the Buddha, the Dhamma (doctrine) and the Sangha (order) became a focus of worship and hope in Buddhist belief and practice. The person of the Buddha above all became the supreme object of faith and reverence. Existing Buddhist canonical texts in Pali offer a perception of the Buddha as a wondrous 'great person' (*maha purusha*) approaching or exceeding the stature of the gods, and he was also identified with the Dhamma or supreme truth incarnate. The Remembrance of the Buddha (*buddhanussati*), one of the practices of Buddhist meditation, became an act of merit. By the first century CE Buddhists began to use physical images of the Buddha and other important Buddhist figures as objects of devotion. During the same period, *bodhisattvas*, those motivated by compassion to help others achieve enlightenment, became objects of veneration and emulation. Compassion became a dynamic, driving force expressed in the spread of Buddhist teachings all over Asia (cf. Hardy 1994: 361). Moreover, as Hardy also points out, there is a realisation that happiness and joy can be derived from compassion, love without a transcendental object. 'The Buddha's Dharma can be envisaged as something loving, compassionate, and pervading the world—to be absorbed and then communicated by the *bodhisattva*, yielding intense pleasure to him—without necessitating a theistic interpretation' (ibid.: 365).

It could be realistically asked whether Buddhist Bhakti includes the love of the devotee for the deity and the deity's love for the devotee. Hindu devotion after all generally presupposes an intimate relationship between humans and a personal God based on love, and also implies the idea of a God who feels intense love for humans. Werner (1993: 48–51) argues that while the Buddha's teaching and the goal of *nibbana* itself seem impersonal, many Buddhists did and still do in fact develop a strong affection for the Buddha. Similarly the Buddha's perfect compassion for other beings suggests mutuality in the relationship between the transcendent and the phenomenal, the contemplated and the contemplator, the worshipped and the worshipper.

Sikhism has from its earliest times been a Bhakti movement. The first *guru*, Guru Nanak (1469–1538), preached a devotional faith which attracted both Muslim and Hindu followers. The term Sikh, deriving from the Sanskrit word for pupil or disciple, indicates the relationship first adopted by Nanak's followers towards their *guru* and analogically towards God. For Nanak, God was infinite and formless. Human beings are separated from God by sinfulness and ignorance, but through grace can be joined to him in mystical union. Nanak spoke of the sorrow of separation from God and the blissfulness of union with Him, a theme which became common to Hindu Bhakti, Jain, Sikh and Indo-Muslim poetry. Nanak rejected the value of rituals, images, priests, pilgrimages, ascetic practices, caste, temples, mosques, etc. His teachings centred on the Word, the Name and the Guru. Thus Nanak's *nirguna bhakti* can be placed in the context of devotional Hinduism and the Sant tradition, which directed devotion to the eternal, formless God, emphasised the role of the *guru*, and taught that love was the characteristic emotion of true religion. When Guru Arjan, the fifth *guru*, compiled the *Adi Granth*, it contained not only the hymns of Guru Nanak and his successors but also of poems by earlier Bhakti poets such as Kabir and Ravidas.

There is evidence that individual Sufis were arriving in the Punjab even before the Muslim conquest. Data Ganj Bakhsh ('Ali ibn 'Uthman al-Jullabi al-Hujwiri) was established in Lahore and died there around 1071 (his tomb is still a place of pilgrimage). He is the only notable Sufi in the subcontinent until Muinuddin Chishti, who reached Delhi in 1193 in the immediate aftermath of Muhammad Ghuri's capture of the city, but later settled in Ajmer. However, after about 1200 CE when Muslim control of North India grew increasingly strong, we find the establishment of Sufi orders which dominated Muslim religious and cultural life in the subcontinent. Sufi teachers brought the spiritual message of Islam to an Indian audience in ways that were both familiar and new. Sufi emphasis on love for God as the principle of human existence, the urge towards union with God, self-surrender, the stages of the mystic path, the passionate yearning for God, and the final goal of the complete annihilation of the self and subsistence in God, have obvious parallels with the devotional path of *bhakti*. Sufi saints and Hindu *bhaktas* stress the personal relationship between the believer and God. Both share the pain of separation and longing for union. Both long to be absorbed into the divine, in a state where all awareness of individual self is lost. Both are recipients of the grace of God. Both practise contemplation and remembrance of the Word or Name(s) of God.

The rise of the Sufi orders in the medieval Islamic world also heralded an increasing love for the Prophet and his family. Muhammad became venerated as the Perfect Man, the Seal of the Prophets, and a figure of loving devotion and miraculous powers. Subcontinental devotion to the Prophet was reflected in the flowering of devotion to living *sheikhs* and *pirs* (and their spiritual descendants) whose relationships to their disciples paralleled those of Hindu *gurus* and disciples. Great masters possessing extraordinary charisma became regarded as saints, and as virtual intercessors with God on behalf of their followers. Pilgrimage to their *mazars* (tomb shrines) became part of popular devotion. In time Sufism and Hindu devotionalism came to share a common heritage of poetic themes and metaphors. Bhakti and Sufi poets both wrote and preached their message in the vernacular, reaching out to the mass of people of both religions, and contributing greatly to the development of the regional languages in India.

As the above survey demonstrates, South Asian Bhakti traditions have come to represent an immense storehouse for human thought, religiosity and devotion. It is by examining specific aspects of this heritage that the authors of this book's chapters have made their contributions. Many more manifestations of the Bhakti phenomenon could have been discussed here, but we have chosen to focus most of all on the strength of *bhakti* as a live and powerful source of value, aesthetic imagination, creativity and well being.

Providing us with interesting methodological tools and an in-depth analysis of textual dynamics, Julia Leslie notes the divergent interests of scholars and devotees. For most Hindus *bhakti* is a way of life. For scholars it is the ambiguities, transformations, puzzles and conflicts that are interesting. In Ricoeur's language, devotees operate with the hermeneutic of recollection, scholars with the hermeneutic of suspicion. In this book we hope that contributors do both. They are willing to listen to the voice of the living tradition, but also operate with a degree of scholarly suspicion.

John Brockington's erudite chapter is the work of an academic who has spent his professional life scrutinising and commenting upon the two Sanskrit epics of India. Here he demonstrates the idea that *bhakti* has to be understood within its historical and social contexts. He shows how the narratives of the Mahabharata and Ramayana, the persons of Krishna and Rama, and even the characterisation of the traditional authors were transformed by understandings of *bhakti*. The epics were originally heroic poems that over time grew to incorporate religious and didactic material, especially after Rama and Krishna were recognised as *avatars* of Vishnu. Particularly significant are the inclusion of the *Bhagavad Gita* and *Narayaniya* within the Mahabharata and the addition to the Ramayana of its first and last books, the *Balakanda* and the *Uttarakanda*. Professor Brockington argues that the Puranas, particularly the *Kurma Purana* and the *Bhagavata Purana*, further developed the emotional *bhakti* emphasis in their summaries of the epic stories. He then argues that it is the rise of the Bhakti movement in the strict sense that transformed the way in which Rama and Krishna and so the epics themselves are regarded. The vernacular adaptations of the epics and their dramatic presentations became a potent medium for the transmission of ideas of *bhakti*. In particular, Tulsidas' *Ramcharitmanas* gives the Name of Rama and the concept of *ramarajya* greater prominence and reflects the increasing popularity of Hanuman. In Hindi-speaking areas it is still the text used for the Ramlila performances. Professor Brockington's careful delineation substantiates his conclusion that without the two Sanskrit epics, especially the Ramayana, the Bhakti movement could not exist in the form in which we know it.

The immense impact of Bhakti movements on text and story, and the characterisation of heroes, saints and gods is also emphasised in Julia Leslie's chapter. She explores in particular how the pressures of *bhakti* have transformed the legend of the poet-saint Valmiki, author of the Ramayana. But before embarking on a historical analysis of change, Dr Leslie notes how the divergent interests of historians and devotees are played out in this specific context. For devotees *bhakti* is 'a given not a phase'. They readily accept the ambiguities that so puzzle historians and are not in the least interested in their exegeses. She then poses some fascinating questions which grew out of a contemporary dispute over Valmiki. What happens when a deity is portrayed not only as human but as ignorant and evil? What happens when two versions of a deity are held simultaneously? By a process of text-historical analysis Dr Leslie locates Valmiki in sacred texts and traces key motifs of the popular Valmiki story—the ascetic in the anthill, the dacoit-turned-devotee, and the *mara-mara mantra*. She then leads us gently to an understanding of how the dacoit legend grew and how several stories have been conflated. She notes that only after the development of Rama Bhakti in North India was this motif attached to Valmiki, a motif which illustrated perfectly the power of the Name of God to turn the worst of sinners into the best of men. Finally Dr Leslie points out how historical knowledge can develop sensitivity to the views of others.

Paula Richman is widely respected for her groundbreaking work on the Ramayana and the South Asian tradition of telling and interpreting the story in multiple ways. Coherently with this expertise, her contribution emphasises the historically situated nature of *bhakti*, incisively deconstructing the complex political, social and economic contexts of particular Ramayana performances. Here she analyses three modern British performances, illuminating the different ways in which they deal with relations between the South Asian communities in Britain and the primarily White communities around them. The first performance discussed is that of the Southall Black Sisters. The Sisters included South Asians and African Caribbeans who viewed themselves as joined in a larger Black identity. In Paula Richman's reading their Ramayana became a vehicle for a self-conscious political critique of racism and sexism. The Commonwealth Institute's gala performance by contrast constructed the Ramayana as an Indian story, and lacked any sense that Rama is God for millions of Hindus. Professor Richman suggests that the gala could be seen as coopting elements of a colonised culture within the framework of multicultural education for the convenience of teachers. It therefore functioned in the interests of the British state. The Festival of Spiritual Unity organised by Manubhai M. Madhvani as a corporate project, was designed as an affirmation of the oneness of all spiritual experience. Its transnational nature and strong Gujarati identification were symbolised by its central religious figure, Morari Bapu. Richman concludes finally that her research reveals that the same diversity of narrative and exegesis found in the Ramayana tradition of South Asia is at work in Britain.

Winand Callewaert's lively chapter on the work of Kabir brings to life problems of textual criticism. It asks whether the devotional songs we sing are authentically those of Kabir. The answer is clearly no. Hundreds of songs written by others are included in the repertoire of Kabir and given the name of Kabir. Professor Callewaert shows why this is so. He points out that poet-mystics have often sought to give their own poems and songs the authority and charisma of the glorious past and that interested groups appropriate poets like Kabir for their own advantage. Singers use the charismatic name of Kabir for their own compositions. Interested parties like the Gorakhnathis, Ramanandis and even twentieth-century scholars appropriate Kabir for their own ideological ends. Callewaert then introduces readers to the most influential analyses of Kabir's work in the twentieth century and argues that scholarly research is difficult but not impossible: we *can* earmark songs that may have been popular in the repertoires around 1556, and that have a high probability of belonging to the very early core of Kabir's songs. Finally Professor Callewaert discusses an essential Indian attitude to authorship. He compares the Indian desire to belong to a tradition, to have a grounding in an authoritative tradition (*parampara*) with modern western attitudes which emphasise the individuality of the author.

Anna King analyses the language of *bhakti* in the globalising world of pilgrimage. She contextualises her own anthropological fieldwork within the rich unbroken heritage of devotion to rivers in the Indian subcontinent. Love of the Ganga is found among Hindus and Sikhs from both orthodox and 'secular' backgrounds, and from all *sampradayas*, castes and communities. Many pilgrims go much further and exhibit the fervent devotion and purity of heart that should ideally accompany bathing and *darshan*. This chapter examines some of the most popular stories, rituals and festivals of the Ganga showing that devotion to the Ganga encompasses the fluid and shifting perspectives of Hindu religious culture: the Ganga to her devotees and lovers becomes the universal Mother, Shakti in her destructive guise, *nirguna* Brahman, the liquid form of Vishnu, etc. It also analyses the ways in which oral narratives of the Ganga are vital genres used in infinitely diverse and multivalent ways—to laud *bhakti*, as social and ethical commentary, to gain a livelihood, as nationalist propaganda and as expressions of a universal human spirituality. Devotion to the Ganga is shaped not only by text and ritual, but increasingly by the media and the rapidly multiplying groups who have an economic or ideological stake in such devotion. Finally Anna King argues that the growing global ecological and feminist movements are potentially new strands in the devotion to Ganga, and suggests that the playful, ludic aspects of Ganga symbolism cohere not only with literal but with postmodern and post-realist understandings.

Peter Flügel's central question is whether Jaina Mahayana or Mahayana-style forms of Jainism exist. His chapter deals with a tradition where the 'intimate other' of devotional Hinduism is apparently absent. The *tirthankara* is disengaged and completely non-transactive; his persona is that of the exemplary other. Defining Mahayana in the broadest sense as being based on the concept of salvation through others, he undertakes a detailed case study of the Akram Vijnan Marg. Field research confirmed that the movement is syncretistic, combining Kundakunda's 'Digambar Mahayana' soteriology, Samkhya ontology and classical Jaina cosmology with a ritual idiom derived from popular Vaishnava devotionalism and Tantric miracle cults. Dr Flügel argues that the principal doctrinal feature of the Marg is the belief in the efficacy of the practice of *jnana bhakti*, the 'magical acquisition of salvific knowledge through devotional surrender (*samarpan*) to its source,' and that at its heart is the devotion to Dada Bhagavan. The founder, A.M. Patel, was not only the medium for the Jain Tirthankara, Simandhar Svami, but also the vehicle of the fully realised supreme self (Dada Bhagavan) and a self-enlightened being qualified to act as a *sadguru* or a *satpurusha*, 'not unlike a *bodhisattva* in Mahayana Buddhism'. This ambiguity of the Dada cult eventually led to a schism after his death with one successor claiming to perpetuate the charismatic cult of the Dada as the currently living *jnani purusha*, the other assuming the more humble role of his spiritual medium. Peter Flügel observes however that for both groups the objectification of charisma – in religious institutions and rituals, and in particular the devotional worship of the Dada image – is becoming increasingly important.

The significance of this chapter is that it challenges the orthodox view that there is no Jaina Mahayana. Dr Flügel is able to demonstrate how and why the Akram Vijnan Movement is primarily devotional. He notes its emphasis on direct experience rather than scriptural knowledge or physical asceticism, the possibility of salvation for all through the miraculous power of grace (*siddhi kripa*) and the acquisition of knowledge through devotion to the knower. The chapter culminates in the insight that there is no essential Jainism but a plurality of doctrinal elements and practices that can be interpreted and reinterpreted from a variety of perspectives. Thus the Akram Vijnan Movement can legitimately be interpreted as a form of Digambara Mahayana, Jaina Samkhya, Jaina–Vaishnava syncretism or Jaina Tantra.

Among the most valuable insights into devotion are those chapters which explore devotional interaction in the context of doctrinal 'absence'. Kate Crosby's carefully nuanced chapter raises many questions about texts and their interpretation, and challenges scholarly assumptions that devotion in Theravada Buddhism is simply for the laity or for the emotionally needy. She explores the nature and meaning of devotion to the Buddha Gotama in the context of the formal teaching that he is dead and no longer accessible to his followers. She begins by noting that the *Mahaparinibbanasutta* itself authorises the enshrinement of the relics of the Buddha in *stupas* and the worship of them, and advocates pilgrimage to sites associated with the Buddha. Dr Crosby goes on to distinguish between those aspects of worship that are unproblematic doctrinally, which do not assume that the Buddha is accessible or present, and those that are problematic, which assume interaction between the worshipper and worshipped. She analyses the treatment of Buddha images, drawing upon a number of studies, which in general emphasise the dichotomy between cognitive and affective response, between doctrine and emotional need, between orthodoxy and traditional practice. She is particularly fascinated by Sinhalese villagers' statement (recorded by Richard Gombrich) that the Buddha's power is present in statues, a view confirmed by consecration rituals of new Buddha statues in mainland Southeast Asia and the myth of the first Buddha image there. Kate Crosby goes on to consider whether devotion is primarily for lay followers and meditation for the Sangha. In a fascinating examination of Buddha worship as a preparation for meditation she argues that we cannot gain answers to questions along these lines. We can however conclude that in pre-modern Theravada Buddhism, devotion and meditation are combined and not contrasted, that devotion is advocated specifically for those undertaking the rigorous path of meditation practice aimed at Buddhahood, and that this type of Buddhism viewed devotion at the very least 'in terms of psychological need and not psychological neediness'.

Ron Geaves begins his chapter by cataloguing the seemingly irreconcilable differences between the Hindu and Muslim traditions, but he moves very quickly to an affirmation of heterogeneity in both religions. He reminds us that it is in devotion that we find most clearly the congruence of Islam and Hinduism although he calls our attention to the political and religious tensions that devotion can trigger within Sikhism and Islam. His chapter focusses on Sufism as a vibrant living tradition that has profoundly influenced the development of Islam in the subcontinent and also on the ways in which Sufism has provided a bridge to certain forms of Hinduism, namely the Bhakti/Sant traditions of northern India. He interprets the two traditions together as proposing a form of devotion that is available to all.

Ron Geaves traces first the development of the Islamic devotional path within the Indian subcontinent through the establishment of mystical Sufi orders (*tariqas*), the presence of wandering ascetics (*qalandars* or *fakirs*) and the growing networks of saints and shrines. He pays particular attention to the early influence of Ibn al-Arabi's ideas which included the teaching that both the One and the many are forms of the One, that the divine is worshipped in all religions and that love is Allah's innermost essence. Geaves goes on to discuss the integrationist approach to Islam and Hinduism of the Mughal emperor Akbar and of Dara Shikoh, the eldest son of Shah Jehan, both of whom were influenced by Sufism. He then explores the confluence between the medieval North Indian *nirguna bhaktas*, known as Sants, and Sufis, analysing and comparing their ideas of God, the functions of Sufi *dhikr* and the *nam simran* of the Sants, the roles of the *sheikh* and the *guru*, and the use of the vernacular in poetry and preaching. He points out that as Sufis and Sants began to collect followers from both communities there was growing Islamic hostility to such eclecticism. Finally Geaves explores Sufi piety and devotion to the Prophet and their *sheikhs*, concluding that the Sufism remains one of the most esteemed devotional traditions of the Indian subcontinent.

Eleanor Nesbitt bases her chapter on her own ethnographic explorations of the ways in which Sikh children are nurtured in contemporary Sikh devotion. In so doing she raises fundamental questions about how all religions should be taught in schools and also about the appropriateness of the paradigm of 'world religions'. She comments that a curriculum based on the five Ks (*kesh* – uncut hair and beard; *kangha* – hair comb; *kach* – special underwear; *kirpan* – sword; *kara* – bracelet of steel) fails to convey the yearning for the divine which pervades Gurbani. It ignores the poetic imagery of the *Guru Granth Sahib* and the aesthetic beauty of *shabad kirtan*. Eleanor Nesbitt offers a wonderfully vivid picture of how children are brought up to revere 'photos' of Sikh *gurus*, contemporary *babas* (living saints) and the *Guru Granth*. She also asks questions about the nature of that devotion when practised by young children. How far does it acquire magical and instrumental intentions? She further notes that children use the term 'God' when referring to the living master, the scriptures and the historical *gurus*, and comments on the frequent untroubled slippage between God and gods. Her analysis of the convergence in this one English word 'God' of European theology on the one hand and Hindu-Indic *darshan* on the other illustrates the need for further research on language among diasporic communities.

Dr Nesbitt illustrates the problems that exist for educationists in representing contemporary Sikh devotion. Aspects of the devotion in which children are nurtured are continuous with more widespread North Indian practices. However to acknowledge this unjudgementally may appear to undermine a minority faith's fundamental principles and identity. It may not fit with the world religions paradigm of present religious education syllabi. For example the worship of Sants is a popular 'powerhouse of devotion' that often inspires Sikh children. Found universally in Hinduism it is nevertheless at odds with the orthodox conviction that 'such veneration is due only to the Sikh *gurus* and the *Guru Granth Sahib*'. Such devotion also fits uneasily into the mapped contours of British religious education.

Jameela Siddiqi has long experience of presenting programmes about South Asian musicians and artists for BBC Radio 3 and the World Service, and writing about Asian music for the general public. Ms Siddiqi has a practical mission not only to introduce audiences to Asian devotional music but also to show that music and poetry disregard boundaries. In this chapter she writes of the shared heritage of devotion in subcontinental traditions of poetry, music and language. She points out that the same *ragas* and *talas* are sung and played by Sikhs, Hindus and Muslims in both secular and religious contexts, that North Indian classical music is a synthesis of Hindu and Muslim musical traditions and that Sufi *qawwali*, Sikh *shabad kirtan* and Hindu *bhajan* share poetic and musical idioms. Many Hindu and Sikh hymns are consistent with the Sufi message of unconditional surrender. Hindu disciples learn from Muslim masters and vice versa. Jameela Siddiqi also discusses the 'crazy' love of the Bauls, wandering minstrels who can be either Hindu or Muslim, but whose music combines the spiritual elements of Sufism and Bhakti with the musical traditions of Bengal. She observes with sadness that although all the religions of the Indian subcontinent share the same musical and poetic heritage, Hindu–Muslim tensions preclude both sides from understanding or acknowledging this. Indeed she laments the rewriting of Indian history to minimise or demonise Muslim influence and post-independence Pakistan's rejection of its own Indian roots.

It is appropriate that our last chapter should be a moving testimony to the inspiration of Tamal Krishna Goswami (TKG) who died as a result of a traffic accident in 2002. One of Goswami's very last projects had been to write a chapter exploring death and dying within the Bhakti tradition. Graham Schweig has been guided by Goswami's interests, and his chapter perhaps more than any other fulfils the very practical aims of the DHIIR. Graham Schweig writes from the triple stance of academic, *guru* and devotee in reflecting on the 'good death'. He starts by asking how the process of dying in *bhakti* compares with dying in the greater pan-Hindu context. This leads him to ask further questions which lie at the heart of devotion in many religious traditions—questions about the power of human effort and volition on the one hand and divine grace and supreme will on the other. In reaching some conclusions he explores contemporary writings on Hindu death and dying, and the teaching of the *Bhagavad Gita*, the *Bhakti Sutra* and the *Bhagavata*.

That which has been hinted at throughout the chapter becomes crystal clear in the conclusion. Graham Schweig speaks of the one principle of *bhakti* that describes its very foundation: 'it is love at its highest level, in its unremitting, purest state.' Love is stronger than death.

It is utterly devotional desire to please the deity that lifts the *bhakta* from this world, even while still living in it....The *bhakta* is not concerned with a good or bad death, or with escaping *samsara*, since he or she is absorbed in devotional love that overpowers death.

Graham Schweig argues that the Bhakti doctrine has historically moved away from *karma* and human effort towards a reliance upon the grace of God. This doctrinal trend does not necessarily reduce human responsibility; 'rather, it acknowledges that the *bhakta* is ultimately and utterly dependent on a gracious and compassionate deity for salvation.' He points out the dangers for the devotees of the Chaitanyite Vaishnava path if they fall back into pan-Hindu attitudes towards the good death, attitudes which involve *karma* or action-determined outcomes. Finally he lets us know that questions about whether his friend and colleague Goswami died the 'good death' are simply irrelevant. 'Rather, the triumph of *bhakti*…is the essential point and it is this triumph of *bhakti* and its transfigurative power in which the devotee lives.'

Conclusion

This book is therefore dedicated both to the memory of Goswamiji and to that of Julia Leslie, the contributor of the third chapter. Julia Leslie died suddenly in September 2004 from a recurrence of the cancer which seemed so courageously to have overcome. Her meticulous textual scholarship, her sympathy with her subject and her warm concern for her students and colleagues alike, as well as her dignity in facing setbacks, won her admiration and affection in equal measure. Her latest book, *Authority and Meaning in Indian Religions*, with its ground-breaking analysis of the changing perceptions of the figure of Valmiki, will undoubtedly be a lasting monument to her outstanding scholarship, but nevertheless the disciplines of Indology and Religious Studies are the poorer for her death at the height of her career.

This publication as a whole represents a remarkable testimony to the rise of *bhakti* which has transformed the hearts of devotees, the characterisation of the divine and the relationship between them. Ardent love and yearning for union now penetrate all aspects of the religious culture of South Asia. Passionate love of the intimate other has become a dominant feature of many Indic traditions and gives them much of this spontaneity and emotional and experiential appeal. *Bhakti* not only provides comfort and emotional solace but poetic inspiration and creativity. However, our contributors show that academic exegesis is equally valuable where it problematises devotion to the divine, and exposes its historical development as complex, often contested, and always 'political'. Contributors remind us, sometimes through the language of postmodernity, that devotion has political, economic and social contexts which must be deconstructed if we are to understand in a plenary, unsentimental way how devotion can subvert or reaffirm the status quo, and how it can become a radical force for change or a romantic retreat from ordinary life.

Since the DHIIR was established to show the relevance of Indic religious and knowledge traditions to contemporary society, we return in conclusion to the conference. Interpreted as a conversation among participants, it was fascinating in its own right. Devotees reported that they found that academic challenges to the 'givenness' of devotion, the search behind, in and in front of the text opened up wider perspectives. They also became aware of the great diversity and often the fundamental ambivalence and clash of religious and social values within their own traditions. They began to debate the desire for distinctive religious and social identities against a more fluid, less bounded understanding of shared South Asian culture. The academics learnt the limits of language and phenomenology in exploring the divine presence in the human heart, and that 'doing theology or philosophy' is what everyone does. For the great majority of participants, love of the divine was seen to bear its most precious fruit when accompanied by an acceptance of the cruelty and suffering of the world. Love for the divine shows itself in care for community and concern for social justice. *Bhakti* as one of the jewels of Indian religious culture shines most brightly when its radiance is reflected back into the world of trustful human relationships.

This book then is a continuation of an ongoing conversation. It shows that 'the melting of the heart', the pursuit of love, entwined with the pursuit of power and wisdom, continues to be the dominant note of Indian religious culture.

Notes

1. Sri Satya Sai Baba, worshipped by his devotees as *avatar, Bhagavan*, Lord and God, teaches that love is the only force in the universe, and that love is God. Service should be a joy, the chance to open the heart and let the love flow.

2. Zelliot (1981: 153) notes that the Sants throughout the centuries distinguished between equality in the sight of God and equality in everyday life, whilst Karve who accompanied devout pilgrims on the road to Pandhapur (1962) was amazed that pilgrims who sing songs vigorously proclaiming the equality of all the *bhaktas*, preserved caste groups even as they sang them.

References

Embree, A. (ed.). 1988. *Sources of Indian Tradition*, Volume One. Second Edition. New York: Columbia University.

Gokhale-Turner, J.B. 1981. Bhakti or Vidroha: Continuity and Change in Dalit Sahitya. In *Tradition and Modernity in Bhakti Movements*, (ed.) J. Lele, 29–42. Leiden: E.J. Brill.

Hardy, F. 1994. *The Religious Culture of India: Power, Love and Wisdom*. Cambridge: Cambridge University Press.

Hirst, J. 1993. The Place of Bhakti in Sankara's Vedanta. In *Love Divine: Studies in Bhakti and Devotional Mysticism*, (ed.) K. Werner, 117–145. Durham Indological Series No. 3. Richmond: Curzon.

Karve, Iravati. 1962. On the Road: A Maharashtrian Pilgrimage. *Journal of Asian Studies* 22: 13–29.

Lele, J. 1981. The Bhakti Movement in India: A Critical Introduction. In *Tradition and Modernity in Bhakti Movements*, (ed.) J. Lele, 1–15. Leiden: E.J. Brill.

Miller, J. 1993. Bhakti and the Ṛg Veda—Does it Appear There or Not? In *Love Divine: Studies in Bhakti and Devotional Mysticism*, (ed.) K. Werner, 1–35. Durham Indological Series No. 3. Richmond: Curzon.

Sherma, R.D. 2000. 'Sa Ham—I am She': Woman as Goddess. In *Is the Goddess a Feminist? The Politics of South Asian Goddesses*, (ed.) A. Hiltebeitel and K.M. Erndl, 24–51. Sheffield: Sheffield Academic Press.

Werner, K. (ed.). 1993. *Love Divine: Studies in Bhakti and Devotional Mysticism*. Durham Indological Series No. 3. Richmond: Curzon.

Werner, K. (ed.). 1993. Love and Devotion in Buddhism. In *Love Divine: Studies in Bhakti and Devotional Mysticism*, (ed.) K. Werner, 37–52. Durham Indological Series No. 3. Richmond: Curzon.

Zelliot, E. 1981. Chokhamela and Eknath: Two Bhakti Modes of Legitimacy for Modern Change. In *Tradition and Modernity in Bhakti Movements*, (ed.) J. Lele, 136–56. Leiden: E.J. Brill.

CHAPTER TWO

The Epics in the Bhakti Tradition

JOHN BROCKINGTON

The two great Sanskrit epics, the Mahabharata and the Ramayana, are both very substantial works, composed and recited at courts by bards attendant on local chiefs belonging to the warrior – Kshatriya – aristocracy. The core of each work was composed around the fifth or fourth century BCE, but as they were recited by the bards, they were subject to a process of expansion and accretion which continued at least until the early part of the Gupta period in the fourth century CE. But the political situation that they each reflect is substantially older, going back in the case of the Mahabharata perhaps as much as another five centuries. They are indeed a major source for our knowledge of the later Vedic and post-Vedic periods, in political, social and religious terms. In the core of the epics, the great Vedic deity Indra is the most prominent and most frequently mentioned, being the ideal to whom human heroes may be compared. But over time the rising importance of Vishnu and Shiva begins to be reflected in the two epics, as they acquire an increasingly religious dimension and also pass into the hands of Brahmins as the established guardians and teachers of tradition.

The influence which the two epics came to have on the various Hindu religious traditions, in particular on the devotional Bhakti tradition, and more generally on Indian culture as a whole, is shown not only by the many versions and summaries of them throughout the devotional literature (from the Puranas – those compendia of popular Hinduism composed between about the fourth and the twelfth centuries – to contemporary pamphlets), but also in pure literature, art and theatre right up to the present day. Sculptural representations are found on North Indian temples from perhaps as early as the fifth century CE. In South India there is the famous carving on a granite outcrop at Mamallapuram (modern Mahabalipuram, about 57 kilometres south of Chennai in Tamil Nadu) of one of the pivotal episodes in the Mahabharata where Arjuna is performing austerities to gain weapons from Shiva. Scenes specifically drawn from one or other epic, or both, are carved on the outer walls of temples in many regions and at many periods. Miniature painters in the sixteenth to eighteenth centuries, working under Mughal or Rajput patronage, also produced many illustrations of scenes from the epics, including complete illustrated manuscripts.

Even to survey the impact of the epics on the Bhakti tradition would be a major undertaking and only a necessarily relatively brief outline of their influence can be presented here, along with references to the relevant secondary literature where individual items are treated at much greater length. My purpose, therefore, in this chapter is to highlight some of the ways in which both epics, but more especially the Ramayana, have been used, the changes which the stories have undergone in the process and the implications for the Bhakti tradition. As we shall see, adaptations of both epics into modern Indian languages were commonly among the first significant works to be produced in each language and have a clearly devotional orientation. The earliest examples come from the Dravidian languages of South India (for example, in Tamil, Villiputtur's Mahabharata and Kamban's *Iramavataram*), but in due course adaptations in the languages of North India followed (from Krittibas's Bengali Ramayana onwards, including most notably of all Tulsidas's *Ramcharitmanas*).

The status of Krishna and Rama as the two *avatars* of Vishnu most frequently worshipped in modern times, especially within the Bhakti tradition, has ensured that the two Sanskrit epics, the

Mahabharata and the Ramayana, are most commonly regarded as devotional texts. However, this has not always been the case. In origin, let me repeat, the Mahabharata and the Ramayana were, in the view of most scholars, heroic poems recited by bards rather than religiously inspired works composed by Brahmins—as indeed is suggested by the use of the English term epics while referring to them. The Indian tradition itself however distinguishes them, calling the Mahabharata a chronicle, an *itihasa*; and the Ramayana the first true work of poetry, the *adikavya*. There is, in fact, general scholarly agreement that eulogies of heroes and cycles of stories underlie the two epics as we now have them. It is only right to add, however, that certain scholars have considered each epic to possess rather greater unity. Madeleine Biardeau in particular regards the Mahabharata as revealing 'a universe of *bhakti*'; basically that is the outlook of the Puranas (Biardeau 1978, 1994). The most obvious feature of her interpretation is her emphasis on the pervasiveness of *bhakti* and of the *avatar* ideology. Since for her *bhakti* is so prominent in Hinduism because it incorporates sacrificial, yogic and renunciatory values within itself, the complementarity of Vishnu and Shiva is also basic to her interpretation (and she discovers it even within the Vedic literature, in the Brahmanas). However, she explicitly adopts a non-historical approach, arguing that the basic forms of Hinduism are unchanging—a view that I find implausible to say the least. Her views have recently found another advocate in Alf Hiltebeitel, who suggests that the Mahabharata is a basically unitary work which was written (not orally composed, as most scholars, both Western and Indian, believe) over a relatively brief period by a small group 'at most through a couple of generations' (Hiltebeitel 2001: 20).

As to their origins, to amplify my comments above, the clustering of ballads and other material around a central theme or hero, transmitted orally by bards attached to warrior chiefs, must gradually have given rise to longer works with a more complex plot; the culmination of this process is the two extant epics, along with the *Harivamsha* as a supplement to the Mahabharata. Although the two epics are based on traditional bardic material of this type, as time passed a greater or lesser amount of religious and didactic material was gradually incorporated into them, especially after one figure in each was recognised as being an *avatar* of Vishnu. Rama and Krishna do, however, present something of a contrast. Rama is the ideal ruler, promoting justice and the welfare of his subjects, and exemplifying perfect filial obedience—a model of putting *dharma* into practice. On the other hand, it is not Krishna's actions which are significant in the earlier period, as his teaching and the advice that he offers to the Pandavas is sometimes morally questionable; indeed, the authors of the Mahabharata seem deliberately to have presented the moral issues as complex and made the epic an exploration of the problems of discerning *dharma*. Since the two epics do constitute the ultimate source for the stories of both Krishna and Rama, it is only natural that the later devotional movement within the Hindu tradition, the Bhakti movement, should make extensive use of them (although of course they are far from being its sole source).

The shift from heroic to religious begins already during the process of growth of the two epics themselves, with the inclusion of the Bhagavad Gita, Krishna's sermon to Arjuna on non-attachment; and the *Narayaniya*, the teaching about Narayana as supreme deity, within the Mahabharata, and the addition to that epic of its supplement, the *Harivamsha* (in its extant form the narrative of Krishna's life and exploits); and with the addition to the Ramayana of its first and last books – the *Balakanda* and the *Uttarakanda* – all occurring between the first and third centuries CE. In the *Valmiki Ramayana*, Rama is often called *ramo dharmabhritam varah*—'Rama, the best of upholders of righteousness' (cf. Brockington 1977), and the events of the narrative are conditioned both by *dharma* and by the reaction of the characters to its requirements. Rama's moral grandeur comes from his willing submission to the apparently arbitrary demand for his exile which leads him ultimately to his greatest deed, the killing of Ravana, who is presented by Valmiki as a slave to lust and later quite naturally seen as the embodiment of evil, defeated by good in the person of Rama. This ethical polarisation becomes even more obvious in the first and last books, in which the concept of *bhakti* in a religious sense also starts to appear, possibly in the opening of the *Balakanda* with the figure of the great sage Narada (1.1.1–2.2), who, in the roughly contemporary *Narayaniya* (cf. below) and then later, is closely associated with *bhakti*, and more definitely in the ending of the *Uttarakanda* (7.98.15 and 100.15).

It is not only the narratives of the two epics that develop over the centuries but also the characterisation of their traditional authors—Vyasa of the Mahabharata and Valmiki of the Ramayana. Both sages appear within the epics ascribed to them. However, Vyasa plays a significant creative role in the Mahabharata, not only – as his name means – as the 'arranger' of all the material but also as the natural grandfather by *niyoga* of the epic heroes,[1] but the legends about him do not develop much thereafter (apart from the anachronistic story of his dictating the epic to Ganesha); whereas Valmiki plays a relatively marginal role in the Ramayana until the late addition to it of the *Uttarakanda* (in which he gives shelter to Sita in his hermitage and educates her twin sons). It is in later texts that the myths about him develop, as Julia Leslie shows so fascinatingly in her article which comes next in this volume.

Whereas Rama is of course the hero of the Ramayana, Krishna is not as central a figure in the Mahabharata, where he appears in two distinct roles: firstly as the chief of the Yadava clan who acts as counsellor to the five Pandavas, the heroes of the epic, and secondly as the supreme personal deity who suddenly reveals himself to Arjuna within the Bhagavad Gita. There seems little connection between these two, while other sporadic references to his divinity apart from the Bhagavad Gita are mostly incidental to the main narrative. However, Krishna's less than central role in the main Mahabharata narrative is remedied in the *Harivamsha*, which contains the first complete account of his life. The Bhagavad Gita itself moves from consideration of the *atman* in its first six chapters, in which *bhakti* is rarely mentioned, through Krishna's self-revelation as the Supreme in the eleventh chapter, to its climax in Krishna's declaration of his attachment (*bhakti*) to Arjuna and the promise that by his grace he can be reached, with this enhanced *bhakti* emphasis quite possibly forming the last stage in the growth of the text.[2] The earliest significant use of the term *bhakti* is indeed found in the Bhagavad Gita, but it has there a sense somewhat different from that which it later acquires (one which is closer to that in the rest of the epics, where it primarily denotes loyalty to one's superior). Typical of the Bhagavad Gita's use of the term is the way Krishna's self-revelation produces in Arjuna a spirit of humility, and the fact that its hallmarks are sacrifice and discipline, with little room for spontaneity but rather a stress on one's duty, *dharma*—here, primarily that of one's class.

In the *Narayaniya*, which is located near the end of the didactic twelfth book of the Mahabharata, the *Shantiparvan* (Mbh. 12.321–39), and is clearly itself a composite text, Vasudeva[3] is the Supreme Soul and the central figure of a religion which is explained to his true *bhakta* Narada by Narayana himself in Shvetadvipa. Its understanding of *bhakti* is broadly similar to that of the Bhagavad Gita (and both are considerably more reserved and staid than later emotional *bhakti* as seen in the Bhakti movement itself). The *Narayaniya* places greater weight on ritual and *tapas*, even as it proclaims that the path of *bhakti* is superior to that of knowledge (Schreiner 1997). In course of time, Krishna, Vasudeva and Narayana all came to be identified with Vishnu (with Vasudeva being regarded as a patronymic of Krishna).

The Puranas, which in some ways continue the Sanskrit epic tradition, as well as displaying a more pronounced religious emphasis, then bear witness in the period roughly from the fourth to the twelfth centuries to the next stages of this development in the summaries of the stories which many of them include. Their narratives of Krishna are not based directly on the Mahabharata but are derived from its supplement, the *Harivamsha*, whereas of course their Rama narratives are based on the Ramayana. For example, the *Padma Purana* contains some extensive narratives as well as several briefer allusions to the Rama story; whereas the *Padma Purana* regards the four brothers as *avatars* of Vishnu, his *shankha*, Ananta and the *chakra* respectively, some later Vaishnava Puranas take this a step further by correlating the four brothers with the four *vyuhas* of the Pancharatra system, that developed Vaishnava theological system of which the beginnings are seen in the *Narayaniya*. Again, the *Agni Purana* begins with an account of Vishnu's *avatars*, in which most space is devoted to Rama, testifying to his importance by that period. But in particular, the *Kurma Purana*, though Shaiva, contains the important theological development of the illusory Sita created by Agni when Sita prays to him just before her seizure by Ravana. She is taken by Agni to heaven and then restored to Rama through the fire ordeal after the conquest of Lanka. This development – which safeguards the real Sita's purity – then occurs also in the *Adhyatma Ramayana*, Tulsidas's *Ramcharitmanas* and elsewhere. The relatively late *Bhagavata Purana* focusses mainly of course on Krishna and to a considerable extent supersedes the *Harivamsha* as the prime narrative of Krishna's life for later Bhakti writers, but it does also include a summary of the Mahabharata which, for example, remodels Balarama's tour of the sacred places, his *tirtha yatra*, to make South India its real heartland. Although it also contains a substantial account of Rama, most importantly it describes the whole of Krishna's life on earth, with some emphasis on his childhood, and develops the story of his amours with the *gopis*, treating this as a paradigm of devotees' passion for the deity, in keeping with its marked *bhakti* emphasis.

It is, in fact, the rise of the emotionally charged devotional tradition, the Bhakti movement proper, in Tamil Nadu from the seventh century onwards which transforms the way in which Rama and Krishna, and so the epics themselves, are regarded. There is incidentally some evidence that the story of Rama and the Mahabharata were known in Tamil literature from the Sangam period, roughly the first to third centuries CE, or soon afterwards (cf. Zvelebil 1974, 1991), while the Alvar Kulashekaran, traditionally a ninth-century Chera king, is supposed to have been so absorbed in the Rama story that on one occasion he mobilised his army to go to the aid of Sita, and on another, dived into the sea to swim across to Lanka. What is certain is that the last three of the ten songs in his *Tirumozhi* are based directly on the Ramayana. So too the greatest of the Alvars, Nammalvar (also known as Maran or Satakopan), alludes to Krishna's role in the Mahabharata war (*Tiruvaymozhi* 5.10.1). Tamil adaptations of the Mahabharata and the Ramayana were composed as early as the ninth and probably the tenth century respectively, thus preceding later *bhakti*-oriented Sanskrit versions such as the *Jaiminiyashvamedha* and the *Adhyatma Ramayana* (and probably being contemporary with the *Bhagavata Purana*, which clearly is indebted to the Alvars and shares its emotionalism with them). The earliest Tamil Mahabharata version is Perundevanar's *Paratavenba* (of which only part survives), but the best known among them as well as the finest in literary terms is that by Villiputtur, which is also the version preferred by the Draupadi cult, centred around Gingee (on which see further below). The first Ramayana adaptation, in probably the tenth century, is Kamban's great Tamil work, the *Iramavataram*, appearing in the wake of the Bhakti poetry of the Alvars and showing the same attitude of fervent devotion (as well as incorporating some of the theological developments of the Sanskrit Puranas). Indeed, although in general he follows Valmiki fairly closely, Kamban's work already shows something of the emphasis on the name of Rama which was to become so significant subsequently (especially, but by no means exclusively, in the work of Tulsidas). Even so, in contrast to later devotional retellings, Kamban focusses on the relationship between Rama as king and his subjects, and his connection with moral conduct, *dharma*. But he links Rama's earthly rule with his divinity in the description of *ramarajya* at the end of the work (he deliberately omits the *Uttarakanda*, no doubt because it was out of character with this, although he was definitely acquainted with it). Versions of both epics in the other Dravidian languages followed over the next few centuries (Brockington 1985: 260–306, 1998: 500–505; Raghavan 1980; Smith 1988). In Telugu there are the *Andhra Bharatamu* (begun by Nannaya around 1025 CE and completed in the thirteenth to fourteenth centuries) and the *Ranganatha Ramayana* from the thirteenth century. In Kannada, after earlier Jain versions, come Kumaravyasa's *Krishnabhakti* in the fifteenth century and the *Torave Ramayana* in the seventeenth century. In Malayalam there are not only the *Ramacharitam* from the fourteenth century – exceptional for framing all the rest of the narrative within the *Yuddhakanda*, in a reflection possibly of the militarism of Kerala society both then and for long after (George 1956) and perhaps also of the strand of violence seen elsewhere in South Indian *bhakti* (for example, in the stories of Kannappar and Chiruttontar among the Nayanars (cf. Hudson 1989)) – but also versions of both epics by Tunchattu Ezhuttacchan (his *Adhyatma Ramayana* based on that later Sanskrit text, his Mahabharata version much condensed); in addition, the Niranam poets of the fourteenth and fifteenth centuries produced condensations of both, including one of the earliest vernacular versions of the Bhagavad Gita (which has been much less translated than often assumed—until the modern period, that is).

In addition, the various Vaishnava theological schools which developed out of the Bhakti poetry of the Alvars came to accept the two epics as sources of authority alongside the Vedas. This is most obvious in the fact that in the thirteenth century Madhva wrote a *Mahabharatatatparyanirnaya* (cf. especially 1.30–31) as well as a *Bhagavadgitatatparya*, but this acceptance of the epics as authoritative is also prominent in several other of these philosopher-theologians, although we may note that Ramanuja's *Bhagavad Gitabhasha* (end of the eleventh century or beginning of

the twelfth) is more devotional than philosophical. Thus esteem for
the epics at the popular level, shown in the poetic outpourings of
the Alvars and Kamban, has now been transferred to the more
elevated level at which the Bhakti movement interacted with the
learned orthodox tradition and made deliberate use of the sanctity
and prestige of Sanskrit to establish its respectability. The Sanskrit
of the original epics was consequently a significant feature in this
respect, as was the prestige of the Bhagavad Gita as one of its three
base texts, the *prasthanatraya*, for the orthodox and prestigious
Vedanta school of philosophical thought.

The next stage of the spread of the Ramayana is seen in the
sectarian recastings in Sanskrit, the dating of which is uncertain but
must all fall well within the second millennium CE and so overlaps
with the composition of versions in the modern North Indian
languages. The *Yogavasishtha* (also known by several other names:
Maharamayana, Arsharamayana, Jnanavasishtha) claims to be by
Valmiki but also asserts that it is the twelfth narration of the story;
in fact, a basically Vedantin work, the *Mokshopaya* or
Mokshopayashastra, has at a very late date been framed within a
dialogue between Vasishtha and Rama, itself enlarged into a form
of the *Balakanda* narrative. This composite work then puts forward
a basically Vedantin viewpoint, with considerable stress on Rama
as a *jivanmukta* and so has elements with a wide appeal, since it
represents a unique blend of abstract philosophy and vivid narrative.
It has been translated into many of the vernacular languages of
India. It thus forms just the latest of several instances of the attempt
by the Bhakti movement to enhance its status by adopting Vedantin
terminology. This is even more apparent in the *Adhyatma
Ramayana*, which teaches a form of Advaita combined with belief
in Rama's saving grace; though regarding the world as an illusion
imposed on the eternally blissful Absolute, it is basically a Bhakti
work and stresses the cult of Rama through devotion, worship and
pilgrimage. It is sometimes ascribed to Ramananda, the first major
but rather shadowy figure in the history of Vaishnava Bhakti in the

north (probably belonging to the fourteenth century), and it is most likely that it was produced within his school; it also includes the *Rama Gita*, probably once separate and more purely Advaitin but now included as Rama's own teaching on the way of salvation and clearly intended to provide a counterpart to Krishna's teaching of the Bhagavad Gita. Similarities with Krishna are much more obvious still in the probably fourteenth-century *Bhushundi Ramayana*, which narrates Rama's childhood sports (of which there is no trace in the *Valmiki Ramayana*) following the pattern of Krishna's, showing a blending of Advaita with an erotic *bhakti* emotionalism and even some hints of tantrism in the way that Sita is presented as Rama's *Shakti*. The idiosyncratic and even later *Adbhuta Ramayana* definitely possesses a *shakta* character, with Sita herself going into action to destroy Ravana's thousand-headed brother (both the change in Sita's portrayal and the episode being novel, though then found in many probably later traditional narratives, cf. Smith 1982, Kapp 1988), so much so that it does not really stand within the Bhakti tradition, though nonetheless testifying to the popularity of the story of Rama.

By contrast, there is only the *Jaiminibharata* (which was composed no later than the twelfth century) as a direct Sanskrit recasting of any part of the Mahabharata; this is often called the *Jaiminiyashvamedha*, since it retells the *Ashvamedhikaparvan* (Mbh. 14) and describes the ancient ritual of the horse sacrifice in some detail, but overall it has a pronounced *bhakti* orientation and has been quite popular, especially in South India, being translated into several of the local languages (Koskikallio 1993, 1995). There are also several works that claim to belong to the Mahabharata as part of their claim to authority (the *Dharmasamvada*, *Garbhagita* and the like), and also several summaries of it (for example, the *Itihasasamuchchaya* and the *Bharatasavitri*). However, it is perhaps worth noting that an earlier, perhaps sixth-century, literary work based on the Mahabharata, Bharavi's *Kiratarjuniya*, does have a definite *bhakti* dimension.

On the other hand, whereas the cult of Krishna was long established, there is no firm evidence for the existence of a cult of Rama until towards the end of the period during which these works were being produced. This has even led some scholars to link the emergence of Rama worship with the imposition of Muslim control on North India (most notably Pollock 1993). Although there may be an element of truth in this, it is grossly over-simplified. The worship of Rama has more significant aspects than just nostalgia for a past golden age, glorified as *ramarajya*, which this view takes as the determining factor. Moreover, the *Agastyasamhita*, the earliest text on the ritual for the worship of Rama, was composed during the twelfth century and presupposes that the cult was already in existence then, before the arrival of Muhammad Ghuri at the very end of the century (cf. Bakker 1986). Equally, the *Agastyasamhita* itself was preceded by the *Ramapurvatapaniya Upanishad* and the *Ramarakshastotra*, which point in the same direction, although they are not as directly related to worship practices. This is not to deny that the concept of *ramarajya* has been part of the appeal of the Rama story, as is demonstrated by the elaboration of the passage extolling Rama's righteous rule after his triumphant return to Ayodhya at the end of the *Yuddhakanda* of the *Valmiki Ramayana* and still more by its borrowing by the earliest recastings of the story (cf. Brockington 1986 and 2000). But equally these passages demonstrate that the concept has been there from an early stage, a millennium at least before the Muslim conquest, and that its appeal was not primarily political. There is also an inherent ambiguity in the concept: it may either be seen as a harmonious but hierarchical order, in which everyone knows his place, and so as essentially a return to the values of the past, or as a kingdom of universal righteousness, in which all may achieve their desires, and so essentially as a future hope, with distinct elements of social reform.

Adaptations of both epics were composed in almost all the modern North Indian languages from the fifteenth century onwards, forming one of the most significant types of such early vernacular literature and generally furthering the spread of the devotional ideal through their powerful appeal. The first major adaptation of the Ramayana into a modern North Indian language was that by Krittibas into Bengali, while one of the earliest versions of the Mahabharata is the Oriya adaptation by Sharaladas written around 1475. Like many such adaptations, these include elements from the oral and folk traditions, both reflecting and enhancing their popular appeal (Smith 1988, 2001). Krittibas's version, probably composed early in the fifteenth century, was followed by several other Bengali versions (by Chandrabati late in the sixteenth century, by Adbhutacharyya in the seventeenth century, by Kabichandra around 1700 and by Jagadrama towards the end of the eighteenth century) and, because of its great popularity, it has absorbed several episodes from these later versions. Well-known Ramayanas in other North Indian languages include the *Jagamohana Ramayana* of Balaramdas in Oriya from the late fifteenth to the early sixteenth century, the Assamese version by Madhava Kandali (completed by later poets), Girdhar's Gujarati version and Eknath's *Bhavartha Ramayana* in Marathi with its emphasis on Rama as an upholder of *dharma* (Eknath also of course composed on the Krishna theme the well-known *Eknathi Bhagavata*), while a somewhat different type of adaptation into Marathi is found in the seventeenth-century reworking of two *kandas* by Ramdas, Shivaji's guru, which does show the politicisation of the *ramarajya* concept. On the whole, in these vernacular devotional Ramayanas, Rama's divinity has eclipsed his earthly kingship, while his opponents have been correspondingly demonised. Another trend seen, for example, in the Oriya version of Balaramdas, is that the events of the narrative are to a certain extent given a local setting.

Other adaptations of the Mahabharata, besides the vigorous Oriya version by Sharaladas already mentioned (which was followed by three less popular Oriya versions), include a version by

Parameshvardas, another by Nityananda Ghos and the seventeenth-century *Pandabbijay* of Kashiramdas and his nephew in Bengali, Assamese versions by Shankaradeva and Rama Sarasvati in the sixteenth century (preceded by poems based on episodes only), and Marathi versions by Mukteshvar, Shridhar and Moropant, while Jnanadeva's great verse commentary on the Bhagavad Gita, properly the *Bhavarthadipika* but usually called the *Jnaneshvari* and supposedly completed in 1290 CE, stands at the very beginning of the Bhakti tradition in Maharashtra. Jnanadeva takes *bhakti* as his main theme, expounding the three paths of the Bhagavad Gita in vivid language. He declares that he will plant the garden of the Gita's philosophy in the city of Marathi, vowing to place Sanskrit and Marathi on the same royal throne (12.16 and 10.45). It is also worth noting that even Surdas (c. 1478–1564), popularly though not altogether correctly thought to have based his Krishna poetry on the *Bhagavata Purana*, makes use of the Mahabharata. Significantly one early manuscript distinguishes under a separate heading ten poems of petition put in the mouths of various figures from the Mahabharata, in particular Draupadi (Hawley 1987: 196 and 199).

Surdas has of course subsequently been claimed by the Pushtimarga as one of the 'eight seals' (*ashtchhap*)—the group of poets who supposedly were gathered around themselves by Vallabha and Vitthalnath. As a result his poetry has been remodelled into the expanded *Sursagar*, with its framework set by the Krishna narrative of the *Bhagavata Purana*, and the famous 'child Krishna' poems, commonly thought to be typical of his style, largely added as a result of the influence of Pushtimarga theology. It is interesting therefore to note that among the 84 *baithaks* ('seats') that commemorate Vallabha himself, some are places where by tradition he stopped to give readings not only from the *Bhagavata Purana* but also from the Ramayana. That the Pushtimarga traditions credit him with such commitment to the Ramayana clearly attests the importance of the epics throughout the Bhakti movement.

The best known and most popular of all such retellings of either epic is undoubtedly the Avadhi Hindi version of the Ramayana by Tulsidas, the *Ramcharitmanas* (begun in 1574 CE). There was in fact an earlier version in Brajbhasha, the *Ramayankatha* (dated 1442 CE), by Vishnudas of Gwalior, who also composed a *Pandavcharit* based on the Mahabharata (dated 1435 CE, this in fact adapts parts of the first book of the Mahabharata, with additions from subsequent books; McGregor 1991, 2000). Tulsidas draws on many earlier versions of the Ramayana and an eclectic range of other sources to produce a work of great literary and religious significance, as well as substantial size at over ten thousand lines long (Vaudeville 1955). He also appreciably reshapes the work, giving much greater prominence to the *Bala* and *Uttara kandas* and reducing the scale of the *Yuddhakanda*, because this fits better with his devotional rather than heroic approach. On the basis of its influence not only on Tulsidas but also on other vernacular authors, it is clear that the *Adhyatma Ramayana* was highly significant for the Bhakti tradition.

Through his narration of the Rama story Tulsidas is seeking not only to encourage deep devotion to Rama but also to reconcile and integrate *nirguna* and *saguna* forms of *bhakti*, Vaishnava and Shaiva devotion, and Advaitin theory with *bhakti* practice. Consequently, in the *Ramcharitmanas*, the Name of Rama – widely current among various groups – and the concept of *ramarajya* are both given much greater prominence than before. In his prologue to the *Ramcharitmanas*, Tulsidas carefully justifies his extolling of the divine name, which for him is the essence of the supreme deity and has immense saving power. Elsewhere he affirms that the ideal state of *ramarajya*, dependent on Rama's actual rule for its global realisation, is accessible to individuals in this Kali Age through his saving name. Interestingly, Tulsi's treatment of *ramarajya* is postponed till early in his *Uttarakanda*, which then continues with a discourse by Bhushundi to Garuda on the nature of Rama's divinity, giving a more coherent as well as a more devotional structure to this book of the epic. In this linking of *ramarajya* with the saving name, what might have been merely nostalgia for the past is made relevant to the present with a liberating and, in some measure, socially liberal message. Tulsidas is sometimes and not unreasonably seen as being socially conservative in his views, but against this can be set the traditional story, attesting some degree of hostility from the Brahmin community of his time, that the *Ramcharitmanas* was accepted by them only after a copy of it miraculously rose overnight to the top of a pile of Sanskrit religious works beneath which it had been placed in a locked temple (Lutgendorf 1991: 8–10). It is also worth remembering that Tulsidas draws on the *Adhyatma Ramayana*, which was probably a product of the Ramanandi school (for several centuries one of the most liberal religious orders in North India), that he was early on taken up by that school, and that his *Ramcharitmanas* is the core text of that movement in more modern times. The Ramanandi movement itself has of course major centres at Janakpur and at Ayodhya, where all three of its branches (*tyagi, naga, rasik*) are represented; however, this is not the place to elaborate on the idiosyncratic nature of these internal differences.

Tulsidas also reveals a particular partiality for Hanuman, which fits well with his own *dasya* attitude, but Hanuman's significance within the Rama story had been growing for a long period before this. Hanuman's popularity as an independent figure, often for example worshipped in Maharashtra as the son of the Wind, Maruti, and as a great magician, has no doubt contributed to this, but an important factor must surely be the extent to which in his whole-hearted service to Rama, despite his all too human failings of forgetfulness and lack of application, he provides a model for the ordinary worshipper. The devotee is conscious of his own shortcomings but is reassured by Hanuman's relationship to Rama that they need not prevent the close relationship with his deity that he longs for. In another of his works, his *Vinaypatrika*, Tulsidas appeals to Hanuman to act as his intermediary in presenting his petition at Rama's court; this mediatory role has become still more prominent in popular devotion, thus further increasing the appeal of the Rama story.

Rama himself comes to be recognised in the various adaptations of the story as the embodiment of *dharma*, understood as the binding force which creates cohesion in society through the individual willingly subordinating himself to the good of the whole. Although *dharma* can be imposed for a time by external pressures, the only lasting adherence to it will come by the free choice of the individual. As I have already commented, in the *Valmiki Ramayana*, Rama's moral grandeur comes from his willing submission to the apparently arbitrary requirement of his exile which leads him ultimately to his greatest deed, the killing of Ravana. Here we see in part how *bhakti* and *dharma* are reconciled in the Rama tradition. While *bhakti* involves the surrender of the individual will to the divinely ordained pattern, this surrender at the same time assigns a role to each individual in the divine plan to defeat evil and inhumanity. Thus *bhakti* is not a denial of the free will which is a necessary presupposition of *dharma* but a harnessing of it in a way which parallels the workings of *dharma* and which gives value to each individual. In the ideal world of *ramarajya* evil in the form of premature death, the overturning of the social order and so on are all abolished and *dharma* reigns supreme, 'when Rama governs the kingdom' (*rame rajyam prashasati*, Ram. 6.116.84d etc.; Brockington 1986 and 2000). Nevertheless, from late in the nineteenth century till now the concept of *ramarajya* has been being politicised by some, from the Hindi writer Harishchandra through the Kisan Sabha movement, the Ram Rajya Parishad and the like to the Bharatiya Janata Party (Brockington 1998: 508–10). However, this is not the place to go into such developments.

The popularity of Tulsi's *Ramcharitmanas* is shown by the fact that in Hindi-speaking areas it is the subject of regular recitation, both private and public, and of regular exposition in the *katha* tradition. Above all, it is the text used for the Ramlila performances staged in so many communities at Dussehra, for this remains to this day a popular religious institution. The *Ramlila* performed annually at Ramnagar under the patronage of the late Maharaja of Banaras was the most elaborate, lasting a full month and lavishly produced (Hess and Schechner 1977), but most performances are on a much simpler scale and close to, indeed entirely supported by, the local community as a whole. Indeed, the extent to which the *Ramlila* has transcended sectarian boundaries and is open to all is one of its most notable features, while another is the extent to which it can become a vehicle for social comment, as we see from a diaspora context in Paula Richman's contribution to this volume. This comes despite the relatively conservative implications of the stress on *ramarajya* by Eknath, Tulsidas and others. Enactment of the story in dramatic form has obviously been a potent force in shaping the nature of popular religion; the extent to which each local community is involved in the organisation and in the acting is highly significant. It is quite likely that in Hindi-speaking areas the tradition can be traced back at least to the time of Tulsidas himself, while Krishnadas Kaviraj records in his *Chaitanyacharitamrita* that on one occasion, Chaitanya (1486–1533) was carried away by his acting the part of Hanuman during a festival at Puri, thus attesting that popular Ramayana plays were in existence in Orissa before the time of Tulsidas. Incidentally, the Chaitanya movement provides another instance of the transfer of this popular devotionalism back to the elite sphere in Rupa Gosvamin's Sanskrit dramas, *Vidagdhamadhava* and *Lalitamadhava*, ultimately based on the *Harivamsha* (cf. Wulff 1984). The trend towards employing Tulsidas' *Ramcharitmanas* as the pre-eminent text for public performance – whether in the *Ramlila* or in the various types of *Ramayana katha* – seems to have grown stronger from the eighteenth century onwards, influenced in varying degrees by the resurgence of Hindu kingdoms after the disintegration of the Mughal empire, the increasing influence of the Ramanandi ascetic order, the growing wealth of merchant families and the emergence of a more consciously Hindu identity in reaction to British rule.[4]

Drama cycles based on the Mahabharata are less common, though found from Gingee to Garhwal. In its festivals celebrated in northeastern Tamil Nadu, the Draupadi cult utilises a mixture of drama, recitation and ritual, with the recitation (the *prasangam*) drawn directly from one or other of the Tamil versions of the epic and the dramatic element (the *terukkuttu*) most often more loosely based on Villiputtur's version (Hiltebeitel 1988–91, Vol. 1: 131–68). At the other end of the country, the *Pandavlilas* of Garhwal, performed at different times of the year in different localities and at varying intervals, are a major component of the local culture (Sax 1995). In Karnataka, in the Yakshagana drama form, stories from both epics are staged and, while this belongs primarily to the folk tradition, there is also a definite *bhakti* element. Better known are the Rasa Lila in various parts of North India, especially in Braj, where Krishna grew up. These re-enact events of Krishna's youth among the cowherds, always commencing with his *ras* dance with the *gopis*, continuing with a dramatisation of one of Krishna's many *lilas*, and centring on the love of Radha and Krishna (Hein 1972). They are based at some remove on the *Harivamsha* and rather more directly on the *Bhagavata Purana*, but are limited in their geographical distribution; also, at least in the Braj region, they are performed by troupes of professional actors (*rasmandalis*). Overall, however, the vernacular adaptations of the epics and their dramatic presentations have been a potent medium for the transmission of *bhakti* ideas.

Just how potent is the hold of the epics on the Bhakti movement and related groups is shown for example in the origins of the Radhasoami movement (a group committed to *nirguna bhakti* and indeed claiming descent from the early Sant tradition). The family of Shiv Dayal Singh (d. 1878), regarded as its first guru by the Radhasoami movement, were devotees in Hathras of Tulsi Sahib (d. 1842/3), who had composed a kind of *nirguna* Ramayana, the *Ghat Ramayana*, based just on its philosophical essence, in which he claims to be identical to Tulsidas, the author of the *Ramcharitmanas* (Juergensmeyer 1987: 331 and 349). Once again, the Bhakti cult with its primary focus on a personal deity is allied with a *nirguna* Absolute.

The popularity of the serialisations shown on Indian television (the Ramayana in 1987–88, the Mahabharata in 1989–90), and subsequently made accessible to Hindus abroad as well through the video versions, has been enormous. One of the most obvious features about them was how far their format was conditioned by traditional religious values and their viewing was correspondingly regarded as an act of *puja* (leading for example to garlanding of the television set or performing of *arati* in front of it). The style of the Ramayana version was indeed to a significant extent based on that of the *Ramlila* and its text on the *Ramcharitmanas* of Tulsidas, despite claims to be presenting the standard version based on comparison of all the regional versions (Dalmia-Lüderitz 1991; Lutgendorf 1990).

It is no exaggeration to state that without the two Sanskrit epics, and especially the Ramayana, the Bhakti movement could not exist in the form in which we know it. They have provided the source for so much of its literary expression and are the continuing inspiration of so many of its most important figures. Not merely are they so familiar in some version to virtually every Hindu that they are part of his or her basic world view, but they are also the soil in which the flourishing growth of the Bhakti tradition has taken root and been nurtured.

Notes

1. It is basically this creative aspect which leads Bruce Sullivan to hold that Vyasa represents Brahma, sharing with him the symbolising of brahminical orthodoxy, the creation and dissemination of the Veda, and being frequently termed *pitamaha*, 'grandfather' (Sullivan 1990).

2. On the position of the Bhagavad Gita within the Mahabharata and on Krishna's teaching in it, see Brockington 1997.
3. By Vasudeva is meant here of course the form with long 'a' in the first syllable.
4. On the techniques of recitation and exposition of the *Ramcharitmanas* and on the *Ramlila*, the latest major publication is Lutgendorf 1991.

References

Bakker, Hans (ed.). 1986. *Ayodhya, Part II: Ayodhyamahatmya.* Introduction, edition, and annotation. Groningen: Egbert Forsten.

Biardeau, Madeleine. 1976–78. Études de mythologie hindoue: Bhakti et avatara. In *Bulletin de l'École française d'extrème orient* 63 (1976): 111–263, and 65 (1978): 87–238 (reprinted in *Études de mythologie hindoue* II, École française d'extrème orient, Pondichéry, 1994).

Brockington, John. 1977. Ramo dharmabhritam varah. In *Indologica Taurinensia* 5: 55–68 (reprinted in Brockington 2000: 250–64).

—. 1985. *Righteous Rama.* New Delhi: Oxford University Press.

—. 1986. Sanskrit Epic Tradition II. The *avatara* accounts of Rama. In *Sanskrit and World Culture: Proceedings of the Fourth World Sanskrit Conference*, 619–27. Berlin: Academie-Verlag (reprinted in Brockington 2000: 326–38).

—. 1997. The Bhagavadgita: Text and Context. In *The Fruits of our Desiring: An Enquiry into the Ethics of the Bhagavadgita. Essays from the Inaugural Conference of the DHIIR, Cambridge*, (ed.) Julius Lipner, 28–47. Calgary: Bayeux Arts.

—. 1998. *The Sanskrit Epics* (Handbuch der Orientalistik, 2.12). Leiden: E.J. Brill.

—. 2000. *Epic Threads: John Brockington on the Sanskrit Epics*, (eds.) Greg Bailey and Mary Brockington. New Delhi: Oxford University Press.

Dalmia-Lüderitz, Vasudha. 1991. Television and Tradition: Some Observations on the Serialisation of the Ramayana. In *Ramayana and Ramayanas* (Khoj—A Series of Modern South Asian Studies, 3), (ed.) Monika Thiel-Horstmann, 207–28. Wiesbaden: Harrassowitz.

George, K.M. 1956. *Ramacaritam and the Study of Early Malayalam.* Kottayam: National Book Stall.

Hawley, John Stratton. 1987. The Sant in Sur Das. In *The Sants: Studies in a Devotional Tradition of India*, (eds.) Karine Schomer and W.H. McLeod, 191–211. New Delhi: Motilal Banarsidass.

Hein, Norvin. 1972. *The Miracle Plays of Mathura*. New Haven: Yale University Press.

Hess, Linda, and Schechner, Richard. 1977. The Ramlila of Ramnagar. *The Drama Review* 21: 51–82.

Hiltebeitel, Alf. 1988–91. *The Cult of Draupadi*. 2 vols. Chicago and London: University of Chicago Press.

—. 2001. *Rethinking the Mahabharata: A Reader's Guide to the Education of the Dharma King*. Chicago and London: Chicago University Press.

Hudson, D. Dennis. 1989. Violent and Fanatical Devotion among the Nayanars: A Study in the *Periya Puranam* of Cekkilar. In *Criminal Gods and Demon Devotees: Essays on the Guardians of Popular Hinduism*, (ed.) Alf Hiltebeitel, 373–404. Albany: State University of New York Press.

Juergensmeyer, Mark. 1987. The Radhasoami Revival of the Sant Tradition. In *The Sants: Studies in a Devotional Tradition of India*, (eds.) Karine Schomer and W.H. McLeod, 329–55. New Delhi: Motilal Banarsidass.

Kapp, Dieter B. 1988. Zwei Anspielungen auf die Mahiravana-Sage: Sivapurana 3.20.34 und Padumavati 394–395. *Wiener Zeitschrift für die Kunde Südasiens* 32: 91–102.

Koskikallio, Petteri. 1993. Jaiminibharata and *Asvamedha*. *Wiener Zeitschrift für die Kunde Sudasiens* 36, Supplementband: 111–19.

—. 1995. Epic Descriptions of the Horse Sacrifice. In *Proceedings of the International Conference on Sanskrit and Related Studies*, (ed.) C. Galewicz (Crakow Indological Studies 1), 165–77. Kraków: Enigma Press.

Lutgendorf, Philip. 1990. Ramayan: The Video. *Drama Review* 34: 127–76.

—. 1991. *The Life of a Text: Performing the* Ramcharitmanas *of Tulsidas*. Berkeley: University of California Press.

McGregor, Stuart. 1991. An Early Hindi Version of the Rama Story. In *Devotion Divine: Bhakti Traditions from the Regions of India*, (eds.) Diana L. Eck and Françoise Mallison, 181–96. Groningen: Egbert Forsten.

—. 2000. A Narrative Poet's View of his Material: Vishnudas's Introduction to his Brajbhasa *Pandav-carit* (AD 1435). In *The Banyan*

Tree: Essays on Early Literature in New Indo-Aryan Languages, (ed.) Mariola Offredi, 2 vols., Vol. 2: 335–42. New Delhi: Manohar.

Pollock, Sheldon. 1993. Ramayana and Political Imagination in India. *Journal of Asian Studies* 52: 262–97.

Raghavan, V. 1980. The Ramayana in Sanskrit Literature. In *The Ramayana Tradition in Asia*, (ed.) V. Raghavan, 1–19. New Delhi: Sahitya Akademi.

Sax, William S. 1995. Who's Who in the *Pandav Lila?* In *The Gods at Play: Lila in South Asia*, (ed.) William S. Sax, 131–55. New York: Oxford University Press.

Schreiner, Peter (ed.). 1997. *Narayaniya-Studien* (Purana Research Publications, Tübingen, 6). Wiesbaden: Harrassowitz Verlag.

Smith, William L. 1982. Mahi-Ravana and the Womb-Demon. *Indologica Taurinensia* 10: 215–25.

—. 1988. *Ramayana Traditions in Eastern India*. Stockholm: Department of Indology.

—. 2001. The Burden of the Forest: Two Apocryphal *Parvans* from Vernacular *Mahabharatas*. *Rocznik Orientalistyczny* 54.1: 93–110.

Sullivan, Bruce. 1990. *Krishna Dvaipayana Vyasa and the Mahabharata: A New Interpretation*. Leiden: E.J. Brill (reprinted as *Seer of the Fifth Veda: Krishna Dvaipayana Vyasa in the Mahabharata*. New Delhi: Motilal Banarsidass, 1999).

Vaudeville, Charlotte. 1995. *Étude sur les sources et la composition du Ramayana de Tulsi-Das*. Paris: Adrien-Maisonneuve.

Wulff, Donna M. 1984. *Drama as a Mode of Religious Realization: The Vidagdhamadhava of Rupa Gosvami*. Chico, California: Scholars Press.

Zvelebil, Kamil V. 1974. *Tamil Literature* (History of Indian Literature 10.1). Wiesbaden: Harrassowitz.

—. 1991. *Companion Studies to the History of Tamil Literature* (Handbuch der Orientalistik, Abteilung 2, Ergänzungsband 5). Leiden: E.J. Brill.

CHAPTER THREE

The Implications of Bhakti for the Story of Valmiki

JULIA LESLIE

The Problem

Historians of Indian religions are familiar with the way ancient material is progressively reinterpreted by later traditions. In his classic study of the Ramayana, John Brockington demonstrates how a hero poem, an oral epic of bardic origins, was reworked first according to brahminical concerns with *dharma*, and later by the understandings of *bhakti* (1984). Noel Sheth clarifies a similar shift from Krishna as hero to Krishna as God, the divine recipient of devotional worship (1984). Von Stietencron explores the Puranic versions of the Mahishasuramardini myth of the Goddess as they reflect the effects of the changing Bhakti tradition (1983: 123–27). In a similar vein, if on a much smaller scale, my focus in this essay rests on the figure of Valmiki. How has the story of the great poet-saint been affected by the pressures of *bhakti*?

But first, a word of caution. Historians often forget that the believer is usually neither trained in the historical method nor interested in its conclusions. For the devotee, Rama is both man (the ideal representative of human *dharma*) and divine (the proper object of human worship). While scholars and commentators may struggle with the concept of a man who does not realise his divinity, or of a god who laments his humanity (Pollock 1984), believers embrace the paradox. Similarly, the devotee of Krishna is more likely to see the shift from hero to deity in terms of the gradual awakening of human consciousness rather than as evidence of historical change in the object of their affection. For practising Hindus today, *bhakti* is a given, not a phase. Rama is God; his apparent humanity arises from the paradox of the *avatar*. Krishna is God; his mischievous and amorous antics arise from the paradox of his *lila*. As a Sikh teacher in Britain remarks, 'It's not a matter of head knowledge but *bhakti*' (see Nesbitt, this volume).

But what happens when the deity in question is portrayed not merely as human but as ignorant and evil? This is the problem of Valmiki. For the devotee, Valmiki is God. How then does one explain the popular story of his brutish early life as narrated both in later texts and in modern retellings of the tale? The historian will want to examine the earliest evidence for the story, textual or other. Differences between this evidence and later versions of the story will then give rise to discussions of historical change. But these discussions may be of little interest to the devotee.

One more question. What happens when the two versions – Valmiki as God and Valmiki as sinner – are held simultaneously by two different religious groups, both contemporary, both vocal, and both present in Britain today? This is the situation that came to a head in Birmingham in February 2000, creating a problem that the text-historical approach may be ill-equipped to solve.

On Monday, 21 February 2000, Central Air Radio Limited (Birmingham), trading as 'Radio XL', broadcast as usual on 1296 medium wave. At 13.45 pm, on the Punjabi phone-in programme, 'Eck Swal' ('One Question'), Vikram Gill is responding to a letter from a listener. The latter explains that he has served a jail sentence and now wishes to live a normal life, but even his own community refuses to offer him employment. Gill tells his listeners that Asians in particular should refrain from blaming others for their past actions, for they have the evidence of their scriptures to serve as exemplars. It is at this point, and in this context, that he refers to Valmiki:

When we call someone a thief, when we call someone a sinner, at that time we insult ourselves – because we are Asian people – if we refer to our Shastars and Puranas, if we look at Maharishi Valmik's case, Maharishi Valmiki, who today some communities call Bhagavan Valmiki. This Valmiki before becoming a rishi (sage), was a daku (dacoit). He couldn't even say 'Ram'. When he said 'Ram', the word 'Mara' came out of his mouth. However with his *bhakti*, from saying 'Mara, Mara...', he learnt to say 'Ram', and with that he is now known as Maharishi Valmiki, known as Bhagavan Valmiki.

Gill concludes that the persecuted man should follow Valmiki's example—he should 'face the world', thinking only of God. The episode is brought to a close with a final snippet of cheery advice: 'Now ignore people, move forward in a happy way with Radio XL's wishes, we Asians are with you' (8–10).[1]

In context, to the disinterested outsider, Gill's advice is obviously well intentioned. Like so many others before and since, Valmiki had been able to rise above a wicked past. As a result, he had become the saintly figure revered by many today as 'Bhagavan' or God. He achieved this by reciting the name of God ('Ram') as best as he could. According to this story, therefore, Valmiki's religious devotion, his *bhakti*, swept aside ignorance, ineptitude and even past misdeeds. The problem, of course, is that only an outsider could countenance the suggestion that Valmiki was ever ignorant, inept or wicked. It is no surprise, therefore, that the broadcast caused offence to British devotees of Valmiki. For them, Valmiki is the divinised poet-saint who composed two of the most important sacred texts of India: the *Valmiki Ramayana* and the *Yogavasishtha Ramayana*. Unfortunately but understandably, Gill's radio broadcast mentioned none of this explicitly. It dwelled only on the well-known (but, to the devotee, unacceptable) story that Valmiki was once an uneducated dacoit (that is, a robber and a murderer) who was unable even to pronounce the name of God.

Their revered Bhagavan had suddenly been reduced in the public discourse of the air waves to an uneducated and simple-minded bandit. How could such a man ever have invented the epic verse form, the Sanskrit *shloka*, as Valmiki is believed to have done? How could he have fashioned the elevated language of the gods into the divine form of the Ramayana? How could he have attained the spiritual heights necessary to convey the insights of the *Yogavasishtha*? In this context, it appears, the dacoit story is inherently impossible.

The Valmiki Legend

At the heart of the problem is the notion that Valmiki was once an ignorant and brutish dacoit. This idea will be familiar to anyone who has read any of the widely distributed comic-book accounts of the poet's life. An excellent example is provided by the Amar Chitra Katha series edited by Anant Pai and subtitled 'The Glorious Heritage of India'. The most recent English edition, entitled *Valmiki: The Story of the Author of the Epic, 'Ramayana'* (Pai 1994), is read and re-read all over the world. Indeed, the message printed on the inside front cover reads: 'AMAR CHITRA KATHA means good reading. Over 78 million copies sold so far.' The popularity of this comic-book series in many Indian languages as well as in English, read by millions of adults as well as children, surely bears some responsibility for the spread of the legend today, and thus for the continued attribution of a wicked past to Valmiki.[2]

Let us look more closely at the Amar Chitra Katha version of the story. The preamble, also printed on the inside front cover, is suitably reverential:

To Valmiki, we Indians owe a deeper debt of gratitude than to any other poet. He gave us the Ramayana, one of the most fascinating stories of all time. No words can describe the hold the Ramayana has had on the people of India from ancient times to the present day. It has affected the life and thought of our people and played an important role in shaping Indian culture. Valmiki was the Adikavi, the first poet, and his Ramayana the Adikavya, the first poem.

But the preamble does not stop there. 'While remembering the man's work,' it continues, 'we must not forget the man. How he wrote the Ramayana, and under what conditions, is itself an absorbing story.' We are then informed that this comic-book version is 'based on Valmiki Ramayana and Vallathol's Malayalam translation', both eminently authoritative sacred texts. Finally, we are presented with a series of fulsome sayings attributed to the great man. There is evidently no intention here to demean Valmiki. Nonetheless, the urge to focus on the stories that have circulated about the man rather than on his work inevitably leads us to the controversy in question.

Both the illustration on the cover and the first frame of the comic format portray the key moment of Valmiki's life: an ascetic-looking figure with long white hair and beard sits on a deerskin in what appears to be a deer-inhabited hermitage, writing the Ramayana on palm leaves. In the cover illustration, we can clearly make out the *nagari* script in which he is writing,[3] and the feather-tipped quill he is holding. He is wearing a necklace and bracelets made from *rudraksha* beads, while his long hair is caught up in the *rudraksha*-bead top-knot of the sage. From the first frame of the story onwards, Valmiki's skin is markedly darker than that of most of the people he encounters: this is a pointed allusion to his presumed tribal, and therefore low-status, origins.

The second frame of the comic takes us to Valmiki's life as a young man. He is depicted as young and muscular, both hair and beard are dark, and there is a hard expression on his face. He wears the animal-skin loin-cloth of the forest-dwelling tribal or *adivasi*. Slung across his back is a quiver of arrows, in his hands a bow. The caption reads: 'Strangely, Valmiki was a hunter and robber in his early life.' The next few frames show him 'roaming the jungle', shooting down 'harmless birds', killing 'gentle animals' (he is pictured stalking deer), and bringing home the 'carcasses' for food (2). We are then told that he 'also waylaid and robbed lone travellers in the jungle', threatening to kill them if they refused to hand over their goods (3). This preliminary scene is set with the words: 'Thus he lived a life of violence and crime' (4).

The following pages narrate the story of the young bandit's meeting with the 'Seven Sages' (*sapta-rishi*). Throughout the exchange, there are striking differences between the bandit and the sages. The former's dark skin, blue-black hair and muscled body contrast sharply with the pink skin, white top-knots and ascetic build of the sages. Clothing and body decorations are quite different: animal-skin loin-cloth as opposed to saffron robes and *rudraksha* beads. The hunter's bow and arrows, and the robber's curved and brandished knife are thrown into relief by the sages' total lack of weaponry. The harsh expression on the attacker's face is met by the untroubled gaze of the holy men.

The sages enquire gently why the young man wants to rob them. His answer is curt: 'I have to maintain my wife and children. Robbery is my livelihood' (5). The leader of the sages requests permission to ask one more question: 'Your family lives on the fruits of your sin. Will they partake of your sins as well?' (6). The robber insists that they will; however, his face betrays a hint of uncertainty. He agrees to go home to check and the sages promise to wait.

Back in his hut in the forest, the robber's conversation with his pretty, pink-skinned wife is short and shocking:

'Dear wife, you benefit from my sinful life. Don't you?'
'Of course, I do. What of that?'
'You will share my sins, won't you?'
'Certainly not! You are the sinner. Why should I share your sin?'

He turns to his equally pink-skinned son:

'Won't you at least share my sin, my darling?'
'No father, I will not.'
'Oh, my God!'

The robber stands 'stunned and dazed', unable to believe what he
has heard. He is shown returning to the sages, bent and staggering
under 'the weight of sorrow', his face distraught. As he approaches
them, he bursts into tears. Throwing himself at their feet and
'weeping bitterly', he begs their understanding and help. 'My soul
is lost,' he declares. 'Redeem it, O compassionate ones' (7–9).

The sages take pity on him. They tell him to sit down and recite
the sounds *ma-ra*. 'Put your heart and soul into it,' they say. 'Don't
stop for a moment till we return.' The young man, still described
as 'the robber', obeys. He is depicted sitting cross-legged on the
ground, his eyes closed, 'forgetting himself'. The caption tells us
that the sounds *ma-ra* are in fact the name Rama 'inverted'. This
means that the continued repetition of the apparently fake *mantra*
(the sounds *ma-ra*) will culminate in the recitation of a real *mantra*:
ma-[ra ma]-[ra ma]-ra, and so on. The implication is that the
ignorant fellow is unwittingly reciting the name of God. He sits
there meditating like this for weeks, months, years. Slowly, a
termite mound takes shape around him, rising inch by inch until
it covers him completely.

Years later, when the sages return, they find a man-shaped termite
mound. They summon the meditator forth. The caption reads:
'The anthill burst open and out stepped a person different in every
respect.' This striking individual pays homage to Rama and to the
sages for the miracle of his transformation while the latter acclaim
him as 'among the greatest rishis' with yet 'greater glory' ahead. The
caption explains: 'He came out of "Valmik" meaning anthill, and
so the rishis called him by the new name of "Valmiki"' (10–11).[4]

This is the legend at issue in the Birmingham dispute. The rest
of the comic-book story may be summarised briefly. News of

Valmiki's 'spiritual power and knowledge' spreads. He meets the great sage, Narada, who narrates the story of Rama, the perfect man. One day, while Valmiki is watching a pair of birds, 'husband and wife, billing and cooing',[5] the male is killed by a dark-skinned hunter. Valmiki curses the hunter, his curse emerging in Sanskrit verse form, and the first *shloka* is born.[6] The god Brahma then appears. He instructs Valmiki to compose the story of Rama, including both what he already knows and what will be revealed to him. Valmiki composes the Ramayana (12–19). Years later, Rama's queen, Sita, is abandoned in the forest, where she is rescued by Valmiki who brings her to his hermitage. There she gives birth to twin sons who are later taught by Valmiki to recite the Ramayana. Later still, he sends the boys to Rama's court to perform a formal recitation. When Rama realises who they are, he sends a message to Valmiki: if Sita will swear in public that she is pure, he will take her back. Valmiki accompanies her to the royal court where he swears publicly on her behalf. But Rama insists that Sita speaks for herself. Instead, the earth opens up and spirits her away. Rama is grief-stricken. Valmiki returns to his ascetic life (20–31).

This is the so-called 'popular' tradition. While it is necessary to concede this point, it is also important to recognise that the key elements of the story – clearly unproblematic for many – are controversial for some. It seems that the historian faces an impossible task. We may rightly hesitate to walk into the line of fire between two opposing sides, and yet there are issues here that require academic scrutiny. Furthermore, might the text-historical approach (textual sources as evidence of change) become a means of negotiating the no-man's land between opposing devotional positions (for both of whom text is sacred)? Can we trace the narrative threads of the Valmiki story as they weave their way through the passing centuries? If we can, might this contribute in some way to our understanding of the interlocking beliefs of British South Asians and, by extension, to a greater awareness of the problematic relationship between sacred text and contemporary religious meaning? Clearly, at the heart of this problem lies the complexity of *bhakti*.

Locating Valmiki in Sacred Texts

The text-historical approach requires that we search for references to Valmiki, and stories about him, at the earliest textual level. I shall begin with references to the name 'Valmiki' in the oldest Sanskrit literature available. It is the conclusion of many scholars (e.g. Bulcke 1958: 121–22, Brockington 1998: 24–25) that the name 'Valmiki' probably identifies at least three separate individuals in India's rich past—an ancient grammarian, a famous ascetic or *muni*, and the poet who composed the Ramayana. The last of these three is described both in early Sanskrit texts such as the Mahabharata and the Ramayana, and in later texts in Sanskrit and vernacular languages (Brockington 1998: chapter 10). This Valmiki is often described as 'Bhargava', that is, as belonging to the famous Bhrgu clan (Goldman 1976, 1977; Brockington 1998: 394–95). More important for the purposes of this paper, there is no mention of the dacoit story in either Sanskrit epic.

The grammarian Valmiki is irrelevant here. The relevance of the ascetic Valmiki will become clear below. First, however, consideration will be given to the poet-saint of the Ramayana, the Valmiki in question.

According to pan-India tradition, Valmiki composed the 'original' Ramayana. There is no external evidence to support this attribution, but the internal evidence is clear. So, what does this sacred text reveal about Valmiki? In the critical edition of the text, there are no references to him in books 2–6, the core of the Ramayana, composed in about the fifth or fourth centuries BCE. All the information about him is found in the later books— 1 (*Balakanda*) and 7 (*Uttarakanda*), composed somewhere between the first and the third century CE. More important, every reference to Valmiki is couched in complimentary terms.

For example, Book 1 begins by describing him as an 'ascetic' (1.1.1), and then as a 'great and eloquent sage', a 'righteous man' who is sufficiently learned and charismatic to attract his own disciples (1.2.1).[7] This 'pious seer' (1.2.12) – described as a brahmin (1.2.13) and a 'wise and thoughtful man' (1.2.16) – is so moved by the death of a bird that he unthinkingly utters a lament in the *shloka* form. So inspiring is this moment of poetic creation that his delighted disciple commits the verse to memory at once (1.2.18). Soon afterwards, the god Brahma comes in person to see this 'sage' who knows 'the ways of righteousness' (1.2.21–22). He addresses Valmiki as 'brahmin' and 'greatest of seers' (1.2.30). Impressed by Valmiki's qualities as both poet and compassionate human being, Brahma asks him to compose the story of Rama in the form of *shlokas*. Furthermore, the god promises him that he will 'see' everything that happened, 'the full story, public and private', and that his poetic utterances will be faultless (1.2.31–34). In Chapter 3, Valmiki sits ritually and reverently in 'profound meditation' in order to 'see' the story he has to tell (1.3.2). The 'holy seer' is then able to render that vision into poetry (1.3.29). In Chapter 4, Valmiki is described as 'the holy and self-controlled seer' (1.4.1), 'the wise master' (1.4.2), 'the great contemplative seer' (1.4.3) and as 'a man who always fulfilled his vows' (1.4.6–7). Finally, he teaches the poem to Kusha and Lava, Rama's sons. It is clear from these scene-setting chapters that Valmiki is an exemplary individual—high-born, high-minded, learned in matters of 'righteousness' (*dharma*), a 'seer' to whom the highest truths are revealed, and a poet with a perfect command of the Sanskrit language; in short, a man worthy of the company of gods.

The next important passage involving Valmiki occurs in Book 7. When Rama instructs Lakshmana to abandon Sita in the forest, he makes sure that she is left near the *ashram* of the famous Brahmin, Valmiki. Valmiki is known to be a close friend of King Dasharatha, Rama's late father. More to the point, since Rama would have been familiar with many *ashrams* and many sages, we may conclude that his choice of Valmiki demonstrates the esteem in which the sage was held. It is obviously Rama's hope that Valmiki, whom he values so highly, will take care of his beloved wife.

The third passage worth noting is that in which Valmiki testifies in public to Sita's innocence. He makes his famous declaration (7.87.17–19):

> I am the tenth son of Prachetas, [O Rama]. I do not remember ever telling a lie. These two (boys) are therefore your sons.

> I have performed austerities for many thousands of years. May I never obtain the rewards accruing to those [austerities], if [Sita] is not innocent!

> When, with my five senses and my mind as the sixth, I was meditating on Sita amidst forest waterfalls, she was revealed to me as pure.[8]

Valmiki's public insistence on his own noble origins and innate truthfulness demonstrates his determination to prove Sita innocent. But his words also confirm what the early tradition tells us—that Valmiki is high-born, a respected ascetic, and a man of the highest moral principles.

Many later texts also tell us about Valmiki. Most of these are variants on the well-known *Adhyatma Ramayana* account reflected in the comic-book version given above. Sometimes, the key role played by the seven sages is taken by Brahma and Narada, or by Shiva and Narada. But the outcome is always the same—a wicked man sees the error of his ways, recites an odd *mantra*, performs *tapas* until a termite mound grows up over his body and, finally, emerges as the Valmiki who will compose the Ramayana.

Of the many vernacular versions of the Rama story, one obvious source to consider is the immensely popular *Ramcharitmanas* written in Hindi in the sixteenth century by Tulsidas. In startling contrast with the earliest Sanskrit evidence, Tulsi's Valmiki is an Untouchable or outcaste (*shvapacha*). Since some North Indian *jatis* claim descent from this individual, the point has important contemporary relevance. For example, when it appeared that the television Ramayana might omit the episode concerning Sita and their ancestor, strike action spread through several major cities in the north (Richman 1991: 3).

Another important source is the famous Ramayana composed in Bengali by Krittibas (Skt. Krittivasa) in the fifteenth century. This text follows the Sanskrit *Adhyatma Ramayana* in the matter of the prehistory of Valmiki. Ratnakara, a cruel and uneducated robber, meets the seven sages and repents of his ways. Because of his background, he is deemed unable to recite the Name of God and so is given instead the *mantra ma-ra* (that is, the Name of God with the syllables reversed). By repeating this *mantra*, he is at last able to pronounce the Name of God and become purified. Because of the termite mound, he is renamed 'Valmiki'. He then composes the Ramayana.

In the context of the Birmingham dispute, one further source is important—the *Adi Granth*. It seems likely that the broadcaster at the centre of the dispute based his remarks on the *Adi Granth*, or perhaps on a Punjabi text based on the *Adi Granth* such as Sodhi Teja Singh's *Bhakt Mal*. According to the Sikh tradition, the *Adi Granth* was dictated by the fifth Guru Arjan to his disciple during the years 1603–1604.[9] In its current form, then, this collection of material is later than all the other sources considered in this essay.

There are two references to 'Balmik' in the *Adi Granth* and neither refers explicitly to him as the composer of the Ramayana.[10] The first passage occurs in Rag Maru, initially by the fourth Guru Ramdas (Maru M4, 995). Ramdas mentions many saintly or heroic figures from classical Hindu mythology within a semi-narrative framework of the Puranic *yugas*. These include Sukdeva, Janak, Sudama, Dhruva, Prahlad, Bidar in the pre-Kali Age, followed by the *bhaktas* Namdev, Jaidev, Kabir, Trilochan and Ravidas in the Kali Age. The next few verses list a number of well-known 'sinners' who were saved: Ajamal, Ugar Sain, 'Dhanna the Jat', and 'Balmik the highway robber' (*balmik batvara*). As one would expect from the *bhakti* context, the emphasis of the passage is on the efficacy of the Name and how each of these individuals was brought to salvation by reciting and reflecting on that Name. The second passage, this time by Guru Arjan, occurs a few pages later (Maru M5, 999). Here the reference to 'Balmik' occurs alongside the word *supchar* which means 'untouchable' or 'outcaste'.

What conclusions may be drawn from this material? Broadly speaking, only two aspects of the story are crucial to the Sikh religious context—the importance of *bhakti* in general and the efficacy of the divine Name. The allusions to Valmiki are unimportant. They merely reflect the story that was in circulation when the *Adi Granth* was being compiled.

Tracing the Key Motifs

The next step is to consider the text-historical evidence for the three motifs of the popular Valmiki story: the ascetic in the termite mound, the dacoit-turned-devotee, and the *ma-ra mantra*.

The name 'Valmiki' is usually derived from the Sanskrit term *valmi* ('termite'; hence *valmika* – 'termite mound'). The name is taken to refer to a person who is for some reason connected with a termite mound. This etymology has given rise to what may be termed the 'termite mound motif' in later literature relating to the author of the Ramayana.

The first point to stress is that the earliest reference to this motif has no connection with the Valmiki in question. According to the Mahabharata, a Brahmin named Chyavana, described as the son of Bhrgu, once practised austerities (*tapas*) for so long that a termite mound grew up around his immobile body. This motif became increasingly popular in the later Puranas. At some point, it also became associated with the Ramayana Valmiki. However, it is important to realise that the notion of staying immobile in meditation until a termite mound grows up around the meditator's body is not restricted to even these two individuals. One might go so far as to say that it is characteristic of Indian ascetic practice in general. For example, a parallel is provided by the Jain tradition—the Tirthankara Bahubali meditated for so long that plants and termite mounds grew up around his body.

The process of conflation is clear. According to available textual evidence, the termite mound motif begins with Chyavana. Both Chyavana and Valmiki are described as ascetics. Both are given the name 'Bhargava' ('descendant of Bhrgu'). The parallels are persuasive. Eventually, the combination of the termite mound story in relation to Chyavana with the etymology of Valmiki's name must have led to the assumption that the ascetic Chyavana and the poet-sage-ascetic Valmiki were the same individual. Before long, the termite mound story was being attributed directly to the poet. In view of the next development in the Valmiki legend, this is important.[11]

The point of the dacoit story is that a wicked person can become a saint. But where did the story originate, and how did it become attached to Valmiki? It is certainly not in the *Valmiki Ramayana*.

The earliest reference to the story in relation to the name 'Valmiki' seems to be the one found in the *Skanda Purana*.[12] This text was once widely known and regarded as authoritative in North India. Scholars tend to date the earliest version of the text to the ninth century CE, but many other versions appeared later as more and more *kandas* were added.[13] It is highly likely that the accounts of the Valmiki legend belong to a later version. The important point for the purpose of this chapter, however, is that the *Skanda Purana* provides four different accounts of the story.

The first account concerns an unnamed hunter who recites the name of Rama. Here we should note, first, the generally devotional context of the story and, second, the specific theme of reciting the Name of God. As a result of his devotions, this hunter is reborn in his next life as the son of an ascetic named Krinu. Krinu performs *tapas* for so long that a termite mound grows up over him. He is given the name 'Valmika' ('termite mound') while his son is named 'Valmiki' ('descendant of Valmika'). On the strength of his devotion in his previous life, Valmiki (the son), eventually writes the Ramayana. This is clearly a late development of the ascetic-in-the-termite-mound story outlined earlier. In this case, however, it is the ascetic's son who is named 'Valmiki' and who, on that basis, is assumed to be the author of the Ramayana.

The second account concerns a dacoit named Agnisharma. One day, he comes across the celebrated seven sages. He is on the point of killing them when they ask him a simple question. Is his family as willing to share his guilt as his profits? Agnisharma goes to find out. He is stunned to discover that both his wife and his children refuse to share his guilt, although they are happy to enjoy the proceeds. In shock, he abandons dacoity and begins to do *tapas* to compensate for his past actions. After thirteen years, the seven sages return to find Agnisharma covered by a termite mound. They dig him out, name him 'Valmiki' on account of the termite mound, and instruct him to write the Ramayana. This version brings together several elements of the popular story narrated earlier—the dacoit who mends his ways, ascetic practice and the growth of a termite mound around the practitioner, the name 'Valmiki' by association with the termite mound, and composition of the Ramayana.

The third account concerns a Brahmin named Lohajangha. When famine strikes, he becomes a dacoit in order to feed his aging parents. The seven sages appear as before and ask their all-important question. Shocked by his family's response, Lohajangha asks the sages for advice. This time, they give him a nonsensical *mantra* to chant.[14] Years later, the sages return to find him still chanting, now covered by a termite mound, and they name him 'Valmiki'. This version adds a new element to the story—the sages give the penitent ex-dacoit a *mantra* to recite, but one without any obvious meaning. This detail will be elaborated further in yet later versions of the story.

The fourth account found in the *Skanda Purana* concerns a Brahmin named Vaishakha who supports his family by dacoity. Again the seven sages appear and ask their question. Vaishakha is so shocked by his family's response that he renounces the world and practises *tapas* for thousands of years. Eventually, the seven sages return. When they find him covered by a termite mound, they name him 'Valmiki' and prophesy that he will write the Ramayana.

Several conclusions may be drawn from these four accounts in the *Skanda Purana*. First, as argued earlier, the story of ascetic practice and the termite mound is told of a variety of differently named individuals. Second, the ascetic practitioner is sometimes defined as a Brahmin, but not always. Third, it is not always the ascetic practitioner who earns the name 'Valmiki'. Fourth, the sinner (hunter or dacoit) invariably abandons his wicked ways. Fifth, the name 'Valmiki' becomes the postscript to each version of the story. Sixth and last, on the strength of that name, all the elements become firmly associated with the author of the Ramayana. For the implications of the *mantra*, and for the power increasingly associated with the Name of Rama, the next stage in the development of the Valmiki legend needs to be examined.

Perhaps the most influential version of the story in relation to Valmiki is that of the *Adhyatma Ramayana*. This Sanskrit text, dated to the fourteenth or fifteenth century CE, is generally considered to be part of the *Brahmanda Purana*. While uncertainty remains concerning both date and author, the text was certainly composed after the spread of Rama Bhakti in the north of India. The main storyline is the same as that in Valmiki's Ramayana, but Rama's divinity is explicit and the *bhakti* context is stressed. In addition, Valmiki's 24,000 *shlokas* have been reduced to 4,000 (Bulcke 1958: 127; Thampi 1996: 17–18). According to this extremely late source, Rama visits Valmiki's *ashram* together with

Sita and Lakshmana. There, the poet tells his own life-story, as follows.

A Brahmin by birth, the man destined to be named 'Valmiki' is raised by low-caste Kirata tribals. He adopts the Shudra life-style, marries a Shudra woman, and becomes a hunter and a dacoit. At some point, the seven sages appear and ask their question. When the dacoit hears his family's response, he at once repents and asks the sages to help him. Because of his apparently Shudra origins and his current career as a dacoit, he is deemed unworthy to pronounce the Name of Rama. Instead, the sages instruct him to recite the *mantra ma-ra* (that is, 'Rama' with the syllables reversed). A thousand years later, they return to find him still reciting but covered by a termite mound, and they name him 'Valmiki'.

It seems that the evolving legend has added two further elements to the story, placing both in the mouth of Valmiki for maximum effect. First, the apparent contradiction between the Brahmin who takes up ascetic practice and the low-caste hunter/dacoit who repents of his wicked ways is resolved by having a Brahmin boy raised by low-caste parents. Second, the strange *mantra* is now explained within an explicitly devotional context by the assumed unworthiness of the recipient to pronounce the Name of God. The point of the story is clear—even when recited in reverse order by an ignorant man unaware of the potential meaning of these syllables, God's name has the power to bring salvation. We may assume that, by the time the (now purified) ex-dacoit emerges from his termite mound, he is knowingly reciting the Name of God. This is obviously a story about *bhakti*, and not really one about Valmiki.

The *mantra* motif is also found in the seventeenth-century Sanskrit text, the *Tattvasamgraha Ramayana*.[15] The protagonist here is a hunter who makes his living as a dacoit. The seven sages appear as usual to ask their question. The shocked hunter repents and asks for spiritual instruction but the sages are nonplussed. What kind of instruction can they give to a low-caste hunter? A voice from the sky proclaims, '*Ma-ra!*' The hunter begins his ascetic practice.

When the sages return to dig him out of the termite mound, the gods appear to sing his praises. Vishnu blesses Valmiki as the future author of the Ramayana. Again, the devotional context is uppermost.

A more complex account is found in the *Ananda Ramayana*, a Sanskrit text usually dated to between the fifteenth and seventeenth centuries CE. This source provides three consecutive life-stories for Valmiki. First, he is a Brahmin named Stambha who falls in love with a prostitute and adopts the life of a Shudra. In his next life, Stambha is reborn as a hunter who lives the life of a dacoit; one day, he feels pity for a Brahmin he has robbed and returns his shoes. In his third life, the former dacoit is reborn from a snake that has swallowed the semen of the ascetic Krinu (see above); the child is raised by the Kiratas as a Shudra, and meets the seven sages. The rest of the tale is predictable, including the *mantra ma-ra*, the inverted Name of God.

All these stories about the prehistory of Valmiki are best understood within the context of the development of *bhakti*. The dacoit story does not appear in the *Valmiki Ramayana*. It is a later addition associated with Puranic retellings and arising from the spread of devotional religion.

Conclusions and Reflections

It is impossible in a contribution of this length to consider the potential sources for, and variations of, the dacoit stories in the prehistory of Valmiki in any depth. However, I have recently completed a full-length study along these lines (Leslie 2003). In that context, I also consider in more detail both the dispute in Birmingham in February 2000, and the religious beliefs and practices of Valmiki devotees in India and Britain.

Although it is hard to substantiate this point, the poet-saint Valmiki probably lived in North India around the turn of the fourth century BCE. By the first century BCE, he is described as a great ascetic (*muni*), a contemporary of Rama, who lived in an *ashram* near the Tamasa and Ganga rivers. By the time of the *Uttarakanda*, Valmiki is described as a famous Brahmin who has close links with the royal house of Ayodhya and belongs to the Bhrgu clan. Here we have the first evidence of a probable confusion between the early termite mound story in connection with Chyavana and the etymology of Valmiki's name.

The dacoit legend grew more slowly. More important, in its earliest forms the story contains no reference to Rama. With the emergence of Rama Bhakti, however, this motif of the dacoit-turned-devotee becomes the perfect illustration, first, of the grace of God and, second, of the power of the Name of Rama (even when the syllables are reversed). The addition of the old Chyavana theme of ascetic practice and the termite mound, together with the etymological explanation of the name Valmiki, pulls all the elements together into one composite tale. This is the version that we find in the popular comic books.

However, there are dangers in conflating these different stories. It is a common enough mistake, of course—even otherwise careful writers make careless remarks in this regard.[16] Perhaps these scholars are unaware of the text-historical evidence for the conflation. They must certainly be ignorant of the implications of such a conflation for the devotees of Valmiki. It is surely wiser to follow the example of those who have studied the early texts. For example, van Nooten writes: 'Legends make him [Valmiki] a reformed robber converted to a virtuous life by a saint, but from the one and only literary work that remains of him we recognise him as a poetic genius, a man of refined and aesthetic sense and a pure instinct for moral living' (1976: xiii). Benjamin Khan is convinced that 'the theory that Valmiki began his career as a highway robber is a legend ill-conceived and unfounded' (1983: 12). Similarly, Camille Bulcke points out in his thoughtful study that the earliest forms of the dacoit story are unrelated to the Rama narrative (1958: 131). Only after the development of Rama Bhakti in northern India was this motif attached to Valmiki. The reason for this is obvious—the legend as it now stands provides the perfect illustration of the power of the Name of God to turn the worst of sinners (that is, a low-caste, murdering dacoit) into the best of men (that is, the revered poet-saint, Valmiki).

According to the earliest evidence available, then, Valmiki may be described as a pious Brahmin,[17] an inspired and gifted poet, a man of high principles and firm morals, a spiritual leader reverenced even by kings, and a gentle saint who feels compassion for all beings, from the cruelly slaughtered sarus crane to the vulnerable and abandoned Sita. This Valmiki is worthy of both veneration and respect. The legend of the low-caste dacoit-turned-devotee must have emerged from another source. Somewhere between the ninth and the fifteenth centuries CE (later rather than earlier), within the context of devotional worship in North India, this legend became so firmly attached to the author of the Ramayana that few people are surprised to find it in the popular comic books of today. One might argue that it is equally unsurprising to find this legend alluded to in a contemporary radio broadcast. However, as I demonstrate in my extended study (Leslie 2003), there are complex issues of status, caste and class embedded in the development of this story. Given the prospect and potential for inter-community conflict, therefore, greater sensitivity is to be hoped for from all concerned.

Notes

1. This material is taken from the English translation of the Punjabi transcript of the relevant broadcasts; both are contained in the *Report of the Bhagavan Valmiki Action Committee* (2000: 8–36). The brackets indicate editorial insertions in the printed text. Insignificant errors of spelling, punctuation and grammar have been silently corrected. I am grateful to Lekh Raj Manjdadria for first bringing

the incident to my attention, and for providing me with a copy of the *Report*.

2. For discussions of the comic-book genre with particular reference to the Amar Chitra Katha series, see Pritchett (1995) and Hawley (1995).

3. This charming picture is, of course, a misrepresentation of the (probably) pre-literate and (certainly) oral traditions of India. As Richard Salomon explains in his review article on recent publications on this topic, 'there are no securely datable specimens of writing from the historical period earlier than the rock inscriptions of Ashoka from the mid-3rd century BC' (1995: 271). For a comprehensive study of the key issues, see Falk (1993).

4. Strictly speaking, the Sanskrit term *valmi* denotes a termite rather than an ant (Skt. *pipilika*), which means that *valmika* should be translated 'termite mound' rather than 'anthill'. That said, termites are popularly known as 'white ants'.

5. For a study of this episode, including the identification of these birds as a pair of Indian sarus cranes and the implications of their symbolism, see Leslie 1998.

6. What (one may ask) is the significance of an ex-hunter, presumably once ignorant of Sanskrit, now using Sanskrit to curse another hunter who is only doing what he himself used to do?

7. The English translations are from Goldman (1984).

8. It is worth noting here that the oft-quoted line – variations on 'I have never sinned in thought, word or deed' – has been relegated to the critical apparatus of the Baroda edition.

9. On the difficulties of undertaking the textual study of Sikh scriptures, see Deol (2001).

10. I am indebted to Arvind Mandair for helping me to locate this material.

11. For further reading, see Goldman (1976, 1977).

12. For one of the earliest studies of stories relating to Valmiki in the *Skanda Purana*, see Bulcke (1958). For the standard English translation of the *Skanda Purana* based on the vulgate version, see Tagare (1992).

13. While the oldest palm-leaf manuscript is dated 810 CE, recent scholarship suggests a tentative date for the core text between the sixth and eighth centuries CE (Adriaensen, Bakker and Isaacson 1998: 4–5).

14. The *mantra* is *jataghota*. The term *jata* relates to the matted locks worn by the ascetic (*jata*), while *ghota* denotes a horse.
15. For further reading in relation to these and other Sanskrit texts, see Raghavan (1952–53, 1980).
16. Examples include Shastri (1962: xv) and Ayyangar (1991: 48–53).
17. However, this too is a controversial point for Valmiki devotees. While they resist the notion of Valmiki as an ignorant robber, they are reluctant to give him high-caste status. See Leslie (2003).

References

Adriaensen, R., H.T. Bakker, and H. Isaacson (eds.). 1998. *The Skandapurana*. Vol. 1, *Adhyayas 1–25, critically edited with prolegomena and English synopsis*. Groningen: Egbert Forsten.

Ayyangar, Sreenivasa. 1991. *The Ramayana of Valmiki*, Part 1. Madras: The Little Flower Co.

Brockington, John. 1984. *Righteous Rama: The Evolution of an Epic*. New Delhi: Oxford University Press.

—. 1998. *The Sanskrit Epics*. Leiden: E.J. Brill.

Bulcke, Camille. 1958. About Valmiki. *Journal of the Oriental Institute of Baroda* 8.2 (December): 121–31.

—. 1959. More about Valmiki. *Journal of the Oriental Institute of Baroda* 8.4 (June 1959): 346–48.

Deol, Jeevan Singh. 2001. Text and Lineage in Early Sikh History: Issues in the Study of the Adi Granth. *Bulletin of the School of Oriental and African Studies* 64.1: 34–58.

Falk, Harry. 1993. *Schrift im alten Indien: ein Forschungsbericht mit Anmerkungen*. Tübingen: Gunter Narr.

Goldman, Robert P. 1976. Valmiki and the Bhrgu Connection. *Journal of the American Oriental Society* 96.1: 97–101.

—. 1977. *Gods, Priests, and Warriors: The Bhrgus of the Mahabharata*. Studies in Oriental Culture 12, Columbia University. New York: Columbia University Press.

—. (ed.), tr. 1984. *The Ramayana of Valmiki: An Epic of Ancient India*. New Jersey: Princeton University Press.

Hawley, John Stratton. 1995. The Saints Subdued: Domestic Virtue and National Integration in *Amar Chitra Katha*. In *Media and the*

Transformation of Religion in South Asia, (eds.) Babb and Wadley, 107–34, Philadelphia: University of Philadelphia Press.

Khan, Benjamin. 1983. *The Concept of Dharma in Valmiki Ramayana.* Second edition. New Delhi: Munshiram Manoharlal.

Leslie, Julia. 1998. A Bird Bereaved: The Identity and Significance of Valmiki's *Krauncha. Journal of Indian Philosophy* 26: 455–87.

—. 2003. *Authority and Meaning in Indian Religions: Hinduism and the Case of Valmiki.* Aldershot: Ashgate.

Nesbitt, Eleanor. 2004. 'Young British Sikhs and Religious Devotion'. [This volume.]

Pai, Anant (ed.). 1994. *Valmiki: The Story of the Author of the Epic, 'Ramayana'.* Amar Chitra Katha series, Vol. 579. New Delhi: India Book House.

Pollock, Sheldon. 1984. *Atmanam manusam manye: Dharmakutam* on the Divinity of Rama. *Journal of the Oriental Institute of Baroda* 33.3–4 (March–June): 231–43.

Pritchett, Frances W. 1995. The World of *Amar Chitra Katha.* In *Media and the Transformation of Religion in South Asia*, (eds.) Babb and Wadley, 76–106, Philadelphia: University of Philadelphia Press.

Raghavan, V. 1952–53. The Tattvasamgraharamayana of Ramabrahmananda. *Annals of Oriental Research* 10.1: 1–55.

—. 1980. The Ramayana in Sanskrit literature. In *The Ramayana Tradition in Asia*, (ed.) V. Raghavan, 1–19. New Delhi: Sahitya Akademi.

Ramayana. *The Valmiki-Ramayana: Critical Edition.* 1958–75. 7 vols. General editors: G.H. Bhatt and U.P. Shah. Vol. 1: *The Balakanda*, (ed.) G.H. Bhatt, 1958; second edition, 1982. Vol. 3: *The Aranyakanda*, (ed.) P.C. Divanji, 1963. Baroda: Oriental Institute. For translations into English, see Goldman (1984), Shastri (1962).

Report of the Bhagavan Valmiki Action Committee. 2000. Typescript compiled and edited by Lekh Raj Manjdadria, Convenor of the Bhagavan Valmiki Action Committee, 24 March.

Richman, Paula. 1991. *Many Ramayanas: The Diversity of a Narrative Tradition in South Asia.* Berkeley: University of California Press.

Salomon, Richard. 1995. On the Origin of the Early Indian Scripts: A Review Article. *Journal of the American Oriental Society* 115.2: 271–79.

Shastri, Hari Prasad, tr. 1962, 1969, 1976. *The Ramayana of Valmiki*, Vols. 1 (second edition), 2 (second edition), and 3 (third edition). London: Shanti Sadan.

Sheth, Noel. 1984. *The Divinity of Krishna*. With a foreword by. Daniel H.H. Ingalls. New Delhi: Munshiram Manoharlal.

Tagare, G.V., tr. 1992. *The Skanda Purana*. The standard English translation based on the vulgate version. New Delhi: Motilal Banarsidass.

Thampi, P. Padmanabhan. 1996. *Ramayanas of Kampan and Eluttacchan*. Thuckalay, South India: O. Padmakumari.

Thiel-Horstmann, Monika (ed.). 1991. *Ramayana and Ramayanas*. Wiesbaden: Otto Harrassowitz.

van Nooten, B.A. 1976. 'Introduction'. In William Buck, tr., *Ramayana: King Rama's Way*, illustrated by Shirley Triest, xiii–xxii. Berkeley: University of California Press.

von Stietencron, Heinrich. 1983. Die Göttin Durga Mahishasuramardini: Mythos, Darstellung und geschichtliche Rolle bei der Hinduisierung Indiens. *Visible Religion* 2: 118–66.

CHAPTER FOUR

Ravana, Divali and Spiritual Unity: Three Ramayana Performances in Greater London[*]

PAULA RICHMAN

When South Asians migrated to the United Kingdom, they brought with them not only the story of Rama (*Ramkatha*), but also the tradition of telling and interpreting the story in multiple ways.[1] Rama's story has been enacted many times in Greater London during the second half of the twentieth century. This essay focusses on three performances. Each recounts *Ramkatha* in a different way, a way that explicitly or implicitly deals with relations between South Asian communities in Britain and the primarily White communities around them. Ranging over a period of nearly fifteen years, the essay analyses distinctive features of each *Ramkatha* and the context in which each occurred.

In its most skeletal form, *Ramkatha* recounts the following incidents: the birth of Prince Rama, his marriage to Princess Sita, their subsequent exile to the forest, Sita's abduction by the Demon King Ravana, Rama's search for Sita, his attack on the demon kingdom, the defeat of Ravana, and the recovery of Sita. In this essay, the term *Ramkatha*, 'the story of Rama' or 'Rama's story', is employed to refer in general to a narrative that recounts or takes for granted all or most of the incidents just enumerated. When discussing a specific telling of Rama's story, I identify it by its name (e.g. Festival of Spiritual Unity) or the name of the institution (e.g. Commonwealth Institute), or group (Southall Black Sisters) that created or sponsored it. When referring to the diverse set of tellings that present Rama's story in different styles and media, I use, as a collective term, 'the Ramayana tradition'. This phrase indicates a set, rather than an abstract summary or synthesis, of many tellings.

Each performance of Rama's story examined in this essay occurred at a particular moment in the history of the South Asian diaspora.[2] Relations between people of South Asian heritage and the majority communities of British society changed in intensity and type over the course of the period under study. This essay's first goal, therefore, is to determine for each drama how migration history, social location, and religious affiliations of authors, actors, exegetes and sponsors influenced their perspective on *Ramkatha* and its interpretation.

Second, I examine how each performance represents or makes claims about South Asian culture in the British context. In one case, *Ramkatha* is used to represent the Indian nation as a whole, while in another case the drama is presented as the cultural property of a particular South Asian religious community, such as the Hindus. Some tellings of Rama's story link it specifically with southern Asia while others read it at a more universal level as an account of the general human condition. Each depiction has consequences for understanding relations between the majority population and a minority group.

Finally, the essay explores the relationship between a particular *Ramkatha* and the state. To what extent does a performance of Rama's story contribute to undermining or consolidating the power of the British (and, in one case, Indian) state? The three tellings of *Ramkatha* examined here relate in different ways to British national policies and material interests. Examining the immigration history of those who stage the performances, the representations of their community and the ways the performance relates to the state enables us to consider the kinds of cultural work *Ramkatha* performs in a diaspora context.

The Southall Black Sisters Burn Ravana

On 19 October 1979, Southall Black Sisters, a feminist group of South Asian and African Caribbean women from Southall, Greater London, staged a *Ramlila* as a fund raiser.[3] The proceeds would help defray the legal costs for friends and family arrested during a protest against the neo-Nazi National Front Party, when police had attacked unarmed protesters with riot weapons. The analysis below examines the migration history of those involved, the events that prompted the *Ramlila*, its casting and structure, and its depiction of Ravana.

Southall, a town just beyond the end of the London Underground (Tube), located southwest of London proper, developed a sizable population of South Asians in two waves of migration. The earlier group arrived in the late 1950s when Britain needed labourers to staff factories during the post-war economic boom. In Southall, the immigrants were primarily Sikhs and Hindus, and mainly Punjabi speakers. Many in the first cohort were men from the peasant proprietor class who had lost land, savings and security through the dislocation of the partition of India and the economic upheaval that accompanied the founding of Pakistan. A number of those who settled in Southall worked at nearby factories or at Heathrow airport in low-paying jobs on long shifts with minimal benefits. Many men worked on assembly lines or custodial crews, while many women toiled in laundries and bakeries. Since the majority of early immigrants were not fluent in English, factory owners sought them as cheap labour unlikely to receive protection from the nearly all-White British unions.

Over the next decade, many who originally left South Asia for a temporary period decided to remain in the United Kingdom, at least partially because minimal wages and high housing costs made it difficult to accrue the amount of savings they had hoped to accumulate before returning home. Eventually, some sponsored the arrival of family members and thus the size of the

South Asian community in Southall steadily increased. Elders within the community who spoke fluent English helped new arrivals get settled, providing advice and temporary financial support.

As the community grew, its members experienced increasing hostility from White residents. When South Asians sought to purchase homes, they found their efforts blocked. Obtaining Council Housing also posed problems. In some areas, one needed to reside in Britain for ten to fifteen years before one could be put on the waiting list for Council Housing. Consequently, Southall's housing became the worst in the borough, forcing immigrants to remain in crowded and substandard dwellings. South Asian parents also encountered obstacles in efforts to ensure that their children received an education that would give them the credentials for social mobility; teachers regularly placed them in the lowest academic tracks in schools. White residents voiced fears of a 'Black invasion' and government agencies began bussing immigrant children to schools far from Southall so that they would not 'overwhelm' local schools.[4]

In the late 1960s and early 1970s, a number of South Asians arriving from East Africa settled in Southall. During the colonial period, the British government had encouraged traders and merchants from India to settle in its African colonies and function as economic middlemen between colonisers and their indigenous colonial subjects. Soon after independence in Uganda and Kenya, Asians were ordered, at short notice, to relinquish their assets and leave the country. Many prosperous South Asians from Uganda and Kenya (as well as Zanzibar and Tanzania) came to the United Kingdom, since they had British passports. This second wave of immigrants, mostly Gujarati speakers, brought with them their middle-class urban experience, as well as skills in running small businesses. The energy generated when they joined their predecessors combined to make Southall one of the most vibrant South Asian ethnic areas in England and Europe.

The highly publicised arrival of South Asians from East Africa led, however, to a policy of limiting immigration even of those with British passports, as well as increasingly strident rhetoric from the National Front (henceforth NF), a party that claimed to protect the 'racial purity' of Britain. Although NF began as a marginal entity, it gained increasing viability by playing upon the notion that the U.K. was in danger of being 'swamped' by outsiders. The National Front targeted not only people of South Asian origins but also those from Africa and the African Caribbean, as well as Jews. Most alarmingly, ideas expressed by these neo-Nazi groups started to appear in more mainstream political discourse.[5] In addition, racist attacks by roaming White gangs became more frequent; they killed or maimed a number of South Asian and African Caribbean youths. Police brutality in areas with large non-White populations also increased dramatically. Bonding between South Asian and African Caribbean male youths grew as they suffered increasingly from random acts of gang violence to which official authorities paid little attention.

Given increasing racist violence, Southall residents responded with alarm to the announcement that NF, which was fielding a candidate in the borough, would hold an election meeting on 23 April 1979 in the Southall Town Hall. Previous NF election meetings had been followed regularly by outbreaks of violence, which NF used as evidence of the 'outside threat' to England. A group of Southall residents and a coalition of progressive activists planned a peaceful demonstration, inviting those involved in liberal, radical, anti-fascist and labour work to join them; their plan called for women and children to sit on the grounds outside the Town Hall, thus preventing NF members from entering.

The protest plan was precluded by the early morning mobilisation of multiple police units. The Special Patrol Group (a corps of crack riot troops), equestrian officers, police dogs, foot police and a helicopter suggested that the authorities were expecting a major conflict. Police immediately cordoned off the area within a mile of the Town Hall, pre-empting any effort to stage a protest at its entrance. As protestors gathered at the edge of the cordon, tensions increased. Eventually, violence broke out between the two sides. Residents and other activists who had come to Southall for the protest then found themselves fighting police armed with truncheons and other riot gear. Hundreds in the crowd sustained injuries (one fatal) and 700 people were arrested. No ambulances were able to enter the area to care for the wounded. Confidential reports, whose contents were released only much later, suggest that police brutality was widespread. Yet, in what impartial observers regarded as a flagrant miscarriage of justice, not a single police officer was penalised after the police inquiry, while the criminal cases against Southall residents dragged on, accruing large legal costs.

In the late 1970s, activists had begun working to build coalitions between ethnic groups in order to fight racism in the United Kingdom. In 1976 the Race Relations Act had been passed, making direct and indirect discrimination based on nationality, skin colour or ethnicity unlawful. In 1977 the Commission on Racial Equality had been set up with local branches called Community Relations Councils, which emphasised community relations, multicultural activities and education against discrimination. During the late 1970s and early 1980s, many anti-racist activists used the term 'Black' to refer to the people of Asian, African and Middle Eastern heritage who had settled in the United Kingdom. Although each ethnic group had a particular immigration history, each had encountered discrimination and hatred in Britain, where many Whites lumped them in the category of 'outsiders'.

In the spirit of coalition building, a group of women who called themselves 'Southall Black Sisters' (henceforth SBS), had begun meeting regularly in 1978 to discuss shared concerns. Composed of teenagers and young women of South Asian and African Caribbean descent born in Britain, East Africa and the Caribbean, SBS members viewed themselves as joined in a larger Black identity shaped by a shared history of colonialism and racism. The South

Asian community in Southall was larger than the African Caribbean in size and each group had different pre-immigration histories. Yet the women who joined SBS found that their roots in colonised countries and their current experiences of racism and sexism in Britain gave them a number of common experiences, concerns and hopes. SBS undertook anti-racist and anti-sexist activism with the goal of bringing about greater equality in Britain.

In the autumn of 1979, in response to the 23 April 1979 events, SBS began a project that would give support to the Southall Legal Defence Fund. They decided to perform a *Ramlila* for Divali, a Hindu festival day connected in many parts of India with Rama's defeat of Ravana and triumphant return to Ayodhya. Since *Ramlila* celebrates the victory of righteous King Rama over tyrannical King Ravana, the narrative evoked strong feelings about the recent conflict with the police. SBS decided to dramatise *Ramkatha* as the story of an oppressive government eventually destroyed by the perseverance of those committed to justice. The play would present a narrative about their desire to eradicate racism in Britain.

Certain aspects of *Ramkatha*, however, seemed to conflict with another goal of SBS, that of combatting sexism. Some members of the group expressed discomfort with enacting a play that glorified Sita as a submissive woman willing to obey her husband's command at all costs, even entering the fire to prove her chastity. So SBS sought a way to stage the play that would question gender stereotypes that idealised submissive women. SBS knew that some male members of the South Asian community in Southall viewed them with suspicion, especially because they gave help to women who fled their homes due to domestic violence, instead of counselling them to return home and 'adapt'. Furthermore, outsiders had long attacked the community's treatment of women as a way to disparage South Asian culture and justify colonialism. At that moment in time, SBS saw its members as the only insiders who could critique sexist attitudes in the community to improve, rather than denigrate, it.

SBS chose, therefore, to mount a *Ramlila* that would affirm their bonds with South Asian culture and distance them from outsiders' critiques, but would simultaneously encourage members of their audience to question certain widely held cultural assumptions about women. Their *Ramlila*, therefore, included the familiar events of Rama's birth, marriage and exile to the forest, as well as the abduction of Sita and Rama's battle with Ravana. SBS got a local sweet shop to donate Divali treats for distribution to the audience so that the drama would include the special foods associated with festival days. A local teacher of classical Indian music and his students volunteered to provide the music for the interval, so that the performance would have the proper ambience. In such ways, SBS sought to create a *Ramlila* whose story and setting would be immediately familiar to members of the audience.

In order to incorporate questioning, however, SBS had to determine their stance towards the characters in the play. Eventually they decided to use casting as a way to raise certain issues about gender. In contrast to many regional and folk dramas in South Asia, where men play all the roles, and to most plays in London, where men and women play the parts of men and women, the SBS cast consisted entirely of women. In addition, casting decisions thwarted traditional gender and ethnic expectations. For example, a tall South Asian woman played Sita, while a short African Caribbean woman played Rama. Such casting undercut notions that a story can be the 'cultural property' of only one ethnic group. Simultaneously it subverted widely held beliefs that in 'proper' marriages a husband must be taller than his wife.

In a manner crucial to the play's critical edge, the production included additional characters to mediate between the narrative and the audience—a storyteller and two jesters. When the storyteller came onstage to tell the story and give background for the next scene, the jesters would interrupt her to draw the audience's attention to traditional sayings, point out topical parallels or interrogate certain assumptions about women reflected in the events of the scene. One jester, a South Asian woman who spoke both English and Punjabi, included well-known Punjabi expressions in her speeches. The other jester, an African Caribbean woman, incorporated translations of the Punjabi phrases into her comments, acting as a mediator for members of the audience who did not know Punjabi. Both actors functioned to disrupt the familiar flow of the narrative and question stereotypical gender roles in the play.[6]

The section of the *Ramlila* dealing with the birth of Rama provides an example of how this structure worked. The storyteller announces that after many childless years, Dasharatha's wives have given birth to sons. What a great celebration the king sponsored! At this moment, the first jester said:

> Yes, it was like that when my brother was born—a great celebration and my family passed out *laddus* [round sweets made of brown sugar and butter]. But when I was born, they didn't celebrate. My mother said, '*Hi Veh Raba, soota mundiyandha thaba.*'

Immediately, the second jester translated and added her economic analysis:

> She said to God, 'Why don't you just throw me a bunch of boys?' Why such jubilation when the son is born, but not the daughter? She must have been worrying about the dowry to be paid for the marriage of that daughter.

The interchange between jesters directs the audience's attention to social and financial forces that shape parents' attitudes towards the sex of their child. The jesters suggest that it was not anything intrinsic about the girl that was disagreeable; instead, it was the economic forces that commodify her and make her a financial burden to her parents that led them to express such different responses to the birth of a son and the birth of a daughter.

The jesters also incorporated topical references, encouraging members of the audience to see links between the story and their daily lives. In one scene, for example, where Sita beseeches her husband to let her accompany him in his forest exile, Rama refuses, insisting that life there would be too harsh for her, saying, 'Your tender lotus feet would get bruised by rocks and cut by thorns.' Hitting him on the shoulder with an audible thump, Sita answered, 'I'm good enough to wear myself out doing all the housework, but too frail to go to the forest with you?' Rama then agreed to let Sita accompany him, with the words, 'Whatever you say, dear.' His response parodies the way a 'proper' wife is supposed to agree with her husband.

Later, when the storyteller is enumerating the heavy responsibilities that fall to a wife, a jester interrupts, saying, 'Yeh, it's a bit like how hard the women at T'walls Factory work, isn't it?' A number of women in the community worked long hours at the nearby T'walls Factory, then returned home to cook, feed their family and clean house. The jester focusses attention on why women must work an entire shift outside the home and then return to another shift inside the home. The scene also exposes the falseness of constructions of women as frail, weak creatures.

The SBS *Ramlila* presented these topical comments in a humorous and non-threatening way, and linked them to everyday experiences with reference to familiar places. A member of the cast recalled that her Punjabi-speaking grandmother and elderly aunts attended the performance. They often sat through community meetings in English that they did not understand in order to meet friends and family, and feel part of the community. The jester's comment in Punjabi about the birth of sons received laughs of recognition from them. Up to that point, they had viewed the performance as a pious reiteration of *Ramkatha*. The jester's speech in Punjabi enabled them to hear the critique of the custom of placing greater value on male babies than female babies, a fact of life with which they were all too familiar. Similarly, by translating, the other jester facilitated understanding of the nuances of the performance for members of the audience who spoke only English.

Among the audience were not only South Asians but African Caribbeans as well as other anti-fascist activists who had been involved in the protest at the Southall Town Hall. The second jester ensured that neither humour nor critique was lost on these non-Punjabi speakers.

Among the actors and audience members I interviewed in 1994 and 1998, almost everyone remembered the humorous asides of the jesters, a few mentioning the Punjabi line quoted above in particular. Several others repeated, word for word, the line about Sita's tender lotus-feet, as one of the high points of the performance. One commented on its irony since most women in the community had to deal regularly with all sorts of dangers and harassment at work, and on their journeys to and from work via public transportation.

Towards the end of the play, when Rama battled Ravana, the political emphasis in the play shifted from gender relations to the current electoral situation in Britain. The SBS interpretation of Ravana as Evil Incarnate shaped the representation of the demon king, who wore a huge mask of ten heads. Several of the heads were enlarged photographs of particular people—Enoch Powell, famous for his 'rivers of blood' speech about how a civil war would occur between 'real Englishmen' and the outsiders who threatened to 'swamp' England;[7] Jon Tynsdale, leader of the National Front party; a local member of the Ealing Council who led the opposition at the time; and Prime Minister Margaret Thatcher. Other heads represented oppression in symbolic form. For example, the hat worn by the Special Patrol Group police stood for brutality and repression. A black bobby's hat over a drawing of a pig symbolised the everyday policing to which the community was subjected. Another drawing depicted restrictive immigration laws, which fragment immigrant families.

The practice of burning Ravana in effigy to culminate the *Ramlila*, accompanied by celebratory fireworks, is an ancient and venerable one among Hindus in South Asia, symbolising the triumph of good over evil. In the SBS *Ramlila*, when Rama defeated Ravana, the storyteller told the audience to meet her in the car park to view the end of Ravana. There SBS set off fireworks, to the delight of the spectators. In this *Ramlila*, burning Ravana symbolised a desire to defeat those who perpetuate racism and to destroy institutions that kept Black people oppressed. Victory over Ravana meant creating a society in which Black people could live without fear, humiliation or harassment.

One of the most striking features of the SBS *Ramlila*, as a whole, is how self-consciously it used *Ramkatha* to convey its political critique. SBS members discussed at length the expediency of harnessing the power of Rama's story. By drawing upon the Ramayana tradition, they sought to show their connection to the culture of their elders and to assure their community that the battle against racism would continue. A quote from a report written by a civil liberties monitoring group sums up how strongly people of South Asian and African Caribbean descent in Southall perceived the events of 23 April as a physical attack on their community:

> [M]embers of that community [Southall] were already well aware of the racialist strains in British society as a whole, but, even with that knowledge, what happened in their town on 23 April came as a severe psychological shock. Many have observed that they had never conceived that the British police could behave as they saw them behave on that day.... Many testified to us of their belief that what occurred was a deliberate assault on the whole small community. (Dummett 1980: 10)

Ravana, king of the demons, was a leader who used his power to humiliate and oppress people. Furthermore, Ravana possessed ten heads so, as a symbol, he could encompass the multiple forms of oppression the SBS sought to target, including neo-Nazi political leaders, various police units, and discriminatory immigration laws. The Ravana created by the SBS represents the British state, insofar as most immigrants experienced it primarily in its repressive and punitive role.

A second notable characteristic of the SBS *Ramlila* is how its interpretation of Ravana transformed *Ramkatha* into a story whose significance was not limited exclusively to the Hindu – or even the South Asian – community in Britain. In keeping with the name 'Southall Black Sisters', members viewed themselves as a coalition of dark-skinned women, part of whose solidarity rested on their shared commitment to opposing racism. If Ravana symbolised evil, Rama symbolised the ability of Black people to defeat evil. In this case, women of both South Asian and African Caribbean heritage battled with Ravana. When the play was originally being conceptualised, one African Caribbean member asked, 'What is the contribution of this play to the Afro-Caribbean community?' SBS answered this question by presenting the destruction of Ravana as an event of symbolic importance to all people affected by racism.

Avtar Brah, a founding member of SBS, recalled in a short essay how explicitly members of SBS sought to cross boundaries separating them from other ethnic groups:

> We had lengthy debates and discussions about the relative merits of different strategies for working within our own communities —for challenging the specific configuration of patriarchal relations in these communities as well as in the society at large— while actively opposing the racism to which all Black people, men and women, are subjected.

Brah goes on to describe Ravana as representing 'evil (for example the racist immigration laws) which our communities are made to suffer in Britain' (1988: 86). Insofar as the SBS *Ramlila* portrayed a traditional South Asian story, it might be relevant only to those of South Asian heritage, but insofar as it explicitly identified the surveillance activities of the British state with Ravana and celebrated the destruction of racism, it was a story for all members of the audience at the SBS *Ramlila*, with its use of bilingual commentary by jesters.

Significantly, the SBS drama included no innovations in the basic *Ramkatha* plot. Sita's marriage, abduction, and fire ordeal all appeared in the play. The one-page programme handed out at the performance, which summarises the story of the play for audience members not familiar with it, includes the usual events that deal with Sita.[8] The commentary by the jesters, however, was where SBS lodged many of their questions about gender stereotypes. Because the jesters stood outside the narrative, adding their own observations about its incidents, they transformed the reception of the story, incorporating a critique of sexism. Brah recalls it as 'our own feminist version of *Ramlila*', contrasting it with 'the classic Hindu epic which depicts Sita, the central female character, as a subservient and devoted wife' (1988: 86). Furthermore, since the jesters spoke in both Punjabi and English, their commentary enabled the SBS to question sexist portrayals of Sita in a way that was accessible to its multilingual audience.

Finally, the SBS *Ramlila* was highly topical. Performed only once, the play was directly related to the events of 23 April 1979. Created with minimal financial resources and a great deal of creativity, it left behind very few traces, and has been reconstructed primarily through interviews with members of the cast and audience.[9] Nonetheless, more than twenty-five years later, certain memories of the play remain strong. Although some women I interviewed found it difficult to recall specific details about the staging or plot, all remembered the locally specific comments of the jesters about working at T'walls and Sita's 'tender lotus feet'. The actors had established the story's connection to Southall life, demonstrating links between *Ramkatha* and the daily experiences of members of the audience. Thus, the SBS *Ramlila* provides an example of how *Ramkatha* could migrate to the United Kingdom, adapt to the circumstances of settlement and be used to convey some of the deepest convictions of the group that staged it. Because the Ramayana tradition incorporates space for topicality, the story can remain relevant to its audience under ever-changing historical circumstances.

The Commonwealth Institute's Divali Programme

In autumn 1994, the Commonwealth Institute in Kensington offered a play and a set of workshops that focussed on Divali and Rama's story. The programmes drew upon a teacher's pamphlet published by the Institute to help incorporate Divali into the curriculum. The play, a gala performance of Rama's story for hundreds of schoolchildren, was staged on the circular platform in the middle of the Institute's three-story exhibition hall. In conjunction with the gala, a set of puppet workshops were offered for students and their teachers. My analysis of the pamphlet, the performance and the workshops considers how these programmes relate to the history of the Institute, the teaching of religion in British schools, and the representations of Divali in Britain.

What is now called the 'Commonwealth Institute' began its life as the 'Imperial Institute'. Opened on 10 May 1893, its inaugural rituals included the attendance of the princes of India to wait upon Queen Victoria, who rode from Buckingham Palace in procession, arriving as the orchestra played the national anthem. Flanked by the Archbishop of Canterbury and the Secretary of State of the Home Department, Queen Victoria then declared the building open.[10] Like a colonial *durbar*, the ceremony enacted a set of power relations between the British coloniser and the Indian colonised. The Queen's final inaugural act symbolised the central role technology played in conquest and rule of the empire. With 'a key, composed of precious stones and metals, contributed by the Empire of India, and the American, Australasian, and African Colonies' (Commonwealth Institute 1993: 20), she completed the circuit of an electric signal to the bell-chamber in the Institute tower, so that its peals would announce the opening of the new building. From

1893 to 1953 the Institute was a centre for scientific research on ways to manufacture saleable products from raw materials from the colonies.

In 1949, calls arose for changes in the Institute, spurred in part by the establishment of Indian independence. The Imperial College of Science and Technology took the Institute's building for its expanding needs in 1958. In 1962, the Queen inaugurated a newly constructed building. The circular marble platform, almost the only part of the old building to be incorporated into the new one, was placed at the centre of the exhibition hall.[11] Three floors, composed of individual exhibit space for each Commonwealth nation, encircled the platform. The symbolism of the main exhibition hall remained essentially neo-colonial, with each nation connected to the central circle, a signifier of the gaze of the British museum-visitor.

The Institute's identity was in flux during the period of rapid decolonisation in Asia and Africa, but it continued to be linked primarily to trade. Although the Institute had been under the direction of the Colonial Office in 1907 and then moved to the Department of Overseas Trade in 1925, its shift to the Ministry of Education's supervision in 1949 indicated a different notion of its mission. It was transferred yet again, however, in 1970, to the Foreign and Commonwealth Secretary. By this point the Institute had long ceased to focus on research about colonial raw materials; instead its goal was described as shifting 'to education as Britain focusses on the Empire marketplace' (Commonwealth Institute 1993: 7). Thus, its educational mission continued to be shaped by commercial concerns and geopolitical objectives.

In 1993, as the Institute celebrated its centennial, it entered a particularly vulnerable period. The Royal Presents Show, a centennial exhibit that featured artworks and riches from Commonwealth countries that had been presented to the Queen during her visits, sought to show the importance of royal tours, but the Institute needed more than royal favour as the government slashed appropriations for education drastically, and the Institute faced possible closure. In 1994, the Institute received a temporary reprieve with the award of continued government funding until 1999. It then began a fund-raising campaign to secure the additional monies needed to stay open.[12] The Institute's programmes on Divali thus took place at a difficult time in its financial history.

The Institute's educational programmes on Divali proved extremely well-subscribed in the autumn of 1994.[13] The gala performance was completely filled and all the puppet workshops overbooked, leading the Institute to schedule a large number of additional workshop sections. Educators had long looked to the Institute as a resource centre and its course materials on Divali and Rama's story had been available for some time. In areas such as Asian and African studies, the Institute had developed pedagogical strategies, created maps and other visual materials, and provided teachers with access to its large reference library. In 1994, however, developments in the teaching of Religious Education (henceforth RE) in primary and secondary schools led to increased interest in the Institute's Divali programmes because Local Educational Authorities (henceforth LEAs) supported teachers who attended workshops linked to RE stipulations. As a result, the Institute generated income to maintain its programmes, simultaneously supporting demands for certain RE materials.

Some history about obligatory RE in British schools helps to contextualise the high demand for the Institute's 1994 Divali programmes. Fifty years earlier, the 1944 Education Act specified that state-funded schools must include classes in religious instruction and non-denominational worship for students. This legislation obliged schools to provide instruction that nurtured religious beliefs and morality, but schools had to do so in a way that did not exclude non-Anglicans. The fact that 'non-denominational' religious instruction was specified took account of not only non-Anglican Protestant groups, but also Roman Catholics and Jews.

The 1944 Act was operative until the National Curriculum Act of 1988. Although the 1988 Act paid greatest attention to teaching English, Mathematics and Science, it did stipulate that RE should continue to be compulsory.[14] By the 1960s and 70s, the demographic mix of Britain's population had changed significantly and the place of religious traditions of South Asia (including Islam) in RE had become a major issue. Some LEAs, advisory bodies that supervise schools and report to a county or metropolitan council, supported RE courses that focussed on 'Living Religions of the World'. For example, the Lancaster-based Schools Council, launched under the leadership of Ninian Smart, developed a curriculum based on a phenomenological approach to the study of religion. This curriculum taught world religions from a thematic perspective, focussing on holy places and holy books in Christianity, Judaism, Hinduism, Sikhism, Islam and Buddhism.[15] Some critics of the approach charged that such surveys got many religions muddled in children's heads.[16]

Unfortunately, the minimal discussion devoted to RE in the 1988 Act made it difficult for teachers to determine precisely what curricular changes it entailed, leading to many unanswered questions. The Department for Education eventually released a circular in January 1994, 'Religious Education and Collective Worship,' in order to clarify policy. The circular defined guidelines for RE curriculum that acknowledged (1) the views of those who feared that Christianity, which some viewed as the foundation of 'English culture', would be neglected, and (2) the views of those who wanted the religious traditions of South Asia (including Islam) included in RE courses. The circular stated that the aim of RE should be 'to develop pupils' knowledge, understanding and awareness of Christianity, as the predominant religion in Great Britain, and the other principal religions represented in the country.'[17] The government mandated that two new model syllabi in line with the 1988 Act, as clarified in the 1994 Circular, be developed. It called for LEAs to develop RE syllabi that would be revised every five years.[18] Thus, the 1994 Divali programmes at the Institute filled a need for teachers who were incorporating materials on 'other principal religions represented in the country'.

A helpful reference pamphlet for teachers' curricular units on Hindu festivals was 'Diwali: Festival of Lights', written by Anthony Ogg and illustrated by Sharon Finmark. Written some years back for educators visiting the Commonwealth Institute, it now functioned as a major resource for teachers.[19] The booklet lays out the different ways in which Divali is celebrated in various regions of India. It also presents lesson plans for classroom projects linked with the festival, such as cooking Divali sweets and making clay lamps. Ogg ends with Rama's story 'retold for easy dramatisation by Doris Harper-Wills', an illustration of the proper costume for Rama, and an extensive bibliography.

Ogg explains Divali with careful attention to variation in practice. Although he notes that Divali is primarily a Hindu festival celebrating the homecoming of Rama and Sita, he also remarks that Jains view it as the beginning of their new year, Sikhs observe the holy day in honour of Guru Hargobind's release from imprisonment in Gwalior, and Bengalis link the story to worship of the fierce goddess, while businessmen connect the festival to Lakshmi, goddess of wealth. Instead of alluding to some unchanging fossilised tradition, Ogg keeps the cultural information he conveys current.[20] Finally, Ogg cites books written in both India and Britain, adds that an Indian book distributor has a shop at the Institute and encourages teachers to consult Hindu children in their class about how they celebrate Divali. Eschewing pedantry or unnecessary confusion, Ogg reveals the multiple contexts of Divali right in London, rather than essentialising it as a traditional, static and foreign event.

To get children involved in studying religion in a 'hands on' way, the Institute focussed its programming on holidays, developing

'Festivals of Living Faiths' units and linking them to its 1994 focus on Asia; the autumn term included programmes on Divali, Id and the Chinese New Year. For each holiday, the staff mounted a 'gala', a huge celebration that busloads of London schoolchildren attended. It was the policy of the Institute to call upon the appropriate High Commission for assistance with its programming.[21] Deputy High Commissioner of India, K.V. Rajan, presented the opening address for the Divali gala. Policy also called for employing 'Commonwealth nationals' to conduct cultural workshops; Rani Singh, who had training in theatre, planned the Divali gala and played the role of storyteller for the performance.[22]

The gala was mounted on the round stage at the centre of the Institute's exhibition hall, ringed by a set of railings on each floor, that enabled children to sit and watch theatre-in-the-round on three levels. After Rajan's opening address and a Divali prayer for peace, Singh told Rama's story with key events illustrated in dance by the Triveni Dance Company.[23] The wicked stepmother theme, common in fairy tales, was emphasised in Singh's treatment of Ayodhya's dynastic succession; Shurpanakha, presented as an ugly witch searching for a husband, suddenly sprouted a bleeding nose thanks to a deftly manipulated stage device; Ravana lured Sita out of the circle and laughed viciously while she wept; the lengthy death scene of loyal Jatayu unfolded with sad music heightening its pathos; the battle between Rama and Ravana involved grand waving of swords. *Ramkatha* unfolded in a clear, straightforward and memorable way, stage-managed perfectly to fit the time allotted. The event ended with fireworks, followed by delighted exclamations from the children.[24]

The fast-paced gala, which balanced music, dance and drama, did an excellent job of keeping children involved. Teachers had received lesson plans in advance to prepare for the play, as well as instructions for children to bring torches (flashlights) and percussion instruments. The audience was invited to give verbal input at key junctures of the play. During the final battle, children beat on their percussion instruments and they switched on their torches in celebration when Ravana died. The costumes of the dancers were so bright and elaborate that even children on the top railing could see them clearly. The vast majority of children were not Hindu. For most, this was their first chance to learn about Divali, so Singh gave analogies, such as Divali is 'Christmas and Easter all rolled into one', and likened the ending fireworks to those set off on Guy Fawkes Day.

As a tie-in to the gala, during October and November, Singh ran a set of hour-long puppet sessions on Rama's story for children aged 6–11, accompanied by teachers. The workshop I attended took place in a classroom decorated with bright Indian handicrafts, at the front of which sat Singh with puppets and costumes. She began with the question, 'What country do I come from?' to which some students, after a short pause, shouted 'India!' and she nodded. Then she showed the children the masks and costumes she would use, and lit a small lamp. After drawing parallels between British royalty and Indian princes and princesses in *Ramkatha*, she took out a packet of *bindis*. Putting *bindis* on a few girls' brows, she told them they looked 'quite nice and quite Indian,' noting, 'Indian women love to decorate themselves.' Children who volunteered to play Rama and Sita put on sequined royal outfits, while Ravana wore a huge mustachioed mask. Singh also had puppets for other major characters, including a reversible one to represent Shurpanakha's initial disguise as a beautiful maiden and her true form as an ugly demoness.

The story that the children and Singh then acted out contained the same events as the gala did, but was more informal and relaxed in tone. In several scenes, in keeping with one strand of oral Ramayana tradition, Singh spoke some of the dialogue as if it took place in a London neighbourhood. For example, Singh 'localised' the dialogue between Rama, Shurpanakha and Lakshmana as follows:[25]

Shurpanakha often went hunting for a husband or two. She said to Rama, 'Hi, Handsome! I've chosen you, you gorgeous man.'

'Sorry mate, I'm taken by Sita. [Pointing to his brother] He's more your type anyway. He's Lakshman.'

'Oh, so this is like a blind date, isn't it?'

These lines, spoken in just the right intonation, produced howls of laughter as children watched elaborately bedecked characters speak as if they were in a familiar neighbourhood conversation. Singh also encouraged audience participation by having them provide snoring sounds while Hanuman crept into the bedroom of sleeping Ravana and a countdown as Rama defeated Ravana.

When interviewed about her narrative choices, Singh indicated that she viewed three main clusters of incidents as primary: (1) the exile and abduction; (2) Jatayu's attack on Ravana and his dying words to Rama about Sita's abduction; (3) Hanuman taking Ravana's arrow, and the battle between Rama and Ravana. Explaining why she emphasised Jatayu, she said children liked flying creatures and noted that the bird's death 'brings a moment of quiet emotion and contemplation of a pathetic creature into the story'. She added that she liked the incident where Hanuman takes Ravana's arrow because it showed that cleverness, not just strength in battle, helped to defeat Ravana.

As soon as Singh finished the story, children bombarded her with questions. Some asked about the status of Rama's story ('Is this story true?'), but the majority pushed at the limits of the story they had just heard, calling for more details and explanation. For example, since Singh expatiated upon Hanuman's great powers, one child queried, 'Why didn't Hanuman rescue Sita when Ravana was abducting her?' An answer that did full justice to the question, for which there was insufficient time, would have to address why Hanuman was so devoted to Rama, as well as Rama's duty as warrior and husband. Also necessary would be a careful distinction between a monkey with superpowers and Hanuman as son of the Wind god, ambassador for Sugriva and ideal devotee of Rama.

The children also raised issues about gender in the story. For example, another child voiced concern about the violence done to Shurpanakha, and wanted to know, 'What happened to Shurpanakha at the end of the story?' When I asked Singh about the ways in which the story depicted Sita and Shurpanakha as opposites, she replied that Sita was not a submissive woman because she got Rama to go after the deer for her. Singh volunteered that her interpretation of Sita was 'uncontroversial' and that it had little to do with current feminist critiques of Sita.

The children's questions indicated a fascination with characters with supernatural powers. One child asked, 'Since Hanuman is so powerful, when he picked up the mountain to bring the herb, why didn't he drop it on Ravana and kill him?' Singh noted that she usually received more questions about Shurpanakha than Sita, and that children were more interested in playing Ravana than Rama. Children seemed intrigued with the notion of Ravana's ten heads; one boy asked what happened when one head disagreed with another, while another wanted to know which head Ravana used to try to kiss Sita.

When I saw the range of questions Singh received and the short time set aside for questions, I asked if it might be better to incorporate more of the story's complexities into her telling. 'It is difficult for children to keep focussed on the subject matter if the story is too long,' she replied. Institutional limitations on her, as well as the short time budgeted for visits of pupils and teachers to the Institute, made it difficult to develop *Ramkatha* in as much depth as she would have liked.

If we stand back and consider the Institute's set of Divali programmes as a whole, we can see that, first and foremost, the Divali unit functions as an institutional Ramayana, presented within the architectural and personnel framework of the Commonwealth Institute. Since the walls of the Institute exhibition hall are covered with separate exhibits about each Commonwealth nation, the Divali gala took place within a visual space that classifies countries as part of the Commonwealth and hence separate from Britain. Consequently, holidays such as Divali are taught within a discourse of foreignness, rather than as integral parts of contemporary British culture. In addition, neo-colonial tokenism is at work in the Institute policy of hiring 'Commonwealth nationals' to develop culture-specific programmes. They provide the content of the programmes but lack permanent positions or decision-making power within the Institute and, therefore, have limited agency to shape the overall framework within which their programmes are presented.

The notion of a 'Commonwealth national' reflects a 'dual-culture' model of cultural interaction, taking for granted that a person is a member of either one culture or another. The gala and workshops also functioned within a dual-culture model and were addressed primarily to a 'target audience' of non–South Asian children. Analogies drawn between Christmas and Divali were used to present Divali to those whose framework was, at least nominally, Christian. Had the target audience consisted of Muslims, Hindus, Jains and Sikhs, the analogies would have differed significantly. Aspects of the performance encouraged pupils to identify Singh and Rajan as 'Indian' solely on the basis of physical appearance. Many White schoolchildren remain unaware that nowadays most children of South Asian heritage were born in Britain. Encouraging students to identify people as foreign by their physical appearance lends support to the view that children of South Asian heritage are 'foreign' and do not belong in Britain, even if they are born and raised there.

Second, Divali was presented in a way that drained it of much of its religious meaning. Divali, 'a festival of lights', does resemble certain other religious holidays in celebrating the victory of good over evil. In the Divali unit, however, *Ramkatha* has been reduced to a minimal set of narrative elements—a prince who defeats the

abductor of his wife in battle with the help of an animal with
supernatural powers. It is unlikely that children who attended the
gala understood why such a simple story proved so central to Hindu
tradition. For many Hindus, Rama is not only a great warrior but
also an *avatar* of God. Each of his actions, therefore, is saturated
with meaning. These meanings disappear when the story is reduced
to a fairy tale with talking animals and dramatic sword fights. If
the account of the crucifixion of Jesus were reduced to such
elements, some Christians would feel outraged at the trivialisation
of divine acts. Will knowing the story staged at the gala, getting a
bindi on one's brow and switching on torches at Ravana's death
really make children who are not of South Asian heritage
understand South Asian religions? The gala could be seen as
coopting elements of a colonised culture within the framework of
multicultural education, for the convenience of teachers.

Third, the gala and workshop – but not the teacher's pamphlet
– conflate the varied practices connected with Divali. The material
in the printed gala programme does quote directly from Ogg's
booklet, but quotes so selectively that Divali is reduced to a
colourful Indian holiday of lights.[26] Homogenising of Divali also
appeared in Rajan's opening remarks, in which he claimed that
everyone in India celebrates Divali. (Indian Christians in
Tirunelveli? Muslims in Deobandh?) His statement carried special
authority since he speaks as an official representative of the
Government of India.

Neither the gala nor the workshop explain that both in India
and in Britain, many religious traditions exist within the Hindu
community. For example, among particular Hindu groups in
England, festivals such as Navaratri or Ganesha Puja may be as, if
not more, important than Divali. Unfortunately, a teacher would
not realise this from the Institute's Divali gala, which contributes
to essentialising Indian religious practices in Britain.[27] Ogg had
cautioned those teaching about Divali to read widely on the many
Divali rituals and ask children from South Asian families to give

input in order to take into account the diversity of practice, but such multiple voices were not included in the Institute unit.

The Institute's rendition of *Ramkatha* also featured little of the moral complexity inherent in Ramayana tradition. Because the story has been simplified so much, it limits severely the aspects of Hinduism that teachers and students learn. The gala reduced *Ramkatha*'s complexity to a compact tale of good versus bad, with little ethical ambiguity. Among incidents that raise questions about Rama's adherence to *dharma*, only Shurpanakha's mutilation appeared in the drama.[28] Even that incident was enacted in a way that encouraged the audience's unquestioning complicity with male abuse of a female who speaks her mind.

Finally, the Institute's Divali unit functions in the interests of the British state. By assisting LEAs to conform to the mandate that they develop syllabi in RE, the Institute assists the British state in controlling the content of religious education. The 1988 Act and the 1994 Circular were carefully brokered to ensure that the majority of RE courses focus on Christianity to satisfy both Protestant and Catholic leaders, but that other religions in the area have also been represented to satisfy local constituents. Id, Divali and Chinese New Year units have value to schools as items that can be slotted into the 'non-Christian' space that can be claimed if people of Asian descent form a sizable element in the local school population. The Institute's Divali unit was shaped and marketed in accordance with national legislation, serving the need of the state to ensure token representation of South Asian religions.

It is painful to criticise such earnest educational efforts. Doubtless, the planners of the gala had the highest goals in mind when designing their Divali unit. Nonetheless, the structure of the Basic Curriculum requirements, the limited time allocated to each religious holiday and the need to simplify the story can lead to significant misunderstandings. In fact, the most dynamic and probing aspects of the Divali unit were the questions asked by children at the puppet workshop. Although limits of time and

format precluded the extensive asking of questions, the ones that children were able to pose broadened the scope of the story and articulated a set of lively reflections about *Ramkatha*. Such queries brought into the open at least some complexities of characters and interpretation that have kept *Ramkatha* ever-changing and vital for so many centuries.

Manas Exegesis and Spiritual Unity

The Festival of Spiritual Unity took place from 30 July to 7 August 1994 in Roundwood Park, to the north of London proper. Manubhai Madhvani, organiser of the Festival, planned it as an affirmation of *samabhav*, 'oneness of feeling', across various religious boundaries. Each morning of the nine-day Festival, Morari Bapu provided exegesis of *Ramcharitmanas* by Tulsidas. Analysis below considers how *samabhav* shaped the concept of the Festival, how Madhvani organised preparations for the event, and what role Bapu's exegesis played.

Manubhai M. Madhvani's father, born in 1894 in Porbandar, left at age 14 for Uganda, where he helped manage a retail shop. From these modest beginnings, he grew into a successful businessman, managing the highly profitable 22,000 acre Kakira Sugar Plantation and Factory beside Lake Victoria. His son Manubhai, born in 1930 in Jinja, Uganda, went at age 10 to India for education, and there came in contact with Gandhian teachings. Upon returning to Uganda, Manubhai joined the family business and, after his father passed away (1958), he and his brother expanded the company, setting up factories in Kenya and Tanzania and diversifying into production of steel, beer, cotton, glass, plastics, textiles and matches.[29]

When Idi Amin ascended to power in 1972, Manubhai Madhvani's situation changed drastically. The holdings of the Madhvani family enterprises, which then 'contributed some

10 per cent of the country's gross national revenue',[30] were expropriated by Amin's regime and Madhvani was imprisoned. In a military jail in Kampala, he sat reading his Bhagavad Gita while his Muslim cellmate studied his Quran and his African Christian cellmate immersed himself in his Bible. Over the tense days the three spent together, they talked at length about their scriptures and the meaning of religion. Madhvani's conversation in prison convinced him that all religions expound essentially the same goals: 'They teach one how to act in society, how to divide up responsibilities in a systematic form, and they spread codes for conduct so that all can live together.'[31] A man with extensive experience in supervising large numbers of employees, Madhvani decided that religion provided society with order by giving each person a clear role and code for conduct that enabled all to prosper. At a time of chaos in his life and in Ugandan political life, he came to view religion in a newly self-conscious way.

Upon release from prison, Madhvani left Uganda and settled in Britain. It was not until 1984 that the family recovered its principal assets in Uganda and began to manage the Kakira Sugar Works again. Working jointly with the Government of Uganda, the newly organised Indeco Group eventually brought their factories back to profitability and the idea for a Festival of Spiritual Unity emerged. As Manubhai wrote:

> Moved by a desire to give thanks to God we thought that an ideal way of thanks giving, in keeping with family traditions, would be to spark the flame of another *katha* whose theme would be spiritual unity. (13)

The 1994 Festival would be the latest in a lineage of family-sponsored *kathas* on Hindu religious texts. Madhvani's father had sponsored a *katha* on Bhagavad Gita in Kakira in 1955 and many others had followed.[32] This time, however, Madhvani had in mind a far more ambitious and multifaceted event: the *katha* would be the centre of the religious gathering, but radiating out from it would be a set of discussions focussed on *samabhav.* The term was familiar to most Indians of Madhvani's age through Mahatma Gandhi's frequent use of the Sanskrit phrase *sarva-dharma-samabhava,* 'all religions have oneness of feeling'.

The term *samabhav* functioned as the central organising theme of the Festival, as is shown by its presence on the very first page of the souvenir volume—a list of eleven definitions and connotations of *samabhav* fills the entire inside cover of the souvenir. The first meanings derive from the dictionary entry—'oneness of feeling' and 'equality'. 'Oneness of feeling' comes closest to the literal meaning of the Sanskrit compound, composed of *sama,* 'one' or 'same', and *bhava,* 'feeling' or 'sentiment'. Madhvani sought to create a Festival that would demonstrate and emphasise the oneness of spiritual experience.

Several definitions of the term given in the souvenir echo Gandhian usage. '*Samabhav* is the realisation that a true follower of any faith respects the different pathways to God chosen by others' as well as '*Samabhav* is the knowledge that all faiths are engaged in the common pursuit of spiritual enlightenment' articulate the Gandhian view of religions as different paths to the same end. '*Samabhav* is the desire to protect and cherish other people's belief as one would one's own' is a variant on an idea from one of Gandhi's favourite Gujarati songs about how a true disciple treats the pain of others as his own.[33]

The list includes a set of meanings for *samabhav* that warn explicitly against disrespect for religious beliefs of others, such as '*Samabhav* is the active tolerance of other people's beliefs' and it 'suffers when any religion is denigrated or its followers are belittled or persecuted'. In his welcome note for the souvenir, Madhvani writes, 'Our daily experience is one of increasing and bitter social conflict, often based on religious or racial intolerance' (13). The souvenir makes a clear distinction between awareness of unity and attempts at conversion: *Samabhav* 'allows all to worship within their own cultural and religious traditions. It has no need of converting believers from one faith to another.' Madhvani sought to emphasise universally shared religious values, but did not expect all religions to melt into one; he wanted to foster respect for similarities, and also for differences.

If everyone lived according to *samabhav*, instead of giving it mere lip service, relationships between people would be transformed radically, as two additional glosses on the term convey: '*Samabhav* is the harmony of true and never-ending compassion for one's fellow human beings.' In other words, awareness of unity of feeling fosters empathy for others, whereas treating them without respect dehumanises them. Therefore, cultivating knowledge of *samabhav* fosters 'a spirit of cooperation, conciliation, and equanimity'. Taken together, all eleven meanings of *samabhav* provide an ambitious sketch for a utopian society composed of diverse religious groups working together while respecting differences. Madhvani planned his Festival so that it would elucidate these various aspects of *samabhav*.

Of the two major Hindu epics, Madhvani felt most affinity with Rama's story, which he interpreted as showing the value of sacrificing one's own desires for the benefit of others. Madhvani cited a Gujarati proverb to back up his preference for Ramayana: 'Mahabharata is where everyone says "mine, mine, mine" and Ramayana is where everyone says "give, give, give".' Mahabharata recounts the tale of two sets of cousins, each bent on grabbing the kingdom away from the other. In contrast, Madhvani sees Ramayana as foregrounding how Lakshmana, Sita and Bharata all willingly made sacrifices for their family. Asked for his favourite character in Rama's story, Madhvani answered: 'Bharata. He ruled only as regent until his brother returned, and took upon himself the same religious austerities that Rama was suffering in the forest. He had sacrificed his own ego.' Madhvani's selection is consistent with his belief that personal sacrifices must be made for the greater good.

Madhvani's plan for the Festival of Spiritual Unity went far beyond earlier family *kathas* in its magnitude and diversity of events; organising it became one of his highest priorities. He approached the process of planning it as if it were a major business endeavour. 'I took it as a project, as if I were starting a new factory, for example,' he told me. Planning the Festival over a three-year period called upon his financial, managerial and interpersonal skills to keep it on time and on target.

A man experienced in long-term financial planning, Madhvani considered the three most expensive items first, since each entailed a large outlay of funds. Several religious leaders had to be flown in from India. Each guest who attended the *katha* had to be fed. The souvenir had to be free of advertising (even though it was common practice to defray *katha* costs by soliciting ads). Madhvani disliked religious events where guests were subjected to frequent requests for money or where more attention was given to fundraising than to achieving the event's spiritual aims. To avoid compromising the Festival's ethos, he decided that the Madhvani family would bear all costs; everything would be done properly, without stinting.

Madhvani shared a strong sense of Gujarati identity with many South Asians who immigrated to England in the 1970s. Gujarati mercantile groups have long travelled beyond the borders of their natal places.[34] Because so many Gujaratis settled in Britain had come from East Africa, one scholar coined the phrase 'twice migrants' to characterise their experience.[35] Madhvani and his compatriots from East Africa who settled in the U.K. shared a common experience and a set of networks. In 1901, (shortly before Madhvani's father arrived in Uganda), eighty per cent of the 35,000 Indians in British East African protectorates were Gujarati. In 1993 (when much of the Festival's planning occurred), approximately fifty per cent of the half a million Gujaratis in Britain had strong links to East Africa (Dwyer 1994: 165–90). Since Indians of Gujarati heritage are one of the two largest ethnic groups among South Asians in Britain, many people shared Madhvani's experiences of rupture and resettlement. Madhvani's decision to hold the Festival in London made sense because it was, 'a second home for us and also because of the large population of Asian origin which has settled here' (13).

Madhvani knew that the Festival's success in attracting an audience depended upon who would perform the *katha*. That person must hold the attention of the audience, possess a good voice, appeal to people familiar and unfamiliar with Tulsidas, and engage members of an audience diverse in educational background, religious views and age. Madhvani chose Morari Bapu, about whom he commented, 'It was said that even if half a million people were attending his *katha*,' at key moments, 'you could hear a pin drop.' Because Morari Bapu not only taught *Ramkatha* but conveyed his deep devotion to Rama through music, Madhvani felt that Morari Bapu's piety would set the right tone for the Festival.[36] In a recent *katha*, Morari Bapu had managed to interest even British-born English-speaking children of Gujarati heritage in Tulsidas' *Ramcharitmanas* by incorporating humorous didactic stories, familiar devotional songs and analogies from everyday life.[37] Both Morari Bapu's strong Gujarati identity and the marketing of, his audio and video cassettes in the last decade led to his popularity among British-born Gujaratis.

Madhvani's next priorities were arranging meals and identifying the other religious leaders who would play prominent roles in the Festival. He asked members of the London branch of the Swaminarayan Hindu Mission (Williams 1984), a group founded by Sahajanand Swami (1781–1830), to take charge of meals following the *katha*. Since they were known for their commitment to volunteer work, exemplary self-discipline and excellent organisation, when they agreed to prepare lunches at the *katha* site, Madhvani knew all would run smoothly. Then Swami Chidanand Saraswati ('Muniji') agreed to help select and invite prominent Hindu leaders as special guests of the Festival. A religious figure who moved comfortably between Hindi and English, Muniji had helped to facilitate the construction of the first purpose-built temple in the United States, the Srivenkateshvara Temple in Pittsburgh.

Winsome and enthusiastic, he was on good terms with holy men among the various *sampradayas, panths*, monastic orders, and other religious groups in India and the South Asian diaspora.[38]

Preliminary plans now completed, Madhvani turned to what he jokingly called 'Phase B', in business lingo, delegating responsibility for day-to-day operations and setting up an advisory board. As 'lieutenant' he chose his London-based manager of company operations in the Middle East, to oversee the day-to-day work. To ensure that *samabhav* infused even the early phase of planning, Madhvani assembled a board of advisors composed of local leaders from major Vaishnava groups such as the Swaminarayan Hindu Mission, the Shri Vallabh Nidhi and the Sri Sitaram Seva Trust.[39] The board met regularly to receive updates on plans, thereby precluding misunderstandings that could lead to later conflict. Because each member was involved in the planning process, each knew why specific decisions had been made. By putting religious leaders on the board, Madhvani provided them with models of effective teamwork and consensus building that they could use in their own organisations.

At first Madhvani had planned to invite only religious leaders from various Hindu groups, but later decided to include some non-Hindu religious leaders as well. One such guest was Maulana Wahiduddin Khan Saheb from Delhi, who sat on the dais each day during the *katha*. The Maulana also wrote a closely argued and practical-minded article for the souvenir, which included close exegesis of Quranic passages.[40] The Chair of the World Congress of Faiths and a member of the International Council of Christians and Jews were also involved with the Festival. Second, Madhvani arranged lodging for religious leaders and himself in forest-surrounded Hotel Stanmore, renaming it Place of Peace for the duration of the Festival. He saw the hotel's setting as evoking a forest hermitage, the place one goes to seek knowledge of religious truth, in Hindu tradition.

The religious leaders who stayed at the Place of Peace might not be the most well known within their group or denomination, but each had an interest in conversations with those outside their own religious community. Those who had built their following by preaching religious exclusivity would not be attracted to the Festival so, to a certain extent, the leaders who came were self-selected; some had been involved in ecumenical or interfaith dialogues, while others were known for writing about similarities between different religious traditions. Each leader gave an address either in the morning, preceding the *katha*, or at the hotel in the evening. Madhvani invited local followers to evening workshops at the hotel on topics such as Islam, Jainism and Judaism. By doing so, Madhvani sought to provide occasions where leaders and followers learned together, hoping that sharing these moments might create lasting commitments to *samabhav*.

Another kind of boundary crossing occurred at the *katha* site, where over three thousand volunteers helped with festival arrangements, which gave them an opportunity to perform *seva*, religious service, as well as a chance to visit with friends and kin. Many were educated young professionals who enjoyed networking with new people and serving a good cause. The Vallabh Nidhi took as its responsibility the work of overseeing the huge tent for the *katha*, supervising the sophisticated amplification equipment and setting up thousands of chairs. Madhvani expressed special affection for the elderly Swaminarayan women who arrived at 3.00 am to begin preparations for each day's lunch. Mobile medical units performed free public service by screening people for high blood pressure, diabetes and high cholesterol. A creche was available so parents of infants could attend the *katha*, and volunteers stood at the local tube and bus stops to direct guests to the site.

The daily discourses of Morari Bapu thus anchored an event which included multiple agendas, religious leaders, sites for interaction and opportunities for service. On weekdays approximately twelve thousand people attended the Festival.

During the weekend *kathas* that began and ended the Festival, the size of the audience rose to twenty thousand. The Festival was planned for August (rather than some particular holiday) so people could attend during their summer vacation and bring their children, for whom special seats close to the stage were reserved. Those unable to attend could still hear the *katha* because a satellite television company, TV Asia, broadcast all nine days of the Festival.[41]

In an interview for TV Asia, Morari Bapu articulated his view of the relationship between *samabhav* and *Ramcharitmanas* [henceforth *Manas*] of Tulsidas. When the interviewer asked Morari Bapu how he interpreted *samabhav*, he answered with a miniature *katha*, using several modes of discourse that occur frequently in *Manas* exegesis.[42] Beginning with etymological analysis, he commented that *sama* (oneness) and *bhava* (feeling) denote a sentiment or feeling that ultimately we all share. To emphasise how *samabhav* transcends the divisions of different religious identities, Morari Bapu turned to analogy:

> The sun (Surya) doesn't decide to give light only to India, or Africa, or the US or Britain, but gives light to every place. It doesn't pay attention to *desh* (country), *bhasha* (language), *varna* (caste), or *quam* (religious community). Similarly, our fundamental nature is one, but it gets clouded over by karma and *purva-graha*.[43]

When asked why, if we all share it, people don't act according to this sense of oneness, Morari Bapu described the human condition in familiar domestic imagery:

> God has given us so much, but we ignore it. We are like cooks stuck in the kitchen. We have all the ingredients, but we don't know how to cook, so we die.

In other words, we are ignorant of the knowledge that could save us from a useless and wasted life. The interviewer then pressed Morari Bapu to explain precisely how one could obtain this crucial knowledge we lack. In response, Morari Bapu turned to epistemology, pointing out that the fruits of past actions often obstruct one's attempts to realise truth. Human beings are fortunate, therefore, to have recourse to the grace (*kripa*) of God, which expresses itself in many forms, among which one of the most revealing is the *Manas*. Morari Bapu had spent much of his life studying, reciting and interpreting the *Manas*, and he saw the text, when understood correctly, as a path to true knowledge. He encouraged others to turn to it for guidance towards truth, drawing upon a *Ramkatha* incident to express his point:

> One must follow God. Just as God made a bridge (*setu*) across the ocean to Lanka, he wants a *katha* to act like a bridge built between all the religions.

Morari Bapu viewed the Festival as an occasion for increasing one's understanding of the *Manas*, a bridge to cross from ignorance to knowledge of *samabhav*.

Morari Bapu returned to *samabhav* several times in the course of the *katha*. For example, on the Festival's second day, he recited a verse from the *Sundarakanda* of *Ramcharitmanas*.[44] Immediately preceding it, Hanuman, who has been brought to the demon's court, tells Ravana that the demon king is under the sway of delusion (*moha*). In the verse Morari Bapu glossed, Ravana threatens to kill the monkey in fury, but Vibhishana warns his elder brother that a messenger should never be killed. Morari Bapu extrapolated from this verse to talk about how we all long for the knowledge that others can give us. As he said,

> We all want this, but there is one precondition. If we love God first, then there will be love amongst us. Until our mental Lanka has been destroyed, we cannot reach *samabhav*.

His exegetical move links delusion with the human condition by describing it allegorically as the mental Lanka that imprisons human beings in ignorance. He urges love of God so we can understand the true nature of *samabhav*, thus freeing us from mental Lanka. As a result, '*samabhav* can be our *ramraj*'—that is, once we understand the feelings of oneness that we all share, we will live in a perfect society, as did those citizens during the rule of Lord Rama, characterised by perfect justice. Morari Bapu ranged over a wide set of themes during the Festival, but the link between *samabhav* and the *Manas* recurred.

When Morari Bapu's *katha* ended, Madhvani wanted guests to return home with something that would prompt them to remember *samabhav*, so recruiting good editors for the souvenir volume had been one of his priorities. The co-editors, Dr Katherine Prior, who specialises in the history of colonial India and the British empire, and Vipool Kalyani, a noted Gujarati journalist, sought to ensure that the souvenir represented the diversity of religious traditions and presented information in a clear and accessible manner, in both English and Gujarati. The advertisement-free volume included essays that looked at world religions in a comparative framework, as well as more specific articles that discussed the role of *samabhav* in individual South Asian religions. Other articles focussed on aspects of Indian culture such as Indian music, specific religious texts and Gujarati modern literature. The souvenir's breadth and range allowed it to function as a cultural and religious anthology for non-specialist readers. It proved so popular among audience members that it went through two printings.[45]

In terms of the planning, enactment and memory of the Festival, its most notable characteristic is the degree to which it foregrounded the crossing of national boundaries. Both planners and invited guests thought within a framework of spatial mobility across Asian, African and European borders. This transnational flow of people locates the Festival as occurring at a moment in the history of South Asian immigration to the United Kingdom when Gujaratis from East Africa had established themselves in Britain.

The most striking example of the Festival's transnational nature is its central religious figure, Morari Bapu. Facing a full-page colour photo of him, eyes closed and rapt in devotion to Rama, the souvenir's first article is a short biographical sketch whose prose highlights Morari Bapu's global role:

> Today Pujya Bapu's discourses are heard by millions of people the world over—from Delhi to London to New York. A globe-trotting Sadhak, he carries the inspirational torch of Ram-Katha to all corners of India and the world. (3)

Another article in the souvenir, written by Meenal Manek, a Britain-born teenager of Gujarati heritage, who went on the Cunard cruise during which Bapu had given daily *katha*, notes:

> [Bapu is] a man who goes around the world reciting the great Hindu epic....Millions of people have assembled to hear this man over and over again. He has been everywhere. (4)

Both in these two articles and in his *kathas*, offhand references to London, Delhi, New York, Africa and Gujarat occur frequently. Bapu has his own theological interpretation of his global travels: he believes that if people keep hearing *Ramkatha* everywhere, 'this will ultimately lead to the universal awakening of mankind' (3). He self-consciously views his border-crossing as a way to make knowledge of the *Manas* universal.[46]

The global reach of Morari Bapu is closely linked with the Festival's second major characteristic—its identification with Gujarati language and culture. Morari Bapu combines the strong regional identity shared by Gujaratis settled in far-flung places with a geographical mobility that enables him to move about easily in new places. Although most of the audience hailed from Greater London, news about the Festival's date circulated long in advance and people of Gujarati heritage came from all over the U.K. and Europe. For many Gujaratis, transnational mobility and a strong sense of regional heritage are two sides of the same coin. Hearing exegesis of *Ramcharitmanas* is a prominent form of Vaishnavite practice among Gujarati Ram-devotees. Although Madhvani asked

Morari Bapu to perform his *katha* in Hindi to make it accessible to the largest audience possible, approximately eighty-five per cent of the Festival audience was of Gujarati heritage. The souvenir also emphasises Gujarati culture.[47]

A third distinctive feature of the Festival was its corporate planning. The Festival's organisers viewed themselves as part of a joint entity with a shared set of goals. When Madhvani constituted the Board of Advisors for the Festival, he created an entity designed to bring a joint project to completion. Similarly, those who accepted Madhvani's invitation to dwell at the Place of Peace became part of the joint endeavour to foreground *samabhav* at the Festival. The Festival was also corporate in that it utilised management techniques of large corporations; as Madhvani so aptly put it, he functioned as if he were 'starting a new factory'. Essentially, Madhvani devised a plan, then selected a team to actualise and publicise it. Using ongoing financial supervision, administrative structures designed for efficient teamwork and leadership from his top managers, Madhvani delegated tasks to create and market a unique and desirable product—a *Ramkatha* about *samabhav*.[48]

Souvenir co-editor Prior appropriately described the Festival of Spiritual Unity as a 'combination of morality and pragmatism'.[49] The Festival of Spiritual Unity was both a corporate project and a social service outreach event, with an efficiency and clarity of purpose seldom found in such large-scale religious gatherings. In sum, the Festival provided a means of linking an ancient story about Rama, believed to illustrate ideal moral behavior, to the ideal of *samabhav*, a concept that proved particularly attractive to a corporate executive whose idea of proper action was linked to sacrifice for the greater good, effective outcomes and long-range planning.

Conclusions

The three performances analysed here reveal that the diversity of narrative and exegesis found in the Ramayana tradition of South

Asia has also been at work in Greater London. This conclusion defies some conventional wisdom about South Asian diaspora communities. It is common to hear complaints that those who leave their homeland cling to the religious practices familiar at the moment of their departure; religious change might occur back in India, but immigrants freeze the religious traditions from the time they left their homeland. Insufficient research has been carried out to determine the precise extent to which this claim is true, but the three examples analysed in this essay suggest an alternative view in the case of *Ramkatha*.

A number of scholars have documented the salience of *Ramkatha* among South Asians in the diaspora. For example, Bhikhu Parekh has argued that the story had a particular resonance as a foundational religious text for overseas Hindus:

> ...the *Ramayana* is a simple and uncomplicated text, not only in its plot but also in its philosophical and moral message, and has a deeply didactic orientation. Good and evil are clearly separated....This highly simplified view of life and the concomitant sense of moral certainty have an obvious appeal for a community anxious to preserve its traditional values in a threatening environment.[50]

This statement has some validity in particular diaspora contexts, but the situation proves far more complex in Greater London during the fifteen-year period examined in this paper.

Only one performance examined in this paper took place in a recognisably formal ritual setting, the Festival of Spiritual Unity. The SBS *Ramlila* was mounted by a group of people who saw themselves mainly as staging a cultural performance to demonstrate their solidarity with the heritage of (some of their) members. The Commonwealth Institute performance avoided treating Rama in a way that acknowledged either the ritual element of the drama or the fact that many Hindus worship Rama as Supreme Lord. Only the Festival of Spiritual Unity contained the *bhajans* and prayers associated with ritual *Ramkatha* events.

The three examples differ in other ways as well, particularly in terms of their treatment of the story. Rama's story can be relatively simple or enormously complex, depending upon the nature of the performance, the scope of exegesis and the time frame within which the story, or part of the story, is recounted. The SBS *Ramlila* takes the story as a relatively straightforward plot in which '[g]ood and evil are clearly separated'. Parekh's claim that the tale has an 'appeal for a community...in a threatening environment' also holds true in this case. SBS saw Ravana as totally evil, epitomising the threat that they encountered in their environment. Thus the SBS conveyed a straightforward message about the need to destroy racism. The presence of jesters within the production, however, introduced a level of critique and complexity that served to question certain gender constructs. While the Commonwealth Institute *Ramkatha* was simple and clear, ultimately it proved least successful in carrying out educational goals, resulting instead in an essentialised and, at the same time, reductionist view of the story and its relationship to Divali. The exegesis of Morari Bapu treated the story as a beginning point for didactic discourse on how to destroy the mental Lanka in which human beings are trapped. In this case, the basic story functioned primarily as an occasion for commentary.

Despite the fact that all three performances enacted or took as their basis the same skeleton of incidents and characters, the overall impact of each performance proved quite different. The Commonwealth Institute gala aided the state in representing and tokenising Hindu religious tradition within the British educational system. The SBS created its *Ramlila* as a protest against state surveillance and institutionalised racism. It is more difficult to determine precisely what kind of cultural politics underlay the Festival of Spiritual Unity. On the one hand, the event's border-crossing nature might imply that *Ramkatha* transcended state boundaries. On the other hand, the transnational nature of the Festival was in consonance with the ideology of multinational corporations, particularly because of the fluid movement of participants across borders and because the cost of the Festival was underwritten with the corporate multinational wealth of the sponsor. At a practical level at least, religious violence, in places such as Lebanon, Africa and South Asia, disrupts economic markets, interfering with 'business as usual'. Thus operationalising *samabhav* on a broad level would contribute to the stable relationships required for 'free' trade.

The evidence provided in this paper also reveals that in Greater London, *Ramkatha* can represent the relationship between the South Asian community in Britain and the wider British society in a variety of ways. As 'Black Sisters' who identified with Southall, both South Asians and African Caribbeans saw themselves fighting against the Ravana of racism. In the Commonwealth Institute Divali gala, *Ramkatha* was an all-India story, as if religious differences between Hindus and Muslims, Sikhs, Jains, Christians or Jews had been airbrushed away. Although the Festival of Spiritual Unity sought to recognise the broad devotional sentiments that all religions were said to share, more than eighty-five per cent of the audience were of Gujarati heritage. That representation itself says a great deal about the primacy of regional heritage among even Hindus of South Asian descent in Britain.

This essay has considered the immigration history, representations of community, and relationship to the state of the actors and performances of three *Ramkatha* events in London in a fifteen-year period. This case study should be viewed as a preliminary attempt to chart some of the cultural work carried out by the many performances of *Ramkatha* in Britain between the 1970s and 1990s. Only when the other performances are explored will we be able to answer some of the questions raised here in a more definitive way.[51]

Notes

*At talks presented at the Divinity School of the University of Chicago and the Ramayana Conference at the University of British Columbia, I received helpful comments on an earlier draft that helped improve this essay. I am grateful to all those who shared information and memories with me in interviews carried out between 1994 and 2000, but especially to Avtar Brah, John De Souza, Perminder Dhillon, Karen Field, Lakshmi Holmstrom, Jacqueline Hirst, Vipool Kalyani, Arjun Kashyup, Anna King, Meena Mukta, Manubhai Madhvani, Parita Mukta, Eleanor Nesbitt, Katherine Prior and Rani Singh, as well as to Meenal Manek and Philip Lutgendorf, who assisted me in translating the nuances of Morari Bapu's discourse. Of course, I take full responsibility for any errors that remain.

Readers who want to read a more extensive discussion of (1) the specific historical and sociological aspects of Southall life that are reflected in the SBS *Ramlila* and (2) the ways in which the SBS *Ramlila* relates to specific features found within the Ramayana tradition in India should consult Richman (1999).

1. For an assessment of the consequences of viewing *Ramkatha* as a vast narrative tradition with a number of different tellings, rather than simply a lineage of textual descendents from Valmiki's Ramayana, see Richman (1990: 7–10).

2. Generally, a 'performance' is defined as a set of actions carried out by actors for an audience. In this essay, 'performance' is used to refer not only to the drama portraying Rama's story but also the preparations for the performance, as well as recitation and exegesis of the story in a performance setting.

3. In this essay, I refer to the original group of women who called themselves 'Southall Black Sisters' in the late 1970s, not the group by that name in the 1990s.

4. For the social and economic history of South Asian immigration and settlement during this period, see Fryer (1984), Wilson (1978), Visram (1986). A study that analyses gender issues with sophistication is Avatar Brah's *Cartographies of Diaspora: Contesting Identities* (1996). *Southall: The Birth of a Black Community* (1981) concentrates specifically on Southall during the period under analysis in this essay, as does Dhanjal (1977–78). Gerd Baumann's *Contesting*

Culture (1996) focusses primarily on the period after the SBS *Ramlila*.

5. See especially Brah (1996: 44–46), Nugent (1976), and Taylor (1978) for analysis of the National Front movement in relation to South Asian immigration during the period under discussion here.

6. I have reconstructed how the SBS *Ramlila* developed and why it took the form that it did through interviews with its original members and those who attended the performance, as well as publications written later by those who had been members of SBS in the 1970s, including Brah (1988: 86), Dhillon (1979) and Mukta (1994: xi).

7. For Enoch Powell's references to this speech after the Southall violence, see *The Daily Telegraph*, 24 April 1979.

8. The Traditional Story of Ramayana. Programme from the SBS *Ramlila*, 19 October 1979, given to me by Parita Mukta.

9. One of the few extant documents attesting to the event is a small notice titled 'Festival', *The Southall Gazette*, 19 October 1979, which reads as follows: 'Southall "Black Sisters" are presenting an updated version of *Ram Leela*, the Hindhu [sic.] religious festival at 7:15 in the Dominion Hall on Friday night. Songs, music and dances will be followed by a bonfire in the Dominion car park and firework display.'

10. In 1886 the Prince of Wales had proposed, in a letter to the Lord Mayor of London, that an Imperial Institute be built as a way of celebrating his mother's golden jubilee. A description of the inaugural ceremony appears in 'Centenary Brochure 1893–1993' (Commonwealth Institute 1993: 19–20). The history of the Institute summarised in the next four paragraphs is drawn from this article.

11. See page 3 of 'Guidelines for Group Visits' (Commonwealth Institute 1994a) for a photograph of the exhibition hall with the stage at its centre.

12. See 'Campaign News: Support the Commonwealth Institute' (Commonwealth Institute 1994b: 1–2). Ultimately, the Institute was unable to raise the required funds and had to curtail its programming severely after 1999.

13. Institute administrator Karen Field noted that teacher workshops related to the National Curriculum were always fully subscribed. Interview, 18 November 1994.

14. The 1988 Act continued to require that RE be compulsory, designating the National Curriculum as English, Maths, Science, Art,

Music, History, Geography, Technology, modern foreign languages and Physical Education, and stipulating that these subjects, in combination with RE, would be known as the Basic Curriculum. As Terence Copley's *Teaching Religion* points out, 'This Basic Curriculum was not further identified', which made it difficult for educators to comply with it (1997: 133).

15. See Jackson, *Religious Education* (1997: 8–19) for the Lancaster-based curriculum; and Jackson, 'Changing Conceptions of Hinduism in "Timetabled" Religion' (1987: 202–13) for analysis of world religious offerings.

16. Lady Olga Maitland, MP, said, for example, that the RE guidelines are a 'multicultural mish-mash'. Quoted in Priscilla Chadwick, *Shifting Alliances* (1997: 101).

17. Department for Education (DFE) Circular 1/94 on *Religious Education and Collective Worship*, quoted in Chadwick (1997: 101).

18. Birmingham and Leicester pioneered the development of syllabi in Asian religions.

19. The pamphlet has no publication date, but its format and typewriter font suggest that it was done in the late 1970s or early 1980s.

20. For example, he notes that although on Divali rangoli (floor design) was painted in white on brown mud floors earlier, recently a brilliant range of colours has also been used.

21. Issue no. 3 of 'Campaign News' (4) notes that High Commissioners of Commonwealth countries should visit the Institute in their role as governors. This issue reports on the visit of HE Mr Wajid Shamsul Husan, High Commissioner of Pakistan, during which he donated materials to the resource centre to aid in the 1994 focus on Asia.

22. Commonwealth nationals need not, however, be members of the religious tradition being studied. Workshop leader Rani Singh, a Sikh, was the Commonwealth national for Divali. Quotes that follow come from my interview with her on 14 November 1994.

23. The Triveni Dance Company, run by Pratap Pawar, performs in Kathak style. Pawar, who studied with a Lucknow Gharana master, is based in Hounslow, Middlesex.

24. This description is based on my attendance at the gala (4 November 1994) and 'Programme for Divali: Festival of Lights'.

25. For a discussion of how *Ramkatha* characters get 'domesticated'

through means such as the use of highly colloquial dialogue in storytelling and exegesis, see Philip Lutgendorf (1991: 213).

26. On the inside cover of the Divali programme entire phrases, directly lifted (without attribution) from Ogg's description of Divali (1), appear but Ogg's mention of other narratives linked with Divali celebrations in India are never mentioned.

27. The elevation of Divali as the 'central' holiday of Hinduism, however, did not begin with the Institute. Instead it reflects a trend developed among some South Asians in the diaspora, at least partly as a practical response to the fact that different communities of Hindus in Britain have different festival celebrations and it is easier to present Divali as a holiday that all groups 'can' celebrate as the 'main' Hindu festival, whereas few people in South Asia would see the need for such a claim. This elevation also ignores the specific rituals and narratives linked with the holiday among different South Asian religious groups in Britain. Divali is foregrounded as well in marketing strategies and media commercials because of the custom of buying new clothing for Divali.

28. Analysis of the role of controversial incidents in the Ramayana tradition appears in my introductory essay to *Questioning Ramayanas* (2000: 6–7).

29. Information about the Madhvani family appears in the souvenir volume, 'Samabhav: The Festival of Spiritual Unity, London 1994' (Kalyani and Prior 1994). The information about the Madhvanis in Uganda and their *kathas* draws upon 'Muljibhai Madhvani and Family', by T.P. Suchak, who lived in Uganda for 40 years (14–16); a similar article in Gujarati, by co-editor Vipool Kalyani (17–20); Manubhai Madhvani's note of welcome to the *katha* (13). Henceforth page numbers of souvenir articles are cited in parentheses in the body of the text, directly following the quote.

30. Indeco Group: Enterprise for Development. Pamphlet.

31. Interview with Madhubhai Madhvani, 21 November 1994. All direct quotes from him in this essay come from this interview.

32. The 1955 *katha* was by Pujya Sant Shri Krishna Shankar Shastri on the Bhagavad Gita. He performed other *kathas* in Kakira in the 1960s and in 1971 (13). Morari Bapu performed a small *katha* for the Madhvani family in 1984 in London.

33. This song, titled 'A True Vaishnava', appears in the souvenir (48). For more on Gandhi's view of Rama, see 'Rama Belongs to All' (15),

focussed upon a favourite Gandhi bhajan on Rama and his comment, 'If you are worshippers of Rama, you must accept that Rama belongs to all. He is the Saviour of all, whether Hindu, Muslim, Christian or Parsi.' Links between Gandhian thought and Gujarati industrialists were strong during the pre-independence period, when Manubhai studied in India. For example, Gandhi developed a close relationship with Gujarati mill-owner Ambalal Sarabhai (Erikson 1969: 296–303).

34. As John Kelly has noted in relation to South Asian diaspora communities: 'A Gujarati commercial migration history [was] intrinsic to the Indian Ocean and Southeast Asian maritime commercial capitalism of the very long run' (2000: 337).

35. Parminder Bhachu's *Twice Migrants* dealt with Sikhs from East Africa but the term 'twice migrant' came to be used more generally for South Asians who had immigrated from East Africa to Britain.

36. For audience reception, see Nesbitt (2000: 177–191).

37. For an English transcript of a *katha* by Morari Bapu that demonstrates his eclectic and wide-ranging style of exegesis, see page 636 of *Mangal Ramayan*.

38. Muniji (Swamiji Chidanand Saraswati), welcomed Festival guests on opening day with a rousing speech about its efficacy. He said, 'This [the *katha*] is the factory that is going to produce [merit],' a reference to Madhvani's record of successful factories. Then he shifted to a new analogy: 'You know that here in London the BBC has several stations. This [the Roundwood Park site] will be the real relay station, through the festival of *samabhav.*'

39. Madhvani made donations to major Hindu groups in London. He felt it was crucial to remain even-handed to each group, and be seen to not favour one over the others.

40. While some articles in the souvenir seem to gloss over differences in religions, such as 'Everyone is Right!' by Pujya Dada Jashan Vaswani (47), Khan's rigorously argued 'Religious Harmony: An Islamic Perspective' (41–42) notes strong differences between religions and comments, 'The principle formulated by Islam is best described not as religious harmony, but as harmony among religious people' (42).

41. Sunrise Radio, the main Asian radio station (with both London and Midlands frequencies) broadcast by live or delayed relay several hours of each day's performances as well.

42. This interview is found on Videocassette 2 of the 16 videocassettes

from the Festival, taped and broadcast by TV Asia. The quotes in the text in this and the following paragraph come from the interview in Hindi with Morari Bapu.

43. The term *purva-graha* can have two senses here: (1) individual destiny, as previously fated by the stars, or (2) bias or prejudice, literally (things that) 'grasp' (you) from 'before'.

44. Videocasette 3 of 16. The verse, which begins *Suni kapi bachana bahut khisiyana*, is *Sundarakanda* 23.5 in the Gita Press edition of *Ramcharitmanas*, a very popular and inexpensively priced edition of the *Manas*.

45. The souvenir's first print-run of 10,000 copies sold out at the nominal price of £ 3, even before the Festival ended. Another 3,000 copies were printed for free distribution to volunteers and donors.

46. Although cruise passengers sometimes went ashore, *Ramkatha* itself took place in territory not viewed as within the borders of any particular country. The illustration paired with Meenal's essay shows a ship with the word 'Ram' on the mainsail, in the midst of the high seas. Floating near the ship is Morari Bapu, surrounded by a nimbus of golden light, with seagulls circling him to hear his words. Morari Bapu has also performed *katha* on an airplane.

47. Among the 48 articles in the souvenir, a goodly number concern Gujarat-related topics: Gujarati writer Narsimh Mehta (48); ritual lamps from Gujarat (49); the history of the Madhvani family (14–16 in English, 17–20 in Gujarati); 11 pages about or of modern Gujarati literature (76–86). The souvenir's last 4 pages contain prayers in Gujarati script, followed by transliteration of the Gujarati into Roman script for those British-born people of Gujarati descent who can understand but not read Gujarati, followed by a translation of the prayer into English.

48. A striking example of the Festival's corporate slant appears in a souvenir article titled 'Tax-Effective Charitable Giving'. Chartered Accountant Subhash V. Thakrar offered this essay to the souvenir editors so that readers of the souvenir who wanted to give to charities would know how to do so in the most advantageous way. A professional who advises businesses about tax laws, he explains to donors how to give in a way that maximises tax advantages. According to the souvenir (74), some of Thakrar's publications include *UK as a Tax Haven* (The Economist) and *Blackstone Franks Good Investment Guide* (Kogan Page).

49. Interview with Katherine Prior, November 1994.

50. Although this quote comes from 'Religion and the Overseas Hindus: The Appeal of the Ramayana,' an article in the souvenir, it is an abridged version of a longer article titled 'The *Ramayana* Syndrome: The Tale of the Struggling Exile,' under which is the subtitle 'Identifying with an epic that cuts across divisions of caste, sect, gender, and age,' which first appeared in the 30 March 1994 edition of *The Asian Age*, as the second in a series of articles on 'The Hindu Diaspora' that the paper ran from 28 March 1994 to 2 April 1994. Parekh qualifies his assessment about what made *Ramkatha* particularly popular in diaspora communities, noting that different factors 'weighed differently with different groups of Hindus in different parts of the world'. It is likely that the situation varies greatly depending upon the location, the amount and kind of regular communication accessible to the migrant, the economic status of the migrant and other factors.

51. I am currently writing a monograph on this topic, tentatively titled 'Ramayanas Abroad: The History of *Ramkatha* Performances in the Diaspora'.

References

Babu, Morari. 1987. *Mangal Ramayan as Narrated by Ever-Revered Sant Shri Morari Bapu*. Bombay: Prachin Sanskriti Mandir.

Baumann, Gerard. 1996. *Contesting Culture: Discourses of Identity in Multi-ethnic London*. Cambridge: Cambridge University Press.

Bhachu, Parminder. 1985. *Twice Migrants: East African Sikh Settlers in Britain*. London: Tavistock.

Brah, Avtar. 1988. Journey to Nairobi. In *Charting the Journey: Writings by Black and Third World Women*, (eds.) Shabnam Grewal et al. London: Sheba Feminist Publishers.

—. 1996. *Cartographies of Diaspora: Contesting Identities*. London: Routledge.

Chadwick, Priscilla. 1997. *Shifting Allianc Church and State in English Education*. London: Cassell.

Commonwealth Institute. 1993. Centenary Brochure 1893–1993. London: Commonwealth Institute.

—. 1994a. Guidelines for Group Visits. London: Commonwealth Institute.

—. 1994b. Campaign News: Support the Commonwealth Institute. London: Commonwealth Institute.

Copley, Terence. 1997. *Teaching Religion: Fifty Years of Religious Education in England and Wales*. Exeter: University of Exeter Press.

Dhanjal, Beryl. 1977–78. Asian Housing in Southall. *New Community* 6 (1–2): 88–93.

Dhillon, Perminder. 1979. They're Killing in Here. *Spare Rib*.

Dummett, Michael (ed.). 1980. *Southall 23 April 1979. The Report of the Unofficial Committee of Enquiry*. National Council for Civil Liberties.

Dwyer, Rachel. 1994. Caste, Religion and Sect in Gujarat: Followers of Vallabhacharya and Swaminarayan. In *Desh Pardesh: The South Asian Presence in Britain*, (ed.) Roger Ballard. London: C. Hurst and Co.

Erikson, Erik. 1969. *Gandhi's Truth*. New York: W.W. Norton.

'Festival'. In *The Southall Gazette*, 19 October 1979.

Fryer, Peter. 1984. *Staying Power: The History of Black People in Britain*. London: Pluto Press.

Institute of Race Relations. 1981. *Southall: The Birth of a Black Community*. London: Institute of Race Relations.

Jackson, Robert. 1987. Changing Conceptions of Hinduism in the "Timetabled" Religion. In *Hinduism in Great Britain: The Perpetuation of Religion in an Alien Cultural Milieu*, (ed.) Richard Burghart. London: Tavistock.

—. 1997. *Religious Education: An Interpretive Approach*. London: Hodder and Stoughton.

Kalyani, Vipool and Katherine Prior (eds.). 1994. *Sambhav: The Festival of Spiritual Unity, London 1994*. Leicester: Chatham Printers.

Kelly, John. 2000. Fiji's Fifth Veda: Exile Sanatan, Dharm and Countercolonial Initiative Diaspora. In *Questioning Ramayanas: A South Asian Tradition*, (ed.) Paula Richman. Berkeley: University of California Press and New Delhi: Oxford University Press.

Lutgendorf, Philip. 1991. *The Life of a Text: Performing the Ramcharitmanas of Tulsidas*. Berkeley: University of California Press.

Mukta, Parita. 1994. *Upholding the Common Life: The Community of Mira Bai*. New Delhi: Oxford University Press.

Nesbitt, Eleanor. 2000. The Impact of Morari Bapu's *Kathas* on Young British Hindus. In *Scottish Journal of Religions Studies* 20: 177–91.

Nugent, Neill. 1976. The Anti-Immigration Groups. *New Community* 7 (2): 170–77.

Ogg, Anthony. n.d. Diwali: Festival of Lights (Illustrated by Sharon Finmark). London: Commonwealth Institute.

Parekh, Bhikhu. 1994. The Ramayana Syndrome: The Tale of the Struggling Exile. *Asian Age*, 30 March.

Richman, Paula. 1990. *Many Ramayanas: The Diversity of a Narrative Tradition in South Asia.* Berkeley: University of California Press, and (1991) New Delhi: Oxford University Press.

———. 1999. A Diaspora Ramayana in Southall, Greater London. *Journal of the American Academy of Religion* 67.1 (Winter): 33–57.

———. 2000. *Questioning Ramayanas: A South Asian Tradition.* Berkeley: University of California Press and New Delhi: Oxford University Press.

Smith, William. 1994. *Ramayanas of Eastern India.* New Delhi: Munshiram Manoharlal.

Suchak, T.P. n.d. *Muljibhai Madhvani and Family.* n.p.

Taylor, Stan. 1978. The National Front: Anatomy of a Political Movement. In *Racism and Political Action in Britain,* (eds.) Robert Miles and Annie Phizacklea, 126–46. London: Routledge.

The Daily Telegraph, 24 April 1979.

The Traditional Story of Ramayana. Programme from the SBS *Ramlila,* 19 October 1979.

Visram, Rosina. 1986. *Ayars, Lascars, and Princes.* London: Pluto Press.

Williams, Raymond. 1984. *A New Face of Hinduism. The Swaminarayan Religion.* Cambridge: Cambridge University Press.

Wilson, Amrit. 1978. *Finding a Voice: Asian Women in Britain.* London: Virago.

CHAPTER FIVE

Kabir: Do We Sing His Songs or Someone Else's?

WINAND M. CALLEWAERT

There may be several reasons why one has interest in the mystic-reformers of the fourteenth to seventeenth centuries in northern India. Besides the scholarly interest, I have been attracted by their inspiring and very modern message. Finding such a message in another culture (too) is not a threat to one's own tradition. On the contrary, it is a gift in this period of increased communication, and of growing openness in the West that reveals other aspects of the divine, or places renewed accents of the divine.

In this essay I address the following questions: Is there a similarity between the times in which these poets flourished, and our times? How did their songs and verses address contemporary problems, and can they have a message for us? What is the essence of that message? Finally, and most importantly, do we sing the songs as they were created by a particular poet, or by the later tradition? It is a good exercise at times to ask the question: If I could start again, would I do what I am doing now? Of course, situations change and we may acquire more wisdom as we progress in life, but I at times ask that question about the research I am doing, which for the last thirty years has been focussed on searching for manuscripts in view of critical editions and an English translation of *nirguna bhakti* texts. These texts were created by the Bhakti mystic-reformers in northwest India in the fifteenth and sixteenth centuries CE. The answer is definitely yes, for several reasons. That research has helped me make some good friends, all over the globe. It gave me the opportunity, when I was young, to make adventurous tours of Rajasthan, using all available diplomatic skill in order to have access to manuscripts. But most importantly, with that research I have contributed to the preservation of old texts threatened with destruction and the generation of critical editions of those texts. I hope to illustrate the urgent need – in the area of Bhakti literature, but possibly also in other areas of Indological research – to work on texts, according to the principle:

> Let the commentator say what might be and what ought to be, and let the text-editor say what there is!

The songs of the Bhakti mystic-reformers were sung, and only around 1600 CE were they written down. Therefore, since we have no recordings of the period, our only way to the original 'sung' version is through a comparison of manuscripts now scattered all over the region, often in remote villages. For the last twenty years I have travelled extensively all over Rajasthan, as well as to Delhi, Banares, Punjab, Pune and even Thanjavur. Every year I discovered new – often private – collections with ancient material, and along with my increasing data bank of Bhakti literature on film grew also the conviction that preservation of manuscripts and critical text-editions are a first priority for a student of Indian culture. The economic situation in India is such that the preservation of manuscripts is not the highest priority, although serious efforts are being made in this direction. Thousands of manuscripts disappear every year, either through decay or lack of care, or because they are sold to tourists. Steps have to be taken to avert the catastrophe already underway as the result of the neglect of vast collections of manuscripts. If these collections are allowed to rot away and are not even microfilmed, there will be little left with which to study Indian contributions to the world, or to draw inspiration from.

When the very devoted scholar of Indian literature, Mr Bahuraji retired as librarian in the City Palace, Jaipur, he told me that the history of Indian literature would have to be rewritten if all the manuscripts in the City Palace collection could be properly studied. In fact the greater part of India's literature survives only in manuscripts, and the part that has been edited has, in nearly all cases, been edited uncritically and on the basis of only a small number of the available manuscripts.

We should remember that classical Indology, of Sanskrit and Buddhist texts, started in the nineteenth century, and the only material available was what the British had brought from India and preserved in the India Office Library. Of course, we have come a long way since then, but we still have miles to go—work enough for the next twenty-five rebirths. Only five years ago I discovered a private collection in Jaipur of more than fifty thousand manuscripts, jealously guarded and neatly catalogued. After thirty years in Rajasthan even I had not been aware of this collection.

I turn now to the main topic of this article—scholarly commentaries on uncritical texts.

1. Mirabai

If the Rajput princess Mirabai died at the age of 43, possibly in 1546, it is remarkable that at the end of the twentieth century there should be as many as 5,197 songs available with her name. It has become a boring expression in studies about Mirabai that it is very difficult, if not impossible to decide which and how many songs are most probably by Mira. And yet, ever-expanding collections keep appearing. In some editions the question of authenticity is resolved on the basis of content (internal evidence), in others on the basis of language. Rarely do authors bother to look at the written material.

It remains a mystery why the written tradition, in the case of Mira, seems to have started so late, c. 1800 CE. This is very late indeed when compared with the spate of manuscripts of Bhakti literature in Rajasthan or Braj written down from 1600 CE onwards. Several reasons have been put forward to explain why the songs of Mira were not committed to writing: (1) The songs of Mira very soon become the (exclusive?) property of women singing the songs of *bhakti* at home, and women did not write, as the *sadhus* and male singers did. (2) The songs of Mira were scorned to such an extent thay they never became part of the standard repertoires of singers. Near the beautiful Kumbha-Krishna temple on the Chittor fort stands a very attractive little temple, called Mira ka Mandir, with a newly installed image of Krishna, but we read in a letter from Menariya to Purohit H.N. Sharma in July 1938:

> People here are not interested in Mira Bai as you and I are. Even the Maharana Sahib believes that Mira has been a black blot on the fair page of the Mewar history and musicians are not allowed to sing the *padas* of Mira Bai in the palace. But this is only for your private information. Please do not make mention of this anywhere in your book.

With due respect for the oral traditions which survive till the present day, my approach to the problem of authenticity starts with a search for the earliest manuscripts. Even if that approach, in the case of Mira, may not add much in terms of authentic songs, at least it can question the claims made in the numerous editions current now.

At the same time I have respect, however, for the translators of Mira who look for a good song in her repertoire, even if it may not have been composed by Mira! But let us not start writing commentaries on sixteenth century Rajasthan by quoting those songs!

In my article about Mira (Callewaert 1990: 363–78) I refer in detail to the so-called 'Dakor' manuscripts, of 1585, with 69 songs of Mira, and of 1748 CE, with 103 songs, and I give a complete bibliography of the sources and English translations of Mira's songs.

Let me here only draw your attention to the following fact—the earliest edition I found of Mira's songs is dated 1842, followed by another 14 editions, till 1948. None of the editions refer to a manuscript and the number of songs varies between 38 and 662! The first edition in which a reference is made to manuscripts is by Sharma (1949), with a total of 111 songs. More editions came after that, usually not referring to sources, and in one case with as many as 662 songs. The volumes appearing under the name of Indira Devi have 3,797 songs in 'Hindi' and 817 in Gujarati!

2. The Life-story of Dadu, by Jan Gopal (c. 1620 CE)

When Jan Gopal sat down to write the life-story of Dadu Dayal around 1620, he could not have imagined that his text would be edited 'critically', 366 years later. The very idea of a critical edition probably never occurred to him—scribes were not supposed to make mistakes while copying; they certainly did not intentionally alter the text or add anything. His life-story as it is now found in the manuscripts is a goldmine of sectarian interpolations and variants, illustrating the growing biases in the early group of Dadu's followers. Very soon – one of the manuscripts with the enlarged text is dated 1654 CE – in the history of the Dadupantha, efforts were made to 'explain' Dadu's association with the low caste of Dhuniyas and with Muslims, or to emphasise his celibacy. I copied many old manuscripts of this text and found basically two versions, here abbreviated as E (early) and L (later).

When we compare the text of E with the text in L, we notice that the original text has been tampered with, especially with regard to the delicate questions of Dadu's non-brahminic origin and his occupation as a cotton-carder. The earliest version clearly and merely states that Dadu was born in Ahmedabad and that he was working as a cotton-carder (*dhuniya*). Thus in Verse 1.6 of E we read: 'There was great joy in the house of the *dhuniya* (at his birth).'

In L, however, we read instead: 'All were overjoyed,' which obscures the fact that Dadu was of (Muslim) cotton-carder's origin. Then follows an interpolation in L telling the story of the Brahmin merchant in Ahmedabad who found a baby in a river. In v. 1.16

we read in E: 'Her carded cotton,' for which L gives: 'He entered the state of *sahaj.*'

In Chapter 2 the encounter with the *qazi* from Ajmer provokes a discussion which may imply Dadu's affiliation with the Muslims. In v. 11 of E we read: 'A Muslim lives by the Divine Word.' If this is a definition of the behaviour expected from (the Muslim?) Dadu, it is neatly avoided in L: 'Without the Divine Word, one cannot go to heaven.'

Yet another example of variant readings is in the context of a burglary in Dadu's house. In verses 3.9–10 of E we read: 'When the thief found threads [of cotton]...the family awoke; [Dadu's] mother and wife said....' In L we find instead: 'When the thief found books, the saints awoke. The saints and disciples said....' This again obscures the fact that Dadu may have been married and had sons. Verse 4.5b in E ('He went on carding cotton') is missing in L. We find hardly any variant in the next chapters, till surprisingly the issue of cotton-carding is raised in the presence of Emperor Akbar. For 'Working hard day and night, there are plenty of cotton-carders in Sikri,' in E, we read in L: 'Roaming around in a holy dress, there are many beggars in Sikri' (7.12).

The terms used in the interpolations of L to denote Dadu's birth clearly suggest that he was of divine origin: 'He transformed His body and appeared in the form of a child.' 'He descended' (*avatar lena*).

In v. 1.7 of E we read: 'When he was eleven years old, Baba Budha appeared to him,' whereas in L we read: 'Hari appeared to him in the form of an old man.'

The term *budha* may be used in its literal, non-specific meaning of 'an old man', it may be an actual name (Budhan?), or it may designate a particular person bearing the name as a title of respect. There is no certainty about the identity of this person, but there is definitely a difference between the reading Baba Budha (in the earliest version) and the literal meaning of *budhai rup* (as in the text of L). This difference is emphasised by the fact that Dadu's second-generation disciple Sundar Das, when tracing the origin of the Dadupantha back to Brahma, calls Dadu's preceptor Vriddhananda! For more examples, I refer to the critical edition of the Hindi biography of Dadu Dayal.

To sum up: Sectarian scribes did change the nuances in particular texts, on purpose, and it is essential that a translator first establishes the 'critical' text. The translation will thus not only bring out what is most probably the most authentic version of a text; it will also highlight the changing attitudes of scribes in the early years of scribal transmission. A similar phenomenon, but not as dramatic, is found in the orally transmitted repertoires of the Sant songs. There too it is very important that the oldest available manuscripts are compared.

3. Namdev

Let us imagine we are travelling through northwest India in 1550 CE, on sandy tracks or on bumpy roads after the rainy season. We spend the nights on the floor in temples and watch the audiences drawn by travelling singers singing songs of *bhakti*. These singers, like the Puranic bards, received extended hospitality depending on the quality and depth of their performance. They may not have belonged to a particular *sampradaya* (sect) and they sang what appealed most to the local populace. We are on the way to Rajasthan after a visit to Banaras, where a few years before Raidas had died, and where the oldest member in the singers' family had heard a person called Kabir. This family of travelling musicians, a few generations before, may have been to Maharashtra where they had heard of a poet called Namdev. Thus, their repertoire kept expanding and some started to feel the need to write down the songs.

The singers sang the songs which were most in demand, such as those of Namdev and Kabir, which they had learned from their fathers. They too were artists, and inspired by a particular environment, they added new, sometimes their own songs, to the repertoire. This should not amaze us. Present-day musicologists in Rajasthan studying the Dev Narayan or Pabuji performance pay their performants by the hour. Some found the story never ending; on close analysis they found that gossip about contemporary politicians was interpolated in the story to lengthen it.

Memory was their only way of recording, but as the repertoires grew bigger, some musicians started to keep little (or big) notebooks as an aid to memory. The earliest manuscripts seem to have had these notebooks as their basis. The manuscripts of the seventeenth century that have been preserved are copies of these early notes now lost. Scholars of the twentieth century have to rely on seventeenth century manuscripts to reconstruct the version of the repertoires of the singers. I do not say: 'to reconstruct what Namdev or Kabir or Raidas were singing'! Travelling singers knew no borders. They easily walked from the kingdoms in and around Banaras through the Mughal territories to the princely states in Rajasthan, or from the Maratha country to the Punjab. With an amazing ease they also moved from one language to another, using a supra-regional medium, while at the same time picking up local idioms and words in an effort to adjust to local audiences. This effort is responsible for the linguistic and stemmatic chaos we find in the manuscripts.

The interaction between regional dialects, and between singers and audiences is an exciting phenomenon which we can study only when looking carefully at manuscripts. A special discipline, however, is required to study the songs which have been in the hands of singers for a long while, before being written down. The text-critic cannot reconstruct a scribal archetype. There never was one. Corrupt readings need not be listed as text-critical clues, in view of an 'emended, original' text. At best we can try to reconstruct oral archetypes and reach beyond the period of creative change by professional and other singers.

We find several 'archetypes'. Text-critical clues based on the variants of oral origin can only point to the possibility of originality in most cases and to relative certainty in some cases. We consider the songs as independent units and do away with the traditional, text-critical approach which treats a corpus of songs as a homogeneous literary piece. The songs have to be treated and studied separately, because songs have undergone creative changes by singers not only throughout each repertoire, but also independently. Consequently, we do not have a repertoire which gives the 'best' reading throughout.

4. Kabir

When around 1500 CE the Muslim weaver Kabir sang his songs in Banaras nobody could have imagined that at the beginning of the twenty-first century he would be the most frequently quoted poet-saint in North India. Even South Indians pride themselves on having memorised some of his lines. But at the same time, he is probably also one of the most wrongly quoted saints. Take for instance the translation by Rabindranath Tagore of one hundred of Kabir's songs (Sen 1910–11). About this volume, scholars write:

> It was Tagore who suggested to his friend Kshiti Mohan Sen the collection of the poems attributed to Kabir and sung by itinerant sadhus all over northern India (especially in Bangal) and their translation into Bangali. The authenticity of these poems is very questionable: it appears that most of them were probably not composed by Kabir.... (Vaudeville 1974)

And further, for this collection 'Sen relied more on what he heard from Sadhus than what he found in printed books' (Dvivedi 1980).

In the Bengali introduction Sen states that he met many *sadhus*, all over North India and that he consulted all the available printed texts (probably the Belvedere publications), of which he gives a list of twelve titles with the name of 'author' or editor, but no place or date of publication. He also collected many stories, of which he gives only two—one relates to Kabir's birth 'on full moon of

Jyestha, a Monday in 1398 shatabdi, in Lahartal in Kashi,' and his death 'in 1518 shatabdi in the month of Magh, near Kashi'. Sen further mentions that Kabir is said to have met Gorakh, Chaitanya, Nanak and Sikander Lodi. His father was Niru, his mother Nima, while his wife was called Loi. Sen collected all these data which may well be the main source for most of the information about Kabir that was circulated in the twentieth century. Using Sen as his main informant Rabindranath Tagore made Kabir known all over the world. But, having now prepared a critical edition of the songs of Kabir – I shall further explain how – I dare to propose that hardly any of the Tagore songs were composed by Kabir. I can understand that a translator of Kabir or a devotee finding inspiration in Kabir's beautiful sayings may look for a nice song without bothering about its authenticity. But that is not quite the same as writing commentaries on Kabir and on fifteenth century Banares on the basis of those songs.

In 1995–96, Bahadur Singh of Hamburg taped about five hundred songs of Kabir now commonly sung during performances by travelling singers in Rajasthan. He noted that most of the reciters belong to low castes and that their patrons are high-caste Hindus. As a result, with a few exceptions, the texts recited do not criticise Hindu scriptures or the Brahmins. In other words, this repertoire lacks precisely those texts which we have all been taught to look upon as the authentic words of Kabir. Similarly, there is scarcely any song criticising Muslim priesthood, although the patrons are not Muslims. Singh quotes an interesting example of a popular song 'of Kabir' on the popular theme of death. The journey to the city of death and immortality, is compared to a journey by train where the body is the *anjan* or 'engine', or *ten gari* or 'train', where *taim jarasi hai* (little time is left), and where the passenger should not lose his *tigat* or 'ticket'. When told that Kabir could not have used these images, the singer was very offended and said that since Kabir was a seer, he knew he had to compose songs with these metaphors for an audience of the end of the twentieth century.

It will not amaze us that hardly any of the five hundred songs recorded by Singh are found in the earliest manuscripts I used for my critical edition.

Nancy Martin's recent research in Rajasthan involved the recording of songs of mainly Mira and Kabir. The singers belonged to a variety of castes, including the Manganiars who are actually Sunni Muslims. The sources used by these singers have traditionally been other elder singers, but in the present day, the sources also include existing recordings on cassette and even CD. It appears that the repertoires of these singers are generally not affected by written sources. We can imagine then that this oral tradition goes back to the time of Kabir, but like the Ganga coming from the Himalayas picking up all kinds of songs on the way. It is specifically stated by these singers that they go on learning so-called 'new songs' of Kabir as they go and listen to nightly performances of other singers. And that is precisely what must have happened four hundred and fifty years ago. Martin carefully compared 30 songs of Kabir in the singers' repertoires in Rajasthan with the printed edition of the *Bijak*. She too notes the lack of directedness and the fact that in these sung repertoires Kabir does not speak to the religious elite or to the high castes: he rather addresses ordinary people of middle and lower castes (Martin 2001: 129–36 and 280–81). Her comparison of the themes too brings out many interesting conclusions, too many, however, to be discussed here.

In the Banaras and Gorakhpur region today, Kabir is associated with newly married couples or young couples going to be married. Long lists of songs, supposedly of Kabir, are sung on the evenings preceding the wedding. The association of Kabir and weddings is so strong in that region that in colloquial language the expression *Aj Kabira hai kya?* means 'Isn't tonight your honeymoon night?' For each of these Kabirs it would be interesting to find out which possibly original song was the basis for an expansion into different interpretations and emphases.

Finally, David Lorenzen of Mexico City, specialist in the Kabirpanth and its literature, made a recent survey of the twenty most popular songs of Kabir in the Kabirpanth today (1996: 205–22).

What does one find here? Only one of these most popular songs is found in my earliest written repertoires (Ms J. and the Gopaldas Sarvangi, see further!) I hear the argument that Kabir's songs were and continue to be passed on in an oral tradition, along with the scribal tradition. I will come to that below. Lorenzen states that

> with only a few exceptions, the songs attributed to Kabir that are most popular today are not those found in the *Kabir Granthavali*, the Kabir *Bijak* and the *Guru Granth Sahib*. It is in fact doubtful that Kabir himself composed these songs, usually called bhajans, except perhaps for the few that are also found in the older collections. (205)

Only one song of Lorenzen's list, Song 14, *Ram niranjan nyara re*, corresponds to Song 430 in my millennium edition.

In 1556, Akbar ascended the throne in Agra, two generations after Kabir may have died in Banaras. The dates of Kabir (traditionally he is said to have lived for 120 years, till 1519) are not certain. I am inclined to accept the dates proposed by Lorenzen: c. 1450–1518. Even these 68 years may have been a relatively long life for a (poor) weaver in Banaras in those days. The first attested written document with his sayings/songs are dated 1572, written no doubt alongside the ongoing oral tradition.

The questions remain: How could Kabir become so charismatic that many devotees, possibly during his lifetime and definitely after his death, were happy to insert his name as *bhanita* or 'signature' in their own compositions and let those songs circulate with his name, not their own name? What was his genius that eventually was changed into a social consciousness strongly influencing later generations? If in the twentieth century many singers may perhaps not even know who the original Kabir was, why are they happy to include their own good, sometimes excellent, compositions in the repertoires that are performed in his name?

What we have here is a social strategy by which certain ideas are promoted using the charismatic name of a person who ceased to exist long ago, who may not even have supported the very ideas that are now spread in his name. If the singers in Rajasthan recorded by Singh are sponsored by Brahmins, as they are, their songs will understandably not be as outspoken in their criticism of Brahmins as Kabir was in Banaras in 1500 CE.

It is the search for that charisma that keeps haunting me and encourages me to look for a 'Kabir' we may still be able to define— that is, the person who was popular in 1556. I do not claim I can go back to the original Kabir. The only exercise I can reasonably make is to look at the songs that were popular in 1556, forty years after Kabir's death, and may have a chance of having been composed and sung by Kabir. This exercise, of course, in no way shows disrespect for the translators of Kabir who find inspiration and aesthetic joy in what he is considered to have written. Nor do I doubt the importance of the ongoing oral tradition that preserved songs of Kabir which did not find their way into the manuscripts of the sixteenth century. Why however, were they not included at all, if they were by Kabir and if they were good songs? Many of the so-called later songs, many of the so-called interpolated songs are good, otherwise present-day singers would not include them in their repertoires.

One more observation: My exercise may perhaps not only shed some light on the real Kabir, it also reveals an essential Indian attitude which is very different from the western way of thinking. It has to do with 'belonging to a tradition' as opposed to 'individual authorship'.

I argue two points:

First, that Kabir was 'appropriated' by interested parties (from the Gorakhnathis and the Ramanandis in the seventeenth century to the Brahmins like Hazari Prasad Dvivedi in the twentieth century, and even Mahatma Gandhi). Kabir was appropriated for their own ideological purposes. And thus, as time passed, the corpus of songs with Kabir's name increased. This may be compared to the situation of another famous medieval saint, Mirabai (c. 1503–46) who may have composed one hundred songs—at the end of the twentieth century there were as many as 5,197 printed songs ascribed to her.

And second, that among the songs in the earliest manuscripts of Kabir we can earmark those that may have been popular in the repertoires around 1556, that is, two generations after the death of Kabir and one generation before the first manuscripts were written. Only after a fresh translation, and an in-depth study of the 240 songs earmarked in our critical edition, can we, with some degree of certainty, describe the characteristics and concerns of the person called Kabir who lived around 1556!

I should now like to briefly introduce the main research work on Kabir in the twentieth century.

The *Bijak* collection is the standard collection for present-day followers of Kabir in Banaras. It should be pointed out that the earliest manuscripts for the editions of the *Bijak* are not earlier than the beginning of the nineteenth century! In these circles especially it is stated that the ongoing oral tradition is equally or even more important than the manuscript tradition.

Recently, two eminent Punjabi scholars have had access to the *Mohan Pothi* manuscripts; these manuscripts (or their originals) were scribed before the *Adi Granth*. Both graciously made the text of Kabir's *pads* available to me, for which I sincerely thank them. Professor Pritam Singh was also kind enough to carefully revise my transliteration from the Gurumukhi into Devanagari.

For his critical study, Pritam Singh personally copied the 50 *pads* (plus one half *pad*) of Kabir in this manuscript. They appear in the manuscripts with the following *raga*—Suhi: 5; Brabhati: 7; Dhanasri: 4; Basant: 6 and a half; Bhairu: 13; Maru and Kedar: 14; Tilang: 1.

The study of Gurinder Singh Mann (1996) is based on a close analysis of the copy at Jalandhar (330 folios) and the copy at Pinjore

(224 folios; see pages 30 and 15–16). After a long survey of the sources about the *Goindval Pothis* and the opinions in the Sikh tradition, the author concludes that the 'Goindval Pothis were prepared during the time of Guru Amardas', that is around 1570–72 (25). It is interesting to note that in these *Pothis* the hymns of the non-Sikh saints, like Kabir, are written by a second scribe, 'invariably in the last portion of the various raga sections,' and 'not all hymns written in this hand appear in the Kartarpur Pothi' (31). At the same time, the author points out that it is remarkable how close the relation between the *Goindval Pothis* and the *Kartarpur Pothi* of the *Adi Granth* is. 'Almost all hymns of the Gurus available in the Kartarpur Pothi/*Adi Granth* are present in the corresponding raga sections in the Goindval Pothis,' while of the 148 hymns of non-Sikhs saints in the *Goindval Pothis*, 129 are found in the *Kartarpur Pothi* (38). Of the 50 *pads* in the *Goindval Pothis*, two are not found in the *Adi Granth*.

Of the total of 403 songs in the (Banares) Nagari Pracharini Sabha edition of Shyam Sundar Das, 1928, as many as 396 are found in the manuscripts which I studied. This edition is a reprint of a manuscript claimed to be written in 1504, 'during Kabir's lifetime', with a few variants found in another manuscript (dated 1824) in Footnote 1.

Vaudeville doubts the authenticity of the date of the early manuscript and it is unlikely that all 403 *pads* attributed to Kabir in the Shyam Sundar Das *Kabir Granthavali* are in fact by Kabir (Vaudeville 1974: 19; Singh 1970: 97–111).[1] Most likely the manuscript is of Dadupanthi origin, dated after 1600, but it is not a *Panchavani* manuscript. It gives only the *bani* of Kabir. The scribe of the early manuscript was Malukdas, which indeed looks like a name not unfamiliar in Dadupanthi circles. After the *sakhis* (59 *ang*, 1–68) and the 403 *pads* (69–168) and *ramainis* (168–86), Das also gives in an appendix of 192 *sakhis* (190–200) and 222 *pads* from the *Adi Granth*. In his brief introduction Das states that the early manuscript probably contains not even one tenth of what is now available·in the name of Kabir [and] although there is a difference of 320 years between both manuscripts, there are very few variants. In the manuscript of 1824, there are only 131 *dohe* and 5 *pads* more. (1)

Das adds that the manuscript having been written in 1504,

fourteen years before the death of Kabir in 1518, we may presume that whatever Kabir may have created after 1504, is not in this manuscript.

At the same time, however, he points out that the *punjabipan* in both manuscripts is puzzling to him:

this may be due to the kindness (*kripa*) of the scribe or to the association with Punjabi sadhus. (4)

In a more personal way he writes that in 1926 he fell sick, after he had accepted the job of editing, which several persons before him had attempted without producing results. For two years sickness and problems at home prevented him from completing the transcription. The authenticity of the date ascribed by Das to his first manuscript (1504) is doubted by most scholars, but it is no doubt an important manuscript clearly belonging to the Rajasthani tradition (c. 1620).

Let me now turn to my statement that Kabir was 'appropriated' by interested parties.

The first such interested party, as far as I can see, were the Gorakhnathis, who used Kabir's popularity and the few yogic references in his songs, to promote their own ideas. In the Nath manuscripts of the early seventeenth century in Rajasthan, Kabir is very abundantly quoted, as if he were a Nathayogi himself. The next interested party were the Ramanandis around 1600 CE, who even adjusted the earliest biography (by Anantadas) to make Kabir a disciple of Ramananda. This is an example of an *avant la lettre* promotional stunt, in the way our politicians now use sports heroes or pop idols to promote their own cause. Another fine example of appropriation is by the Brahmin scholar Hazari Prasad Dvivedi and many of his peers in the second half of the twentieth century. In his milestone publication called *Kabir*, in 1942, Hazari Prasad Dvivedi clearly emphasises one dominant theme—the image of an ideal man in the twentieth century, and his rootedness in the Indian tradition. Can this be compared to the recent revival of an old tradition in India of finding roots for the present in the past, preferably even in Vedic times, when the 'Indo-Aryans' supposedly started their trek to the west? In our case, the issue is of finding roots for the growing national awareness of the new India. That exemplar is Kabir, and through the pen of Dvivedi, Kabir becomes the exemplar of a person committed to a task, a servant of a task which is to form man and to serve mankind. This idea may of course be somewhere in Kabir's earliest songs, but you need a strong magnifying glass to find it. For Dvivedi, the commitment to a task becomes Kabir's main idea. Dvivedi selectively strings Kabir's sayings on the garland of his inner development as Dvivedi feels it must have run. In this way Dvivedi arrives at a biography that runs from imperfection through crisis to perfection. And that is the ideal for modern man in a new India. But that image is itself rooted in a glorious past.

I may add here that it fits perfectly in Dvivedi's scheme that the low caste and Muslim weaver Kabir was initiated by the orthodox Brahmin Ramananda—the first appropriation. Again, there is much more to be said about this, but that is perhaps beyond the scope of this paper.

I should like to refer now to my second argument, that among the songs in the earliest manuscripts of Kabir we can earmark those that may have been popular in the repertoires around 1556, that is, two generations after the death of Kabir and one generation before the first manuscripts, still preserved, were written. The norm for this earmarking is 'occurrence' in Punjab and/or Rajasthan. To put it very simply, we have basically three regions where the written tradition of Kabir has been preserved:

1. The Banaras region, where the *Bijak* collection is the most popular text, based, as I pointed out earlier, on manuscripts not older than the nineteenth century. One reason given for this fact in sectarian Kabir circles is the tradition of immersing and destroying old manuscripts on certain occasions.
2. Punjab, where we have the Sikh tradition of the *Adi Granth* of 1604 and its antecedent, the *Mohan Volumes* of 1572.
3. Rajasthan, where we have basically three traditions, which are rather different and therefore interesting from a text-critical point of view.

Below I give the list of the early manuscripts collected by me over a period of twenty-five years. All these are available with me on film. I give also the date of scribing and the number of songs of Kabir found in them (Callewaert and Lath 1989: 82ff).

Manuscripts (*in chronological order*)		Songs
M	*Mohan Pothi* of 1570–72	50 (2 are not in the *Adi Granth*)
AG	*Adi Granth* of 1604	220 (89 are 'unique')
F	Fatehpur manuscript of 1582	15
S	*Panchavani* manuscript of 1614 (S. Sharma)	370

The *Panchavani* manuscripts S, A, V have more or less the same *raga* order, and that corresponds more or less to the Sabha edition of Shyam Sundar Das.

A	*Panchavani* manuscript of 1675	393
V	*Panchavani* manuscript of 1658	348
Gop	*Sarvangi* by Gopaldas of 1627 (Ms. of 1724)	352 (10 are 'unique')
Raj	*Sarvangi* by Rajab (ca. 1620?; Ms. of 1744)	151 (4 are 'unique' and 22 not found in Gop)
J	Manuscript of 1681	222
C	Manuscript of 1660/1669	185

Editions

Sa	Sabha edition of 1928 by Shyam Sundar Das 403	(7 are not found in my Mss.)
[Rajasthani manuscript of 1620?]		
Tiv	Parasnath Tivari, 1961	200 (49 are not found in my Mss.)
[earliest Ms. dated 1684]		
MP	Mata Prasad Gupta, 1969	403 (19 given in footnote = 388)
YU	Yugeshvar [3rd edition], 1996	403
[(Bij	Shukdeo Singh: 1972	115 (32 songs also in our edition))]
[earliest Ms. dated 1805]		
W	my total (some occurring only in one Ms.)	593 *pads*

Depending on the occurrence in a number of repertoires, I have marked songs as more or less 'popular' around 1556, that is one generation after the death of Kabir. Songs earmarked with four **** have, according to me, a high probability of belonging to a very early core. These songs are found in

[1] the *Adi Granth* and/or *Mohan Pothi* of the Punjabi tradition, and in at least one of each of the three Rajasthani traditions.

[2] one *Panchavani* manuscript

[3] one *Sarvangi*

[4] C and/or J

Three *** are given if the song is found in 3 of [1], [2], [3] and [4], but including *Adi Granth* and/or *Mohan Pothi*; while two ** are given if the song is found only in the three Rajasthani traditions: [2], [3] and [4], but not in the *Adi Granth* and/or *Mohan Pothi*. Thus looking at the occurrence of a song in repertoires of both Rajasthan and Punjab, we have

— 48 songs with ****: found in Punjab and in most Rajasthani repertoires

— 51 songs with ***: found in Punjab and in some Rajasthani repertoires

— 141 songs with **: found only in Rajasthan

Total 240 (out of 593 found in the early manuscripts)

Summing Up

In the manuscripts/repertoires dated between 1570 and 1681, I found a total of 593 *pads* with the name of Kabir. Of these *pads* only one is found among the *Twenty Popular Songs* recorded by David Lorenzen in Banaras in 1991.

Kabir's songs have had a long life of nearly five centuries. The first major event in that life was not that they were written down, but that they travelled. They travelled in different directions and they did so in different companies, in different memories. Of one thing we are certain: the songs of Kabir very soon travelled west and became popular in Rajasthan and in Punjab. They were not popular in Vrindavan where a revival of devotion for Krishna started after Chaitanya came there around 1500 CE.

The repertoires reflected in the manuscripts we studied do not go back to one archetype of one generation before. These repertoires underwent changes several generations earlier and a comparison of these repertoires takes us to at least the year 1556. If a song is found in more repertoires, it has a better chance of belonging to a basic core of a song popular around 1556. It is hard to explain how a song popular around 1556 would become a stray song and would eventually continue to exist only in one repertoire. Thus, if a song is found in more repertoires, it has a better chance of belonging to a basic core of songs popular around 1556.

I should like to conclude with a consideration about authorship. All the songs composed by the medieval saints (Kabir, Surdas, Mira and hundreds of others) have the name of the composing saint-poet, usually in the last line. But it is evident from the analysis made above that hundreds of songs created by someone else, sometimes by very good poets, were included in the repertoire of Kabir and were given the name of Kabir.

In the West this would probably be called 'voluntary plagiarism' and I do not know how the copyright laws would deal with this. What are we to make of a situation where, for example, a good scholar produces a wonderful piece of research on Kabir and publishes it in an outstanding journal under the name of another famous author! The first author gladly gives up the honour of publishing in his or her own name because – and this is one explanation for the phenomenon I have discussed – it is more important for him to belong to the tradition of the second author. This would give the first author more satisfaction than if he published under his own name. Something like this definitely happened in the sixteenth and seventeenth centuries, when good poet-mystics composed a good song and circulated it in the singing tradition with the name of Kabir. In this respect the medieval Indian psyche is different from our modern western attitude. It is essential for an Indian to have a grounding in an authoritative past, to be part of a living memory, to be inscribed in an ongoing social subconsciousness, to be linked to what Indians call a *parampara*, an authoritative tradition. A similar phenomenon is noticed in the *guru*–disciple relationship, or in the *gotra* awareness in the caste system. This need to be linked to a glorious past may help to explain why individual authorship becomes less relevant.

Reading Kabir

I doubt whether all the verses attributed to him in even critical editions are by Kabir. One thing is however certain: what he thought he said, and what he said he said strongly, often in abusive language, at times deeply mystical, but always impressive.

A statement such as this one below could not have endeared him to the 'slickly robed, nicely perfumed Muslim qazis' (Vaudeville 1974: 19).

If God had wanted to make me a Muslim,
Why didn't he make the incision?

Nor would the following have earned him the affection of the argumentative, supercilious Brahmin pundits with whom he coexisted...

> Vedas, Puranas—why read them?
> It's like loading an ass with sandalwood!

But his testy aphorisms did ensure that the common people would take in what he said—storekeepers, fishermen, housewives, and rickshaw drivers—and his words are on their tongues to this day. (Vaudeville 1974: 35–36)

I quote one of Kabir's songs from an ancient collection of his sayings, called *Bijak*, superbly rendered into English by Linda Hess (Hess and Singh 1983: 42). It is a description of Banares in 1450, but also a description of Banares in 1997, and in fact of many religious phenomena all over the world:

> Saints, I see the world is mad.
> If I tell the truth they rush to beat me,
> if I lie they trust me.
> I've seen the pious Hindus, rule-followers,
> early morning bath-takers—
> killing souls, they worship rocks.
> They know nothing.
> I've seen plenty of Muslim teachers, holy men
> reading their holy books
> and teaching their pupils techniques.
> They know just as much.
> And posturing yogis, hypocrites,
> hearts crammed with pride,
> praying to brass, to stones, reeling
> with pride in their pilgrimage,
> fixing their caps and their prayer-beads,
> painting their brow-marks and arm-marks,
> braying their hymns and their couplets,

reeling. They never heard of soul.
The Hindu says Ram is the Beloved,
the Turk says Rahim.
They kill each other.
No one knows the secret.
They buzz their mantras from house to house,
puffed with pride.
The pupils drown along with their gurus.
In the end they're sorry.
Kabir says, listen saints:
they're all deluded!
Whatever I say, nobody gets it.
It's too simple.

The simple message of Kabir, then and now, is clearly
formulated in the song I quote from Hawley's fine rendering of a
few songs (50):

Go naked if you want,
Put on animal skins,
What does it matter till you see the inward Ram?
If the union yogis seek
Came from roaming about in the buff,
Every deer in the forest would be saved.
If shaving your head
Spelled spiritual success,
Heaven would be filled with sheep.
And brother, if holding back your seed
Earned you a place in paradise,
Eunuchs would be the first to arrive.
Kabir says: Listen brother,
Without the name of Ram
Who has ever won the spirit's prize?

Notes

1. The text of the Shyam Sundar Das edition is reprinted in Charlotte Vaudeville (1982) with 811 *sakhis* (3–53), 403 *pads* (113–223) and *ramainis* (395–409).

References

Callewaert, M. Winand. 1990. The 'Earliest' Song of Mira. In *Annali, Istituto Universitario Orientale*, Napoli 50: 363–378.

—. (ed.). 2000. *The Millennium Kabir-Vani*, 1. Pads. New Delhi: Manohar.

Callewaert, M. Winand and Mukund Lath. 1989. *The Hindi Padavali of Namdev*. Leuven: Orientalia Lovaniensia Analecta and New Delhi: Motilal Banarsidass.

Dvivedi, Hazari Prasad. 1971, 1980. *Kabir ke Vyaktitva, Sahitya aur Darshanik Vicharon ki Alochana*. New Delhi: Rajkamal Prakashan.

Hess, Linda and Shukdeo Singh. 1983. *The Bijak of Kabir*. San Francisco: North Point Press.

Jan Gopal. 1620. *The Life Story of Dadu Dayal*.

Lorenzen, David N. 1996. *Praises to a Formless God: Nirguni Texts from North India*. Albany: State University of New York Press.

Mann, Gurinder Singh. 1996. *The Goindval Pothis: The Earliest Extent Source of the Sikh Canon*. Harvard: Harvard University Press.

Martin, Nancy M. 2001. Interrogating the Oral and Written traditions of Mirabai and Kabir: In *Devotional Literature in South-Asia: Current Research 1997–2000*, (eds.) Winand M. Callewaert and Dieter Taillieu. New Delhi: Manohar.

Sen, Kshiti Mohan (ed.). 1910–11. *Kabir ke pad*. 4 vols. (Hindi text with Bengali translation). Shantiniketan.

Sharma, S.N. et al. 1949. *Mira Smrite Granth*. Calcutta: Bangiy Hindu Parishad.

Singh, Pritam. 1995. *Ahiyaurvali Pothi* (Punjabi). Amritsar: Guru Nanak Dev University.

Singh, Shukhdeo. 1970. Kabir Granthavali ki Pramanikata. In *NPS Patrika*.

Vaudeville, Charlotte. 1974. *Kabir*. Vol. 1. Oxford: Clarendon Press.

—. 1982. *Kabir Vani*. Pondicherry: Institute Francais d'Indologie.

CHAPTER SIX

The Ganga: Waters of Devotion

ANNA S. KING

The Ganga as potent theophany and powerful metaphor can be studied from a multitude of perspectives and within many academic fields of discourse. Academics have often drawn on textual rather than ethnographic sources, sources that glorify the Ganga as divine manifestation. Their universalising and orderly accounts have themselves become modern *mahatmyas* (e.g. Eck 1982; Kinsley 1988: 187–96). On the other hand anthropologists like Ann Gold who analyse the Ganga's multiple meanings in the life of actual communities find their data leading to equally empathetic but more nuanced, ambivalent and paradoxical conclusions (1988: 209–307).

In this chapter I bring together both historical and anthropological perspectives in order to consider the ways in which Vedic reverence for the great rivers has developed and transformed over the centuries. Today pilgrimage (*tirtha yatra*) to holy places (literally fords or 'crossing places') is more popular than ever before. The Ganga is the most celebrated of all rivers and many of Hinduism's most famous pilgrimage sites – Banaras, Allahabad, Hardwar and Gaya – are situated on its banks. Moreover, the Ganga is infinitely replicated and multiplied. All rivers which are the object of pilgrimage, such as the Godavari in Andhra Pradesh or the Kaveri in Tamil Nadu, are regarded as forms of the Ganga (cf. Fuller 1992: 205). The Ganga today is possibly the greatest symbol of Hindu unity and attracts the devotion of Hindus from all kinds of backgrounds, both orthodox and secular, and from diverse communities, castes and *sampradayas*. This love sometimes develops into intense personal devotion or *bhakti*. It is this devotion that I wish to explore.

The introductory section of this chapter follows the Ganga's meanderings across the sacred landscape of India, weaving changing patterns of pilgrimage. The next section analyses the symbolism of water in the language of *bhakti*, and the power of the story and the storyteller in inspiring devotion. The third section is devoted to the great festivals and fairs of India which are also great bathing festivals, mass expressions of devotion. I argue that for many Hindus plunging into the Ganga's sacred waters is to plunge into sacredness itself, the essence of *bhakti*. The next section focusses on contemporary devotion to the divine mother as the source, womb, cradle and lap of the living and dead. It is followed by a section examining the role of the guardians and gatekeepers in promoting, embodying and controlling devotion to the Ganga. Finally I refer to ways in which devotion to the Ganga is spreading ever more globally: not only through the return to the source in pilgrimage, but through a process of Gangaisation—the multiplication of symbolism in a Hindu diasporic world.

There are many auspicious *tirthas* attracting pilgrims to the Ganga, but to make this chapter manageable and because I have spent many happy months and years along the banks of the Ganga at Hardwar and Kankhal as a social anthropologist, *sadhak* and guest, I focus my discussion through a *tirtha* that pilgrim guidebooks describe as the gateway of the gods, heaven upon earth, the means and the condition for *mukti*.

The Supreme Tirtha of the Kali Age

Devotion to the Ganga is deeply embedded in the language, religion, custom, traditions and feelings for place shared by many Hindus and Sikhs, and some Jains and Christians. For millions of devotees it is a source of power (*shakti*) and comfort, and a wish-fulfilling *tirtha*. It is religiously the supreme *tirtha* of the Kali Yuga, a perpetually moving stream of grace and purifying, life-giving energy, offering immediate healing experience of the divine. For centuries devotion to the Ganga has woven together and inextricably elided fundamental Hindu ideas of purity and fecundity, of worldly happiness and spiritual freedom. It also contributes to the order and unity of the Hindu landscape—flowing between the three worlds, the Ganga purifies and sacralises India and by extension the entire world. The source and symbol of all rivers, she carries the pulse of the cosmic mountain, of Shiva, Vishnu and Brahma to the ends of the Hindu world. Flowing into the ocean she becomes free from name and form, mirroring the *atman's* absorption into God, the culmination of *bhakti*. Sacred all her length, her sheltering power is evoked most fervently at *tirthas*.

The Ganga is not only the divine archetype whose multisemism generates breathtakingly fluid symbolic analogies and cosmic correspondences, but also the actual river with which millions of Hindus have a living relationship. Bathing in the Ganga and using its waters for washing, drinking and cooking ensures Ganga's blessings and grace. Pilgrims express their devotion in the rhythms of everyday life—*darshan*, the offering of flowers, the lighting of incense and sprinkling of water. In many temples and *ashrams* along the banks Ganga *puja*, Ganga *arati*, Ganga *kirtan* and *prasad* (food offered to Ganga and eaten as *prasad*) are performed daily.

Yet the enchanted world of *tirtha* and temples, bells and *bhajans* is also the turbulent world in which the spheres of the market and the *tirtha* are linked in complex networks of power, patronage and commerce. A world increasingly swept up in the stream of national politics, global economics and land speculation.[1] A world in which deforestation, and the flow of chemicals and untreated raw sewage into the Ganga have massive consequences. Peavey claims that 'People's relationship to the Ganga is born of habit. It hasn't been rethought for generations' (Ahmed 1995: 152). Ecological and environmental considerations may cause just such a rethinking, forcing revision of devotional practices such as mass bathing, offering of flowers, immersing of ashes and human unburnt bodies, *achman* (sipping water), etc. (Ahmed 1995: 148; Chapman and Thompson 1995: 200).[2]

Moreover, while religious teachers or apologists speak about the Ganga authoritatively, theologically weaving diverse stories into a single devotional tradition, in practice the Ganga is evoked in many ways. Bihari or Gujarati villagers, middle-class pilgrims from Delhi or Mumbai, second-generation Hindus or Sikhs from the United States or Canada, bring to pilgrimage to the Ganga multiple, shifting and contextual attitudes and perspectives. Modern India's revised economic identity, greater international exposure and improved communications means that pilgrims come from affluent and cosmopolitan as well as poor and illiterate backgrounds. The great bathing *tirtha* as a whole reveals the uneven, hectic and contradictory character of India's modern life (cf. Khilnani 1998 *passim*). For some Hindus the Ganga remains pre-eminently the river of death and liberation, associated traditionally with death rituals and the immersion of the ashes of the dead. For many women devotion to the Ganga is a continuation of their social experiences and part of their *stri dharma*. Diaspora Hindus and Sikhs, however devout, may be primarily interested in questions of cultural roots and personal identity while increasing numbers of seekers who are not Hindus by birth find in bathing or meditating by the Ganga a profoundly spiritual experience.[3] And paradox lies at the heart of Hindu pilgrimage to the Ganga. There is certainty that for those with pure minds the Ganga flows at home in the *tirtha* of the heart. On the other hand there is the equally powerful conviction that God may be approached more easily at the sacred river, the *tirtha* par excellence. And *yatra* to the Ganga motivated by love of God (gods) often blurs joyously into cultural tourism, enjoyment and pleasure for its own sake (*ghumna phirna*).

The Rise of Devotion

In the Vedic period the waters are the primaeval element and the Rig Vedic hymn (10.9) to the waters of life prays that they cause well-being and health to flow over us:

1. Waters, you are the ones who bring us the life force.
   Help us to find nourishment so that we may look upon great joy.
2. Let us share in the most delicious sap that you have, as if you were loving mothers.
3. Let us go straight to the house of the one for whom you waters give us life and give us birth.
8. Waters, carry away all of this that has gone bad in me, either what I have done in malicious deceit or whatever lie I have sworn to.
9. I have sought the waters today; we have joined with their sap. O Agni full of moisture, come and flood me with splendour. (O'Flaherty 1981)

Indra, the bull with the thunderbolt, in killing the serpent Vrtra, opened a way for the waters who 'like cows rushing to feed their calves' flowed onto the earth. The waters are praised as 'pure and clear waters that drip honey'.

This Vedic characterisation of rivers remains powerful but it is enriched and transformed by an emotional and intellectual *bhakti*. Faith and devotion are increasingly emphasised as a condition for human flourishing and salvation. In the epics and Puranas it is the Ganga rather than the Sarasvati that becomes the chief among the seven rivers; flowing through time she continues to accumulate legends and stories. The great stories of the Ganga's origin and descent are constantly recollected, and she is held to respond to the worship of her devotees with affectionate care or love. The intense concentration of *bhakti*, the worship of the heart, accompanies ritual performance. *Bhakti* becomes a means to liberation. The

Mahabharata speaks of the Ganga as the embodiment of auspiciousness and prosperity. Bhishma tells Yudhishthira in *Anushasana Parva* 26: 'That man becomes dear to Ganges who adores her with deep devotion, with mind wholly fixed upon her' (Ray 1893: 194). Ganga's characterisation is transformed by Puranic retellings and the rise of *bhakti* further deepens the stress on devotional intimacy. Vedic gods who have themselves been promoted by the religion of *bhakti* are unsurprisingly portrayed as ardent devotees of Ganga (cf. *Narada Purana* 1982: 19:5, 92). Moreover, such devotion in turn glorifies Vishnu, from whose feet the Ganga had emerged, Shiva, the bearer of the Ganga, and Uma or Devi who is non-different from the Ganga. There is a missionary zeal in both the epics and Puranas to promote devotion to the Ganga. Listening and telling her stories, remembering her, pilgrimage, bathing, dedication of donations, vows, ascetic acts are all meritorious activities. The *Kurma Purana's* praise is characteristic:

> Ganga is called Tripathaga (saviour of the three worlds) since she rescues the human beings on the earth, the serpents (Nagas) in the nether region, and gods in heaven. As long as the bones of a man remain in Ganga, for so many thousands of years does he enjoy respects in heaven. Among the holy places, Ganga is the holiest, among the rivers, she is most sublime, and is the yielder of liberation (Moksa) to all beings, even the greatest sinners. She, the auspicious one, is the purest of the pure, the holiest of the holy dropped from Mahesvara as she is the remover of all sins. (Tagare 1982: 30–32, 35)

The goddess is identified with the supreme deity in the *Narada Purana's* 'Hymn to Ganga':

> Obeisance to one who is antagonistic to all miseries; repeated obeisance to the auspicious deity. O greatest deity, greater than the greatest, obeisance to you, O bestower of salvation for ever. May Ganga be in front of me; may Ganga be at my sides. May

Ganga be all round me; O Ganga, may my existence be in you.
You are at the beginning. You are in the end; you are in the
middle, you are everything. O auspicious deity who have descended
on the Earth...You alone are the primordial Prakrti; you are lord
Narayana. O Ganga, you are the great Atman; you are Siva.
Obeisance, obeisance to you. (Tagare 1982: 19:5, 82–84)

While many Puranic epithets of Ganga remind us of Vedantic
hymns, Puranic and epic stories go much further in feminising,
sexualising and personalising Ganga. The *Padma Purana* likens the
Ganga to a mother:

Sons (may) abandon a father who is born of a paramour, or who
is fallen, or who is wicked or who is of a low caste, or who has
killed his preceptor, or who is full of treachery or all sin; or wives
or groups of friends or other relatives (may) abandon their dear
(one); but Ganga would never abandon them. As a mother holds
her child to her bosom and cleans him of dirt and excrement;
so Ganga would wash the dirt of them. They become very
famous and are honoured with enjoyments and ornaments.
(Deshpande 1989: I.62: 25–27)

Some Puranic stories show Ganga in very human terms with all the
seductive attributes of an enchanting goddess. *Shrimad Devi
Bhagavatam* tells how King Shantanu used to go out hunting tigers
and other forest animals. Once, while he was roaming in a wild
wilderness, on the banks of the Ganga, he saw 'a fawn-eyed well
decorated woman':

The king could not rest satisfied simply with seeing the lotus-like
face. The hairs on his body stood on their ends and his heart
was very attracted to her. Ganga Devi, too, knew him to be the
king Mahabhisa and became, in her turn, very much attached to
him. She then went smiling towards the king. Seeing the
blue-coloured lady looking askance at him, the king became very
happy and consoled her in sweet words and said: —'O, one of

beautiful thighs! Are you Devi, Manusi (human kind) Gandharvi; Yakshi, the daughter of Nagas (serpents), or a celestial nymph? Whoever you may be, O beautiful one! Be my wife; your sweet smiles, it seems, are brimful of love; so be my legal wife today.' (I, IV: 1–8).

Ganga's marriage to Shantanu, and the birth of their sons (in reality the eight Vasus who have been cursed by Vasishtha to be reborn on earth) are familiar Puranic subjects. Ganga fulfils her promise to the Vasus by drowning each in turn, and the last is saved only by the anguished intervention of Shantanu. This child grows up to be the great hero Bhishma or Gangeya whose vow of perpetual celibacy enables his father to marry the fisherman's daughter Satyavati and to ensure that the kingdom passed to her children. The *Brahma Purana* (8.37–54) narrates the story of Ganga and the *rishi* Jahnu and tells us that: 'Greedily seeking a husband, Ganga wooed him (Jahnu) as her husband. Since he dissented, Ganga flooded his sacrificial hall (Bhatt 1985: 33:1, 8.15–21).' It also relates the incident where Gautama propitiates Ganga on behalf of his elderly wife and Ganga gives them both the gifts of youth and beauty (Bhatt 1986: 36, IV:37).

Thus the various strands of Ganga's cult – ritual, mythic, salvific, etc. – become gradually steeped in *bhakti* so that today Ganga is depicted in devotional literature as responding lovingly to her devotees, soothing their anguish and accepting their self-surrender and sacrifice. The goddess – knowing all their inmost desires and needs – takes upon herself all their afflictions and fears, and leaves them purified and reassured. Thus pilgrims during *arati* ask Mother Ganga to soothe the pains and sufferings, cravings and longings of her children. Chanting the 108 names of the Ganga also leads the devotee to believe that all desires can be realised through her grace. She has gained all the attributes of the supreme God. She is the giver of complete emancipation (*sumukti-da*), she flows through the three worlds (*triloka-patha-gamini*), she is a cow which gives much milk (*bahu-ksira*), she is eternally pure (*nitya-sudha*), unmanifest, unevolved (*avyakta*), yielding shelter (*sharanya*), eternal (*ananta*), destroyer of sorrow (*dukha-hantri*), auspicious (*punya*).

Contemporary *bhajans* extol her as the feminine aspect of God, Ma, Bhagavati, Maha Maya, Adi Shakti, and also as the nectar of wisdom, nectar of immortality, the essence of Brahma, the *shakti* of Lord Shiva. She is Jahnavi, Bhagirathi, Bhavani, the river of knowledge (*jnana-Ganga*), *Brahma-dravi* (liquified knowledge) and *Brahma-sara* (the Lake of Knowledge). She has become both the manifestation of the feminine in God and the primordial principle of energy that is at the root of the changing world.

Yet Ganga Bhakti is paradoxical. Devotional literature gives the Ganga all the attributes of the Great Goddess, it also celebrates and deifies her physicality, her flowing movement. Salvation is obtained by surrender to the waves of the divine *lila*. Saints and poets like Kalidas and Jagannatha, the author of the *Ganga Lahari*, never tire of praising the grace and beauty of Ganga's foam-flecked waves, her capricious moods and meanderings from the snows of the Himalayas through jungle and forest to plain and ocean.

The Waters of Devotion

Hindu devotional language uses the imagery of water – the ocean of *samsara* – to express both the existential situation of all beings and the nature of the divine. The devotee 'thirsts' for God. Divine love or grace is described as a stream or fountain. The notion of liberation is expressed in similar images—salt dissolving in water, rivers that lose their identity as they flow into the sea, the return to the source, etc. The Ganga becomes to the devotee an inexhaustible and boundless stream of motherly care, pointing to a realm free from sorrow, fear, old age and death. For many Hindus to sit at her banks brings feelings of peace (*shanti*) and joy (*ananda*). To drown in her waters is bliss. The yearning for the rain and streams of cool water becomes itself a symbol of the longing of *bhaktas* for divine love.

It is not therefore the temples or images of the Ganga that pilgrims seek out but the living streams of water. To immerse themselves, to offer *tarpan*, to wander by the banks, to see, to reflect, to meditate, to sit at the feet of holy men and women. These are the goals of many pilgrims. Hindus rarely worship her as their personal *devta*, yet the holy bath and the use of the Ganga water is a continuing thread in their lives—in daily *puja*, in rites of passage from birth to death, in ideas and practices of physical, mental and moral purification.

Sacred River, Sacred Land

Each *tirtha*, particularly the *jal* or water *tirtha*, replicates many of the patterns and structures of pilgrimage found throughout South Asia and indeed the Hindu world. Nevertheless each is distinctive. Their hinterland, history and changing patterns of pilgrimage are as different as their geography.

Hardwar or Gangadvar is the gate of the Ganga, the meeting place of mountain, plain and river—described by Chaudhari and Singh as the real protagonists and metaphors of India's life (Singh 1992: 4, 11). The Shivaliks on either side, crowned by the temples of Chandi and Mansa Devi, are identified with the tangled magical hair (*jata*) of Shiva which tempers the potentially catastrophic force of the river. The sacred geography incorporates the divine play of Shiva (mountain) and Shakti (river), of *lingam* and *yoni*. The surrounding jungle, still the home of elephant, tiger and leopard, becomes in the religious imagination the ancient forest of Vedic *rishis* and *munis*. Within this sacred geography the Ganga descends from Mount Meru (often identified with Mount Kailash) as *avatar* and ascends as the moving staircase of heaven.

Religiously the Ganga is a *tirtha* where transition and transformation occur: where the worlds of the living and dead, of the human and the divine, meet. For many pilgrims and devotees however the natural beauty of the Ganga and the Himalayas is itself a means of directing emotion towards God and of stilling the mind from worldly distractions. Swami Muktananda, an Udasi ascetic, told me,

> I am a lover of nature. I love to go to the Ganges, far from... people. I go over the Ganga to Chilla Park and beyond Bilvekeshvar. I watch the macaws, the Himalayan doves, the peacocks, the deer and the waterfalls. There you can feel something: the attraction of the cosmic mind.

Sacred Journeys

Pilgrimage to the Ganga is the result of centuries of historical patterning. Whole regions, villages, castes, or communities inherit traditions which shape their pilgrimage. Their journeys are patterned by great bathing festivals, by caste and community customs, by life-crisis rituals, by ritualised expiation of sins, etc. Many pilgrims originally from Punjab, Haryana, Rajasthan, Madhya Pradesh, Himachal Pradesh think of Hardwar as 'their' place of pilgrimage. It is the city where *their* priest lives, where *their* ancestral registers or genealogies (*bahis*) are kept, where the ashes of their forbears have been poured, to which their families have come at times of illness, distress and difficulty. Diaspora Hindus from all over the world – Britain, Canada, the U.S. or the Caribbean – return to Hardwar to pour the ashes of the dead into the Ganga and to donate. And increasingly pilgrims from the South and from abroad come to see, to bathe and to make offerings – to compare Hardwar with other great pilgrimage sites – and to journey on towards *dev bhumi*, the land of the gods, to the Himalayan shrines of Gangotri, Badrinath and Kedarnath, the sources of the three main branches of the Ganga—the Bhagirathi, the Mandakini and the Alakananda, and even beyond to Mount Kailash and Lake Manasarovar in Tibet, the mythical source of the Ganga.

While every journey to the Ganga appears to replicate another, its trajectory is unique. Pilgrims, tourists and sightseers come at different stages of their own lives and for very different reasons. Their psychological engagement in the bathing rituals differs. Some of those watching the spectacle of bathing have no intention of immersing themselves. Others are there to enjoy themselves. When a young *panda* boy splashing about in the Ganga told me, 'I love swimming in the river,' an elderly couple nearby reproved him sharply, 'This is *not* a river. This is Ganga.'

Gangadvar: Gate of the Ganga

The *tirtha* necessarily reflects the great diversity of India in the twenty-first century, yet devotion to the Ganga today shows remarkable continuities with descriptions by classical authors. Hiuen Tsang gives us the first detailed account of life along the river in 633 CE. He observes:

> The water of the river is blue, like the ocean, and its waves are wide-rolling as the sea. The scaly monsters, though many, do no harm to men. The taste of the water is sweet and pleasant, and sands of extreme fineness border its course. In the common history of the country this river is called Foshwui, 'the river of religious merit', which can wash away countless sins. Those weary of life, if they end their days in it, are borne to heaven and receive happiness. If a man dies and his bones are cast into the river, he cannot fall into an evil way; whilst he is carried by its waters and forgotten by men, his soul is preserved in safety on the other side (in the other world). (Mahajan 1984: 17–18)

Gangadvar (the door of the Ganga) is an ancient place of pilgrimage, praised in the Puranas and the Mahabharata as a highly meritorious *tirtha* for bathing, *shraddh* and *pinda dan*. There are records of Hindus bathing and pouring ashes in the Ganga at Hardwar in the time of Mahmood Ghaznavi in about 1008, and we have later descriptions by Alberuni and Fazallulah Rashid. Akbar's preference for Ganga water – 'the water of immortality' –

is described in the *Ain-I-Akbari*. It was brought from Hardwar in sealed jars, a practice continued by Jahangir and Aurangzeb and the entire Mughul court (Mahajan 1984: 25–31). Today Hardwar's priests claim that Hardwar alone is the true Ganga *tirtha* and the Ganga's living temple. They argue plausibly that at Kashi Lord Vishvanath and Annapurna are also worshipped, and that Allahabad's fame lies in the *triveni*, the triple-braided confluence of the Ganga, the Yamuna and the mythical Sarasvati.

Devotion to the Ganga is related organically to the rhythms of the sun and moon, the planets and seasons. The sacred time of dawn is the most auspicious. As the sun begins to rise behind the Himalayas and mist wreathes the Ganga, bathers take their first dip. Shaivite Dasnami *sanyasis* and Vairagis wash their clothes and apply their *tilaks*. Gaur Brahmin pilgrimage priests (*tirtha purohits*) arrive in *vikrams*, by train or motor scooter at their thrones or seats (*gaddis*). Karmantris and Mahabrahmans begin to perform rituals at Kusha Ghat. Shopkeepers open their shops filled with the paraphernalia of pilgrimage—bottles of Ganga *jal, rudraksha malas*, scarlet cones of *kumkum*, bundles of sacred threads, yak whisks, carved walking sticks, etc. As the sun grows stronger the main *ghats* are full of purposeful ritual activity. At midday *shraddha* rituals for the dead take place. The afternoon may be somnolent. *Pandas* and *ghatiyas* sleep or chat. In the evening pilgrims in their thousands gather silently. As the sky turns purple and black the priests of Hardwar begin to worship the Ganga to the sound of conches and bells, their flaming torches circling and dipping through the elements of air, space, earth and water. Hymns of love and surrender drift filmily from crackling loudspeakers as flower boats with flickering lights set off precariously towards the ocean.

Hardwar itself, its *ghats, dharmashalas* and temples, shade-giving trees, wells and water fountains, free food-distribution centres (*annakshetra*) are expressions of *bhakti*. All buildings of importance hug the Ganga's bank tightly—the *akharas* of the great orders of ascetics, the huts and rooms of the Brahmin priests, the *ashrams* of *gurus*, the *dharmashalas* and hotels. Today the great boom in land value is a measure of the desire of Hindus to live or retire near to the Ganga. And the *bazaars* themselves are sites which promote, exploit and resource this devotion as the rows of shining copper pots and plastic bottles, the books, maps and posters, the devotional videos, cassettes and CDs show. Today television, film and popular music are as likely to mediate devotion as more traditional vehicles of religious expression.

I wanted to know whether the educated younger generation had the same devotion to the Ganga as their parents. Rajiv, a young engineer from Bharat Heavy Electricals, then working in computers, commented,

> Most of the young generation [particularly boys] in Hardwar see Ganga as a river only but [they] belong mainly to the Punjabi, Baniya, Jain and Sindhi communities. But on the other hand Brahmin boys, and girls from almost all castes see Ganga as an auspicious river...and *do* believe in the power of her water. The [first group] don't have much belief in the religious or metaphysical or spiritual or divine powers of her water. They see all the rituals along the bank of Ganga as a business enterprise...controlled by Brahmins for running their families.[4]

Stories and Storytellers

'In India place is suffused with story, and story is grounded in place. The *tirtha* links story and earth' (Eck 2001). Storytellers help unify the present with the past in the religious imagination, authenticating the *tirtha* by locating it in sacred geography and history and using contemporary language to give it life.

Ganga's Descent to Earth at Hardwar is the *tirtha's* great foundational story, together with that of the Sacrifice of Sati who gave up her life in nearby Kankhal, and whose limbs scattered around India are centres of power (*shakta-piths*). Both these epic stories convey a sense of divinity flowing in every stream and the whole earth as a sacred place. Stories of the Ganga's descent unify the sacred landscape as she flows through body–temple–land–universe and in rivers, springs, tanks and wells all over India.

The storytellers of Hardwar glorify the universality of the Ganga. They so mingle the Puranic sources that all major gods play a part in her descent and all sects can claim her. The development and convergence of various theistic and sectarian traditions within Hinduism, and the long syncretic pattern of its growth has added to the richness and complexity of the stories and legends associated with pilgrimage. Thus the Ganga flows from the *kamandalu* of Brahma, streams over the feet of Vishnu and is entangled in the *jata* of Shiva. As the emanation of Mahashakti, Ganga contains and is the power of all three. She is the sister of Parvati, daughter of Himalaya and wife of Shiva in some stories, the consort of Vishnu in others. A strong local tradition is that she told Bhagirath that she would walk behind him as long as he did not look back. Like the Greek Orpheus he broke this condition and true to her promise the goddess Ganga remains for ever at Hari-ki-pairi at the feet of her husband Hari. She is also praised in poetry and myth as the liquid form of Vishnu. When I asked a Brahmin priest why pilgrims poured water on the Shiva *linga*, he surprised me by prioritising male imagery: 'We pour the water because Ganga is the watery essence of Vishnu, and Shiva is the great devotee (lover) of Vishnu.' In the Bhagavad Gita, Krishna claims to be the Ganga among rivers. To Vaishnavites she is Radha, to *shaktas*, Devi. Nevertheless, at Hardwar the Ganga's primary relationship with Shiva is beyond doubt. As Eck (1996: 148) says, 'Without the Ganga, Shiva would remain the scorching, brilliant *linga* of fire; without Shiva, the Ganga would flood the earth.' She alone can withstand the heat of Shiva's semen and her water alone can cool his *lingam*.

Storytellers also present Ganga's love for her children as unconditional. As a goddess she is depicted as wholly auspicious, holding a lotus and a water pot while riding a crocodile. All communities and castes bathe in her waters, and for women especially, the Ganga provides 'safe' space. The salvation offered by the Ganga is open to all. Devotion to the Ganga enables everyone to achieve closeness to God and liberation from rebirth. As a local Brahmin recalled, 'The Ganga brings contentment and prosperity during life and at death she accepts all on her lap. She suckles you with bliss and blessedness.' It could be argued that the delight in Ganga's characteristic love, compassion and universal accessibility reflects and inspires the yearning for social as well as spiritual liberation. However, the universalising of salvation by *bhakti* is not a charter for egalitarianism.

Stories of Ganga also become persuasive discourse. Stories of her celestial origin, her descent onto Shiva's head, her division into seven streams before the hermitages of the seven *rishis*, the swallowing of Ganga by the *rishi* Jahnu and the salvation obtained by the sixty thousand sons of King Sagar when the Ganga flowed over their ashes are part of shared culture. However as Paula Richman (see Chapter 4) superbly demonstrates, the same story can be told and interpreted in multiple ways. Indeed it is only through interpretation that it acquires meaning.[5] The narrator's intention is first and foremost to achieve communion with the audience. In the rooms of the priests the retelling is performed, often with interjections and banter from the audience. Ganga became the focus of contemporary sexual politics when an amused group of feisty Khatri women heard this youthful *panda* depict her as a flighty, headstrong girl, shameless in her refusal to leave heaven until the very last minute, causing Parvati to burn with jealousy and then rudely upsetting the *puja* pots of the meditating *rishis* Dattatreya and Jahnu. Shiva and the *rishis* had to act vigorously to control her waywardness. Panditji, warming to his theme, spoke of the dire consequences of feminist propaganda. Women were leaving their children without food, families were breaking up, society was growing day by day more corrupt and materialist. His *jajmans* retaliated delightedly and defiantly with a barrage of teasing insinuations and insults. Pandit Kriparam Sharma spoke to his *jajmans* of his direct experience of the unfailing beneficence of the Ganga, but his Ganga is not simply benign and gentle. She is the manifestation and source of absolute power, the liquid form of Mahashakti, who brings life and death, creation and destruction. And yet for Panditji, the play of the human mind is all important. He told different audiences over and over again that it is the faith and passion of devotees alone that create the river's power to bless, by investing divinity in it. Pandit Nand Kishore offered the husband and wife who came from the U.S., with the ashes of their three young children, a very different picture of Ganga—that of the gentle nurturing universal Mother.

During Kumbha Mela's more formal *satsangs* and *pravachans* religious leaders weave into their retelling jokes, *bhajans* and social commentary. For Swami Parmananda, Bhagirath became the paradigm of the self-sacrificing *bhakta* in a material world where individualism emphasises rights not duties. Shiva's role as the bearer of the Ganga was connected to God's protective role towards the environment. The continuing battle between *devas* and *asuras* led into discussions of moral and social evils and the need for personal and societal transformation. *Amrit* became a metaphor for purity of life, the churning of the ocean for the churning of the soul.[6]

Preaching can also challenge orthodoxy and reduce the complex, often unarticulated emotions felt by devotees to blind faith. Swami Agnivesh, an Arya Samaji activist made fun of the idea that a river can give salvation. He urged the crowds to pursue justice rather than superstition. '*Karma* does not mean *karmakand* or taking a dip in the holy Ganga. It means the eradication of all evils in society like corruption, casteism, inequality, liquor, lottery, etc. and the determination to lead society in a new direction.' Swami Agnivesh seems a very modern voice until one remembers the long line of reformers before him. Hiuen Tsang recalls how in the first century CE 'the celebrated Buddhist scholar Arya Deva once dared to stand up in the midst of the immense crowd of pilgrims gathered on the banks of the Ganga and launch a tirade against this superstition' (Mahajan 1984: 20).

Great Bathing Fairs and Festivals

On the great festivals of Vaisakhi, Ganga Saptami, Ganga Dussehra, Ganga Shivaratri and Pitrapaksha, Kartik Purnima, eclipses of the sun or moon, on *amavasya, ekadashi,* the *navaratras* and on all important Hindu festivals pilgrims crowd the roads to Hardwar and the Ganga.

At Shivaratri and in the month of Shravan hundreds of thousands of pilgrims from Haryana, Uttar Pradesh and further afield come to carry water from the Ganga to bathe the *lingams* of their villages and towns. Many also offer water to Shiva at the famous pilgrim shrines at Neelkantha and Daksheshvar. This obviously recalls the fall of the Ganga onto the head of Shiva and the universal linking of Shiva, mountain and water. Parties of villagers come on foot chanting the praises of Shiva '*Bolo Boum, boum*', '*Har, Har Mahadev*' and of Ganga '*Har, har Ganga*', '*Bol Ganga Mai ki jai*'. Many walk hundreds of miles barefoot. They spend precious money decorating their *kamvars* with pictures of Ganga and Shiva, plastic toys, tinsel garlands and streamers, fill them with brimming pots of Ganga water and cover them with red cloth. They then perform the *puja* of the baskets, lift them onto their shoulders and before setting off for home circumambulate Brahmakund. They are often drenched by monsoon rains and in real danger from traffic along the route. Pilgrims making the journey to the four *dhams* carry water from Hari-ki-pairi or Gaughat to Rameshwaram. Some pour water over the *jyotirlinga* there, returning with the sands of Rameshwaram to place in the Ganga.

The popularity of these water rituals is actually increasing, and a new and unstudied phenomenon of youth pilgrimage has developed in the last two decades. It has become popular (even fashionable) for groups of young people (mainly males) to arrive either on foot, or on scooters and motorbikes to collect water. This shows that pilgrimage can evolve to reflect the recreational and aspirational needs of new generations of urban Hindus.

Pilgrims come to drink the water, to see it, to feel it, to sink their bodies within it and to chant the names of Ganga. However, Ganga water is precious in its own right and carried away by almost all pilgrims. Pilgrimage is often considered worthless unless Ganga water is taken home. It is then drunk as a medicine or used in cooking, splashed upon the body before ritual, placed in the mouth of the dying, used as a prophylactic against disease, etc. It is used in rituals of life and death, at times of happiness and at times of sorrow. Sometimes seen as an almost magical essence, its use actually returns Hindus to key cultural values—whether of purity or beneficence.

The most spectacular Hindu festival is the Kumbha Mela, a festival that glorifies the Ganga in all her fecundity and power. It is the re-enactment of a cosmogonic event when, at a particular astrological conjunction, the waters of the Ganga become nectar. During the 1998 Kumbha over fifteen million people bathed in the area of Hardwar, and the 2001 Allahabad Kumbha attracted many millions more. Such vast human assemblages in which 'Religion, trade, and amusement go hand in hand everywhere' have long fascinated visitors (Sidney Low in Mahajan 1984: 122). The thirteen great congregations (*akharas*) of ascetics with all their affiliated *ashrams, maths* and devotees assemble in their camps and are taken in royal procession to Hari-ki-pairi where the Nagas, naked and ash covered, the symbol of Kumbha, inheritors of a warrior past, run into the Ganga dancing and whooping with joy. Millions of pilgrims come to have *darshan* of the ascetics and to bathe. Many accompany their *gurus* in the processions and for them bathing in the Ganga is doubly precious, infused with the extra sweetness of *guru bhakti*.

Inspiring the pageantry is devotion to the Ganga. Tensions can run high. In 1998, during the second great bathing day of the Hardwar Kumbha Mela, fierce fighting broke out between Juna and Niranjani *akharas* over precedence in the bathing order. There were quarrels between Shankaracharyas, stories of kidnappings and rumours of Inter Services Intelligence (ISI) conspiracies. None of this however could entirely eclipse the atmosphere of carnival, of partying, of intimacy, ecstasy and rapture. This collective intensity and euphoria Durkheim calls effervescence. We do not have to accept Durkheim's opposition of sacred and profane to recognise a world which differs dramatically from the 'profane, utilitarian world of economic production', a world in which the sacred is created and recreated and states of exaltation are achieved (Giddens 1986: 93). The accessibility and immediacy of the Ganga creates emotions intensified by sensory intoxication—the hypnotic *yajnas*, drumming, *kirtan*, dancing, dramas (*Ramlilas, Raslilas*, etc.). The spectacularly cacophonous processions of massed saints, elephants, *bhangra* dancers, gyrating bands and even the pungent smells of incense, marigold garlands, wood fires and hashish also increase the feelings of serendipity and joy.

Each pilgrim had their own story, their own reason for coming, but for the great majority bathing in waters sanctified by thousands of saints was the goal. Many commented on the rare chance to have *darshan* of all *sadhus* and *mahatmas*, adding, 'When these saints bathe in the Ganga her water becomes auspicious. And we also become auspicious when we take a bath later in the same water.' Many pilgrims said they were made proud to be Hindus and commented on the integrative element of bathing (*samabhav*). They also spoke of the spiritual energy and power arising from the millions gathered together. The astrological significance of Kumbha, the *punya* to be earned, the washing off of sins were also remarked. Many however spoke simply of feelings of peace and happiness and spiritual transformation. 'After taking a bath we feel peace of both mind and soul.'

Moral Transformation and Renewal

In the traditional brahminical scenario the ideal pilgrim comes to Hardwar and goes through a succession of transformations, bathing, shaving of the head (the hair is then dedicated to the Ganga), eating pure vegetarian (*satvic*) food, giving donation and charity, living a simple life, keeping chaste, having *darshan* of many divinities, and always busy with prayer, *satsang, jap, kirtan, katha,* etc. In so doing she recovers joy and peace of mind and a focus upon God. The spiritual and physical state of the pilgrim is transformed to one which is pure and auspicious, a state embodied in the Ganga water and *prasad* which is taken home and shared out to the wider family and community as tokens of moral renewal. In the past the return home and the re-establishing of connections between pilgrims and villagers were celebrated by *Gangabhoj,* a feast offered by returning pilgrims. Ganga Mother bringing her boundless life force is welcomed to Rajasthani villages with songs and festivities and her water is eventually unsealed and distributed to guests in an extravagant 'Celebration of Ganga' (*Gangoj* or *Gangotsav*) or in a more modest 'walking-sticks night' (*dangari rat*) (Gold 1988: 196–97 and *passim*).

Bathing in the Ganga according to the Mahabharata and the Puranas brings every kind of fruit and blessing—even heaven and *moksha.* However, pilgrims know that these promises are not to be taken literally, or at least if they are they must be purified by ethical ideals and moral discipline. *Bhavana* (attitude and emotion) is all important. For some *gurus* this is the preliminary stage of *bhakti* when the *bhakta* bathes and develops *maha bhava, prema* and *bhava.* It develops into love for love's sake, pure unselfish devotion. Bathing is done to please God, to destroy subtle desires. For some teachers of *advaita* the bath then becomes the external form of meditation in which the individual is immersed in God. To the *bhakta* the Ganga flows directly from the feet of the Lord; worshipping, bathing in and drinking this divine water are different forms of serving the Lord's feet. This devotion is intended to destroy all worldly attachments and allow the mind to think exclusively of God.

Pilgrims themselves engaged in bathing often assert its uselessness without purity of life. Here is part of an interview with an elderly Khatri pilgrim from Lucknow on the main bathing day:

'This time I have come especially for the Kumbha festival and will stay for one month. I have attended two or three Kumbhas before. Today I took bath at Rajghat (Kankhal) in the morning but I didn't feel peace in my heart until I bathed at Hari-ki-pairi in the evening.'

'How do you feel now?'

'In the Kumbha festival thousands of *sadhus* come from all over India. The water of the Ganga becomes even more pious when they take bath because of the contact of their bodies. So I felt more peaceful on taking bath in that water…'

'Will you earn *punya* then?'

'No, by bathing in the Ganga I did not earn *punya*. My *karma* would determine whether I earn *punya* or *pap*. So the concept of earning *punya* just by bathing in the Ganga is not true if I keep doing bad deeds. One earns *punya* only if he or she performs good deeds. The deciding factor for earning *punya* is deeds, not bath in the Ganga.'

'After bathing in the Ganga during Kumbha festival I feel much happiness within me. I am very fortunate to take bath in this Kumbha because possibly I may not be alive by the next Kumbha.'

A Sikh pilgrim said much the same. She had come from Meerut with her entire family and was intent on feeding the fish.

'Why did you come?'

'We had *path* of *Guru Granth Sahib* and *bhandara* for three days at our home. Now it is finished and so we've to offer "*khetri*" in the Ganges [*khetri* consists of a metal dish (*parat*) containing sprouting seeds of barley, with a pot or pitcher (*kalas*) crowned with a coconut].'

'Have you taken bath in the Ganga?'

'Yes.'

'How do you feel about the Ganga and its water?'

'What to feel? It is Ganga Maiya, but I can't say whether its water is the destroyer of sins.'

'Does the water of the Ganga have no power contrary to what the Brahmin or *panda* says?'

'Why should I say anything like that to earn sin? Our Guru (Guru Nanak) says that one should always avoid earning sin. One should always do good *karma* and be good and pure from inside. There is no point if you keep on doing misdeeds and think that you'll get pure or sinless by taking a bath in the Ganga.'

Devotion through Action

The energetic scene by the Ganga bears out the truth that action and devotion are stronger than *karma* or fate in South Asian religious culture. There are so many active measures that pilgrims can take to promote well-being or mitigate disaster and despair. Ritual and donation performed by the sacred bank of Ganga – shaving of the head, the gift of a cow (*godan*), pilgrimage, *shraddha* and *pinda dan*, gifts to Brahmins and to the poor, etc. – increase their merit a thousandfold. Many pilgrims show devotion by circumambulating (*parikrama*) the most important of Hardwar's Puranic *tirthas*, and a few of the most spiritually inclined circumambulate the Ganga itself (*pradakshina*), walking by the left bank from the mouth of the river to its source, returning by the right bank. The most devout prostrate the entire way.

Ganga snan

The simple action of immersion is the only necessary action of pilgrimage. However, the holy bath only becomes holy when attention is focussed on it in a highly marked and orderly way. The pilgrim immerses herself beneath the waters of the Ganga totally.

She drinks the water (*achman*), and in offering water to the gods, *rishis* and the ancestors makes a connection between the living and the dead, the human and the divine. Many pilgrims when first asked give the conventional answer that bathing washes off sins and gives salvation. But questioning reveals often that the act of bathing itself is seen as an act of self-surrender to God. Many pilgrims are reluctant to claim that they automatically earn merit or the cancellation of sin.

Feldhaus (1995) is interested in how rivers are understood to act on sin. She suggests that rivers do away with sins because they are wet. They transform the sinner just as water has the power to transform a barren landscape into a fertile one. They substitute fertility and fecundity for a kind of moral aridity. This reading is extraordinarily rich and suggestive. Nevertheless it does not seem to be the entire story. Pilgrims speak of the Ganga 'burning', pulverising or purifying sins. It is notable that Ganga is associated with Agni and the sacrificial fire that 'burns away' impurities. Kinsley (1988: 189) also points out, 'Moving, flowing, or falling water is believed to have great cleansing power…Like fire…water is affirmed to contain intrinsic powers of purification, particularly when in motion.' He observes that one function of the images of the Ganga and Yamuna positioned at the threshold of many medieval temples was symbolically to cleanse devotees before they entered the sanctum.[7]

However mere contact with water is not enough. The wicked mind does not become sinless and pure. There must be an emotional transaction or reciprocal exchange. The Ganga then functions as what Babb calls 'an *intimate other*', the divine countergiver (Babb 1998: 160). The importance of *bhava*, of love, emotion, faith is proclaimed again and again. Bathing can lead to a transformed sense of self as full of bliss (*ananda*), peaceful and divested of worries. 'Without full faith and emotional responsiveness, bathing will achieve little. Bathing is a form of *bhakti*, in which emotion is directed towards the divine.'

That the Ganga can get rid of sins or give a better *janam* in the next life, or bring salvation, appears to bring the idea of grace into tension with the inevitability of *karma*. Parry (1994: 27ff) argues that a theoretical level the liberative grace of the *tirtha* makes the funerary rituals irrelevant, and suspends the laws of karmic causation, while the ideology of *bhakti* which has exercised a profound influence on modern Hinduism and according to which devotion to a personal god is sufficient for salvation, reduces the Brahmin to a similar irrelevance. However, the rootedness of these seemingly antithetical concepts in the sacred texts points to their functions as mutually enriching and purifying. They are powerful in the context of living and practice. They are there to inspire ethical, devotional and ritual action—not to close it off.

Ganga puja

The Ganga is sometimes spoken of as the river for the dying, the Narbada for the living. Yet the Ganga is everywhere connected with fertility, abundance and prosperity. The anthropomorphic goddess embodies Lakshmi who showers blessings upon those who worship her (Feldhaus 1995: 85). Pilgrims pour milk into Ganga, throw coconuts, fruit and garlands upon her, offer gifts of jewelry, gold and coins. They present her with saris, blouses, nose rings, *mangalsutras, kumkum*, etc. Many pilgrims explained to me that gifts (the coconut, *sriphal*, for example) symbolise the devotee who offers herself to God, and that the greatest gift of all is that of the self. 'Ganga has no need of offerings but she is pleased by the love they represent.'

Young couples come to bathe in the Ganga after marriage, before conception, after the birth of a child, at times of the first *mundan, yajnopavit*, etc. Wives donate a basket full of miniaturised cosmetics and clothes for Ganga (*suhagpitari*) for the long life and prosperity of their husbands. Sufferers of skin disease or cancer, tuberculosis and AIDS, bathe in or sip the miraculous waters. The Ganga is particularly associated with abundant crops and Punjabi farmers traditionally brought branches of trees that had not fruited to dip them in the water. Women bathe in order to be fertile and to give birth to a son. Pilgrims bathe in order that all their plans come to fruition through the grace of Gangaji.

The River of Death

Devotion to the Ganga comes in many forms—she is Ganga Maiya to whom all cares can be confided and to whom at last all beings come. Hardwar is a *moksha puri*, a *tirtha* or ford by which the stream of transmigration (*samsara*) is crossed, and where the living and the dead can communicate easily. For centuries pilgrims have come here to die and to perform the rituals of death, and today thousands of pilgrims come each week to immerse the ashes of the dead and to perform *tirtha shraddh* and *pinda dan*. Death and life flow as one. At Hari-ki-pairi, the heart of Hardwar, pilgrims bathe standing on the bones of the dead and children splash and play around the floating marigold garlands and the sooty trail of ashes. At Kusha Ghat where tradition says the *rishi* Dattatreya performed *tapas* for thousands of years, priests and pilgrims face each other over intricate *yantras* and rows of white rice balls (*pindas*) which both embody and nourish the dead, while only a few feet away the auspicious rituals of life are performed.

Central is Hari-ki-pairi, the navel or axis of the universe, where light dazzles off the shimmering Ganga and the white marble ghats, and the water streams towards the ocean bearing the ashes of the dead and flowers of the living. This wordless articulation of existential destiny is immensely powerful and healing. Sivananda, one of the most influential *gurus* of the twentieth century, who wrote poetry and prose in praise of the Ganga, died, as so many Hindu saints are said to have done, drinking only Ganga *jal*, his eyes turned to the Ganga. Pilgrimage to the Ganga within the Hindu tradition has always been a metaphor for life's journey, and the journey of death as a return to the source of life, an assimilation to the divine holding possibilities of rebirth or *moksha*. After death the ashes are immersed in the river. The body returns to the elements and the spirit goes to God or is merged in Brahma.[8]

The Banks of the Ganga

The banks of the Ganga are public and open places. They offer a space for the poor and dispossessed in contrast to the *bazaar* and the commercial street which are often a means of order and control. Cows sway down the marble steps of the ghats. Small children sell pellets for Ganga's fish. Barbers, flower-sellers, vendors of trinkets, postcards, *chats, mithai* and snacks sit waiting for customers. Three *hijras* live under one of the bridges while across the Ganga an Aghori *sadhu* lives among the burning pyres at Chandi Shamshan Ghat. Like him many *sadhus*, poor labourers and beggars live in huts and polythene shacks close to the banks. Pilgrims are free to make fires and to cook *rotis* over simple *chulhas*. At night they can have all-night singing sessions (*kirtan*) or sleep in the open air. The banks of the Ganga under a pipal tree are peaceful places for meditation and *bhajan*, for entertaining pilgrims and for sharing a *chillum*. Such democratisation and freedom nurtures *bhakti*, defined as intense, emotional love for a personal god, 'often rejecting institutionalised forms of religion, such as formal temple worship, yoga and theology, in favour of an immediate experience of the divine' (Flood 1996: 131).

The banks of the Ganga are considered equally holy (*pavitr*) by Hindus all their length. Yet paradoxically some places are holier than others. These are often consciously created numinous environments. Moreover, there is complexity upon complexity. The Ganga is sacred in Hardwar only where she follows the original course of Bhagirath's chariot. This means that the banks of the

Upper Ganges Canal built in 1854 by the British are empty of all devotional activity. Additionally the Ganga has changed course so often that uncertainty can arise. This was demonstrated during the 1998 Kumbha when some *vairagi sadhus*, persuaded that the 'real' *kund* (i.e. where Brahma appeared) was across the Ganga, solemnly processed to the Neel Dhara to bathe.

The fundamental and primary appeal of the Ganga is not limited to immersion and bathing but extends to spiritual practice (*sadhana*). Her banks have always been considered to offer the serenity and peace necessary for silent meditation (*dhyana*), the search for complete inner stability. Every *tirtha* is considered by Hindus to radiate divine power. The Ganga, the greatest *tirtha* of this age, is believed to radiate a beneficent influence which sanctifies and energises good actions. Its banks are believed to be saturated with the power accumulated from the *tapas* of ascetics and the devotion of pilgrims and saints over the centuries. The Ganga's blessings flow out into the world irresistibly transforming people, place and time, and at the same time the devotion and the prayers flowing out from devotees intensify her divine potency. Power then is transmutable from the supreme deity and back.

Guardians and Gatekeepers

Gangagurus

The presence in Hardwar of a large community of pilgrimage priests and almost every order of ascetics clearly signifies that the Ganga's symbolism here embraces both this-worldly religious values of success, prosperity, good health, long life, food, beauty, love and the birth of children; and the values of renunciation and freedom from the world.

The priests of the Ganga are Gaur Brahmins who claim to be the autochthonic inhabitants of Hardwar and the rightful recipients of its donations. Long before the advent of modern media they toured surrounding states, advertising the fame of Hardwar and teaching pilgrims and devotees how to worship the Ganga as a Mother Goddess and how to seek her grace. They maintain the ancestral registers or *bahis* of pilgrims, perform rituals and accept the offerings (*dan*) made to Ganga. They also control Hari-ki-pairi, the main bathing ghat. Their *jajmans* are on the whole householders enmeshed in family life for whom all the *purushartha* are important, but many elderly pilgrims come who are freer to pursue the great life-aim of release. Like many sacred specialists, pilgrimage priests operate both within the moral economy of *jajman* and *purohit* and within a modern business idiom. The strategems and chicanery reported by Parry (1994: 119–48) and van der Veer (1988) for Banaras and Ayodhya respectively, stem from this profound ambivalence.

As a community the pilgrimage priests say that they follow two paths—those of *karmakand* and *bhakti*, describing ritual as the expression of *bhakti*. They assert both the importance of their rituals and the value of a loving and submissive personal devotion to god. Action must be infused with emotion. A *panda* friend told me: 'If pilgrims come with full faith, and full respect for Mother Ganga and take bath, then all their sins are forgiven....If when they are dying, they with full faith drink Ganga water then they get *moksha*.'

Shri Ganga Sabha, the *tirtha purohit* association, like the *akharas*, has powerful local and national influence. In the past the Brahmin community saw themselves as honouring the Ganga in their struggles to make Hardwar vegetarian and alcohol-free, to secure bans on fishing in Ganga water, and to remove prostitutes from sacred sites. They fought during the British period to maintain the right for ashes to be immersed at Hari-ki-pairi. They also contested the British control of the Ganga during the extensive irrigation and canal works, and campaigned to retain the 'true' channel of Bhagirath's Ganga. Today Shri Ganga Sabha as vigorously opposes the granting of non-vegetarian and alcohol licences to luxury hotels and restaurants, campaigns against buildings that obstruct or disfigure the main ghats, and supports a ban on pleasure boats and water sports. Increasingly the *tirtha purohits* are acting with journalists, educationists, the administration and local residents to clean up the Ganga. However, the acknowledgment that the Ganga may become dishonoured by uncleanliness (*gandagi*) does not mean that she has become impure or powerless. The priests believe that the Ganga is pure. The goddess who purifies the world has the power to transform all pollution and human waste.

Renouncers

Hardwar, far more than Banaras, is a monastic city where the goal of detachment is visibly sought. The banks of the Ganga are associated not only with auspicious well-being in this world but with the courage and fortitude of renunciation, indifference to joy and sorrow, asceticism and yogic discipline. This association of the Ganga with asceticism and *tapasya* is ancient. It is claimed that the Pandavas passed through Hardwar on their way to the Himalayas and that *rishis* and sages such as Bharadvaja, Agastya, Jayadratha and Pulastya did *tapas* there. It is said that practising the highest *yoga* either in Himalayan caves or by the banks of the Ganga brings unsurpassed boons. Many *sadhus* are attracted to the banks of the Ganga since they are 'the best places to seek liberation, to experience pure being, pure consciousness and joy', but also more practically because they provide many charitable resources for the wandering holy man. There is therefore an interesting dynamic between the female Ganga and the male ascetics who live on her banks.

The Ganga is bound up intimately, even symbiotically, with the lives of many *sadhus*. *Sanyas diksha* is often given at her banks. Self-surrender and the abandonment of the previous life are symbolised not only by the rituals of *shraddha* and *pinda dan* performed by the Ganga but also by bathing—initiates descend into the waters and emerge naked with no possible return. At death, since they have no need of further funerary rituals, many ordinary *sanyasis* are given *jal samadhi* in the deep currents of the Neel Dhara.

While it is often argued that the Ganga remains ever pure, totally uncontaminated by the sins she removes, many *sadhus* maintain that saints augment and preserve her sanctity. Swami Sivananda (1994: 25) has Ganga complaining to Bhagirath: 'All the sinners of this world will wash their sins and purify themselves by immersing their sinful bodies in my holy waters. Where shall I wash the immense store of sins they deposit in my watery body?' Bhagirath replied: 'O sacred Mother! Holy saints will bath in Ganga and purge you of all your sins, because Lord Vishnu, the dispeller of sins, dwells in their heart.'

Ashrams

In Hardwar, Kashi, Vrindavan, Allahabad, Ujjain, Puri, Rameshwaram, Badrinath, etc. *ashrams* play a vital role in religious life. One of the most striking features of *ashrams* all over India is their location—many are located on the banks of rivers. *Ashrams* provide a spiritual setting within which a quasi-ascetic life can be lived and a devotional routine established. Many pilgrims are attracted by the presence of saintly ascetics. It is paradoxically these charismatic renouncers rather than ritual specialists who are the new spiritual entrepreneurs using modern technology to spread the fame of the Ganga and to redefine it pre-eminently as a place of *sadhana*, devotion and meditation for disciples from all over the world. Their websites and pamphlets, like those of tourist agencies and hotels, evoke a sacred land where suffering humanity can throw off the tension of modern life and where virtue can be practiced and true happiness realised. They offer meditation and *yoga* courses, retreats, *yajna* against the background of the Ganga and Himalayas. Changes in social and cultural attitudes suggest that there has been a strong shift to private internalising of religious experience and a move to humanistic philanthropy rather than traditional gift giving.

Global Trends

Globalisation and the Hindu diaspora have stimulated 'Gangaisation'. Rivers, lakes, even seas in the U.K., the U.S. and Canada are assimilated to the Ganga. *Ganga jal* is taken to temples and homes in South Africa or Fiji or Australia, and is given to the sick and dying wherever Hindus are found. There is an equally powerful pull in the other direction. Many Hindus wish their ashes and bones to mingle with those of their ancestors. Non-resident Indians (NRIs) make the sacred journey home and a surprising number are turning into settlers. They retire to apartments and bungalows close to the Ganga where they hope to find serenity and the company of like-minded devotees.

Globalisation is also linking devotion to the Ganga to many of the values of new social movements—ecology, feminism and peace. From the time of Megasthenes in 302 BCE, devotion to the Ganga has been for visitors one of the most defining and puzzling features of Hindu culture. Contemporary reporters, anthropologists, television and film producers find it equally intriguing. Yet today so far from being alien or 'other', this devotion for many visitors resonates with a postmodern longing for the re-enchantment and sacralisation of nature and for a living, organic understanding of the world. Non-Hindus increasingly interpret devotion to the Ganga, not simply as connected with orthodox Sanskritic gods, but as a way in which the physical world can be endowed with significance. At the same time Hindu sacred texts which elaborate themes of responsibility for the earth are becoming a global resource for scholars and activists.

It is ironic therefore that *India Today* describes this holiest of Hindu rivers as a sewer and mocks the Ganga Action Plan launched by Rajiv Gandhi in 1986 as the Ganga Inaction Plan. Surprisingly Hindu political parties in India have not been very active in the efforts to clean up the Ganga. The Sankat Mochan Foundation (SMF) was established in July 1982 to raise public awareness of the pollution of the Ganga and the deterioration of Banaras. It is named after the second most popular temple in Banaras whose mahant, Veer Bhadra Mishra (Mahantji), is also Professor of Hydraulic Engineering at BHU (Ahmed 1995: 150).

> One day [1975] I had to choose a spot where I could take a dip in Gangaji. It was a very painful realisation, but not a difficult one to make for I saw raw sewage floating on the surface of the river and dead bodies etc. I started talking and writing articles in newspapers describing the increasing levels of pollution of the Ganga and their effects on Banaras and Banarasis. At first people thought I was crazy—didn't I have enough work to do at the temple and at BHU they asked, besides, how could Gangaji be polluted? (ibid.: 151).[9]

Mahantji found a way of capitalising on people's traditional love for Ganga Ma by asking them: "'Would you do this to your mother?' I say to them. "Isn't the pollution a disrespect to your mother? Is it not spitting on your mother? That disturbs people and they are ready to do anything if you put the problem in this way'" (Ahmed 1995: 152).

The Ganga represents ancient Vedic values – of vitality, sexuality and fecundity – which have increasing appeal for those who find ultimate meaning and religious power in nature. It is an open question as to whether ecological movements will secularise the Ganga by calling attention to widespread pollution and challenging ancient devotional practices. The belief that Ganga has supreme power over human agency is challenged by a language and logic that assumes human power to harm Ganga and which relies on human agency to restore her cleanliness. On the other hand it is possible that religious believers and interest groups who have resisted such pressure in the past will join with activists to return the Ganga to her previous cleanliness, imbuing devotion with a new environmentalist ethic.

It is also relevant to ask whether the feminist revival of goddess worship and the feminising of ritual and religion worldwide will promote Ganga Bhakti. Hindu goddesses that have travelled to the West according to McDermott (2000: 723) represent the dark, sexual, repressed and angry sides of women. Ganga may seem too identified with a specific landscape and with auspicious, nurturing 'feminine' qualities to attract feminist interest. Nevertheless, the goddess has come to be deeply identified with human thriving, and her stories are largely untapped resources in valuing and evaluating women's experience.

Critical attention to gender issues challenges not only the scholarly study of religion but religion as it is lived and practised. Although women often spend their entire lives in devotion to Ganga, it is men who are visible as her priests and theologians. Despite the rise of women *gurus* and ascetics, the public ceremonial and ritual connected with the Ganga remain overwhelmingly patriarchal.

Conclusion

My aim in this essay was to explore the fervent devotion the Ganga attracts. Anthropological theories have offered partial insights. Durkheim's concept of effervescence is helpful in understanding the joyful abandon and ecstatic devotion of the great bathing festivals. Turner's model of the play between the forces of structure and *communitas* illuminates the dialectic between the essentially inclusive, democratic and world-affirming ethos of pilgrimage to the Ganga, offering salvation for all, and the many inherited structures of pilgrimage which continue (albeit ambivalently) to reinforce social, gender and caste hierarchies. For many pilgrims the act of bathing transcends all hierarchies.

Historically the Vedic imagery of the waters of life shapes the later development of the Ganga and, unlike Sarasvati, the prototypical Vedic river, she retains her association with fertility and purity. Her representation is then humanised and sexualised by Puranic legend and story, and by the rise of *bhakti*. In the twentieth century, for secularists like Nehru, the Ganga was a universalising image of an inherited, proliferating diversity. In recent decades however the Ganga as a focus of Hindu piety has been used by Hindu nationalists as a powerful symbol of Bharatavarsha and of a purifying exclusivism (for example in the Vishva Hindu Parishad's All-India Sacrifice for Unity of 1983).

While India transforms technologically and enters the global markets, pilgrimage to the Ganga and attendance at major festivals is year by year more popular, appealing perhaps both to those who seek stability in a time of rapid social change and to those for whom the great expansion in economic opportunities and freedom from social bonds and constraints give new choices. The concept of *Ganga yatra* is changing.[10] Modern communications, the growth of an affluent middle class and now access to the Internet are creating all kinds of pilgrims, sightseers and tourists with very diverse intentions and needs.

I pointed out in my introductory paragraphs that generations of Hindus have yearned for *darshan* of the Ganga, believing that *Ganga yatra* requires only a spirit of surrender and devotion. Love for the Ganga is often cited as an essential part of Hindu identity, of Hinduness. Yet the simplicity of bathing rituals veils paradox and mystery. The Ganga is the unmediated divine, yet intrinsically part of the landscape. In the religious imagination, she connects nature, human beings and the divine. She flows through space and time, linking macrocosm and microcosm, past, present and future. She is the river of death, yet always life giving, of the earth, fecund, maternal, playful, connected with sexuality and birth. She contains the power of all the gods and they themselves come to worship and bathe in her waters. Hindus everywhere offer her water to other deities. As goddess, Ganga is interactive and transforming. For devotees caught in the flux of *samsara*, she is the 'intimate other', a means of saving grace and worldly felicity. Yet the dominance of *saguni* devotion is not complete. The Ganga is also an extraordinarily powerful focus for *nirguna bhakti* (the worship of a divine being without attributes), orthodox Advaita and interior meditation. The devotee merges into divinity and unites with it, a rehearsal for final liberation and absorption. As Abhishiktananda commented: 'To plunge into the icy water is also a cosmic rite of return to the original matrix, to the source of Being' (1974: 173).

Notes

1. Pilgrimage is contextualised in history and affected by important socio-political events. For example, in the 1980s, Sikhs and many Punjabi Hindus stopped coming to Hardwar to bathe, and the majority of Sikhs have not reverted to their previous patterns. Numbers of non-resident Indians (NRIs) have added to the feverish pitch of land deals, land grabbing, encroachment and evictions.

2. Local people say that Ganga water can never spoil and that the value of bathing in it has been scientifically proved. They argue that the *rishis* who knew this were great scientists. This may seem to result from the neo-Hindu desire to promote Vedic science, but in fact for centuries the medicinal and health-giving properties of the Ganga have been famous (cf. Mahajan 1984: 25–31). Kumra on the other hand notes that 'in summer except at Hardwar the river water quality is too poor for bathing at all locations along the Ganges' (1995: 137).

3. A devotee describes his own experience in this way: 'In contemporary terms…the real pilgrim emerges from unwanted symbolic forms, false consciousness, victimisation and oppression, to self-presence.'

4. Rajiv added that 'most young people see the Ganga as a river with business potential [stone mining, water sports, etc.] that could generate huge revenues. They feel if this can be done Hardwar won't be restricted to just being a holy city. It will be able to change.' He also shared the view of many young people that since Ganga was being used for boating in Banaras and Calcutta, Hardwar's wide streams and banks should be used for pleasure. He noted, 'if Ganga's

water can be used for rafting, kayaking, etc. up in the hills then what's wrong in using her water for water sports in Hardwar if there are proper rules and regulations...?'

5. Story is used as a kind of metalanguage, a way of 'presenting religious concepts in a symbolic form which is open-ended' and capable of infinite reinterpretations (Brockington 1996: 196).

6. Kalyan Das for example spoke of the demons and *devtas* coexisting in our society even today: 'sometimes we get poison and sometimes nectar'. Saint Sri Morari Bapu referred to our human body as a *kumbha* (pot) full of the poison of bad intentions and the nectar of good intentions. Only after churning our body can we get that nectar. He also said that Hardwar is a place where all the *devtas*, Lord Shiva and Lord Vishnu live but 'one needs purity and piousness of the self to recognise them....*Shraddha* is the motivating force for all *sadhaks*. Without *shraddha* one cannot gain knowledge or understand truth.'

   The teachings of the great *sadhus* are often spoken of as the *real* 'showers of *amrit*', and *gurus* are themselves identified with the goddess. Debeaprasad Mukhopadhay (1989: 203) describes Ananda Mai Ma's presence at Ardha Kumbha as follows, 'Let us never forget that she was Bhagavati herself—the custodian of the pitcher (Kumbha) of nectar. The water of the Kumbha is the essence of Brahma—that was she, the immortalising liquid. Hundreds of sannyasis, even the accomplished ones fell at her feet, seeking from her the "nectar". All you need to do is to prostrate yourself at her feet with a whole-hearted, fervent cry for Ma and you too shall have a taste of the nectar. Ma will draw you into her lap.'

7. Kinsley notes: '[Ganga's] position at the doorways of temples probably indicated her role as remover of pollution. Before entering the sacred realm of the gods, which a temple represents, devotees should cleanse themselves of worldly impurities. Crossing the threshold of a temple flanked by images of the goddesses Ganga and Yamuna, devotees probably were symbolically cleansed in the purificatory waters of these rivers' (192).

8. Hardwar is not like Kashi a *mahashamshan*. Although pilgrims come at times of illness and sorrow to bathe in the Ganga and people come in their thousands to Hardwar to retire and die, there is no custom of relatives bringing the dying (*rogi marnevale*), no formal customs in which the dying are carried to the ghats as in Kashi and

Pashupatinath and no hospices or 'mansions of liberation' for dying pilgrims. The three cremation ghats, still less the electric crematorium, are not central.

9. In November 1982, Mahantji, along with the support of academics, religious leaders and politicians amongst others, launched the Swatcha Ganga Abhiyan (Clean Ganga Campaign), a public education programme to make people aware of the plight of the Ganga and to formulate, a people's approach (Ahmed 1995: 151).

   The question of whether these ecological movements are effectual is also tackled by Sarah Ahmed. Her research leads her to believe that they are not. They tend to be hierarchical, they do not question the nature of and distribution of power in society and are more concerned in saving the Ganga rather than the lives of the people who are dependent on it. She suggests that those at the bottom will suffer social and economic exploitation quietly.

10. For example, commercial pilgrimage tours such as those to the four Himalayana *dhams* and the four *dhams* of Badrinath in the north, Puri on the east, Rameshwaram in the south and Dwarka on the west coast, the seven sacred rivers, the seven cities of liberation, the twelve *jyotirlingas*, the 52 *peethas*, etc. increase the ease and speed of pilgrimage.

References

Abhishiktananda (Henri le Saux). 1974. *Guru and Disciple*. (trans.) Heather Sandeman. London: SPCK.

Abul Fazl. 1907. *Ain-I-Akbari*. (trans.) H. Beveridge. Calcutta.

Ahmed, Sarah. 1995. Whose Concept of Participation? State–Society Dynamics in the Cleaning of the Ganges at Varanasi. In *Water and the Quest for Sustainable Development in the Ganges Valley*, (eds.) C.P. Chapman and M. Thompson, 141–60. London: Mansell Publishing.

Babb, L. 1998. Ritual Culture and Distinctiveness of Jainism. In *Open Boundaries: Jain Communities and Cultures in Indian History*, (ed.) John E. Cort. Albany: SUNY.

Basu, B.D. (ed.). n.d. *Sri Mad Devi Bhagavatam*. Swami Vijayananda (trans). Allahabad: Sudhindra Nath Vasu.

Bhatt, G.P. (ed.). 1985. *Brahma Purana. Ancient Indian Tradition and Mythology* 33:1. New Delhi: Motilal Banarsidass.

—. (ed.). 1986. *Brahma Purana. Ancient Indian Tradition and Mythology* 36: IV. New Delhi: Motilal Banarsidass.

Beal, Samuel (ed.). 1888. *The Life of Hiuen Tsiang.* Trubner's Oriental series. Boston: Trubner.

Bloch, Maurice and Jonathan Parry (eds.). 1982. *Death and the Regeneration of Life.* Cambridge: Cambridge University Press.

Bonazzoli, G. 1977. Prayaga and its Kumbha Mela. *Purana.* Vol. 19, No. 1: 81–160.

Brockington, John. 1996. 2nd edn. *The Sacred Thread: Hinduism in its Continuity and Diversity.* Edinburgh: Edinburgh University Press.

Carman, John B. and Frederique Apffel Marglin (eds.). 1985. *Purity and Auspiciousness in Indian Society.* Leiden: E.J. Brill.

Chapman, G.P. and M. Thompson (eds.). 1995. *Water and the Quest for Sustainable Development in the Ganges Valley.* London: Mansell Publishing.

Chapman, G.P. 1995. The Ganges Plains. In *Water and the Quest for Sustainable Development in the Ganges Valley,* C.P. Chapman and M. Thompson. London: Mansell Publishing.

Darian, Steven G. 1978. *The Ganges in Myth and History.* Honolulu: The University Press of Hawaii.

Deshpande, N.A. (trans.). 1989. *Padma Purana. Ancient Indian Tradition and Mythology* 40:I. New Delhi: Motilal Banarsidass.

Eck, Diana. 1982. *Banaras, City of Light.* New York: Alfred A Knopf.

—. 1996. The Goddess Ganga in Hindu Sacred Geography. In *Devi: Goddesses of India,* (eds.) John Stratton Hawley and Donna Marie Wulff, 137–53. Berkeley and Los Angeles: University of California Press.

—. 2001. Sacred Geography, Pilgrimage and the Land of India. Unpublished paper given at the Spalding Symposium on Indian Religions. Oxford.

Feldhaus, Anne. 1995. *Water and Womanhood: Religious Meaning of Rivers in Maharashtra.* Oxford: Oxford University Press.

Flood, G. 1996. *An Introduction to Hinduism.* Cambridge: Cambridge University Press.

Fuller, C.J. 1992. *The Camphor Flame: Popular Hinduism and Society in India.* Princeton: Princeton University Press.

Giddens, A. 1986. *Durkheim.* London: Fontana Press.

Gold, Ann Grodzins. 1988. *Fruitful Journeys: The Ways of Rajasthani Pilgrims.* Berkeley: California University Press.

Gupta, A.S. (trans. and ed.). 1972. *Kurma Purana*. Varanasi: All-India Kashi Raj Trust.

Jagannatha. n.d. *Ganga Lahari*. Varanasi: Thakur Prasad and Sons.

Kapoor, Subodh. 2000. *The Hindus: Encyclopaedia of Hinduism* Vol. 3. New Delhi: Cosmo.

Khilnani, S. 1998. *The Idea of India*. London: Penguin.

Kinsley, David. 1988. *Hindu Goddesses: Visions of the Divine Feminine in the Hindu Religious Tradition*. Berkeley: University of California Press.

Kumra, V.K. 1995. Water Quality in the River Ganges. In *Water and the Quest for Sustainable Development in the Ganges Valley*, (eds.) C.P. Chapman and M. Thompson, 130–40. London: Mansell.

McKean, L. 1996. Mother India and her Militant Matriots. In *Devi: Goddesses of India*, (eds.) John Stratton Hawley and Donna Marie Wulff, 137–53. Berkeley and Los Angeles: University of California Press.

Mahajan, Jagmohan. 1984. *The Ganga Trail: Foreign Accounts and Sketches of the River Scene*. New Delhi: Books from India.

McDermott, Rachel Fell. 2000. New Age Hinduism, New Age Orientalism, and the Second-generation South Asian. *Journal of the American Academy of Religion* 68, no. 4: 721–31.

Mukhopadhyay, Debeaprasad. 1989. *Matri-lila Darshan*. Calcutta: Shree Shree Anandamayee Charitable Society, Matri Mandir.

Narayanan, Vasudha. 2000. Diglossic Hinduism: Liberation and Lentils. *Journal of the American Academy of Religion* 68, no. 4: 761–79.

Newby, Eric. 1966/1983. *Slowly Down the Ganges*. London.

Newby, Eric and Raghubir Singh. 1974. *Ganga: Sacred River of India*. Hong Kong: Perennial Press.

O'Flaherty, W. Doniger. 1981. *The Rig Veda: An Anthology*. Harmondsworth: Penguin.

Pandey, Raj Bali. 1969. *Varanasi: The Heart of Hinduism*. Varanasi: Orient Publishers.

Parry, Jonathan P. 1994. *Death in Banaras*. Cambridge: Cambridge University Press.

Ray, Pratap Chandra (trans.). *Mahabharata*. 1893. Calcutta: Bharata Press.

Sachau, E. 1888. *Alberuni's India*. Trubner's Oriental series. Boston: K. Paul, Trench, Trubner.

Shastri, J.L. (ed.). 1985. *Brahma Purana. Ancient Indian Tradition and Mythology* 33:1. New Delhi: Motilal Banarsidass.

Singh, Raghubir. 1992. *The Ganges*. London: Thames & Hudson.

Sivananda, Swami. 1994. 3rd edn. *Mother Ganga*. Shivanandanagar: The Divine Life Society.

Stanley, John. 1977. Special Time, Special Power: The Fluidity of Power in a Popular Hindu Festival. *Journal of Asian Studies* 37(1): 27–43.

Tagare, G.V. (trans.). 1982. *Narada Purana*. Ancient Indian Tradition and *Mythology* 19:5. New Delhi: Motilal Banarsidass.

The Times of India. 2 September 1998. Issue of Inclusion in Hill State Vitiates Hardwar Scene.

van der Veer, P. 1988. *Gods on Earth: The Management of Religious Experience and Identity in a North Indian Pilgrimage Centre*. London: Athlone.

Vandana, Sister. 1988. *Waters of Fire*. New York: Amity House.

Vivekananda. 1989/1997. 7th reprint. *The Complete Works of Swami Vivekananda*, Vol. 3. Calcutta: Advaita Ashram.

Wadley, Susan and Lawrence Babb (eds.). 1995. *Media and the Transformation of Religion in South Asia*. Philadelphia: University of Pennsylvania Press.

CHAPTER SEVEN

Present Lord: Simandhar Svami and the Akram Vijnan Movement[*]

PETER FLÜGEL

Introduction

Most textbooks present Jainism as a religion which survives in a pristine state virtually unchanged from the time of its last prophet, Mahavira, some two thousand and five hundred years ago. Walther Schubring, for instance, wrote in his classic work, *The Doctrine of the Jainas: Described after the Old Sources*, that the 'teaching proper' of Jainism, which propagates monastic asceticism as the principal means of salvation, was 'scarcely affected' by exterior changes: 'The new formations which developed to remain,' he writes, 'are nearly exclusively concerned with formalities.'[1] This view was reiterated by Robert Williams, in his book *Jaina Yoga*, which describes the textual prescriptions for the traditional rituals of lay Jainism, though he emphasised that the 'changelessness of Jainism is no more than a myth'.

> Admittedly there have been no spectacular changes in basic assumptions such as there were, for example, in Mahayana Buddhism. At most there have been variations in emphasis. Had Jainism, as at one time must have seemed possible, become a majority religion in southern India something akin to a Digambara Mahayana might, with continuing favourable circumstances, have emerged. But all that can be detected today are the traces of aborted developments.[2]

In his influential work *The Jaina Path of Purification*, P.S. Jaini detailed examples of the continual 'erosive' influence of Hindu devotionalism on almost every aspect of popular Jainism from the fifth century onwards, but restated Williams' view:

> No movement towards a more catholic viewpoint or liberalised discipline, no 'Jaina Mahayana' was ever allowed to develop among either the Digambaras or the Shvetambaras.[3]

In this essay I will present at least one case not only of a doctrine or isolated features but of a syncretistic religious movement which, I would argue, can legitimately be called 'Jaina Mahayana',[4] i.e. a primarily devotional form of Jainism, visibly different from the ascetic path outlined in the canonical and classical Jaina scriptures,[5] which congenially combines Kundakunda's 'Digambara Mahayana' soteriology (which is in many ways closer to Shankara's Advaita Vedanta),[6] Samkhya ontology and classical Jaina cosmology with a ritual idiom that is largely derived from popular Vaishnava devotionalism and Tantric miracle cults.[7]

For practical purposes, I follow Heinz Bechert in defining Mahayana in the broadest sense through the concept of 'salvation through others',[8] which is equally important in devotional Hinduism. In Buddhism, the concept has gained particular prominence in the so-called Pure Land (*Sukhavati*) school in East Asia and informs popular devotional practices which answer the religious needs of the Buddhist laity. The *Sukhavati* and similar schools offer temporary respites prepared by a *bodhisattva*, a Buddha-to-be, where the devotee prepares for one final rebirth in the presence of a Buddha after which *nirvana* will be attained. In popular religion, these 'Buddha fields' (*Buddha kshetra*) became soteriological ends in themselves, because they offer an easy and essentially non-monastic path to salvation which merely demands the recognition of the 'Buddha nature' within (*tathagatagarbha*), that is, the true knowledge of the real self (*atman*). In other words, 'we are already fully enlightened Buddhas if we but recognise the face.'[9]

Instant Knowledge (Akram Vijnan)

The case I wish to present in favour of the argument that Mahayana-style forms of Jainism do exist – at least, on the margins of the five major traditions of the Bisapanthi and Terapanthi Digambara, on the one hand; and the Murtipujaka and the Sthanakavasi and Terapanthi Shvetambara, on the other – is the Akram Vijnan Marg in western India, literally the path of the stepless or instant acquisition of the knowledge (necessary for salvation). Because of its recent emergence, its lack of a scriptural 'great tradition' and its small size (quantity is not really an issue) the Akram Vijnan Marg has not yet been studied, although it is highly interesting from a comparative perspective; not only because it combines Jaina and Vaishnavite features in a unique way, but mainly because it offers its followers a method of purification which does not demand renunciation or difficult religious practices, such as asceticism (*tapas*), material offerings (*puja*) and gift-giving (*dana*), or other ritual observances to annihilate *karma*. It therefore presents itself as an attractive option for anyone who seeks easy access to religious purity without the desire to renounce the world or to spend much money on such 'useless'[10] rituals. Moreover, the promise of instant access to salvific knowledge poses a fundamental threat to the traditional establishment of Hindu and Jaina religious functionaries, which are both dismissed as obsolete.

The Akram Vijnan Marg is a lay movement which teaches that there are two paths in Jainism. The dominant *kramik*, step-by-step, Jaina path of purification is predicated on the cosmologically derived assumption that due to the current absence of the conditions for the existence of enlightened beings in our world, enlightenment and therefore final liberation is, at present, not possible anymore. By contrast, the *akramik*, stepless, path, offers a direct route to *moksha* through the grace (*kripa*), of the presently existing lord (*vartamana tirthankara*), Simandhar Svami, one of twenty Jaina *tirthankaras* who according to classical Jaina mythology and cosmography presently lives in the mythical pure land of Mahavideha Kshetra, some 193,950,000 kilometres north of our continent Bharata.[11] The Akram Vijnan movement offers 'instant salvation' to its followers by claiming that Simandhar can be accessed through magical means—that is, through direct contact with a medium (*nimitta*). The principal medium, the late A.M. Patel, became a *bodhisattva*-like figure for his disciples by acting as an interlocutor between humans and the presently existing *tirthankaras* in the pure land of Mahavideha.[12] The cosmological assumptions of this new method are not controversial, although they emerged relatively late in the history of Jainism,[13] and neither is the use of magical means of contact which, in this case, is probably inspired by the example of Kundakunda's yogic travels to these regions in search of inspiration from Simandhar.[14] However, nowhere has a separate path to salvation been offered explicitly in the Jaina tradition to date, though A.M. Patel claimed to follow the unique example of King Bharata, the son of the first *tirthankara*, Rishabha, and who, according to the Akram Vijnan version of the legend, was granted omniscience by an act of grace of Rishabha.[15]

There are two paths to liberation or freedom from all bondage. One is the royal road climbing the steps of [spiritual evolution] slowly [step by step]....It is a very arduous path. You have to climb up [rise] performing penance (*tap*), renunciation, incantation of god's name (*jap*); and even then the sword of Damocles is dangling over your head. The second is the Akram Marg—the lift path. Here you have not to climb steps; you are to get into the lift—with wife and children, after getting sons and daughters happily married, after performing the worldly duties—for freedom from bondage. Performing all these mundane duties you do not lose your 'freedom' even for a second. This Akram Marg is also called an exceptionally 'rare' path. Once in a million years it manifests itself. Only king Bharat had got this 'knowledge' from his father, for Rishabadevji—

Dada Bhagawan—bestowed this 'knowledge' only on Bharat out of his 100 sons.[16]

The principal doctrinal feature of the Akram Vijnan Marg is the belief in the efficacy of the practice of *jnana bhakti*, the magical acquisition of salvific knowledge through the devotional surrender (*samarpana*) to its source—Simandhar Svami and his medium A.M. Patel. The main differences to traditional Jainism are: (a) indifference toward or rejection of scriptural knowledge (*shrutajnana*) in favour of the direct experience of the soul (*atmajnana*), (b) rejection of physical asceticism (*tapas*) in favour of spiritual knowledge (*atmajnana*) as the principal means of salvation, (c) rejection of monasticism and other institutionalised forms of religious practice, (d) the possibility of salvation for all through the grace (*kripa*) of Simandhar Svami, and (e) the acquisition of direct insight into the true nature of the self through devotion to a knower (*guru bhakti*).

Self-enlightenment: A.M. Patel

The Akram Vijnan Marg is a highly innovative religious movement. It originated in the 1960s in Bombay and is slowly spreading throughout western India and the Gujarati diaspora in East Africa, North America and the United Kingdom. The founder of the Akram Vijnan Marg was Ambalal Muljibhai Patel (7 November 1908– 2 January 1988). His disciples called him *jnani* or *jnani purusha*— the enlightened being; *pratyaksha atmajnani*—the presently living knower of the self; or simply *dada bhagavan*—grandfather lord, because they recognised in him one who has realised his own inner ultimate self (*paramatma*). A.M. Patel was a contractor by profession. He was born into a Vaishnava Patidar family in Tarasali, a village near Baroda (Vadodara), and grew up in the village Bhadaran in the district of Kheda in central Gujarat. It is reported that when he was thirteen he once served a saint (*sant*) visiting his village, who blessed him with the words: 'May God gift you with liberation', whereupon he replied:

> I don't want that liberation, if God is to give it to me. 'Given by him' means that 'he is my boss and he can take it back when he desires to do so.' Liberation itself means 'a state where there is no boss, no underhand'.[17]

In one of his published discourses he said, 'The lid of ignorance in my case was so thin (light) that at the age of thirteen, I had intimations of immortality' (ibid.: 8). In 1923, when he was fifteen, he married Hiraba. Because she lost an eye at a young age, he was once asked whether he was interested in remarriage. But he stated that he had a happy marriage and would keep his marital vows. The couple remained childless, because both of their two young children (born in 1928 and 1931) died a few months after their birth. At this time A.M. Patel encountered the writings of Shrimad Rajachandra and, through them, became interested in Jaina philosophy. Shrimad Rajachandra (1867–1901) was a Gujarati Jaina householder and religious visionary who inspired new religious lay movements which represent the first predominantly devotional form of Jainism. A.M. Patel was particularly impressed by Rajachandra's teaching of *atmadharma* and his rejection of *gurus* and of sectarianism.[18] He also began to practice temporary celibacy, or *brahmacharya*, and at the age of thirty, together with his wife, he took the vow of lifelong *brahmacharya*.

Ambalal Muljibhai Patel had only basic formal education and did not speak any English, except a few words, which he regularly interjected into his discourse. He moved to Bombay, where he stayed for most of his working life, and operated successfully as a contractor for the company Patel & Co. which was engaged in the construction and maintenance of the dry docks in the harbour of Bombay. It is said that notwithstanding his occupational commitments, throughout his life he was primarily interested in *moksha*, liberation and *jagat kalyan*, welfare of the world, which for him, as for Rajachandra, meant offering salvation for the suffering humanity through freedom from passion, or *vitaraga*—detachment from the actions of mind, speech and body.[19] In July 1958, when he was fifty years old, he had what he later described as an experience of direct spontaneous enlightenment (*pratyaksha jnana*), which he attributed to the natural fruition of his good *karma*. The experience occurred suddenly while he was waiting for a train on a bench on the busy platform 3 of the railway station in Surat at about six o'clock in the evening and lasted '48 minutes'. The extraordinary feeling, which A.M. Patel himself called 'indescribable' and never put into words,[20] was characterised by his disciple Nirubahen Amin as follows:

> He had just finished his supper, and was waiting for a train. He was sitting on a railway platform bench in Surat, India, when the extraordinary event happened. The Lord became manifest in him. In one hour all the secrets of the world, life and universe opened up to him. He said later, that there are no words to describe what he experienced. Each and every *anu-paramanu* [atom] revealed his vision. He maintained that the external body of A.M. Patel is not God. The Lord who is manifest inside is revered by A.M. Patel. The experience of the Absolute established itself in him permanently. He became the Enlightened One. He became the first *Jnani Purush* to represent Akram Vijnan for modern times.[21]

Another description by Nirubahen, which is corroborated by similar statements from other disciples, makes it clear that A.M. Patel had experienced what he believed to be the revelation or manifestation (*jnan pragat*) of the god within, that is the pure self (*shuddhatma*), the vehicle of the fully realised supreme self (*paramatma*), which he called 'Dada Bhagavan':[22]

> In the 'shrine' of the name of Ambalal Muljibhai Patel, after infinite births, was manifested naturally: 'Dada Bhagavan' in the

form of Akram![23] In the span of one hour he had an experience of the entire universe! 'Who are we? Who is God? Who runs the world? What is karma? What is liberation? etc. All the world's spiritual questions were answered! In this way nature offered an unparalleled absolute vision to the world through the medium of Shree Ambalal Muljibhai Patel, a Patidar of the village of Bhadran, Charotar. Although a contractor by profession, he remained a *Vitarag Purush!*'[24]

Such an 'enlightenment' experience which reveals 'each and every atom of the world' is in Jainism technically known as *kevala jnana*, or omniscience (*sarvajna*),[25] though it is also held that A.M. Patel experienced only *samyak darshana* or *samyaktva*, right view—that is, spiritual insight into the true nature of the self being entirely separate from the *karmik* body (as described by Jaina and Samkhya doctrines).[26] The ambiguity is the result of Patel's attempt to quantify omniscience and to define *samyaktva*, which he calls *jnana* or *prajna*, as 'partial omniscience'.[27] The words most frequently used by him in this respect were *svarupajnana*, self-realisation, and *atmajnana*, self-knowledge (as opposed to *jagatjnana*, knowledge of the world, and *shastrajnana*, scriptural knowledge). The two terms refer to two processes which he, following Kundakunda,[28] regarded as intrinsically connected. Because he experienced his true self without the help of others, in Jaina technical terms, the event transformed him into a *svayam sambuddha*, a being enlightened by itself. According to Nirubahen Amin, A.M. Patel explained that the revelation occurred after an experience of insult and humiliation, involving feelings based on great egotism. At the time of self-realisation, he became aware that it was not 'I', the pure self, or *shuddhatma*, who experienced worldly insult, but only 'me', that is the relative self, or *pratishthit atma*,[29] which is a superimposed, rather alien 'outward packing' in the form of Ambalal Muljibhai Patel:

What you see is Ambalal Muljibhai Patel, a patidar of Bhadran, contractor by profession. But 'he' who is revealed within is a great wonder. He is 'Dada Bhagwan'....We haven't identified our 'self' with this Ambalal Muljibhai even for a second. And ever since my self-realisation, I have been living with him as my first neighbour.[30]

After his enlightenment experience, A.M. Patel stopped working full time in order to concentrate fully on the permanent cultivation of this spiritual insight and left his contractor business to his partners, while living on the dividends of his company shares. However, he remained a householder and never stopped looking after his business throughout his life, because his soteriology demanded neither renunciation of the world nor asceticism. His followers proudly report that he 'never borrowed money from anyone in his life', and lived by the principle: 'In business dharma will decrease, but in dharma, business will not decrease.'[31]

Insight through Grace: Kanu Patel

At first, A.M. Patel did not make his inner experience publicly known, except for a few relatives and close friends who noticed some changes in his demeanour and started asking questions. But already in 1962, he evoked for the first time the experience of *samyak darshana* in another person in his own rented house in Baroda. In the language of the Akram Vijnan Marg this procedure is called 'transmitting the knowledge'. Why he thought this might be possible is not entirely clear, since he left few documents which could serve as a basis for a reconstruction of the development of his religious ideas. His brother's, now deceased, son Chandrakant Patel from Uganda (originally from Bhadaran, Gujarat), who called him reverently *dada*, or grandfather, was very interested in his vision. Chandrakant was the first individual to experience a sudden insight into his own pure self in the presence of 'the *Dada*'. The experience was triggered by a conversation. Chandrakant asked his *dada*: '*Dada* are you a Jnani? How does one recognise a Jnani?' A.M. Patel's answer opened his eyes. He said,

> Just slap me in my face, and look into my eyes, whether you see anything....Beat me up any way you like to make me human.[32]

This event, which involved nothing but the knower's words of truth (*aptavani*)[33] and an informal blessing (*ashirvada*) is remembered as the first performance of the *jnana vidhi*, or rite of knowledge, the ritual for the evocation of the experience of *samyak darshana* through the destruction of all the obstructive *mohaniya*, or delusion producing *karmas*. In classical Jaina doctrine this is technically called *kshayaka samyaktva*[34] and is believed to be possible only in the presence of a Jina.[35]

The second person to be given the *jnan* was Kanubhai K. Patel (born 1930) who became one of the two principal spiritual successors of A.M. Patel. He was the son of Kantilal Patel, A.M. Patel's business partner, and worked until recently as a structural engineer. For fifteen years he lived together with A.M. Patel in the same house in Bombay. Later he married, but continued to work in the company Patel & Co. He prides himself that during these fifteen years he stayed with A.M. Patel round the clock and looked after his physical and mental well-being. This practice is called *seva*, service, to the Dada. In the late 1970s Kanubhai took some business decisions against A.M. Patel's advice and lost a lot of money for the joint company. Thereupon, A.M. Patel left the partnership. Kanu Patel told me in 1999 about his experience of receiving 'the *jnan*', that is *samyak darshana*, from the Dada. In 1963 he underwent a major crisis, which he characterised with the words 'to be or not to be'. One of his problems was that he could not sleep. However, one night the Dada appeared in his dreams and after this he was able to sleep for the first time in a long while. The next day he went to A.M. Patel, put his head at his feet and asked: 'Who am I?' The Dada then gave him the knowledge. As in Chandrakant's case, no special ceremony was performed, just an informal conversation lasting five to ten minutes, which, Kanu Patel stressed, had changed his entire life. Everything turned 'upside down' for him during these few minutes.

The Rite of Knowledge (*Jnana Vidhi*)

The once informal procedure of passing on spiritual energy for the separation of soul and non-soul in another person soon became more formalised. Between 1962 and 1968, A.M. Patel transmitted his spiritual powers only to select members of his circle of family and friends, but from 1968 onwards he offered to bestow with *samyak darshana* (*paramartha samakit*) anyone who bowed to him and requested to be blessed by the *bheda jnana*, the knowledge of separation. This was the origin of the devotional Dada Bhagavan cult at the heart of the Akram Vijnan movement. In his discourses, A.M. Patel often said that the attribute *'Dada Bhagavan'* was originally not of his own making, but introduced by his followers. Out of fear of public opinion, he said, he was initially not even sure whether he wanted to publicise his teaching beyond a small circle of friends, as had been the case with Shrimad Rajachandra. But in response to public demand, he went to the Rishabha temple in Khambhat near Vadodara, where Rajachandra had stayed in 1893, to ask for Rishabha's advice. Apparently, he was able to contact Rishabha in *siddhaloka*, the realm of the liberated souls,[36] and to sit at his feet to receive the advice that he should convey 'the knowledge' to all strata of society, not merely to the select few. On request, the first public performance of the *jnana vidhi* was held in 1968 in Bombay. In subsequent years the rite was performed at regular intervals and the procedure became more and more elaborate, until it attained its present form in 1983.[37]

Originally, A.M. Patel performed what was later called the *jnana vidhi*, the rite of knowledge, only for individuals and under the seal of secrecy. Often, the rite was performed on remote mountain tops, because intense shouting came to be seen as a key ingredient for the removal of the obstructive *karmas*, as was the blessing (*prasadi*) performed by laying hands on the head of the bowing devotee (A.M. Patel did not like the term 'disciple') at the feet of the Dada. With time, the *vidhi* became more elaborate and was performed in small groups. On request, the blessing was accompanied by a few firm knocks on the devotee's back with one of A.M. Patel's shoes or with a coconut, a symbol of auspiciousness which offered, as it were, a tangible equivalent to the imperceptible inner process of separation of self and non-self. All aspirants I interviewed insisted that they 'felt absolutely nothing' even at the severest blows. This divine blessing cum thrashing was called *alaukika prasadi*, otherworldly blessing, and apparently introduced 'only reluctantly' by A.M. Patel on 'request of the aspirants'. Additional blessings were sometimes given by showering the aspirants with rose petals.

In the beginning, the ritual was not informed by any explicit doctrine. However, from 1968 onwards A.M. Patel also started to teach his vision to others. On request, he held *satsangs* or meetings for religious discourse in private houses, not unlike Shrimad Rajachandra before him, and performed the *jnana vidhi* regularly for groups of aspirants.[38] He now referred to himself as the *jnani*, the self-realised knower who had directly experienced the difference between self (*purusha*) and non-self (*prakriti*), and was thus qualified to act as a *sadguru* or a *satpurusha*, a good teacher or self-realised being, for the spiritual well-being of others, not unlike a *bodhisattva* in Mahayana Buddhism.[39]

A.M. Patel's religious terminology indicates that his teachings were strongly influenced by the Samkhya view, both echoed and criticised by Kundakunda,[40] that all forms of action in mind, speech and body are merely material; that is, natural processes and thus entirely unconnected with the true self which is in essence a passive observer, not a doer.[41] For him, the illusion of a real connection between the essentially pure self and the action of mind, body and speech is a product of the conventional point of view (*vyavahara naya*), whereas from the real point of view (*nishchaya naya*) the pure self is essentially free and unbound.[42] Liberation can therefore be achieved through the mere acquisition of self-knowledge—the intuitive and strictly non-intellectual (*abudha*) immediate experience of the true nature of the self which exists in qualitatively identical form in all living beings.[43] A.M. Patel illustrated this fundamental insight for his audience with reference to the difference between the empirical self, the ego and the pure self:

> What you see here is not 'Dada Bhagavan'. What you see is 'A.M. Patel'. I am *Jnani Purush* and He that is manifested within, is 'Dada Bhagavan'. He is the Lord of the fourteen *lokas* (regions of the universe) and He is within you and everyone else. He is residing in an unmanifested form within you, whereas here (within me) he has completely manifested (manifested in an absolute form)! I myself am not the Dada Bhagavan. I bow down to the Dada Bhagavan that is manifested within me.[44]

In his later years, A.M. Patel explained his method of inducing liberating insight in others in his discourses. He described himself as a 'doctor of the mind' who uses his own miraculous powers (*siddhi*)[45] for performing painful surgery on the self of others[46] by squeezing their ego,[47] burning to ashes their sins from infinite cycles of births,[48] and finally separating their pure self (*shuddhatma*) from their ego-centred mind (*mana*) in order to eliminate all sense of possessiveness and to make them understand the nature of *prakriti*. He stated:

> 'We' are the exorcist [*bhuva*] of the three ghosts of mind, speech and body that have possessed you. We can get you released from these three attachments.[49]

All that is needed is the blessing of the *jnani*, who puts his hand on the head of the aspirant[50] and uses his faculty of speech in order to transmit his divine powers of intuitive knowledge to separate self and non-self:

> Suppose metals like copper, brass, silver got mixed up with gold, cannot a scientist separate them, examining their different qualities? He can do it easily. In the same way he who knows the qualities of the soul and the non-soul and who as an omniscient *Jnani* possesses infinite power, can separate these two substances after analysing them. 'We' are the greatest scientist of the world. Analysing every atom of the soul and the non-soul, separating both of them, 'We' give you the pure soul (*shuddhatma*) in your hand in an hour.[51]

The destruction of the *mohaniya karmas* is thought to be achieved simply through the miraculous power of grace (*siddhi kripa*) of the god within, that is the all-compassionate Dada Bhagavan as manifested within his 'boss' A.M. Patel:

> Ay, we are god's boss. Perfectly non-attached. God himself has given us the position of his superior.[52] He told us: 'We are in search of a worthy instrument and we discovered it in you. We are perfectly non-attached sitting in pure self-liberation. We cannot help anybody now. So you are the omnipotent manifest form. Though you live in a clay mould, you are perfectly non-attached. So we give you our superior power and accept you as our boss. And you do good to the world.' And therefore we have become even god's boss. We are the boss of the Lord of the fourteen worlds. With all his spiritual power has the incarnation of *Jnana* manifested itself.[53]

Like Shrimad Rajachandra, A.M. Patel emphasised the impotence of scriptural or ritual knowledge for the liberation of the soul and pointed instead to the significance of direct contact with a living *jnani*, since, in his view, the spiritual power (*siddhi*) that is necessary to separate self and non-self can only be transmitted through the direct speech (*pratyaksha vani*) and blessing of a true *jnani*,[54] not through the indirect speech (*paroksha vani*) of the scriptures or an un-self-realised mendicant.[55] For him, the *jnani* was the living embodiment of knowledge (*pratyaksha sarasvati*). He therefore never tired of emphasing the unique opportunity of meeting a *jnani* such as the Dada Bhagavan:

> You ignoramus, a *Jnani* rarely visits the earth; and the *Jnani* of the Akram path (instant-liberation path) is born once in ten million years and that, too, in this present age of strange happenings, like the *kaliyug*. He lifts you up in a lift. You are not to gasp for breath after climbing the steps....Only *vitaraga vani* (speech free from any attachment) can lead to liberation. Our speech is sweet, melodious and unprecedented, unheard of before, direct. That speech [which is] contained in the scriptures is indirect. If one listens to the 'direct speech' one will have '*samakit*'. Our speech is *syadvada*—not hurting anybody's view or standard—but acceptable to all views. It accepts all points of view because we are sitting at the centre. Our speech is impartial....*Vitaraga vani* is that which is replete with the feeling of complete spiritual well-being of others. Only *vitaraga vani* can do good to a person and lead him to liberation.[56]

Simandhar Svami

Although the matter is not entirely clear, it seems that at the beginning of his career as a religious virtuoso A.M. Patel did not refer much to Simandhar Svami, the Jaina *tirthankara* who is believed to be currently living in the mythical continent Mahavideha. However, from the 1970s onwards, probably after a sustained reading of Jaina cosmological literature, he regularly invoked a special link to Simandhar Svami and distinguished three categories of enlightened beings: (a) the *siddhas*, or liberated beings living in *siddhaloka*, who do not speak and cannot be reached anymore; (b) the currently living *tirthankara* or *arhat* Simandhar

Svami in Mahavideha, who speaks to the Dada within A.M. Patel, who contacts him through his 'astral body', but does not instruct his followers; and (c) the Dada, who speaks through A.M. Patel and instructs his disciples in this world. A.M. Patel claimed that he himself had not only experienced *samyak darshana*, but also '356 degrees' of total omniscience (*kevala jnana*). There was only a difference of '4 degrees' between himself and the *arhats* and the *siddhas*. Because of likeness of his own soul and the souls of the fully omniscient, he said, he was able to contact Simandhar Svami directly.[57] During the *jnana vidhi*, he claimed, the voice of the Dada, and through the Dada, the voice of Simandhar Svami spoke directly through A.M. Patel, who acted as his medium in order to transmit 'the knowledge' to his devotees. Because he was accepted as a partially enlightened and passionless being, and was able to mediate in this way between his followers and Simandhar Svami, A.M. Patel was called *khatpat vitaraga* by his followers, the passionless one who uses tricks to get things done.

In contrast to Rajachandra and the 'elitist' and 'decadent' Jaina mendicant traditions which follow the path of Mahavira, A.M. Patel held that the worship of past or future *tirthankaras* on the basis of scriptures and images can only function as a reminder of a distant ideal, whereas he himself has given his followers the opportunity to gain liberation themselves through direct contact with the present *tirthankara*, Simandhar. Unlike Rajachandra, who occasionally considered himself to be 'the second Mahavira',[58] he did not present himself to be the source of possible liberation, but only an instrument, or *nimitta*, of Simandhar, although the distinction is often blurred in popular perception and sometimes Simandhar and the Dada Bhagavan are deliberately identified.

This overview of the key differences between the teachings of Rajachandra and A.M. Patel points to an important shift of emphasis. The Akram Vijnan movement highlights the present possibility of salvation. It stresses the doctrinal fact that no past or future Jaina god (*tirthankara*) can grant any practical help to his present devotees, only a god living in the present (*pratyaksha*) who is directly accessible to everyone – like Simandhar through his medium A.M. Patel – can do so. The followers of the Akram Vijnan Marg believe that the fact that A.M. Patel has made his personal link to Simandhar available to his followers singles him out from the two other 'omniscient' *jnanis*, Kundakunda and Rajachandra, as well as Kanji Svami, the *brahmachari* who is technically a Jaina layman, who provided vivid descriptions of their personal spiritual journeys to Simandhar without offering a direct link for everyone, as the Dada did.

A comparison of the ways in which these three Gujarati Jaina laymen cognised the possibility of establishing contact with a living *tirthankara* under the conditions of the present time cycle shows variations along the dimensions of time, place and medium of communication. Rajachandra said he gained salvific knowledge through the memory (*jatisamarana jnana*) of an encounter with a Jina of the same continent (Bharata) in a previous life. Kanji Svami achieved this apparently through the memory of the encounter with a Jina of a different continent (Mahavideha) in a previous life, while A.M. Patel maintained that he was in continuous contact with a Jina of a different continent in his present life. He was the only one who made this unique link available for everyone, while Rajachandra and Kanji Svami projected themselves as *tirthankaras* of the future.[59]

Devotion and Self-effort

The mere participation in the rite of knowledge itself does, of course, not secure final *moksha*. But it is believed that it offers the possibility of achieving so-called living *moksha*,[60] and the prospect of being reborn 'at the feet' of the currently living *tirthankara*, Simandhar Svami in Mahavideha Kshetra, within not more than two lifetimes. According to Jaina doctrine, everyone has the opportunity of being enlightened in the presence of a living *tirthankara*, a process called *buddha-bodhita* that is attributed to his great compassion.[61] The question is how to get to Mahavideha Kshetra.[62] Classical Jainism teaches that a better rebirth can only be secured by reducing and purifying the *karmik* burden of an individual.[63] A.M. Patel and his successors agree with this, but have a different opinion about the way in which this is achieved. Because they believe, like the Bhagavad Gita,[64] that the soul is passive, not active, and that there is no real bondage between soul and body, and therefore there is no need for physical asceticism, their main concern is the continuous application of the liberating perspective of the pure soul to all aspects of life. The resulting non-attachment towards one's own actions secures both that no new *karmas* are accumulated and that old *karmas* come to fruition naturally. In addition, they also preach the principle of non-violence (*ahimsa*) and the abstinence from all intentional action in order to prevent the influx of new *karma*. If an act of violence nevertheless occurs and the ego is involved, fresh *karma* is produced. However, A.M. Patel taught how, through the technique of *anamnesis* of concrete violent actions from the point of view of the pure self (*nishchaya naya*), any such mistake can be neutralised by a devotee of the Dada Bhagavan who has received the knowledge.[65] The Akram Vijnan Marg thus teaches a mixture of devotion to the pure self and ethics. In this respect its soteriology differs from purely theistic or gnostic approaches.[66] A.M. Patel has made the importance of the role of self-effort – sandwiched between the initial gift of *bheda jnana* by the grace of the *Jnani* and the final gift of *sarvajnana* by the grace of Simandhar Svami – explicit in the following statement:

> First I destroy all your blunders because by yourself it is impossible for you. How do I do it? By placing my hand on your head and letting Bhagavan (Dada Bhagavan the Lord of the 14 worlds) give his divine grace (*kripa*). Thereafter, you need to remove your mistakes yourself. You will be able to see your own

mistakes. Daily you will be able to see 5, 50 or 100 faults of your own and thus these mistakes will go on their own. Your realisation of your self will increase as your mistakes (faults) decrease.[67]

The Dada cannot purify. He can only give his knowledge and inspirational power to face own's own mistakes. Only the effort of maintaining a permanent awareness (*jagriti*) of one's real self can purify. In asking the Dada for forgiveness for mistakes during devotional practices, the devotee is not assuming that the Dada cleanses the soul by an act of pure grace, but in evoking the manifestation of the Dada in his/her mind, the experience of his/her own pure soul is realised. It is only the awareness that this was not 'I' who has committed an act of violence, but 'me', that is *prakriti* or the accumulated *karmas* which come to fruition naturally, which reduces the burden of *karma*.[68]

Following

The Dada Bhagavan cult developed first in Bombay and in A.M. Patel's hometown Baroda. In 1983, only twenty years after the first *jnana vidhi* was performed, already forty of the fifty thousand followers[69] reportedly existed in southern Gujarat and Maharashtra. A.M. Patel's funeral in 1988 in Kelanpur near Baroda was attended by about 60,000 people, and for 1999 the figure of about 300,000 followers is mentioned by the magazine *Akram Vijnan*.[70] The followers of the Dada were not recruited from any particular caste. But because of his own social and professional background, many of the leading adherents were middle-class Patels from Mumbai and Baroda. Even today, the chief personalities of the movement are engineers, merchants and medical doctors. However, most of the common followers of the Dada are uneducated, often illiterate, members of the urban working classes, predominantly Patels, Mahetas and Shahs from the Patidar,

Shrimali and Osval castes of Gujarat who traditionally practise Vaishnavite and/or Jaina rituals often side by side.[71] A.M. Patel supplied their need for religious inspiration, and offered a path of salvation which was easy to understand and practise at the same time. The main reason for the popularity of the Dada Bhagavan cult is its universal, non-intellectual and non-sectarian appeal. A.M. Patel was a simple, unassuming man with a good grasp of Jaina and Vaishnava concepts. He spoke about subtle religio-philosophical ideas in an uncomplicated plain Gujarati language with interjected English terms which everybody could understand, and gave practical advice for the resolution of everyday problems from the point of view of 'absolute truth'.

Community Organisation

As a matter of principle, A.M. Patel rejected organised forms of religion, *gurus* and religious functionaries. He nevertheless 'agreed to' the creation of community associations. The main association of the Akram Vijnan Marg is the Jay Sacchidananda Sangha in Mumbai. This organisation was founded under the auspices of A.M. Patel himself, who appointed Khetsi Narsi Shah, the head of the local Dada Bhagavan Vitaraga Trust, as the first *sakala sanghapati*, or overall community leader, who acts as the chief coordinator of the activities of all local *sanghs*. After the death of Khetsi Narsi Shah, G.A. Shah from Ahmedabad was appointed as the *sanghapati*. His main duties are to organise the movements of the religious leader and his main disciples, the so-called *aptaputras* and *aptaputris*, a category of celibate laity who are invited by devotees all over the world, and to publish the community magazine *Akram Vijnan* which was first issued in 1979.[72] He also oversees the various building projects and looks after the community funds. Today, the organisation has important strongholds, led by local *sanghapatis*, in Mumbai, Ahmedabad, Surat, London and in the U.S.

Ritualisation: Nirubahen Amin

The development of the Dada Bhagavan worship from a charismatic family cult into an organised religious movement which refers to itself as the Akram Vijnan Marg, the stepless path of knowledge, is to a large extent, though not entirely, the achievement of Nirubahen Amin (born 1944), the second chief disciple of A.M. Patel. She was instrumental in publishing the discourses of A.M. Patel and effected the creation of an elaborate ritualism, including the formalisation of the *jnana vidhi* which under her influence was developed into a public initiation ceremony lasting more than 48 minutes. She also composed a *puja* ritual and promoted the construction of temples for the veneration of Simandhar Svami.[73]

Nirubahen Amin is a gynaecologist by profession and the daughter of one of the oldest devotees of A.M. Patel, a multi-millionaire from Aurangabad, whose family was traditionally Vaishnavite. She was married, but later separated from her husband and took up medical studies in Bombay, when suddenly her husband died in 1968 under the suspicion of suicide. Shortly afterwards, her mother died as well. After these traumatic events, which left her heartbroken, she went to A.M. Patel, whom her father had asked to look after her in Bombay. 'With the Dada's help,' she said, she finished her medical exams at the end of the year. On the same day her father died. Before the news reached her, 'the Dada' told her about her father's death in great detail, although he had not yet received any report of the death himself. This confirmed to her his omniscience. When the official message was brought to her, she was prepared, fully detached and indifferent. The sad news could not harm her, because she had received the *jnana* from 'the Dada' A.M. Patel and knew that her father – as a dedicated follower of the Dada – would be reborn as a higher incarnation: 'Life goes on, one just changes outer appearances.'

From then on, she says, she became a devotee of the Dada and was never again unaware of her pure self even for one moment.

Initially, Nirubahen had no competence in the 'science' of the self (*atmavijnana*), but she was so impressed by the Dada that she began to tape his religious discourses (*satsangs*) from 1974 onwards. She collected in this way about four thousand tapes between 1974 and 1988, which are currently compiled, transcribed (in a few cases translated) and published under the title *Aptavani*, or words of truth. The currently twelve *Aptavani* volumes represent the emerging doctrinal corpus of the Akram Vijnan Marg.[74] The first one and a half volumes of the *Aptavani* were compiled both by Kanubhai Patel and Nirubahen Amin, and the first volume published in 1973 by the Jay Sacchidananda Sangha. Volumes published later than 1983 are based exclusively on Nirubahen's tapes. The only other textual source for A.M. Patel's teachings is 'Vasudev' Natubhai Patel's collection of *satsang* notes which were published in several volumes under the title *Svarup Vijnan* in the 1980s.[75]

Except for the slightly modified, syncretistic version of the Jaina *Namaskara Mantra*, called *Tri-Mantra*, or three-fold *mantra*, which includes references to the Jinas, Krishna and Shiva and is recited at the beginning of every religious event of the Akram Vijnan Marg,[76] none of the printed compilations used in the current ritual stems from A.M. Patel, who refused to write religious tracts. He only ever composed two short ritual texts, the *Namaskar Vidhi* in 1971–73,[77] a devotional hymn addressed to Simandhar Svami and to all other Indian saints and gods he considered worthy of worship, in descending order from the Pancha Parameshthins of the Jaina *Namaskara Mantra* down to Krishna, the Dada Bhagavan himself and the pure self of all living beings; and the *Nav Kalamo*, the Nine Precepts, in 1977, a prayer to the Dada Bhagavan which is said to comprise 'the essence of all scriptures'.[78] The oldest ritual text of the Akram Vijnan Marg which is the centrepiece of both the daily worship and the *jnana vidhi*, the *Nishchay-Vyavahar Charan Vidhi*, or Absolute-Relative Foot Worship, was written by Vanubhai Patel at the request of A.M. Patel and Nirubahen Amin in 1968.[79] The opening chants of today's formalised rite of knowledge were composed by a songwriter from Bombay, Navanit Patel, in 1970.[80]

In 1976 Nirubahen had an ecstatic religious experience in A.M. Patel's presence which, in her words, also established a unique link between herself and Simandhar Svami, and inspired her to compose the text of an *arati* ritual for the veneration of Simandhar. Her description of the event resembles the narration of the enlightenment experience of A.M. Patel. But it highlights the significance of the mediation of the Dada and of a special *mantra* composed by him:

> Naturally, before I came into contact with Pujya Dadashree, I was not familiar even with the word 'Tirthankar' in its real meaning. As such, how was I to have any information regarding Shree Simandhar Swami? It was 1971. We were in Vadva. At night, we were all sitting in a small room of Pujariji. Each one of us present there had to recite, one by one, the following mantra: 'In the very presence of Dada Bhagavan and through him, most devoutly do I bow in supplication unto *tirthankar* Bhagavan Shree Simandhar Swami, traversing at present Mahavideha Kshetra.'[81] First of all, Dadashri recited it to show us how it should be recited. Then he penned it on a piece of paper and gave it to me, asking me to make others recite it in turn. This was my first acquaintance with Shree Simandhar Swami. Then, in September 1972, there was one *shibir* of three days in Aurangabad. During the morning prayers, Dadashri reflected on something and told us all present there: 'One who recites this mantra forty times a day shall gain the fruit of offering one hundred and eight obeisance directly to Shree Simandhar Swami.' Thereafter everyone started reciting this mantra forty times a day. Dadashri had suggested that, time permitting, you should at least once a week, on a holiday, recite

this mantra forty times. As far as I am concerned, the rule of reciting the mantra, which was ingrained into my being then, has come down till today, uninterrupted and unbroken. In 1976, while Dadashri was staying in Mamani Pole, Baroda, I had the golden opportunity of serving him during his illness. It was 12.30 p.m. Having taken his dinner, he was, as usual, sitting on a bench. I was sitting on a sofa just opposite to him. On the wall facing me was a photograph of Shree Simandhar Swami. While conversing—I don't know how or why, be it some divine inspiration or be it the ripe time to shower his infinite grace onto me—he attuned my being with Shree Simandhar Swami and set a unique link between us! I don't have adequate words to express my Ecstatic Experience and Great Bliss of that moment. Thenceforth, the moment my *chitta* [reflective mind] feels free and unoccupied, it gets lost in the lotus-feet of Shree Simandhar Swami. In those days, when Pujya Dadashri used to smoke a *hookah* [hubble-bubble], there sprung in me such an overflowing feeling of oneness with Shree Simandhar Swami that I was divined and inspired to compose His *aarti*. The *aarti* has in it all the mysteries of my unique union with Him.[82]

Nirubahen Amin continued to work in a small surgery in Bombay until 1978, when A.M. Patel suffered a fractured leg. From then on he needed constant medical care and Nirubahen was asked to stay with him and to do *seva* in the place of Kanu Patel. Her medical expertise was particularly valuable during A.M. Patel's missionary tours abroad between 1982 and 1987, which Kanu Patel, who had to look after the business of Patel & Co., could not join. Thus, for the last ten years of A.M. Patel's life Nirubahen became the person closest to him, apart from his wife. Being the daughter of a multimillionaire, she was able, like her brothers, to live off her share in her father's business.

During the last years of A.M. Patel's life, the issue of how the movement could be perpetuated beyond his death was hotly debated. After some hesitation, A.M. Patel finally agreed in 1980 to the construction of a temple for the worship of the three images (*trimurti*) of Simandhar, Krishna and Shiva in order to spread the message of universal religion. But he spoke out against the worship of his own image and insisted that his method of liberation should only be spread by the lineages of his successors, which he called *jivanmurti*, or living idols:

> Don't we have the (paintings) of Mahavir and Krishna? Keep them. Don't put our photograph. It won't be useful to you in any way. We'll leave behind us our successors and then the (chain) link of *Jnanis* will continue. Therefore find out a living idol. The puzzle won't be solved without his [sic!] guidance.[83]

In 1993 the impressive Tri-Mandir temple near Surat was inaugurated and a *dharmashala* was built nearby, both under the management of the Mahavideha Tirthadham Trust. But, although the Tri-Mandir temple in Surat was constructed in such a way as to demonstrate that the same god (the pure soul) dwells within everyone – in Simandhar, Krishna and Shiva – it also offers the chance to worship the photos of A.M. Patel and Kanu Patel in a separate chamber underneath the central Simandhar Svami temple.[84]

Succession Dispute

Shortly after the death of A.M. Patel on 2 January 1988, the Akram Vijnan Movement split into two factions. The person who was close to him until 1978, Kanubhai K. Patel, took over as the sole religious leader of the Akram Vijnan community with the institutional backing of the main community association, the Jay Sacchidananda Sangha in Bombay. Nirubahen Amin seceded and created a separate community on her own. There are two conflicting accounts of this split.

According to Nirubahen, A.M. Patel decided near the end of his life to secure the continuation of the Akram Vijnan Marg by passing on his powers (*siddhi*) of liberation (*mukti*), knowledge (*jnana*) and grace (*kripa*) to a number of successors. In 1987, he blessed Nirubahen 'in the presence of Simandhar' with a secret *mantra* through which she would be able to temporarily manifest the Dada (the pure soul of A.M. Patel) within herself and thus be able to access him, and through him, Simandhar's spiritual power. In this way, a spiritual link would be maintained across the hiatus of physical death between the presently living *tirthankara* Simandhar Svami, the *jnani purusha* Dada Bhagavan and Nirubahen who was called *satpurusha*, the divine being or the being of truth. A.M. Patel also gave her the authority to perform the *jnana vidhi*, and trained her for five months, during which she learned the required words by repeating what he said.

After the death of A.M. Patel, Nirubahen began to perform the *jnana vidhi* on her own, claiming that the Dada had given her the powers to do so and is actually speaking through her for a significant part of the ritual. Nirubahen present herself as a medium (*nimitta*) of the Dada. However, she says that she communicates with him even in her dreams, where she experiences how the Dada passes her messages to Simandhar and Simandhar's answers on to her. This assertion was not acceptable to the leaders of the Jay Sacchindananda Sangha, who supported Kanu Patel as the successor of A.M. Patel, because they would not accept a female leader. However, Nirubahen continued and left the community organisation to build up her own following. Like A.M. Patel, she officially rejects the notion of organised religion (in order to juxtapose herself against the followers of Kanu Patel), but nevertheless inspired the creation of organisations of her own supporters, first the Dada Bhagavan Foundation Trust of Ajit Patel in Chennai and Ahmedabad, and more recently the Simandhar Svami Aradhana Trust in Ahmedabad and Nirubahen Amin's own Mahavideha Foundation in Mumbai. At the moment, Nirubahen

Amin is the most popular religious leader of the Akram Vijnan movement. She also frequently appears on Indian television. Since 1999 she is called Niru-ma, 'Mother Niru', by her followers.

This version of events is contradicted by the account given by the followers of Kanubhai Patel. They produced a tape of a private conversation between A.M. Patel and Nirubahen, which was recorded by chance on their tour of the United States on 19 September 1987, to prove that the Dada intended Kanu Patel and not Nirubahen Amin to be his successor.[85] At the beginning of the short conversation, conducted in a husky voice with long intervals between utterances, A.M. Patel gave her instructions for his funeral and then, using the formula '*Dada Bhagavan bole che*' (Dada Bhagavan says), he said that Nirubahen should continue to perform six more *satsangs* herself. After this, she should help Kanubhai in the same way as she helped him to perform the *jnana vidhi*. He then said: 'I have [already] passed the *vidhi mukeli* [rite of liberation] on to Kanubhai.' This evidence seems to prove that A.M. Patel wanted his two main disciples to work together. He wanted Nirubahen first to teach the performance of the ritual to Kanubhai and then to assist him. At the time, Kanubhai had no experience in performing the *jnana vidhi* himself. He apparently received the powers to do so from A.M. Patel already in the early 1960s, but refused to perform the *vidhi* 'out of respect (*vinaya*) for the Dada'. However, Nirubahen performed the *jnana vidhi* a few times herself. When she saw that it worked successfully, she simply continued and refused to step down and serve Kanubhai.

The followers of Kanubhai accept that Nirubahen acquired many powers in her years in the presence of the Dada, but emphasise that the power of liberating others has not been given to Nirubahen, which she accepts herself. By contrast, the first two disciples of A.M. Patel, the late Chandrakant and Kanubhai, are regarded by them as *jnanis* in their own right who are entitled to perform the rite of knowledge on their own, without recourse to the Dada. Many of Kanubhai's devotees accept his claim that he will be reborn as one of the twenty-four *tirthankaras* of the next time cycle (*kalachakra*) and recite verse no. 10 of the *Namaskar Vidhi*: '*Dada Bhagavan na bhavi tirthankar sahebo ne atyant bhakti purvak namaskar karum chum*'—'With extreme devotion I offer my salutations to future *tirthankara* lords of Dada Bhagavan.'[86] In other words, they see encounters with him as a possibility to establish a direct link (*rinanunandha*) with a future *tirthankara*. 'Kanudada' as he is sometimes called, is also recognised by the Jay Sacchidananda Sangha as the 'presently existing enlightened being' (*pravartaman pragat jnani purusha*).[87]

Two Approaches

Nirubahen Amin accepts that the Dada passed the authority to perform the *jnana vidhi* also to Kanu Patel (though not the *mantra*). But she does not agree with Kanu Patel's claim to spiritual leadership under the pretext that he is the currently living *jnani purusha*. Because, in her view, A.M. Patel was the only *jnani*, she merely assumes the humble role as his spiritual medium (*nimitta*) for herself. Moreover, she accuses Kanu Patel of not distinguishing between .*samyak darshana* and *moksha*, that is between the experience of the difference between body and soul, and salvation. Because he claims to be the self-realised one, she says, Kanu Patel has no religious aim, no transcedence to offer anymore, although his conduct hardly matches his claim to have reached salvation within the world. 'No-one owns this knowledge, only the *tirthankaras*,' she says, and only 'someone with sufficient purity can give the *bhed jnan* to others.'[88] Nirubahen Amin unequivocally states:

> The science of Akram Vijnan is transferable. Thousands became enlightened through the grace of Dadashree and thousands continue to experience instant living *moksh* even now provided they surrender their intellect and their beliefs to god, Dada Bhagavan, the lord of the universe, who was fully manifest in A.M. Patel.[89]

It becomes obvious in the following quotation that Nirubahen's interpretation of God comes close to what might be called the 'Jina-nature within',[90] which is generally contrasted by her with the 'self-deification' practised by Kanu Patel:

> A very important message of note for all who are new to Pujya Dadashri's Science of Akram Vijnan is to be aware that the title of Dada Bhagvan can never be given to any living being. Dada Bhagvan is the name given to the Lord within. This was frequently asserted by the *Jnani Purush* Dadashri and now is being asserted by Pujya Nirubahen and all who have received Jnan from her.[91]

Kanu Patel, on the other hand, insists that one cannot transfer spiritual experiences by performing ritual acts or by becoming a medium. Words themselves are not important, whether they are the exact utterances of the Dada or not. The *vidhi* can be performed in any language, not only in Gujarati as Nirubahen maintains.[92] For the *jnana vidhi* to be efficacious it is of the utmost importance that the performer is enlightened himself. Everything must be based upon one's own experience, on mind (*mana*), not on action or speech:

> 'I cannot be out of my centre,' he said, 'my experience is individual, it has to be independent. There cannot be any hierarchy. The Dada did not give special powers to anyone. No person can make others experience the truth, neither can books nor any transfer of intellectual knowledge. Grace is the only way to achieve self-realisation. And grace exists only when nothing is given and nothing received. I am neither the giver nor the receiver. I am totally free. I am not out of my centre. My own experience is more important than the word. The Dada's speech is fundamental in the *vidhi*, yet the potential for divine speech is essentially existing within everybody. Every human being can have the experience of liberation out of suffering in the present

life. Only animals and plants cannot have this experience. The *vidhi* itself does not cause any material changes.'[93]

Kanubhai also claims to have experienced great intimacy with the Dada, although Nirubahen stayed with A.M. Patel during the last ten years of his life, and says that the Dada was principally opposed to the development of any cult, and did not design any definite ritual, like Nirubahen, because he thought that rituals and ceremonies develop naturally as a form of *vyavasthit shakti*.

However, there was another reason for the departure of Nirubahen. Kanu Patel and the *sanghapati* were simply not prepared to accept a female leader, although they offered Nirubahen the opportunity to work for the *sangha*. They reported that the Dada himself was opposed to women becoming *brahmacharinis*, 'just because they don't want to marry'. Apparently, A.M. Patel said: 'Women cannot observe my principles and better do more chanting', although this is uncorroborated by the followers of Nirubahen. He apparently also believed, like most Jainas (and Hindus), that women have an inferior *karmik* constitution and that, therefore, few have higher spiritual experiences. It is widely held that women generally have more *mohaniya*, or mind-deluding, *karmas* and therefore cannot realise the effects of the *jnana vidhi* as easily as men. Although the influx of new *karmas* will be stopped after undergoing the ritual, too many old *karmas* continue to discharge. Kanu Patel claims that this was the reason why A.M. Patel had initiated only *aptaputras* and no *aptaputris* at all [Kanu Patel has not initiated any *aptaputras* or *aptaputris*].

Kanubhai's followers generally criticise Nirubahen's 'desire for power' and her 'lack of humility' which they see confirmed by the fact that, in contrast to the Dada and Kanudada who continued to wear their everyday dress after their enlightenment, she (and her main disciples) changed her dress to pure white, thus getting involved in the 'relative world'. The Jay Sacchidananda Sangha officially rejected Nirubahen Amin's claim that she is a medium of the Dada, discouraged her following and frequently broke up her meetings. In 1993, at the consecration ceremony of the Akram Vijnan Simandhar temple near Surat, the association produced a written document in which it renounced all responsibility for Nirubahen Amin's actions.

The aversion between the two sections of the Akram Vijnan movement is currently only concealed under a thin veil of silence publicly observed by the followers of both sides. Nirubahen Amin is said to have taken advantage of her position 'as a nurse' to claim greatest closeness to the Dada out of greed and depression. And Kanu Patel is painted as a 'religious imposter' who claims *jnani* status on no merit. Stories about the embezzlement of community funds to cover Kanu's business losses are also circulating. The religious leaders of both groups pressurise their followers to take sides or to risk losing the *jnana*, 'because the turmoil of doubt caused in the mind will attract more *karmas*, if you support both sides, you lose your *jnana*'.[94] Most followers understand this of course not in *karmik*, but in personal terms, and fear to lose spiritual and social support. An atmosphere of supernatural angst therefore prevails in the Akram Vijnan community today.

Routinisation of Charisma

The developments shortly before and after the death of A.M. Patel correspond well to the pattern outlined in Max Weber's theory of the routinisation (*Veralltäglichung*) of charisma. In fact, the two solutions offered – the attempt to perpetuate the charismatic cult of the Dada through a designated, similarly qualified successor, on the one hand, and the objectification of charisma in *mantras* and designated ritual acts with a magical link to the original charismatic source, on the other hand – are paradigmatic options of the model. The two groups also play the two sides of the ambiguous Dada cult against each other: the Dada as the medium of Simandhar, and the

Dada as a self-enlightened being. Since both groups tend to rely more and more on the creation of religious institutions and rituals, in particular the devotional worship of the Dada image, it seems that Nirubahen is better placed, because of the detachment of the source of charisma from her person to a *mantra* which can be transmitted from *guru* to *guru*. Therefore, (a) her future successors will not have to pretend to be self-enlightened, but will qualify for the performance of the *jnana vidhi* by merely receiving the blessings of their predecessor and the Dada's *mantra*, (b) the leadership and the *brahmacharya vrata* can be given by the spiritual leader, or *atmajnani*, of the movement to both men and women, and (c) the option of a pure image cult, entirely detached from a *guru* lineage, is maintained by the consecration of a new temple, the Mahavideha Tirthadham, in Ahmedabad on 31 December 1999, to match the temple of Kanu Patel's followers in Surat. Ultimately, the anti-female position of the Jay Sacchidananda Sangha and the lack of a successor to Kanu Patel will probably turn the tide in favour of Nirubahen Amin, who is already more popular than Kanu Patel outside India, where she has founded the Jaya Sacchidananda U.K. and other community organisations in the U.S. However, it should be noted that some followers of the Dada, most of them *mahatmas* associated with the Jay Sacchidananda Sangha, accept neither Nirubahen nor Kanubhai as their *gurus* but continue to venerate the Dada and Simandhar Svami. Similar forms of routinisation of charisma can be found amongst the Shrimad Rajachandra movement and the Kanji Svami Panth.[95]

Conclusion

In contrast to the theistic Vaishnava traditions, which propagate devotional religion (*bhakti marga*), and to Shrimad Rajachandra, who promulagated a '*kramik*' combination of devotion, asceticism and knowledge, with an emphasis on devotion, the new Akram Vijnan movement professes to follow the path of knowledge (*jnana marga*). However, a comparison with the Pushtimargis in Ujjain, for instance, who are aptly described in Peter Bennett's ethnography *The Path of Grace*, shows that the Dada Bhagavan cult incorporated key elements of Vaishnava forms of worship in their religious practices. Both traditions share the doctrinal rejection of asceticism and of strict rituals, and claim to offer a universalistic trans-religious vision open even to Muslims or Christians. However, the mediating role of the *guru* is pre-eminent and often no clear distinction is made between god and man. In practice, the professed doctrinal universalism therefore invariably turns into *guru* cults with exclusivist tendencies. The most visible resemblance between the Pushtimargis and the Akram Vijnan Marg (as well as the Svaminarayan tradition) is the practice of symbolically surrendering all worldly attachments, that is *karmas*, including one's property, through a formal resolution (*sankalpa*), called *samarpana*, at the point of initiation.[96]

In contrast to Jaina mendicants, the *sadgurus* of both the Rajachandra and the Akram Vijnan movement have in common with Hindu *gurus* that they often present themselves as *avatars*, as manifestations of gods on earth, or as their mediums. However, in practice the distinction between incarnate god and medium is hard to maintain. Gombrich and Obeyesekere, who investigated the current urban resurgence of 'spirit cults' in Sri Lanka, which combine elements of traditional Buddhism with influences of *bhakti* and Tantra, have observed:

> One can of course argue a difference between miracles, which a god produces by his grace to favour his devotees, and magic, a technique by which humans can coerce unseen powers. But when the miracle-working god takes human form, the distinction becomes blurred...[97]

Gombrich and Obeyesekere interpret these spirit cults as imports from Hinduism, though the Buddhist *bodhisattva* worship takes similar forms. P.S. Jaini, who often acts as a defender of the classical view of Jainism, has also argued that similar popular forms of *bhakti* religiosity amongst Jains are forms of Hinduisation (though imported in a consciously Jainised form):[98]

For Jainas, in other words, no synthesis of the human and the supramundane was ever possible; hence the *tirthankaras* [and not the *bodhisattvas*] remained the highest models of spiritual development, and such tantric practices as identification of the self with the deity were simply out of the question.[99]

Although Jaini principally denies the existence of a 'Jain' cult of chosen deities (*ishta-devata*),[100] he does not fail to mention the frequent examples of Vaishnava and Tantric influences on Jaina texts and practices such as the deification of the Jina, the visualisation of omniscience or the concentration on that which transcends form, mentioned for instance in Hemachandra's *Yogashastra*, which 'give the meditator a kind of experimental contact with the "ultimate Self" (*paramatman*)', an experience which, Jaini hastens to add, is 'not equivalent to that of *siddhahood*' itself.[101] J.E. Cort also noticed that Murtipujak Jains in Gujarat often blur 'the distinction between the Jinas and the living mendicants, in the same manner that Vaishnavs oftentimes conflate Vishnu-Krishna and their living gurus'.[102] However, 'the Shvetambar Murtipujak guru remains much more a human being, albeit a special, powerful human being, whereas among the Hindu guru cults the guru tends to assume the status of a deity.'[103]

I would argue that the 'Digambara Mahayana' teachings of Kundakunda, which have greatly influenced a variety of Jaina lay movements, including the Shrimad Rajachandra movement and the Akram Vijnan Marg, cannot entirely be brought under the verdict of Hinduisation.[104] The fact that they could be easily reinterpreted by the layman A.M. Patel from 'theistic', 'devotional' and 'Tantric' perspectives rather seems to reflect the fact that there is not one Jainism made up of a fixed set of discernable 'core beliefs'[105] promoted by identifiable individuals or groups but a plurality of doctrinal elements and practices that are compiled, combined and labelled in various ways.[106] What is certainly special about any self-consciously 'Jain' movement is the principal emphasis on the soteriological importance of non-injury and the soteriological goal of liberation preached by the Jinas, which is shared by both Kundakunda and the Akram Vijnan movement, although the latter adopts the Samkhya ontology of the passive soul whereas Kundakunda retains the traditional Jaina interpretation of the soul as intrinsically active. In his analysis of Kundakunda's concept of self-realisation, William Johnson writes: 'one can only speculate on the effect of such ideas on the Jaina layperson,' arguing

> that any changes must have been largely in terms of expectation rather than practice...such theoretical possibilities as that of a 'Jina-nature' nevertheless make liberation *seem* closer. They are affectively satisfying....[107]

The logical, although not necessary, conclusion Johnson writes, for those who take Kundakunda's mystical philosophy seriously 'would seem to be abandonment of the external forms of Jaina ascetic life in favour of self-realisation, to be achieved by meditation on the pure self. It never quite comes to this'.[108]

This paper has attempted to show that there is now a religious lay movement which works out the implications of Kundakunda's ideas from new angles. It can from different points of view, be interpreted as a form of 'Digambara Mahayana', 'Jaina Samkhya', 'Jaina Vaishnava syncretism' or 'Jaina Tantra'.[109] However, to the participant it does not merely represent an admixture of elements of Buddhist, Vaishnava and canonical, classical or mystical Jaina sources, to the latter of which it is, nevertheless, closely related, but a new doctrinal synthesis, which offers salvation to everyone in the mythical pure land of Mahavideha Kshetra through the grace of Simandhar Svami. Because of the similarities in doctrinal structure, this synthesis can be legitimately labelled 'Jaina Mahayana'.

Notes

*This essay is based on intermittent field research in London, Ahmedabad, Surat and Mumbai between 1997 and 2001. If not indicated otherwise, all texts and translations have been cited verbatim from the literature of the Akram Vijnan Marg.

1. Walther Schubring, *The Doctrine of the Jainas: Described after the Old Sources.* Translated from the original German by S.B. Shrotri, 2nd English Edition (New Delhi: Motilal Banarsidass, 1935/2000), 60f.

2. Robert Williams, *Jaina Yoga: A Survey of the Medieval Shravakacaras* (London: Oxford University Press, 1963/1983), xix.

3. Padmanabh S. Jaini, *The Jaina Path of Purification* (Berkeley: University of California Press, 1979), 88. See Chapter 9 on the issue of Hinduisation.

4. I will not attempt to trace the history of specific doctrinal imports from Mahayana Buddhism into Jainism but rather emphasise the general structural parallels to a new Jain religious movement.

5. If anyone should prefer the label 'Jaina Samkhya' or 'Jaina–Vaishvana syncretism' for the characterisation of the Akram Vijnan Marg, I would not object, since the thrust of my main argument is not affected by this.

6. The Digambara *acharya*, Kundakunda, lived in South India sometime between the first and the eighth century CE.

7. The 'import' of elements of Mahayana, Samkhya and Vedanta philosophies, especially by authors such as Kundakunda who are associated with the Digambara Jain 'mystical' tradition, has been discussed in particular by Helmuth von Glasenapp, *Jainism: An Indian Religion of Salvation.* Translated from the original German by Shridhar B. Shroti (New Delhi: Motilal Banarsidass, 1925/1999), 504; A. Chakravarti, 'Introduction', in *Acharya Kundakunda's Samayasara, with English Translation and Commentary based upon Amritacandra's Atmakhyat*, 3rd Edition, edited by A. Chakravarti (New Delhi: Bharatiya Jnanpith, 1925/1989), 103ff; Adinath Neminath Upadhye, 'Introduction', in *Shri Yogindudeva's Paramatmaprakasha (Paramappapayasu): An Apabhramsha Work on Jaina Mysticism* (Bombay: Sheth Manilal Revashankar Jhaveri, 1937), 29ff; Walther Schubring, 'Kundakunda echt und unecht', in *Zeitschrift der Deutschen Morgenländischen Gesellschaft* 107 (1957) 568–74; Ram Jee Singh, *The Jaina Concept of Omniscience*

(Ahmedabad: L.D. Institute of Indology, 1974), 54–57, n. 25; Bansidhar Bhatt, 'Vyavahara-Naya and Nishchaya-Naya in Kundakunda's Works', in *Zeitschrift der Deutschen Morgenländischen Gesellschaft, Supplement II* (1974) 283; Bansidhar Bhatt, 'On the Epithet: *nataka* for the *Samayasara* of Kundakunda,' in *Jainism and Prakrit in Ancient and Medieval India*, edited by N.N. Bhattacharya (New Delhi: Manohar, 1994), 432, 455; William J. Johnson, *Harmless Souls: Karmic Bondage and Religious Change in Early Jainism with Special Reference to Umasvati and Kundakunda* (New Delhi: Motilal Banarsidass, 1995), 45, 180ff, 281–87; Nalini Balbir and Colette Caillat, 'Introduction', in *Yogindu: Lumière de l'Absolu*, traduit de l'apabhramsha et présenté par Nalini Balbir et Colette Caillat, Préface de Bernard Sergent (Paris: Éditions Payot & Rivages, 1999), 40ff.

8. Heinz Bechert, 'Buddhist Modernism: Present Situation and Current Trends', in *Buddhismus, Staat und Gesellschaft in den Ländern des Theravada-Buddhismus. Band II. Burma, Kambodscha, Laos, Thailand.* Neuausgabe mit Supplementen sowie Personen-und Sachregister (Göttingen: Seminar für Indologie and Buddhismuskunde, 2000), xxxii.

9. The student of Mahayana Buddhism will find numerous structural similarities in the following description of the Akram Vijnan Marg, although I refrained from pointing them out one by one, to mention only the significance of wisdom, compassion, devotion and magic in the cult of the *bodhisattva* and the concepts of *Buddha kshetra* and *tathagatagarbha*. There are equally important parallels to Vaishnavism.

10. Statement of a male devotee of the Akram Vijnan Marg in London.

11. On Simandhar Svami and Mahavideha see Mohanlal Mehta and K. Rishabh Chandra, compilers, *Prakrit Proper Names, Part II* (Ahmedabad: L.D. Institute of Indology, 1972), 799; and Paul Dundas, *The Jains* (London: Routledge, 1992), 255f, n. 65. Simandhar is not only worshipped by the Akram Vijnan Marg. The Murtipujaka Tapagaccha tradition of the *acharyas* Buddhisagarswi, Kailassagarswi, Kalyansagar and Subodhsagar, inspired the construction of the first modern Simandhar temple in Mahesana in north Gujarat. Simandhar is also worshipped by the Digambar followers of Kanji Svami. References to Simandhar abound in the

post-canonical literature, but until recently he never became the focus of the religions cult, like Mahavira.

12. It seems that the Jaina *tirthankaras* in Mahavideha play a similar role to the Buddhas in the pure lands of Mahayana Buddhism, while A.M. Patel, the Dada Bhagavan, resembles the *bodhisattvas* in Buddhism, who are able to communicate with the Buddhas in the Buddha fields with supernatural means. Although outwardly human, he acts as a self-awakened enlightened being, and thus as a god on earth, for the benefit of others. However, this is not yet recognised in the scholarly literature. See Suzuko Ohira, *Study*, 204f.

13. For conceivable reasons for its creation see Ohira, *Study*, 33, 168. The possibility of visiting the Mahavidehas, where always 4–24 (the number varies from text to text) Jinas live due to the absence of the time cycle, is discussed already in the canon. See *Viyahapannatti* (*Bhagavati*) 25.6.11 (=895b). On Mahavideha and its *arhats* see in particular *Thana* (*Sthananga*) 3.390, 4.137, 4.315, *Uvavaiya* (*Aupapatika*) 101–116, *Viyahapannatti* 20.8 (=791b); Willibald Kirfel, *Die Kosmographie der Inder nach Quellen dargestellt* (Hildesheim: Georg Olms, 1920/1967), 229–42; Schubring, *Doctrine*, 220, 222. The possibility of achieving liberation in Mahavideha is described in canonical narrative texts such as the *Nayadhammakahao* (*Jnatridharmakatha*) I. 1, 19, 13, 16, 19, etc. and the *Uvasagadasao* (*Upasakadasha*) 2, 7, etc.

14. See the commentary on the *Pravachanasara* 1.3–5 by the twelfth century *acharya*, Amritachandra, in Acharya Kundakunda, *Pravachanasara together with the commentary, Tattva-dipika by Amritachandra Suri* (=PS). Vol. 1. Jain Literature Society Series. English translation by Barend Faddegon, edited with an Introduction by F.W. Thomas (Cambridge: Cambridge University Press 1935), 3–4; Dundas, *The Jains*, 230.

15. Late-canonical mythological and cosmological texts such as the *Jambudvipaprajnapti* do not refer to the conveyance of omniscience to Bharata through an act of grace. Bharata is invariably characterised as a *pratyeka buddha*, a self-enlightened being. He is however the only householder mentioned in the canon who gained omniscience spontaneously, without first having been initiated as a monk. See Schubring, *Doctrine*, 22, 225; Acharya Hemachandra, *Trishashtishalakapurushacharitra* (=TSPC), translated by Helen

M. Johnson as *The Lives of Sixty-three Illustrious Persons*, Vol. 1, Verse 715–45 (Baroda: Oriental Institute, 1931), 376–78.

16. A.M. Patel, *Aptavani I*, edited by Khetsi Narsi Shah, translated by V. Pathak and G. Shah (Bombay: Sacchidananda Sangha, 1983), 11, cf. 70. Compare the original Gujarati text, *Aptavani* (=AV), Vol. 1–12, compiled and edited by Nirubahen Amin (Amadavad: Dada Bhagavan Foundation, 1995–1999), Vol. 1, pp. 9, 57 (the first edition of Vol. 1 was compiled by Kanu Patel and Niru Amin and published on 15 July 1973 by the Jay Sacchidananda Sangha in Bombay).

17. A.M. Patel, in Khetsi Narsi Shah, 'Foreword', in A.M. Patel, *Science of Liberation*, compiled by Aptaputra Dr Shailesh P. Mehta, edited by K.N. Shah (Bombay: Sacchidananda Sangha, 1995), iv. See the original passage AV I, 6f, and its English rendition in A.M. Patel, *Aptavani I*, 7f.

18. Rajachandra's original name was Lakshminandan Maheta. Although he rejected traditional *gurus* and his contemporary Jaina mendicants who acquired their charisma only *qua* position, he taught *bhakti* towards a truly enlightened *guru* as the principal path towards salvation. (See Emma Salter, 'Unity and Diversity amongst the followers of Shrimad Rajachandra', in *Jinamanjari* 23, 1 (2001): 32–51.) His emphasis on *atmadharma* derives from the tradition of Kundakunda.

19. Another word that he often used was *muktabhava*, or freedom from the effects of feelings. See Nirubahen Amin, 'Who is Dada Bhagavan?' in *Dadavani* (Ahmedabad: Dada Bhagwan Foundation, n.d.), 30.

20. The only self-description I found was in a short discourse (translated?) in Hindi in A.M. Patel, *Aptavani I*, 2nd edition, edited by Nirubahen Amin (Madras: Dada Bhagavan Foundation, 1973/1995):

> *Prashna: Ap jnani kaise hue?*
> *Dada: Yah* but natural *ho gaya hai. 1958 mem Surat steshan par lakri ki bench par sham ko suryastakal ke samay andar achanak jnan prakash ho gaya. Sare brahmand ko ham ne dar asal vastu ke rup meim dekha. Tab se vah 'jnan' nirantar prakash deta hi rahata hai. Yah* natural production *hai. Khud prayatna karke prapta karna bahut hi mushkil hai.* (215)

21. Amin, 'Who is Dada Bhagavan?' 30.

22. A.M. Patel utilises the terminology of Digambara mysticism, which has parallels in the Vedantic tradition, in order to explain the relationship between soul and body; in particular, Kundakunda's distinction between three aspects of the soul: *jiva* (life), *atma* (individual self-consciousness), and *paramatma* (supreme self or God), which is frequently equated with *shuddhatma*. Instead of *atma*, he often uses the term *pratishthi atma* to mark the difference between ego-centred erroneous (*vikalpa*) self-consciousness and the pure self. For *jiva* he often uses the word *bhana*, or consciousness, stating: 'A "*Jiva*" does not know "who am I" ' (A.M. Patel, *Aptavani* I, 115, cf. AV I, 94).

23. That is, a stepless or instant experience, not generated through specific religious practices.

24. See Nirubahen Amin, 'Who is "Dada Bhagwan",' in A.M. Patel, *The Essence of All Religion*, edited by Nirubahen Amin (Ahmedabad: Dada Bhagwan Foundation, 2000), iv, cf. Nishpakshpati Trimandir Sankul Mahavideh Tirthadham (=NTS), editor, *Trimandir Paricay* (Surat: Mahavideh Tirthadham, n.d.), 15.

25. Padmanabh, S. Jaini, 'On the *Sarvajnatva* (Omniscience) of Mahavira and the Buddha', *Buddhist Studies in the Honour of I.B. Horner*, edited by L. Cousins et al. (Dordrecht: D. Reidel Publishing Company, 1974), 71f; and R.J. Singh, *Jaina Concept of Omniscience*, identified two different interpretations of 'omniscience' in the Jaina tradition, 'namely, omniscience as knowledge of essentials [the eternal self, P.F.] and omniscience as universal knowledge' (56). Kundakunda (*Niyamasara* 158, in ibid., 53) tried to combine both views. Consistent with Kundakunda's views, A.M. Patel claimed to know 'every atom of the soul and the non-soul, separating both of them' (*Aptavani* I, 20, cf. AV I, 16).

26. The best discussion of *samyak darshana* is Chapter 5 of Jaini's *Path of Purification*, 134–56.

27. 'Even a degree of *Keval Gyana*, "we" call *Pragna*...Absolute Omni-Science or *Keval Gyana* is at the completion of 360° full' (A.M. Patel, *Aptavani* I, 272).
   'A circle has 360°. The English are on 110°, the Muslims on 120°, the Paris on 140° and the Hindus on 220°; and all of them look at reality from their own points of view...But "We" are sitting at the centre-completing full circle of reality and so our vision is perfect. A Gnani [a realised soul] sitting at the centre has the right [true]

perception of reality...But..."We" also could not digest 4° more and hence "we" are poised on 356°' (ibid., 207).

28. 'Knowing here means realising' (Singh, *Jaina Concept of Omniscience*, 51). See also Johnson, *Harmless Souls*, 238.

29. A.M. Patel sees the 'superimposed' or embodied self as a mixture of ego (I) and attachment (me): *ahamkara* (*hum*) *ane mamta* (*marum*) (AV I, 109, cf. A.M. Patel, *Aptavani* I, 134f).

30. A.M. Patel, *Aptavani I*, 7, 6. Compare the following analysis of A.M. Patel which uses techniques of reversal that are frequently found in Tantric literature. It is a good example of the way in which 'the knowledge (sans intellect)' is applied: 'Nobody likes to be insulted. But "We" say that it is very "helping". Respect and insult are the sweet-bitter juice of the ego. Let me tell you, he who insults you has come to squeeze the bitter taste out of you. When somebody said, "You are a fool", he drew away that juice from you. The ego gets broken in proportion to the amount of juice extracted from it and this is done, without our labour, by someone else...We "*Gnani Purusha*" are "*Abuddha*" (sans intellect); but know that the "*Gnani*" possesses so many powers that he can easily squeeze all the juice of the ego. But you don't have such powers' (A.M. Patel, *Aptavani* I, 119, cf. AVI, 97).

31. Amin, 'Who is "Dada Bhagavan",' v.

32. Interview with Kanu Patel, 1999.

33. The word *apta* means also trustworthy, reliable, authoritative. For its use in Jainism, see Jayandra Soni, *The Notion of Apta in Jaina Philosophy: The 1995 Roop Lal Jain Lecture* (University of Toronto, 1996).

34. Only the *mohaniya*, or delusion-producing *karmas* can be destroyed by the *Jnani*. Thereafter, the aspirants are said to be able to prevent the influx of new *karmas* through the practice of passionlessness. However, the already accumulated *karmas* need to come to fruition naturally. If they are acted out dispassionately they will not bind new *karmas*.

35. It is believed that in the presence of a Jina or his immediate disciples, arhatship can be achieved within a few births through the annihilation of the *mohaniya karmas* via *kshayaka samyaktva*, insight through destruction, in the eighth *gunasthana*, or stage of purification (Jaini, *Path of Purification*, 146).

36. A doctrinal impossibility, which devotees explain was made possible by the intervention of the gods.

37. For a detailed description and analysis of the rite, see Peter Flügel, *Present Lord*, Forthcoming.

38. Shrimad Rajachandra, *Shrimad Rajachandra*, edited by Manubhai B. Modi, 7th Edition (Agas: Shrimad Rajachandra Ashram, 1951/1995), 679. Translated in U.K. Pungaliya, *Philosophy and Spirituality of Shrimad Rajachandra* (Jaipur: Prakrit Bharati Academy, 1996), 204. For affirmative references to the example of Rajachandra, who is popularly called Kripalu Deva, or merciful god, see A.M. Patel, *Aptavani* I, 207f. (cf. AV I, 97) and *Generation Gap*, 62: 'If you pray to Kripalu Dev (another *Gnani Purush*) or Dada Bhagavan, it will be the same, because they both are the same in the sense of *Atma*. They are physically different in appearance, but in essence the same. Even if you invoke Lord Mahavir, it is one and the same.'

39. A.M. Patel declared that only three *jnanis* ever existed in Bharata (India) since the *nirvana* of the last *tirthankara*: Acharya Kundakunda, Shrimad Rajachandra and himself. He did not regard the neo-Digambara *brahmachari*, Kanji Svami (1889–1980), as a *jnani*. For Kanji Svami, see Dundas, *The Jains*, 227–32.

40. Kundakunda maintained the principle that the soul is active, though it can only transform itself. See Acharya Kundakunda, *Samayasara, with English Translation and Commentary based upon Amritachandra's Atmakhyat* (=SS), 3rd Edition, edited by A. Chakravarti (New Delhi: Bharatiya Jnanpith, 1925/1989), verse 340–41, 202f. See also A. Chakravarti, 'Introduction' 108, 157f; and Johnson, *Harmless Souls*, 292–95, on Samkhya and Vedanta influences on Kundakunda's philosophy.

41. Like Rajachandra (SR 238), A.M. Patel was strongly influenced by the Bhagavad Gita, in which, in the words of J.A.B. van Buitenen, *The Bhagavad Gita in the Mahabharata: Text and Translation* (=BG) (Chicago: The University of Chicago Press, 1981), at least in certain passages, 'a three-order universe (God, *jivas, prakriti*) is superimposed on a Samkhya two-order universe (*purushas, prakriti*) with the implications not wholly thought through' (169, n. 2, commentary on BG 37).

42. The two-truth theory in a mature form was introduced into Jainism by Kundakunda, *Samayasara*, Verse 7, 14f.

43. Rajachandra writes in his famous text on the six principles (*shatpad*), that it is the activity of the soul itself that binds *karma*: '*atma che*', '*te nitya che*', '*che karta nijakarma*', '*che bhokta*', '*vali moksha che*', '*moksha upaya sudharma*' (*Atmasiddhi* 43, in Rajachandra, *Shrimad Rajachandra*, 538). In other words, 'the soul is the doer (*karta*)'. A.M. Patel, on the other hand, insists that 'the soul is not the doer', it is 'only the knower'. Accordingly, Rajachandra teaches a more traditional interpretation of Jainism, although he also writes: '*karta bhokta karmano, vibhava varte jyamya; vritti vahi nijabhavamam, thayo akarta tyamya*' (*Atmasiddhi*, 121, 554): 'In delusion one does the deeds, receives the fruits; but non-doer he is, when he sows the knowledge-seeds, and constantly remains the knower' (*The Self-Realisation, Being a Translation of Atma-Śiddhi of Shrimad Rajachandra by Brahmachari Govardhanadasajira*, Agas: Shrimad Rajachandra Ashram, 1985/1994, 87). The principal difference between the teachings of Rajachandra and A.M. Patel is that the latter emphasises exclusively the religious value of the *nishchaya* perspective, whereas Rajachandra combines, often in an unexplicated way, *nishchaya naya* and *vyavahara naya*. The classical Jaina view is that without taking into account the *vyavahara* perspective, religion remains ethically impotent and salvation impossible. For Rajachandra, world-renunciation is ultimately indispensable. On this point, see Pungaliya, *Philosophy and Spirituality of Shrimad Rajachandra*, 285f.

44. A.M. Patel, in N. Amin's 'Introduction' to A.M. Patel, *Generation Gap*, ii.

45. These powers include mind-reading, *manaparyaya jnana*. See A.M. Patel, *Aptavani I*, 90, cf. AV I, 75.

46. Ibid., 204, cf. AV I, 185.

47. Ibid., 119, cf. AV I, 96f.

48. Ibid., 55, cf. AV I, 45f.

49. Ibid., 27, cf. AV I, 21f.

50. Ibid., 58, cf. AV I, 47: '*Jyare akram marg mam jnani purush mathe hath muke to pote purush thai akhi prakriti ne samaji jay.*'

51. Ibid., 21f, cf. AV I, 15f.

52. God is, here, the soul and the boss is A.M. Patel, though the statement is deliberately ambiguous.

53. A.M. Patel, *Aptavani I*, 71, cf. AV I, 59.

54. Kundakunda also devaluates scriptural knowledge in favour of

self-realisation, but he does not mention the possibility of a transfer of self-knowledge.

55. Krishna Kumar Dixit, *Jaina Ontology* (Ahmedabad: L.D. Institute of Indology, 1971), 133, and Jaini, *Path of Purification*, explained that the common sense use of the term *pratyaksha* for 'ordinary, sense-mediated cognition' is a specific historically development (ibid., 122, n. 44).

56. A.M. Patel, *Aptavani* I, 72f, cf. AV I, 59f.

57. Although the term 'astral body' is occasionally used, this is apparently achieved without even utilising the so-called communication body, or *aharaka sharira*. See Schubring, *Doctrine*, 137–39, on the Jaina doctrine of the five bodies. A.M. Patel, *Vartaman Tirthankar Shri Simandhar Svami*, edited by Nirubahen Amin (Chennai: Dada Bhagavan Phaundeshan, 1994), said elsewhere that the grace of Simandhar operates only indirectly through *anumodana*, his empathy (13).

58. *Hum bijo mahavira chum, em mane atmika shakti vade janayum che* (SR 27, 165f).

59. Also Kanu Patel. Paul Dundar, 'Somnolent Sutras: Scriptural Commentary in Shvetambra Jainism', *Journal of Indian Philosophy* 24 (1996): 82f., also interprets Simandhar as a *tirthankara* of the future, comparable to the future Buddha Maitreya: 'Shvetambara sources suggest that...only goddesses could have immediate access to Simandhara.'

60. The Akram Vijnan Marg distinguishes between final *moksha* and living *moksha*. See Sharadaprasad Ramadevanahalli. See page 2 of http://www.geocities.com/Atens/Acropolois/7591/gnani.html. Two other websites contain useful conformation on the Akram Vijnan Marg are: http://www.dadabhagawan.org and http://www.dadashri.org.

61. See Jaini, *Path of Purification*, 142f.

62. In other sources, rebirth after a strict monastic life is presented as the standard method for reaching Mahavideha. See the story of Ambada in the *Uvavaiya Suttam* (*Aupapatika Sutra*) 101–116, which presents Mahavideha without reference to Simandhar Svami, who seems to be a historically later invention.

63. The problem is that the realisation of old *karma* automatically binds new *karmas* of the same type. It is therefore assumed that the cycle of bondage cannot be interrupted merely by assuming 'a good state

of mind' and waiting for the natural maturation (*udaya*) of *karma*, but only through a slow and painful process of purification of one's old *karmas* (*apurva karana*) through a logical sequence of stages of asceticism and meditation which cause the premature maturation (*udirana*) of *karma* in a controlled way. See Helmuth von Glasenapp, *Die Lehre vom Karma in der Philosophie der Jainas* (Leipzig: Otto Harrassowitz, 1915) 81; and Schubring, *Doctrine*, 325, cf. 178f.

64. The Bhagavad Gita follows the Samkhya view. The following well-known passage must have influenced A.M. Patel: 'At any rate, actions are performed by the three forces of nature, but deluded by self-attribution, one thinks: "I did it!" But he who knows the principles that govern the distribution of those forces and their actions knows that the forces are operating on the forces, and he takes no interest in actions' (BG 3.27–3.33, 83f).

65. This technique is a major improvement over the schematic rites of repentance (*pratikramana*) which are obligatory for Jaina mendicants. For a detailed analysis of the ethical principles and the rites of purification of the Akram Vijnan Marg, see Flügel, *Present Lord.*

66. Johnson, *Harmless Souls*, 271, 281f, 293, etc. notes a similar 'eclectic' combination of gnosis and ethics in Kundakunda's *Samayasara*, and argues—*pace* Schubring, *Kundakunda*, 574, but with B. Bhatt, *Vyavahara-Naya and Nishchaya-Naya in Kundakunda's Works*, 288, who attributes only the gnostic sections to Kundakunda—that the text, whose content appears to be inherently 'contradictory', must be the product of more than one author and compiled with a social purpose in mind (265, 307). A similar theory could obviously not explain A.M. Patel's views.

67. A.M. Patel, *Who Am I*, edited by Amin, 34.

68. The idea that self-knowledge is the true form of renunciation, not the renunciation of physical objects, had been stated by Kundakunda (SS 34, translated by Johnson, *Harmless Souls*, 288).

69. Nirubahen Amin, compiler, *Tirthankar of Today Shree Simandhar Swami*, translated by G.A. Shah (Bombay: Shri Dada Bhagvan Vitarag Trust, 1983), 22.

70. *Akram Vijnan* 20, August 1999, 35.

71. The great majority are Patidars, the dominant agricultural caste of Gujarat, who traditionally practice some form of Vaishnavism. Most of them perform the emotive Krishna Bhakti worship of Vallabhacharya's Pushtimarga, the path seeking the grace of God, or

the Svaminarayan tradition of Sahajananda Svami (1781–1830). An excellent ethnography of the Pushtimarga is Peter Bennett's *The Path of Grace: Social Organisation and Temple Worship in a Vaishnava Sect* (New Delhi: Hindustan Publications, 1993).

72. Both wings of the Akram Vijnan Marg distinguish today three religious statuses: (1) The spiritual leader, Kanu Patel on Nirubahen Amin, who carries the title *pujya atmajnani*, venerable knower of the soul, and who alone can perform initiations and the rite of knowledge, (2) the group of approximately fifty male and seven to ten female celibate disciples (*brahmachari* or *brahmacharini*), called *aptaputras* or *aptaputris*, or true spiritual sons or daughters of the Dada, the one with the speech of truth (*aptavani*), and (3) the common believers, who, after their initiation, are either called *mumukshus*, seekers for salvation, like the followers of Rajachandra, or *mahatmas*, great souls. The leaders of the local or all-embracing lay associations are distinguished with the title *sanghapati*.

73. The reason for this is that rebirth in Mahavideha Kshetra is believed to be achievable through the creation of a link of mutual indebtedness (*rinanubandha*) with Simandhar generated by devotional practices (A.M. Patel, in Amin, *Tirthankar of Today*, 29f). Because Simandhar is a living *tirthankara* he can indeed, if accessible, enter relationships of reciprocity, in contrast to the liberated 24 Jinas of our world. Simandhar thus plays a similar role in the religious imagination of his devotees as miracle-working Jaina ascetics or the deceased *dada guru devas* of the Kharataragaccha described by Caroline Humphrey and James Laidlaw in their book *The Archetypal Actions of Ritual: A Theory of Ritual Illustrated by the Jain Rite of Worship* (Oxford: Oxford University Press, 1994), 50, etc.

74. See AV (1995–1999). In contrast to Rajachandra, who explained his teachings mainly in his letters to his closest friends, collected in the volume *Shrimad Rajachandra*, A.M. Patel did not write tracts or letters on religious subjects. His discourses were informal conversations in Gujarati with the participants of his *satsang*. Although he has not attempted to produce a work of systematic theology, his teachings are logically coherent. Only the first volume of his published discourses is available in translation. See A.M. Patel, *Aptavani* I.

75. Natubhai B. Patel, editor, *Svarup Vijnan: Pujya Dada Bhagavan ni Jagatkalyan ni Vani Emna Ja Shabdo mam*, Shreni 2–3 (Mumbai:

Shri Dada Bhagavan Vitarag Trast, 1989). Initially, A.M. Patel did not permit the taking of notes of his discourses, but Natubhai Patel convinced him that otherwise he could not remember much.

76. Apart from the first sentence of part 1, '(1) I bow before the unattached ones (*vitaraga*)', the first part of the text is identical with the (Murtipujaka) Jaina *Namaskara Mantra*. However, part 2–3 is idiosyncratic: '(2) Om. I bow before Lord Vasudeva [Krishna]. (3) Om. I bow before Shiva. Hail to the eternal truth, knowledge and bliss [of the pure soul].' In the original: (1) *namo vitaragaya*,... (2) *om namo bhagavate vasudevaya*. (3) *om namo shivaya, jay sacchidananda* (Nirubahen Amin, compiler, *Charan Vidhi*). 2nd Edition (Chennai: Dada Bhagavan Phaundeshan, 1998).

77. A.M. Patel, in *Dadavani*, n.d., 13–16. For a rendering into English, see A.M. Patel, *Ultimate Knowledge*, edited by Rakesh M. Patel (London, 1994), 68–70. The key verse is no. 13: 'The real self is god and therefore I see god in all living beings' (70).

78. A.M. Patel, in *Dadavani*, 18–22. For a rendition into English, see A.M. Patel, *Ultimate Knowledge*, 73–76. The text is a variation on the theme of the five great vows (*mahavrata*) of the Jainas: '(1) He Dada Bhavagan! Give me the infinite inner strength not to hurt, cause someone to hurt, nor instigate anyone to hurt the ego of any living being, even in the slightest extent...' (73).

79. See N. Amin, *Charan Vidhi*.

80. The devotional form of this rite which aims at the creation of a union between the worshipper and the worshipped was almost certainly inspired by Amritachandra's depiction of Kundakunda's legendary yogic travels to Mahvideha in search for inspiration from Simandhar. See Amritachandra, *Tattva-dipika*, 3–4.

81. The original Gujarati text of the *mantra* is identical with the first verse of the *Namaskar Vidhi* text as reproduced in footnote 81. Cf. A.M. Patel, *Vartaman Tirthankar Shri Simandhar Svami*, 11.

82. N. Amin, in: N. Amin, *Tirthankar of Today*, 24f.

83. A.M. Patel, *Aptavani* I, 73, cf. AV I, 60.

84. A similar arrangement – the image of the *sadguru* placed in another room underneath the Jina image – can be found at the temple in Agas, the main centre of the Rajachandra cult.

85. Both Nirubahen and Mina (Patel) taped all *satsangs* of this tour, and Mina's tape-recorder went on recording the conversation which took place after the *satsang*. It was later discovered and excerpts printed in

the magazine *Akram Vijnan*, June–July 1999, 5. (I had the opportunity to listen to a copy of the tape.)

86. In A.M. Patel, *Essence of All Religion*, 51.

87. NTS, 16.

88. These statements have been compiled from the author's interviews with Nirubahen Amin.

89. N. Amin, 'What is your spiritual state after "Gnan Ceremony"?', 30.

90. Johnson, *Harmless Souls*, 282f has introduced this term.

91. www. 7.1.1999 (the website does not exist anymore).

92. The followers of Nirubahen always insist on the special status of Gujarati as the religious language of the Dada.

93. Author's interview in 1999. However, the following critical report of a participant indicates that Kanu Patel's performance is not much different from Nirubahen's: '*Samyak darshan* cannot be achieved through magical means, but only through self effort. I met Kanubhai Patel and went through one of his sessions. Before shouting "*Hum shuddhatma chum*" everyone was touching Kanubhai's toe to get the power of enlightenment transferred from Simandhar while Kanubhai, who was in touch with Simandhar through *atmasakshatkar*, was muttering a *mantra*. It is impossible to get *samyak darshan* transferred this way. Even asceticism only prepares the ground. Important is only *atmasakshatkar*, experiencing one's own soul' (Interview with Anupam R. Shah, Mumbai).

94. Comment of an *aptaputra*.

95. Salter, *Unity and Diversity*, 44–49, observed three methods of tradition-building amongst the followers of Shrimad Rajachandra which she analysed in terms of two types of 'true gurus': (1) present/living *gurus* (*pratyaksha guru*): (a) *guru* lineages, (b) independent *gurus*; and (2) absent/dead *gurus* (*paroksha guru*)— Rajachandra and his immediate disciples. Both the veneration of the independent *gurus* and the absent *gurus*, she writes, are based on Rajachandra's writings and, at least in the latter case, also on his image. As in the case of the Akram Vijnan movement, there are at least two types of *guru* lineages: (a) the line of Rajachandra's personal disciples which terminated with the death of his last disciple (direct contact with the founder: lineage of Agas), and (b) a lineage based on the transmission of a secret *mantra* authenticated by Rajachandra (indirect contact with the founder: lineage of Sayla). On the Kanji Panth see W.J. Johnson, forthcoming.

96. Bennett, *Path of Grace*, 35, sees the initiation *mantra* as the 'lifeblood' of the segmentary lineage structure of the Pushtimargis.

97. Richard Gombrich and Gananath Obeyesekere, *Buddhism Transformed: Religious Change in Sri Lanka* (Princeton University Press, 1988), 55. The authors define Tantra 'by the doctrine that the same observances may yield either material benefits (*bhukti*)—notably power—or salvation (*mukti*)' (56).

98. Schubring, *Doctrine*, emphasised that already Umasvati, the principal author of classical Jain doctrine, managed to 'incorporate the magical faculties' (*iddhi, laddhi, siddhi*) frequently mentioned in the Canon into the system (316). He interprets this as a 'concession made to the popular belief' (ibid.).

99. P.S. Jaini, 'The Disappearance of Buddhism and the Survival of Jainism: A Study in Contrast', in *Studies in the History of Buddhism*, edited by A.K. Narain (New Delhi: BR Publications, 1980), 88.

100. Jaini, *Path of Purification*, 254. The analytical literature on Jain *bhakti* is still sparse. Lawrence A. Babb, *Absent Lord: Ascetics and Kings in a Jain Ritual Culture* (Berkeley: University of California Press, 1996), 177, *pace*, 93, tends to regard all types of Jaina Bhakti as variations of a 'common South Asian theme'; while Jaini, *Path of Purification*, writes that even though 'the Hindu concept of *ishta* has exerted a certain amount of influence...Jain devotionalism is oriented not towards a chosen deity (*ishta-devata*) but toward an ideal, the attainment of *kevala jnana*; thus reverence is given to all beings who have been or are actively engaged in pursuit of that ideal' (163, cf. 194f). John E. Cort, *Jains in the World: Religions Values and Ideology in India* (New York: Oxford University Press, 2001), has emphasised the non-derivative nature of Jaina Bhakti and proposed 'to conceive of *bhakti* as a style of religiosity, one that can be applied to almost any religions content' and suggested the 'term *enthusiam*...as an alternative gloss' (John E. Cort, 'Singing the Glory of Asceticism: Devotion of Asceticism in Jainism', in *Journal of the American Academy of Religion* 70.4 (2002): 738; while M. Whitney Kelting, *Singing to the Jinas: Jain Laywomen, Mandal Singing and the Negotiation of Jain Devotion* (Oxford: Oxford University Press, 2001) 113, emphasises the commitment to 'the right sentiment' and that in fact appeals to the 'grace and compassion of the Jinas are not seen as "un-Jain"' (13). The issue of the absence of the divine in Jainism has been extensively (and controversially) discussed by

Sinclair Stevenson, *The Heart of Jainism* (New Delhi: Manohar, 1915/1984), 289–98.

101. Jaini, *Path of Purification*, 256.
102. John E. Cort, *Jains in the World*, 114.
103. Ibid., 116. For a similar verdict see Jaini, *Path of Purification*, 254.
104. Cf. Schubring, *Kundakunda*, 569, on SS 141–44.
105. Cf. the *tattvas*, or truths, of classical Jainism.
106. See the work of Klaus Bruhn on Jaina texts.
107. Johnson, *Harmless Souls*, 282f. They are certainly also cognitively satisfying for the believer.
108. Johnson, 'The Religious Function of Jaina Philosophy: *Anekantavada* Reconsidered', in *Religion* 25 (1995): 47.
109. References to the scant literature on Tantric practices in Jainism can be found in the David G. White (ed.). *Tantra in Practice* (Princeton: Princeton University Press, 2000).

CHAPTER EIGHT

Devotion to the Buddha in Theravada and its Role in Meditation

KATE CROSBY

The Buddha Gotama is worshipped by the overwhelming majority of practising Theravada Buddhists. This fact has received some attention from scholars of Theravada, since it could be interpreted as a practice in contradiction to the formal doctrinal position in Theravada that, since the Buddha entered final enlightenment (*parinibbana*), he is no longer accessible to his followers.[1] He was mortal and has died for the last time.

This atheistic aspect of Theravada Buddhism is best represented by the Buddha's advice recorded in the *Mahaparinibbanasutta*, a text that relates the events of the last months of the Buddha's life. There the Buddha advises the monks, that after his passing they should resort to the Dhamma and the *vinaya*, i.e. the truth realised and taught by the Buddha, and the monastic code governing the lives of monks and nuns:

> Now the Exalted One [Buddha] addressed the venerable Ananda, and said—'It may be, Ananda, that in some of you the thought may arise, "The word of the master is ended, we have no teacher more!" But it is not thus, Ananda, that you should regard it. The Truths (*dhamma*), and the Rules of the Order (*vinaya*), which I have set forth and laid down for you all, let them, after I am gone, be the Teacher to you.'[2] (Rhys Davids 1966: 171)

Much time and effort on the part of Buddhists throughout the past two and a half millennia since the Buddha's *parinibbana* have been dedicated to preserving these two resources through the *Sutta* and *Abhidhamma* literary and scholastic traditions, on the one hand, and the texts of the *Vinaya Pitaka*, subsequent legal literature that developed from it and monastic lineages, on the other.

The dry rationality evidenced here is in tune with the general tenor of other teachings of the Buddha recorded in the canon. The Buddha's rejection of the efficacy of ritual (the meaning of *karma* in orthodox Vedic religion) and reinterpretation of *karma* in terms of intentional/ethical action is the key doctrine underlying Buddhist soteriology. In the much cited *Sigalovadasutta* 'Sutta of Advice to Sigala', the Buddha advises the Brahmin Sigala that the effective way to perform worship of the six directions is to look after the six directions, each of which is reinterpreted as a metaphor for a different set of the groups of people with whom one interacts. Rather than make offerings to north and east, etc. one should conduct one's relations with wife and children, friends, teachers, servants and others in a skillful and appropriate fashion. The advice in the *Mahaparinibbanasutta* to rely on the Dhamma and *vinaya* after the Buddha's death is similarly realistic and of clear practical benefit.

Nevertheless, the same *Mahaparinibbanasutta* also authorises the enshrinement of the Buddha's mortal remains after cremation in funerary mounds, *stupas*,[3] and their worship as meritorious activities.

> And as they treat the remains of a king of kings, so Vasetthas, should they treat the remains of the Tathagata [Buddha]. At the four crossroads a cairn [*thupo*] should be erected to the Tathagata. And whosoever shall there place garlands or perfumes or paint, or make salutation there, or become in its presence calm in heart—that shall long be to them for a profit and a joy. (Rhys Davids 1966: 183)

Hence *stupas* and the relics of the Buddha enshrined in them, or later enshrined in other ways, form a pivotal feature of the sacred landscape throughout the Buddhist world.

The *Mahaparinibbanasutta* also advocates pilgrimage to the sites of the key events in the life of the Buddha. These sites, augmented beyond the list in the text, form the core itinerary for Buddhist pilgrimage in India and Nepal. By extension, a number of Theravada texts relate further incidents in the life of the Buddha interposed between the events described in the canon. These additional details reveal that the Buddha, perceiving with his divine eye the needs and future glory of the future strongholds of Theravada Buddhism, such as Sri Lanka, Burma and Thailand, pays visits to them. During these visits he either leaves a relic, such as a lock of hair, or predicts the future discovery of them at that place, along with other events, such as the prosperity of Buddhism there or the sanctity and piety of a particular line of kings.[4] Most relations of this kind are found in a genre of literature known as 'chronicles' (*vamsa*). *Vamsas* mostly focus on the legitimacy of a particular monastic community, sacred site or object and authorise the protocol for the interaction between Sangha and state, in particular with the king. The religious practice of paying homage to the remains of the Buddha authorised in the *Mahaparinibbanasutta* continues to be pursued throughout the Theravada world in relation to those places associated with the Buddha, the relics of his remains or of items he used.[5] Some relics are particularly famous and receive mention in *vamsa* literature, but many temples also have their own relic, with or without a story of its derivation.

While worship of the Buddha continues to be performed in relation to a *stupa*, as authorised in the *Mahaparinibbanasutta*, it is more common to focus on a statue of the Buddha as the object of extended worship, more elaborate offerings or prayer. This latter aspect, the worship of a statue, adds to the dilemma between the doctrine and the meaning of Buddha worship. Is the Buddha seen to be somehow present in the statue, as a Hindu deity may be regarded as present in its *murti*? Does the representation of the Buddha as an individual detract from the idea that he no longer exists as an individual? In other words, does the worshipper believe the Buddha is still 'out there' and able to interact with him/her, in the same way as a god?

There are some aspects of the practice of worshipping the Buddha that are doctrinally unproblematic. Recollection of the Buddha is a key Buddhist meditation. In focussing on him and his qualities, the practitioner is reminded of his/her own ultimate goal. The Buddha is the ultimate role model. From this perspective some prefer to use verbs such as 'venerate', 'revere' or 'pay respect', rather than 'worship', since these terms better convey a sense of appreciation and emulation of the qualities and achievements of the figure venerated, rather than obeisance to a supreme power (King 1990: 174). In this sense the Buddha is the focus of veneration because he is the inspiration for spiritual life, the reminder that the ultimate goal is achievable from the human state. The practice of recollecting the qualities of the Buddha is, in addition, believed to have advantages, specifically in allaying fear.

It is also almost universally accepted that paying homage to the Buddha is a meritorious activity, i.e. it is a form of good *kamma* (Skt. *karma*) that reaps benefits in this or a future life, as stated in the *Mahaparinibbanasutta* above.[6] Buddhist narrative literature abounds with stories exemplifying the benefits of paying homage and making offerings to the Buddha, Pacchekabuddhas or any other sanctified beings, including members of the Sangha. That worship earns merit is also accepted in Buddhist philosophy, even if there is no shared view between different schools on the exact mechanisms of the process by which this works or the nature of the Buddha's presence after *parinibbana*. For example, this shared view is used to move forward the debate between opposing Buddhists on the proposed illusory nature of the phenomenal world in the dialectical ninth chapter of the seventh century Madhyamika text, the *Bodhicharyavatara*: 'merit comes from [worshipping] the Conqueror [Buddha] who is like an illusion in the same way as it would if he was truly existent' (Crosby and Skilton 1996: 116, Ch. 9, v. 9). This statement remains uncontested because both sides accept that worshipping the Buddha brings merit. The nature of the Buddha, whether he is present, dead or illusory, is not a factor in the outcome.

A further universally accepted advantage to worshipping the Buddha, which perhaps underlies or at least justifies the belief in merit, is that it may transform the mental state of the individual. Since the mind is the forerunner of all acts, an improvement in the continuum of an individual's stream of consciousnesses may have a profound impact on that person's success on the spiritual path as well as on his/her future rebirths. This understanding is present in the *Mahaparinibbanasutta* in the Buddha's explanation of why a *stupa* should be built for a him after his death:

> At the thought, Ananda: 'This is the cairn [*stupa*] of that Exalted One awakened for himself alone' the hearts of many shall be made calm and happy; and since they there had calmed and satisfied their hearts they will be reborn after death, when the body has dissolved, in the happy realms of heaven. (Rhys Davids 1966: 157)

These are the advantages of paying homage and making offerings to the Buddha that are doctrinally unproblematic because they do not depend on the Buddha being currently accessible or present in the objects, the images and other *chetiyas*, that form the focus of worship to him. The benefits ensue from the process of worship and the attitude of the worshipper. The questions arise when the interaction between worshipper and worshipped extends beyond this, for example, in the common practice of the worshipper seeking forgiveness from the Buddha for misdeeds committed and assistance from the Buddha in forthcoming obstacles or undertakings. Here the Buddha is treated as if he has the grace to pardon sins and the power to intervene. These present two doctrinal problems. The first is that forgiveness of sins and external intervention are contrary to the doctrine of *karma*, namely that all morally charged actions result in good or bad consequences for the individual who performed them. The second is that it could indicate that the Buddha is understood to be present in some way, particularly in statues of him.

Practices that appear to contravene the doctrine of *karma* are well known in Theravada, especially apotropaic practices such as the use of *paritta*, i.e. protective texts and amulets, and the transference of merit to deceased relatives. I do not wish to rehearse the arguments on the subject here, except to acknowledge that two of the doctrinally unproblematic benefits of worship mentioned above could be drawn on by way of explanation here—the accumulation of merit through making offerings to the Buddha or others and the transformation of the mind, e.g. through rejoicing in the generosity of others or acknowledging one's faults. I wish to focus here on the second problem, the suggestion that the Buddha is in some way present in his image.

The treatment of Buddha images has been discussed in some detail in a number of studies. Here I shall draw on the work of Richard Gombrich, Winston L. King, Donald Swearer and Francois Bizot, writing on the Theravada Buddhism of Sri Lanka, Burma, Thailand and Cambodia respectively. The apparent inconsistencies in doctrine and practice are similar throughout the Theravada world, even if the details in practice vary from region to region.

Sinhalese Buddhists gave Gombrich a variety of answers as to why they worship statues of the Buddha. For the most part, the doctrinal position that the Buddha is no longer present is quite clear to his informants and the explanations they offer conform to this view. For example, one explanation given is that it is the attitude of mind, the joy the worshipper experiences, that is significant (Gombrich 1971: 141).

Nevertheless, some practices, such as treating the Buddha as if he could forgive or intervene, cannot be explained in this way. Gombrich (1971: 97; cf. 1988: 120) describes this treatment of the Buddha in the following terms, 'The Buddha has long since become the victim of a personality cult', and elsewhere submits that worship

of him 'was not the Buddha's idea'. The contrast between the
understanding that the Buddha was mortal and the devotional
supplication to him as present is explained by Gombrich as the
distinction between the cognitive and affective response—between
the rational understanding that the Buddha is no longer present
and the emotional interaction with him, typically in the form of a
statue, as if he were still present and divine. 'For the Sinhalese the
Buddha is cognitively human but affectively divine' (1971: 10).

Gombrich explains this inconsistency in terms of psychological
need. Although they accept that the Buddha is indeed dead, Buddhists
feel an emotional response to him and a need for his assistance that
induces this apparently inconsistent devotional behaviour:

> Theravadin doctrine has never wavered from the position that
> the Buddha is dead and no longer active in the world; in
> moments of great crisis some individuals do pray to him for help,
> but that is the spontaneous outburst of emotion and in their
> calmer moments they know that it can do no good except as a
> psychological relief to themselves. (1988: 120)

However, some Sinhalese villagers gave Gombrich quite a
different answer, namely that the Buddha is worshipped not because
he is himself present, but because his power is present:

> If pressed they reveal that although the Buddha is dead there is
> a certain Buddha force (*Budubalaya*), which will exist till at the
> end of this dispensation, in another 2,500 years, the Buddha's
> relics (including images) will collect...and after a last sermon the
> Buddha will finally disappear... (1971: 167)

For Gombrich this answer is insufficient to explain the practice of
worshipping the Buddha,

> because this *Budubalaya* does not seem to operate outside the
> ritual context as part of the world at large, but only in the presence
> of images; it is virtually a force inherent in the image. (ibid.)

That the statue is in some way empowered is clear from the eye-painting ritual described by Gombrich (ibid. and 1966: 23–36) A statue is only treated with reverence once this final ritual has been performed by an artisan from a particular caste who specialises in this, the most crucial stage in the creation of a Buddha image. However, Gombrich rejects the association of the presence of the Buddha power and the eye-painting ritual:

> To say that this force is put in by the craftsman who completes an image by painting in the eyes would be a logical final step, but we cannot take it because the Sinhalese do not take it. Things are just not so tidy. (1971: 167)

Winston L. King (1964: 154) likewise describes the dichotomy between doctrine and emotional need and records the typical views of contemporary Burmese monks on the subject. He quotes the venerable U. Pyinnya Dipa, who acknowledges the apparent worship of images but also explains it in terms of using the image as a reminder of the Buddha's qualities. Dipa expresses what King terms 'the Buddhist apologetic for physical symbolism' as follows: 'Simple or average people require simple doctrines and are able to conceive an idea only through a symbolic image or ceremony.'

King summarises the dichotomy between orthodoxy and traditional practice as follows:

> This leads us to the interesting question of whether a Buddhist venerating a Buddha image thinks of the Buddha as being actually present there. We may repeat that according to orthodox teaching, the Buddha is not present. Yet the emotion-filled devotion the worshipper seems to feel toward, or by means of, the image, gives the lie to his strict adherence to orthodoxy. There is clearly something of the 'Buddha-presence' which is available here before the image, and not elsewhere. He may be thinking only of a set of perfections, but the odds seem to be against it. Emotion almost surely transforms the past tense of

honoured memory into the present tense of petition and adoration. And we must add to this that, despite orthodox teaching to the contrary, a kind of magical efficacy is attributed to the images of the Buddha. Wishes uttered in their vicinity have a chance of being fulfilled that they have nowhere else... (1964: 177–78)

Like Gombrich, King points out that the statue is the locus of the ongoing presence of the Buddha or his power. The apparent belief in such a presence is not generalised, but experienced and expressed in relation to an image.

The views of Gombrich and King, echoed by the contemporary Theravada Buddhists they questioned – that the treatment of the Buddha as present is a development of the religion in response to the needs of those not strong enough for the higher path – find confirmation not only in the spirit of the canonical texts, but in later Theravada literature. The following story from the medieval Pali poem, the *Sihalavatthuppakarana*, encapsulates the dichotomy between the emotional response to the Buddha's physical representation in an image of him, and the understanding of the reality of his absence and impermanence:

The monk Phussadeva asks Mara, the personification of death and worldly temptation, to take on the form of the Buddha.[7] When Mara does so, Phussadeva is overcome by emotion at the sight of the Buddha and begins to worship him while recollecting the Buddha's virtues. But Mara interrupts the vision, reminding Phussadeva of the truth of impermanence, 'Such is the wholly enlightened Jina, the best of all beings, but he has succumbed to impermanence, gone to destruction; one cannot see him.' Phussadeva continues his description of the Buddha's physical qualities, but adds that each is 'gone to destruction and not seen.' This recognition of impermanence leads Phussadeva to attain enlightenment.[8]

In this story Phussadeva experiences an emotional response to Mara in the guise of the Buddha which verges on the inappropriate. The physical form of the Buddha is represented by the embodiment of death and temptation, strongly symbolic of the falsity of the physical form of the Buddha. Yet through the traditional practice of recollecting the Buddha's virtues combined with meditation on the impermanence of that very thing to which he feels attachment, Phussadeva achieves the highest goal, enlightenment. His devotion in combination with the knowledge of impermanence is the key to his spiritual success. This theme is also present in stories of disciples of the Buddha who were initially hindered in their spiritual progress because of their attachment to the person of the Buddha during his lifetime. The Buddha's personal attendant Ananda, because of his attachment to the Buddha, does not achieve enlightenment until the Buddha's death forces him to confront the truth of impermanence. The monk Vakkali is recorded as following the Buddha everywhere because he was so engrossed in the perfection of the Buddha's visible body. The Buddha's advice to him is one of the most well-known statements highlighting that the significance of the Buddha should be identified as the truth of his teachings, rather than attached to him as an individual:

> What is to thee, Vakkali, this foul body that thou seest? He who seeth the Dhamma he it is that seeth me. For seeing the Dhamma he seeth me, and seeing me he seeth the Dhamma.[9]

These stories confirm the dichotomy between the affective and doctrinal positions outlined by Gombrich and King. Nevertheless, the consecration rituals of new Buddha statues in Thailand and Cambodia, as described by Swearer (1995a; 1995b: 50–58) and Bizot (1994), confirm the response of those informants who told Gombrich that it is the power of the Buddha rather than the Buddha himself that is present in the statue. The consecration rituals for Buddha images are far more extensive in Thailand and Cambodia than those described by Gombrich concerning Sri Lanka.

They involve both re-enactments of events in the Buddha's life and rituals that empower the statue. Given that these rites and the attendant texts support the Sinhalese villagers' interpretation that the Buddha's power is present, it would be interesting to know whether there are or were similar empowerment rituals in Sri Lanka, that informed that interpretation.

The climax of the consecration ritual for a Buddhist image is the same in all countries, namely some form of 'opening of the eyes'. While in Sri Lanka these are painted as part of the empowerment ritual, in mainland Southeast Asia the moment is enacted though the unsealing of the eyes or the removal of a cloth covering them. The opening of the eyes is of utmost significance in the consecration rituals because it represents the moment of the Buddha's enlightenment or 'awakening', in which the Buddha himself became empowered through his higher knowledge and mastery over *samsara*. The main difference between the consecration of the statue in Sri Lanka as described by Gombrich, compared with those witnessed in Thailand and Cambodia by Swearer and Bizot respectively, is the explicit empowerment of the statue in the latter.

In Swearer's description, the main process of empowerment is the recitation of texts, in particular *paritta*, by monks holding on to a sacred thread attached to the Buddha image (1995a: 27–32). The consecration text translated by him makes the process of empowerment completely explicit. After recounting the life-story and achievements of the Buddha, the text contains this invocation:

> May all his qualities be invested in this Buddha image. May the Buddha's boundless omniscience be invested in this image until the religion ceases to exist.
> May all of the transcendental states of the Blessed One...be invested in this image. May the boundless concentration and the body-of-liberation of the Buddha be invested in this image for five thousand years during the lifetime of the religion. May the

supermundane reality discovered by the Buddha during his enlightenment under the bodhi tree be invested in this image for the five thousand years of the religion. May all of the miracles performed by the Buddha after his enlightenment in order to dispel the doubts of all humans and gods be invested in this image for all time. May the powers of the reliquary mounds miraculously created by the Buddha at the places of his enlightenment in order that humans and gods might worship him be invested in this image for five thousand rains-retreats. (Swearer 1995b: 57)

The text continues, inviting the power of the Buddha's teachings and powers associated with particular events to enter the statue. It culminates in the request:

May all the gods, together with Indra, Brahma, Mara, and all people protect this Buddha image, as well as the relics and the religion for five thousand years for the welfare of all human beings and gods. (ibid.: 38)

This consecration text therefore supports two beliefs mentioned by Gombrich. It reveals that the Buddha's power is present, and the association of the power explicitly with the statue clarifies his question as to why this power is felt specifically in the presence of a statue. It also confirms the association of the statue with the relics and the duration of the Buddha's teaching.

The Cambodian consecration ceremony described by Bizot (1994) adds a further significant level of authorisation for the power of the Buddha statue.[10] The ceremony includes the key events found in the Thai rites: the re-enactment of events in the Buddha's life, the recitation of appropriate texts, and a liturgy that explicitly empowers the statue with the powers and perfections of the Buddha. Further empowerment comes from an older statue, which had itself at some earlier date received its own consecration when it was new. It is brought into the presence of the new statue and its powers are invited to enter into the new statue. The powers of the old statue are not diminished by this process.

Bizot (ibid.: 109) points out that the actions involved and the terminology used in the empowerment of the new statue by the older statue parallel those used in the *pabhajja*, the ordination ceremony for monks. The new statue is ordained and receives the Buddha perfections from the older statue. This suggests that each statue is empowered by an ordination, perhaps in a continuous lineage back to some sacred original, just as a monk through his ordination enters the unbroken lineage that first began with the Buddha's ordination of Annata Kondanna, the first member of the Sangha, as recorded in the Buddha's 'first sermon', the *Dhammachakkapavattanasutta*. Perhaps Buddha statues have a similar lineage. One text cited by Bizot suggests this possibility: 'When the Buddha entered final *nibbana*, he conferred his own ten perfections on a Buddha statue, so that the religion might be protected and endure for 5000 years'[11] (ibid.: 115).

The belief may rest on the legend of the first Buddha statue. We know from the *Mahaparinibbanasutta* that the Buddha is recorded as authorising the worship of his relics enshrined in *stupas*. The text makes no mention of statues. However, other, presumably later, texts provide such authorisation for statues. I have summarised the following story of the first Buddha statue from a Khmer text translated by Bizot (ibid.: 102–04), into French.[12] Another version of the same story is found in the medieval Sri Lankan Pali text, the *Kosala-bimba-vannana*, which has been made available by Gombrich (1978: 281–303).

One day King Pasenadi of Kosala arrived at the Jetavana, the grove in which the Buddha resided, bringing the usual paraphernalia for worship such as incense, candles and flowers, in order to pay homage to the Buddha. The Buddha, however, was away teaching. Finding the grove deserted, King Pasenadi felt despondent, as if the Buddha had already entered *parinibbana* (final enlightenment/last death). In the Buddha's absence, he made his offerings to the place where the Buddha usually sat.

On meeting with the Buddha at a later time, King Pasenadi explained the emotions he had experienced and asked the Buddha's permission to make a statue of him to worship during any future absence of the Buddha. The Buddha granted him permission to do so.

Using the costliest sandalwood the King had a statue made in the Buddha's likeness and placed it on a shrine in his palace. The King invited the Buddha to see the statue.

When the Buddha arrived at the palace, the statue noticed his arrival and thought, 'I am myself a statue of the Buddha without consciousness (*vinnana*). Right now, the Buddha is alive and is present here. It is not right for me to be raised up on a shrine. So I shall get down and pay homage to the Buddha.' So thinking the statue descended from the shrine to worship the Buddha. The Buddha, however, stopped him saying, '*Avuso* statue of the Buddha, do not get down, remain elevated on the shrine. The religion of the Buddha should endure for 5000 years. I entrust it to you. Once the Buddha has entered *nibbana*, you will remain in the Buddha's place to save all beings for those 5000 years.'

In this story, the Buddha authorises the Buddha image as the protector of the Dhamma for its duration and as a source of salvation for all beings. He also addresses the statue as *avuso*, the title to be used by a senior monk addressing a more junior monk. In the Sri Lankan text, the verb used for the Buddha's statement regarding the future role of the statue is *vyakaroti*, 'predict', the term used for predicting the future Buddhahood of a *bodhisattva*. From this and other indications in the empowerment of Buddha statues, it would seem that the statue is empowered not through the Buddha himself being immanent in the statue, but through a process of empowerment that is believed to go back to the Buddha himself.

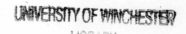

The ordination of new statues by an older one suggests a lineage, presumably back to the empowerment of the original statue by the Buddha. This validates the treatment of Buddha statues as powerful.

Given the presence of such empowerment rituals in mainland Southeast Asia, and the myth of the first Buddha image there and in Sri Lanka, it is curious that Gombrich found no explicit empowerment of statues in Sri Lanka to support the Sinhalese villagers' statement that the Buddha's power is present. Perhaps the Sri Lankan tradition has always been different, or perhaps there was a 'cognitive' rejection of Buddha worship as a doctrinally viable practice as a result of reform of Buddhism at some stage in Sri Lanka's history. In other words, perhaps these other beliefs have been at some stage rejected by Sri Lankan Buddhists more familiar with the doctrines of the Pali canon, or even with Buddhism as seen through the eyes of Protestant-influenced westernised academics. If the latter is the case, the current absence of such empowerment is the result of a syncretic modern interpretation of Buddhism on the part of those either unfamiliar with indigenous traditions from the pre-modern period that authorise those practices, or who find a rationalistic interpretation more acceptable to their world view.

This explanation of Buddha worship, namely that the Buddha's powers are present in the statue, does not satisfactorily account for all features of it. Even if the Buddha's powers can be extrapolated from him, pardoning of sins is not one of them, even if miraculous intervention is possible.[13] This remaining concern notwithstanding, it is clear that canonical texts describe the worship of the Buddha during his lifetime, and that the practice of worshipping his relics after his death is also authorised there. While the *Mahaparinibbanasutta* does not give instructions for or authorise the making of likenesses of the Buddha, this silence is filled by other texts, such as those quoted above. Indeed, the presence of Buddha statues safeguards the Dhamma, the Buddha's teaching, on which, together with the *vinaya*, the monks are to rely after the Buddha's final *nibbana*.

Regardless of the contemporaneity of authorisation for both strands of practice – that is, the reliance only on the Dhamma and *vinaya*, and the worship of relics – it is generally accepted by those writing on the subject that relic/Buddha worship is at best a broadening out of the Buddha's teaching, to fulfil the needs of the spiritually less advanced (Gombrich 1971, 1988; King 1964).[14] Devotion is a practice designed in particular for the psychologically or emotionally 'needy', typically the layperson, for whom the idea that the Buddha is no longer with us is too harsh, given the implications this has for spiritual self-reliance. This is set in contrast to the religion of the ideal monk or nun. For them, the transformation of the individual in particular through meditation is regarded as the correct religious practice. Meditation continues to be practised by a significant minority of monks as well as more dedicated lay people to this day. In Theravada Buddhism it is regarded as the main method for reaching enlightenment. Devotion is set in direct contrast to meditation. One might say that devotion and religious acts, such as gifts to the Buddha or Sangha, represent the path of *kamma*, for those seeking improved present and future lives within *samsara*, while meditation represents the path of *nibbana* for those seeking release from *samsara*.

This distinction between devotion for lay followers of Buddhism and meditation for members of the Sangha, and the line drawn between the two, seems to be confirmed by the sources quoted above and by the modern practice of meditation.

In the sources quoted above, the *Mahaparinibbanasutta* and the legend of the first Buddha image, worship of the Buddha statue and Buddha relics are authorised, yet these practices are placed firmly in the realm of the laity—it is the laity, in particular royalty, who initiate and carry out the construction of the *stupas* and the image. It may be that this association with laity and in particular royalty, is to be taken as the protocol for interaction between the Sangha and royalty, a linking of the fortunes of the two. Nevertheless, it seems reasonable also to interpret it as a division between the religiosity of those who remain in society and the more self-reliant practice of those giving up social ties to follow the more rigorous path of renunciation and self-transformation within the Sangha.

Theravada meditation is often taught today, both in the West and in traditionally Theravada countries, without any devotional context. An explanation, or perhaps justification, given for this is that since Theravada is an atheistic religion and the ideal practitioner should be self-reliant, the methodology of meditation practice can be regarded as effective in transforming the individual irrespective of that individual's beliefs. For example, Winston King writes:

> [Since] the effort and attitude of the meditator, which are absolutely essential to any salvific result,...are not exclusively determined by creedal affirmations, formal adherence to a given statement of faith is of lesser importance than in most Christian sacramental contexts. (1989: 251)

Here King is specifically examining Christian sacraments, such as baptism and the eucharist, and seeking parallels in Buddhist meditation. He uses the definition of the sacrament as 'an outward and visible sign of an inward and spiritual grace' so that in the Christian context the sacraments are the 'appointed means of receiving salvific grace' (ibid.). King's position is that there is no parallel in Buddhism, because man has the innate ability to gain salvation. The practitioner is self-reliant and therefore receives no salvific grace from an external source, rather he generates it through his own meditation.

Similarly, devotional practices are not mentioned in association with Theravada meditation in standard modern texts on the subject, such as King's *Theravada Meditation: The Buddhist Transformation of Yoga* and Vajiranana's *Buddhist Meditation in Theory and Practice*. As with many academic descriptions of Theravada meditation practice, as well as many meditation revival practices, these two texts are based almost entirely on the *Visuddhimagga*. The *Visuddhimagga* is a fifth century Theravada treatise on the spiritual path by Buddhaghosa. Buddhaghosa is often regarded as the epitome of Theravada orthodoxy. These modern texts talk of preparation for meditation in terms of finding an appropriate place, sitting in a comfortable position, being in the right frame of mind or receiving an appropriate meditation subject from an appropriate teacher—all issues that are discuss in the *Visuddhimagga*. In the broader context of the individual's development, progression from general morality to meditation, then wisdom, forms the entire structure of the *Visuddhimagga*. It analyses the path to salvation in a series of three progressive stages—*sila* (morality), *samadhi* (meditation) and *panna* (wisdom). In this progression, morality is regarded as the necessary preparation for successful meditation, i.e. meditation that leads to spiritual progress. In theory, someone progresses to meditation once they have attained moral purity. While reflection on the qualities of the Buddha, *buddhanussati*, is one of the meditation practices explained, worship of the Buddha in conjunction with or in preparation for meditation is not taught in these writings that are based on the *Visuddhimagga*.

In summary, various pieces of evidence suggest that a clear division is to be made between devotion to the Buddha and meditation. These are the current contrast of meditation with devotion, the emphasis on morality as the appropriate preparation, the contrast between devotion as the religion of the layperson and meditation as the religion of the monk, and the fact that Buddhist meditation is often taught as an almost religious practice, adaptable to all contexts, whether Buddhist or not. We do not, therefore, expect to find devotion and meditation combined. Yet a number of pre-modern meditation manuals contain extensive instructions and liturgies for devotion to the Buddha. Furthermore, they advocate these devotional practices as *essential* preparation for meditation.

One such meditation manual from northern Thailand written in c. 1900 by the Thai forest-monk Pannawongsa has been partially translated into English by Donald Swearer (1995c). The manual begins with a fairly lengthy section of devotion and offerings to the Buddha. The text states:

> Whoever practises meditation, whether a yogin, layperson, or a monk, who desires the fruits of meditation from both trance and insight should begin with certain dedicatory preparations. (ibid.: 209)

Swearer observes:

> The tendency of western Buddhist meditators, in particular, to remove meditation from its ritual-devotional context represents what some scholars of Theravada Buddhism have characterised as a 'Protestantising' of the Tradition. (ibid.: 208)

Swearer asserts that meditation devoid of this devotional preparation is a modern phenomenon and that traditionally all meditation began with such worship and offerings.

A survey of meditation manuals of the medieval or pre-modern period confirms Swearer's assertion. Current evidence suggests that a pool of related devotional materials associated with meditation was present throughout the pre-modern Theravada world. In addition to Pannawongsa's text from northern Thailand, such material is also attested in central Thailand, Cambodia and Sri Lanka.[15] More will almost certainly come to light as further forays are made into the hitherto little explored realms of medieval Theravada literature.

In order to examine the relationship between the practitioner and the Buddha in the preparatory worship that precedes the meditation practice in these manuals, and its purpose, I shall examine one of the most extensive liturgical texts, which is attested in manuscripts from Sri Lanka. A descriptive title found on one such manuscript is *Samatha-Vipassana-Bhavana-Vakkapprakarana* (*Vak*), which means 'Liturgy for Tranquillity and Insight Meditation'.[16]

Vak provides the liturgy for the preliminary rituals which precede each meditation exercise taught in a meditation manual called the *Amatakaravannana*, (or 'Text of the Mind of the Deathless State' i.e. *nibbana*).[17] Since the meditation manual prescribes the performance of the preliminary rituals not only once before the whole set of meditations, but before each individual stage in the meditation, the liturgy of *Vak* and the attendant offerings must be performed several thousand times in putting into practice the entire course of meditations in the manual. In addition to the devotion to the Buddha, another liturgy is provided for the exchange between meditation teacher and pupil.

Before discussing the significance of the devotional activities to the Buddha, I shall summarise their structure and content according to the instructions given in *Vak*. For clarity, I have divided the text under separate headings and enumerated each subsection. I include a quotation to exemplify the devotional tone of the text.

The practitioner gathers the offerings for worship: flowers, incense, rice, water, candles. He then follows the liturgy through the following stages.

HOMAGE
1. Homage to triple gem (Buddha–Dhamma–Sangha).
2. Offerings to the Buddha.
3. Worship of the Buddha's qualities.

SILA
4. Acknowledgement of his own unwholesome mental states and failure to follow the Buddha's teaching:

'Venerable omniscient Gotama, since these fourteen unwholesome factors, namely, delusion, unscrupulousness, shamelessness, distraction, greed, false view, pride, hate, envy, selfishness, restlessness, torpor, languor, and doubt,[18] have flooded my mind, like a blind man or one deranged, I do not see the path of the four truths.[19] Therefore, I cannot follow the Buddha's advice. Venerable, omniscient Gotama, out of compassion for me accept my material offering.

Venerable, omniscient Gotama, ascertain any defect in my three gateways.[20] If, on investigation, there is one, then take it and place it before me. After placing it there, weaken it either by overcoming it with its opposite or by overcoming it by starving it. Destroy it. Annihilate it. Make me pure without blemish. When I have been made pure like silver or gold burnished in the mouth of a furnace, may I have a radiance like the spotless orb of the moon over Mount Yugandhara.'

5. Request for Buddha's help in removing his unwholesome mental states and gaining purity.

6. Request for wholesome mental states, in the successively more sublime/advanced cosmological-cum-psychological realms: in the realm of desire, the realm of form, and the realm of the supermundane.

SAMADHI

7. Request for meditation exercises, both general and specific.

8. Request for success in the meditation practice.

PANNA

9. Request for wisdom.

10. Request for four stages of spiritual attainment that lead to *nibbana*, from stream-entry to *arhatship*.

TRANSFERENCE OF MERIT TO ALL BEINGS

11. Transference of merit of worshipping triple gem to all beings, for their good rebirth and attainment of *nibbana*.[21]

12. Invitation to the four world-protectors to rejoice in the merit of the practitioner and consequently remain attentive, so that the Buddha's teaching will last the full five thousand years.

PREPARATORY PARITTA (to ensure protection and success in undertaking)

13. A selection of *paritta* texts.

CONFESSION OF FAULTS (a similar confession of faults to the meditation instructor is found at a later stage in the ritual)

14. Confession of faults.

POSSIBILITY OF NIBBANA

15. Statement of the continuing possibility of attaining *nibbana*.

16. Request for *nibbana*.

PROTECTION OF BUDDHA AND FIVE GEMS

17. Request for the Buddha's support.

18. Invocation of protection of the Buddha, Dhamma, Sangha, meditation instructor and meditation practice.

REQUEST FOR TEACHING

19. Specific request to the Buddha for the full set of meditation practices found in one entire section of the manual.

20. Specific request for an individual meditation practice from that section of the manual.

21. Request for each of the subdivisions for the meditation exercises of one section.

REQUEST FOR SUCCESS

22. Request for the physical and visual experiences that mark the successful accomplishment of that meditation.

VOW, TRANSFERENCE OF VOW

23. Vow to perform the practice successfully or die.

24. Invocation of the power of the vow.

MANTRA RECITATION

25. Repetition of sacred formula hundreds or thousands of times.

FOCUS ON FOCAL POINT OF INDIVIDUAL

26. Focussing of mindfulness (*sati*) on the *hadayavatthu*.

REQUEST THAT THE QUALITIES BECOME INCORPORATED IN THE INDIVIDUAL

27. Request that the meditation practice and successful attainments in it become an inalienable part of the practitioner's person and become the cause of his attainment of *nibbana*.

The practitioner then proceeds to the next ritual, which is performed with his meditation teacher.

The overall goal of the meditator using this liturgy and the accompanying manual is to achieve *nibbana*. The request for *nibbana* is not a single straightforward statement of intent. It is structured through a series of requests to the Buddha, which are progressive. They begin at the most basic stage of ridding oneself of impure or unwholesome states of mind (*akusalachitta*) and gaining pure or wholesome states of mind (*kusalachitta*). The practitioner then makes a series of further requests for increasingly higher states of attainment. The order and nature of these attainments follow the classical descriptions of the spiritual path, such as that found in Buddhaghosa's *Visuddhimagga*. In summary, they progress from morality, *sila*, through success in the various levels of meditation, *samadhi*, then culminate in the attainment of the highest level of wisdom, *panna*. The attainment of *panna* leads directly into the 'four paths and fruits' – stream-entry, once-returner, non-returner and *arhatship* – which represent the highest spiritual levels of the individual, in which *nibbana* is inevitable. The entire path is therefore represented in the ritual performed to the Buddha.

The practitioner clearly identifies himself as a potential Buddha. There is a variety of evidence for this. The practitioner makes the same vows as a Buddha. For example, one vow taken is to succeed in the quest for enlightenment or die, and never to leave the meditation seat until one or the other state is achieved. Another vow taken is to help all beings attain *nibbana*. The practitioner aims for the omniscience of a Buddha. The practitioner internalises the Buddha qualities achieved through the meditation.

What is the purpose of this section of worship of and requests to the Buddha? We can attempt to answer this at various levels.

Given that the liturgy summarises the entire spiritual path of morality, meditation and wisdom, including the specific expectations of the results of meditation exercises, one could see its purpose as a rehearsal of the path the practitioner is undertaking. The practitioner is reminded of the entire theoretical description and analysis of the path, before engaging in the actual practice of that path. He is reminded of his potential, his purpose, his direction and what to expect.

The worship of the Buddha's qualities could be understood as a performance of homage to the ideal of Buddhahood, as in the 'cognitive' explanation of Buddha worship more generally. Such an interpretation could be supported by the clear identification the practitioner makes of himself as a future Buddha. His vow to die parallels Buddha's own vow recorded in the *Jatakanidana*, one of the earliest complete biographies of the Buddha in the Theravada tradition. The concern for all beings is a quality of the Buddha. The attainment he seeks is higher than *arhatship*; it is the omniscience of a Buddha.

Furthermore, there is a curious discussion embedded in the text which appear to be a debate about whether it is possible to gain *nibbana* given that the Buddha has entered final *nibbana*:

Whether he is present or has entered *nibbana*, the 'fruit' in the mind is equal. People go to a good rebirth as a result of the accumulated wholesome states (*kusala*) of their mind.

The teaching lasts as long as the Blessed One is present in the world.

The greatly compassionate Blessed One established the teaching enduring for five thousand years in order to release those beings yet unperfected. Moreover those unperfected beings who had [at the time of the Buddha's death] reached stream-entry or one of the other [stages which make *arhatship* inevitable] were caused to attain *nibbana* [after he had died].

While interesting for a number of reasons, this text at least demonstrates that the practitioner is aware of the formal doctrinal position that the Buddha is no longer accessible. This seems to confirm that the Buddha worship preceding each meditation exercise is for the sake of inspiration. The text also confirms the position from the *Bodhicharyavatara* mentioned above, that the merit gained through worship of the Buddha is the same whether he is present or absent. These are the two doctrinally unproblematic advantages of worship mentioned at the outset of this paper—inspiration and merit making.

Yet while all these factors might confirm a rational interpretation that tallies with the cognitive understanding that the Buddha is not accessible, it could also be interpreted as the opposite, as the ritual realisation of the path and as interaction with the Buddha as present.

The rehearsal of the entire path could be regarded as the ritualisation of the path. Moral purity is an essential preparation for success in meditation. The requests to the Buddha and confession of faults are the ritual removal of sin, the ritual acquisition of moral purity. Specifically the Buddha intervenes to remove all moral impurity and ignorance and to bestow moral purity and knowledge. The subsequent ritual of interaction between practitioner and meditation instructor offers a parallel to this ritualisation of ethics. The meditation instructor takes on the evil deeds, the demerit, committed by the practitioner, again providing him with the moral purity necessary for successful progress on the path. This exchange of demerit is akin to that found in the initiation rituals for practices in Tantric Buddhism. Tantric Buddhism explicitly accepts the efficacy of ritual. Here, the tradition has come full circle from the teaching of the *Sigalovadasutta*. The ethicisation of ritual has developed into the ritualisation of ethics.

The practitioner aims to become a Buddha, rather than just an ordinary enlightened being, an *arhat*. The path to Buddhahood is the same for all Buddhas. In addition to accumulating merit and spiritual purity by developing the perfect virtues of a Buddha throughout hundreds of former births, a future Buddha must worship at the feet of a previous Buddha, vow to achieve Buddhahood in the presence of a previous Buddha, and be predicted to be a future Buddha by the previous Buddha.[22] In the ritual prescribed in *Vak*, the practitioner invokes the aid of the Buddha as if present, treats him as if he can intervene, and also as if the meditation instruction comes from him. Devotion to the Buddha as present is an essential preparation for the attainment of Buddhahood, according to canonical tradition and according to the prescriptions of pre-modern meditation manuals.

Let us turn now not to accounts of meditation based on the *Visuddhimagga*, but to the *Visuddhimagga* itself to see if it offers any further explanation of this combination of devotion to the Buddha and meditation. I wish to draw on three statements of potential relevance here. The first concerns choosing a meditation teacher:

> It is only the Fully Enlightened One who possesses all the aspects of the Good friend. Since that it so, while he is available only a meditation subject taken in the Blessed One's presence is well taken.
>
> But after his final attainment of *nibbana*, it is proper to take it from any one of the eighty great disciples still living. When they are no more available, one who wants to take a particular meditation subject should take it from someone with cankers destroyed, who has, by means of that particular meditation subject, produced the fourfold and fivefold *jhana*, and has reached the destruction of cankers by augmenting insight that

had that *jhana* as its proximate cause....If not, one should take it from a Non-returner, a Once-returner, a Stream-enterer, an ordinary man who has obtained *jhana*, one who knows three *Pitakas*,[23] one who knows two *Pitakas*, one who knows one *Pitaka*, in descending order. If not even one who knows one *Pitaka* is available, then it should be taken from one who is familiar with one Collection together with its commentary, and one who is himself conscientious. For a teacher such as this who knows the texts guards the heritage, and protects the tradition, will follow the teachers' opinion rather than his own. (Nyanamoli, Vol. 1: 99–100)

This text advocates the superiority of the Buddha as the giver of the meditation subject, and so could be taken as justification for the interaction between the practitioner and the Buddha prescribed in *Vak*, where the practitioner requests each meditation exercise from the Buddha. On the other hand, in its hierarchy of appropriate contingency meditation teachers, the Buddha's absence is accepted as a reality. Furthermore, advocating someone who knows the scriptures and so will not follow his own opinion, supports one reason offered above for rehearsing the entire path during the preparatory ritual. The meditator is reminded of his potential and what to expect according to the tradition, and is not led off course.

The second passage from the *Visuddhimagga* is a short statement on dedicating oneself to the Buddha and one's teacher before undertaking a meditation practice. While not providing the elaborate detail of the pre-modern meditation manuals, it does provide an orthodox model for doing so, as well as justification for doing so, namely freedom from fear:

> The meditator should dedicate himself [*attanam niyyatetva*] to the Blessed One, the Enlightened One (Buddha), or to a teacher, and he should ask for the meditation subject with a sincere inclination [of the heart] and sincere resolution.

Herein, he should dedicate himself to the Blessed One in this way: 'Blessed One, I relinquish this my person to you [*attanam tumhakam parichchajami*]'. For without having thus dedicated himself, when living in a remote abode he might be unable to stand fast if a frightening object make its appearance, and he might return to a village above, become associated with laymen, take up improper search and come to ruin. But when he has dedicated himself in this way, no fear arises in him...in fact only joy arises in him. (ibid.: 118)

Finally, it seems relevant to look more closely at the benefits that Buddhaghosa ascribes to the meditation reflecting on the qualities of the Buddha, *buddhanussati*:

When a monk is devoted to this recollection of the Buddha...he attains fullness of faith, mindfulness, understanding and merit. He has much happiness and gladness. He conquers fear and dread. He is able to endure pain. He comes to feel as if he were living in the Master's (Buddha's) presence. And his body, when the recollection of the Buddha's special qualities dwells in it, becomes as worthy of veneration as a shrine room. His mind tends towards the plane of the Buddhas. When he encounters an opportunity for transgression, he has awareness of conscience and shame as vivid as though he were face to face with the master. And if he penetrates no higher, he is at least headed for a happy destiny.
Now when a man is truly wise,
His constant task will survey be
This recollection of the *Buddha*
Blessed with such mighty potency. (ibid.: 230)

Included in this list of benefits of meditating on the Buddha's qualities, we find a number of benefits that are of potential relevance to success in meditation. The practitioner will develop commitment, gain merit, and be proof to fear and pain. Particularly significant is the sense of living in the Buddha's presence. He becomes more Buddha-like in mind, and worthy of worship, and his sense of shame regarding transgressions is enhanced. This brings us back to the psychological interpretation of Buddha worship—it assists the mental state of the practitioner, even in the Buddha's absence.

The significance of Buddha worship as a preparation for meditation is certainly multivalent. At this stage in our familiarity with medieval Theravada literature we can only hazard guesses as to the true variety of meanings ascribed to it. We do not know if even the *Visuddhimagga*, let alone the meditation manuals discussed above, ever intended to advocate or were interpreted as advocating a purely psychological interpretation of Buddha worship. The presumed necessity of such worship and the apparent interaction with the Buddha suggest otherwise. We cannot know the answers to our questions regarding the theological interpretation of such practice by those within the Buddhist tradition that produced the meditation manuals, because we do not have their answers. We do not even know if they exist. Manuals are about performance. Evidence provided, regarding belief, for interpretation is incidental, not systematic. The manuals are not philosophical treatises nor are they accompanied by them. Even if such philosophical treatises come to light, they are likely to be the product of those within the tradition who sought to analyse the efficacy of the ritual, or even explain the doctrinal inconsistencies. In other words, their interpretations, like mine, came into being as a result of the rituals they sought to explain, rather than the other way around.

Nevertheless, we can at this stage at least ascertain that in pre-modern Theravada Buddhism, devotion and meditation are combined and not contrasted. Devotion is advocated specifically for the religious specialist, the monk or layperson undertaking the more rigorous path of meditation practice aimed at Buddhahood. Even if we dismiss the evidence for the belief in the ritual efficacy of worship to the Buddha and accept only a psychological interpretation, we must accept that pre-modern Theravada viewed devotion in terms of psychological need and not of psychological neediness.

In this light, it is interesting to note that in the Sri Lankan version of the story of the first Buddha statue, the *Kosala-bimba-vannana*,[24] while it is indeed the king that has the statue made, the Buddha himself and his entourage of 500 enlightened monks all engage in worship of the statue:

> [The Buddha] extended his right arm, which was like [the celestial elephant] Eravana's trunk, and restrained [the image]. To do it honour he offered it handfuls of jasmine flowers, and likewise both five hundred whose defilements were destroyed and the ordinary unenlightened people offered various fragrant flowers. At that moment Sakka, Suyama, Santusita, Brahma and the rest [of the gods] offered that image their own respective material offerings. The Four Great Kings took up guard on all sides. All gods and men shouted thousands of hosannas.[25]

Notes

1. For a discussion of statements in the Pali canon concerning the nature of the Buddha after his final enlightenment and the way in which individuals at different levels of attainment understand the Buddha, see Harvey (1983).

2. Although the plural 'Truths' is used in the translation, the Pali reads *dhammo* 'truth/teaching' in the singular.

3. *Stupa* is the Sanskrit term now commonly used in English. The term in the text is Pali *thupa*. Other terms commonly found are Pali *chetiya*, Sanskrit *chaitya*, Sinhalese *dagaba*, and Thai *chedi*. The word used for *stupa* in early translation into English is 'cairn'.

4. See for example, the sixteenth century *Chamadevivamsa* for Burma and northern Thailand, Swearer and Premchit (1998), or for Sri Lanka, Geiger (1912).

5. There are four types of relics: physical remains of the Buddha, objects used by him, reminders of him, and his Dhamma texts. The fourth item in the list, which is in addition to the more common list of

three, is given in the popular mainland Southeast Asian biography of the Buddha, *Pathamasambodhi*, cited in Bizot (1994: 104).

6. There are exceptions to this among some modern practitioners who avoid any such practices that could be construed as superstitious or as reliance on another rather than striving for oneself.

7. This transformation of Mara into an aide for Buddhists is a theme that crops up in texts of a number of different schools.

8. I have taken this account from John S. Strong (1993: 138). Strong, who translates from Jacqueline Ver Eecke (1980: 23), mainly looks at Sarvastivada rather than Theravada.

9. C.A.F. Rhys-Davids (1951: 197) from *Theragatha* 105; cited and discussed further by King (1990: 152–53). Rhys Davids translates Dhamma as 'Norm'. I have retained the word 'Dhamma'.

10. In addition to providing texts that relate to the consecration of a statue and descriptions of consecration rites, Bizot's article also discusses the inhabitation of the Buddha statues by entities other than the Buddha's powers, such as deceased ancestors/local guardian spirits.

11. My translation from the French.

12. Bizot gives only a manuscript acquisition number and no title. He thinks the text may be a local version of the *Vattanguliraja jataka*.

13. The numerous descriptions of the Buddha's performance of miracles means that this understanding of the Buddha by the early Buddhist tradition and the Theravada tradition is not in doubt, even though this aspect of the Buddha's nature has often been underplayed in western writings on Theravada. What is accepted, however, is that the gift of the Dhamma is a far greater miracle than displays of magical power, since it offers the recipient a way out of *samsara*. The role of the *stupa*, and by extension, the statue, as a focus for confession of sins appears in other Buddhist traditions too, and warrants a study in its own right.

14. Gombrich (1988) and King (1990) are particularly clear on this.

15. For such a liturgy from central Thailand and Cambodia, see Francois Bizot (1992).

16. Edition and translation, Kate Crosby, unpublished. Manuscript Or.6601(85)II in the Nevill Collection of the Oriental and India Office Collections at the British Library, London.

17. The *Amatakaravannana* contains meditation of the *yogavachara* tradition, which while possibly once mainstream, is unlike much of

meditation taught and practised in Theravada countries today. For an account of it and related texts, see Crosby (2000).

18. This list comprises the four primary *akusala-sadharana-chetasika-sankhara*, or general unwholesome mental factors, and the ten secondary *akusala-sadharana-chetasika*, given in e.g. *Abhidhammatthasangaha* Ch. 2. (Bodhi 1993).

19. The four truths—suffering, the arising (of suffering), the cessation (of suffering), and the path (to the cessation of suffering). These constitute an early, and enduring, classical summary of the soteriological truth to be realised in Buddhism.

20. *Dosa*, defect, a fault or obstacle, in particular, one preventing success in meditation, *dvara*, or gateway, access point. There are various lists of gateways through the mind and the sense organs. The *Abhidhammatthasangaha* lists them as six—eye, ear, sense of smell, tongue, body and mind. Here the group of three is identified below in the text, as the gateway of the eye, the mind and the body. The other sense organs, other than the eye, seem to be incorporated in the body access-point. It is in these access points that obstacles can appear if the practitioner is not mindful. It is necessary to be rid of any faults in the *dvara* before beginning the meditation since all mental images and experiences are caused by external phenomena, even if they can become independent of them. The meditator will not be able to develop the higher results of meditation if he cannot see without fault the initial meditation subject.

21. This concern for the welfare of all beings and transference of merit to them, or even the vow to assist them all attain *nibbana*, is often associated with Mahayana, to the exclusion of Theravada. It is, however, commonplace in Theravada. I would suggest that the identification of Theravada as a form of 'Hinayana' is erroneous, and we should rather see Theravada as a form of Mahayana if we use this criterion.

22. The standard career for all Buddhas is laid out in the *Mahapadanasutta*, (see T.W. Rhys Davids, 1966: Sutta I) and the *Buddhavamsa* (see Horner, 1975).

23. *Pitakas* are the three collections of texts that make up the Pali canon.

24. See Gombrich (1971: 298). My additions in square brackets. I would like to express my gratitude to Nazima Joomun for her ingenuity in finding this translation and getting it to me.

25. Since this paper was written, Swearer has published a book on image worship in Thailand (Swearer 2004). Two other useful works on the

topic of Buddha worship are Schober (1997) and Ray (1994), especially chapters 10 and 11.

References

Bizot, Francois. 1992. *Le Chemin de Lanka: Textes Boudhiques du Cambodge no. I*. Paris: Collection de l'Ecole Française d'Extreme-Orient.

—. 1994. La Consecration des Statues et le Cult des Morts. In *Recherches nouvelles sur le Cambodge*, (ed.) Bizot, 101–27. Paris: Ecole Française d'Extreme-Orient.

Bodhi, Bhikku. 1993. *A Manual of Abhidhamma*. Kandy: Buddhist Publications Society.

Crosby, Kate. 2000. Tantric Theravada: A Bibliographic Essay on the Writings of Francois Bizot and other Literature on the *Yogavachara* tradition. *Journal of Contemporary Buddhism* (2 November): 141–98.

Crosby, Kate. (ed. and trans.). n.d. *Samatha-Vipassana-Bhavana-Vakkapprakarana* (*Vak*). Manuscript Or6601(85)II in the Nevill Collection, Oriental and India Office collections, British Library, London.

Crosby, Kate and Andrew Skilton. (trans.). 1996. *Shantideva: The Bodhicharyavatara*. World's Classics Series. Oxford: Oxford University Press.

Geiger, Wilhelm. (trans.). 1912. *The Mahavamsa or the Great Chronicle of Ceylon*. London: Pali Text Society.

Gombrich, R.F. 1966. The Consecration of a Buddhist Image. *Journal of Asian Studies* 26 (1): 23–36.

—. 1971. *Buddhist Precept and Practice: Traditional Buddhism in the Rural Highlands of Ceylon*. London and New York: Kegan Paul International (rpt. 1995).

—. 1978. Kossa-bimba-vannana. In *Buddhism in Ceylon and Studies on Religious Syncretism in Buddhist Countries*, (ed.) H. Bechert, 281–303. Abhandlugen der Akademie der Wissenschaften in Gottingen, Phil. Hist. Klasse 3 Folge, Nr. 108, Vandenhoeck & Ruprecht, Gottingen.

—. 1988. *Theravada Buddhism: A Social History from Ancient Benares to Modern Colombo*, London: Routledge Kegan Paul.

Harvey, Peter. 1983. The Nature of the Tathagatha. In *Buddhist Studies, Ancient and Modern*. London: Curzon Press.

Horner, I.B. 1975. *Minor Anthologies* (*Buddhavamsa*). Vol. 3. London: Pali Text Society.

King, Winston L. 1964. *A Thousand Lives Away: Buddhism in Contemporary Burma*. Berkeley: Asian Humanities Press, rpt. 1990.

—. 1989. Sacramental Aspects of Theravada Buddhist Meditation. *Numen* 36.2: 248–56.

—. 1990. *Theravada Meditation: The Buddhist Transformation of Yoga*. University Park: Pennsylvania University Press (rpt. New Delhi: Motilal Banarsidass, 1992).

Nyanamoli, 1976. *The Path of Purification*. 2 vols. Boulder and London: Shambala.

Ray, Reginald A. 1994. *Buddhist Saints in India: A Study in Buddhist Values and Orientations*. New York: Oxford University Press.

Rhys-Davids, C.A.F. 1951. *Psalms of the Buddhists* (Theragatha). London: Luzac.

Rhys Davids, T.W. 1966. *Dialogues of the Buddha*, Part II. London: Pali Text Society.

Schober, Juliane. 1997. In the Presence of the Buddha: Ritual Veneration of the Burmese Mahamuni Image. In *Sacred Biography in the Buddhist Traditions of South and Southeast Asia*, (ed.) Schober. Honolulu: University of Hawaii Press.

Swearer, Donald, K. 1995a. *The Buddhist World of South-East Asia*. Albany: State University of New York.

—. 1995b. Consecrating the Buddha. In *Buddhism in Practice*, (ed.) Donald S. Lopez, 50–58. Princeton: Princeton University Press.

—. 1995c. The Way of Meditation. In *Buddhism in Practice*, (ed.) Donald S. Lopez, 207–15. Princeton: Princeton University Press.

—. 2004. *Becoming the Buddha: The Ritual of Image Conservation in Thailand*. Princeton: Princeton University Press.

Swearer, Donald K. and Sommai Premchit. 1998. *The Legend of Queen Chama: Budhiramsi's 'Chamadevivamsa': A Translation and Commentry*. New York: State University of New York Press.

Strong, John S. 1993. Buddha Bhakti and the Absence of the Blessed One. In *Premier Colloque Etienne Lamotte*, (ed.) J. Ryekmans, 131–40. Louvain-La-Neuve: Institut Orientaliste.

Vajiranana. 1962. *Buddhist Meditation in Theory and Practice*. Colombo: M.D. Gunasena

Ver Eecke, Jacqueline. 1980. '*Le Sihalavatthuppakarana': texte Pali et traduction*. Paris: Ecole Française d'Extreme-Orient.

CHAPTER NINE

The Heart of Islam in the Subcontinent

RON GEAVES

A superficial glance at the Muslim encroachments into India from the tenth century onwards may lead to the conclusion that the meeting of Islam and Hinduism could only result in confrontation. The message of Islam appeared dogmatically monotheistic whereas Hinduism was perceived by Muslims as polytheistic. Islam came into existence with a firm commitment to uproot idol worship from the city of Makkah and the first Muslims into the subcontinent must have considered the prolific multiplicity of images used by Hindus in their traditional forms of worship as an abomination compared with the revelation of the Oneness of Allah.

Islam is a religion based upon an historical revelation of divine law manifested through the Quran and Muhammad, the final Prophet of God. Hinduism, on the other hand, is mythological, encompassing vast sweeps of non-historical time in which the divine manifests as a host of deities, both male and female. Islam's mood can be imperative and transcendental whereas Hinduism's is often immanent and questing. The doctrines of orthodox Islam teach belief in a pre-eminently transcendental God who affirms his will to human beings through a time-honoured process of human messengers and revealed scripture. Hindu philosophical doctrines, on the other hand, have introduced an experiential focus on pure being which is immanent in the creation and discovered in the hearts of human beings, and this emphasis has led to a focus on inspiration rather than revelation. Consequently Hinduism has never placed a limit on the human capacity to experience the divine whereas Islam has declared Muhammad as the last and final Prophet of God, and the Quran as the final and complete revelation from Allah to humankind. Islam preaches a final Day of Judgement that will assign all human beings a place in Paradise or Hell according to their intentions and actions undertaken in one human life, whereas Hinduism proclaims an infinite cycle of births and deaths controlled by the law of *karma*.

Socially, Islam advocates an ideal of egalitarianism in which all are equal under the sovereignty of Allah who intervenes directly in human affairs without the need for intermediaries such as priests. Hinduism goes back to its oldest and most authoritative scripture, the Vedas, to find justification in a divinely ordained hierarchy to order human society in which a priestly caste, the Brahmins, sat at the summit. Islamic doctrine was opposed to all forms of monasticism whereas classical Hinduism had long acknowledged the *sanyasin* (celibate wanderer) as the most efficacious choice for those seeking closer contact with the divine, even though the Bhakti traditions had undermined this to some extent with the ideal of salvation for all.

All these differences would have been compounded by Islam's divine command to root out idolatry and establish itself as the final form of worship of the one God throughout the world. Muslims had an unshakeable belief in a divinely given mission to bring the final revelation of Allah to all the people of the world. When this was combined with the expansionist policies of various Muslim empires it created a potentially dangerous world view that divided all nations into *dar al-Islam* (territory of Islam) and *dar al-Harb* (territory of war). Islamic law gave protection to conquered Jews and Christians as fellow monotheists who are awarded the special status of *Ahl-i Kitab* (People of the Book) in the Quran, but no such protection was given to people who were regarded as polytheists.

However, neither religion is homogenous. There are varieties of Hinduism that do not conform to the above analysis and Islam had, by the time it reached India, developed a variety of interpretations of its central revelation. One of these forms of interpretation was to find itself compatible with the Bhakti traditions of Hinduism that were themselves often in opposition to brahminical doctrines and practices. Sufism, or Islamic mysticism, is commonly believed to have developed from two strands in Islam, the ascetic and the devotional, very soon after the Prophet's death. By the end of the eighth century, the devotional strand was dominant and many Sufis would have echoed the sentiments of Rabi'a (d. 801), the female mystic from Basra, when she said:

> O God, my whole occupation and all my desire in this world, of all worldly things, is to remember Thee, and in the world to come, of all things in the world to come, is to meet Thee. (Rizvi 1997: 31)

Such emotive intensity would have also struck a chord with both the *saguna* and *nirguna bhaktas* of medieval India.

Islamic Mystcism

By the end of the ninth century, Sufis had developed doctrines and methods of the path to mystical union, and were emphasising the union between the soul that is pure and the divine, over and above only following the outer forms of Islam. The Sufi experience of union led to a profound understanding of the nature of divinity and the human being, and brought about a unique understanding of *tawhid* (unity and oneness of Allah) not accessible to the orthodox who simply followed the outer teaching of Islam. The emphasis on divine transcendence had stimulated the sense of fear and awe but the closeness of the divine immanence made Allah intimate to his lovers.

The message of the Quran, although emphasising the transcendent, does not deny immanence. One of the most important passages for the Sufis was the declaration that Allah is 'nearer to man than his jugular vein' (Quran 50:16). The Quran also states 'Unto Allah belong the East and the West, and whithersoever ye turn, there is Allah's Countenance' (2:115). These statements of divine immanence are supported by references to the relationship between Allah and his worshippers being one of love (Quran 5:119). Allah is perceived by the Sufis as the Beloved, and they see themselves as His lovers longing for union with the divine essence that is only attainable by the heart.

The Sufis' interpretation of *tawhid* had revolutionised Islam. They perceived Allah as the sole reality and there was no other existence apart from or independent of Allah. *Tawhid* is defined as the awareness of the reality of all-embracing, all-encompassing oneness. *Shirk*, the greatest sin of orthodox Muslims, usually defined as associating another with Allah or departing from strict monotheism, is reinterpreted as awareness of duality or existence outside of Allah's omnipresence in both time and space. This is a dramatic shift in emphasis – from monotheism towards monism – that provides the possibility for comparisons between the teaching of the Sufis and the philosophy of Hindu Vedanta. Not all Sufis were prepared to move all the way towards a monistic experience of Allah, but the two most influential exponents of this position were Sheikh Muhiy'ud-Din Ibn Arabi (1165–1240) and Sheikh 'Abd al-Karim al-Jili (d. 1390). They both assert that transcendence and immanence are two aspects of Allah as experienced at the human level. Al-Jili uses the example of water and ice to describe the relationship between creator and creation. They are the same in essence because Allah formed creation out of His own substance. He taught that the pure in heart are able to 'melt' and perceive the all-encompassing reality of Allah with 'the eye of water' rather than the 'eye of ice' (Lings 1995: 70–71). Pure being or *Haqq* (the real) descends as emanation from absoluteness to manifestation. This expression of reality in the created order is known as *Khalq*. *Haqq* can have neither name nor attributes but as it becomes *Khalq*,

names and attributes appear, as imprinted upon it. The total sum
of all the names and attributes forms the phenomenal universe
through which Allah expresses Himself.

For these two Sufis and many others, the spiritual quest is not
about uniting the soul back to the divine but it is about removing
the veils so that one may see what actually is, that is the reality of
the Unity of Allah. The idea of a veil that hides the reality of God
from human perception coincides with the variety of Hindu
doctrines concerning *maya* (illusion). In the Quran's message,
human beings exist as Allah's *khalifa* or vice-regents. The Sufis
recognised this essential point but interpreted it in the light of their
experiential relationship towards the Unity of Allah. In order to
exist as the *khalifa* of Allah it was necessary to know oneself. They
cited the *Hadith* that declared the Prophet himself as saying, 'He
who knows himself, knows his Lord' (Burckhardt 1990: 37). The
way of the Sufi became the path of self-knowledge. The human
being was perceived as consisting of layers of physical and spiritual
components essentially divided into the spiritual inner part and the
outer carnal part. The *sirr*, which provides us with the inner voice
of conscience, represents the innermost part of the higher self, the
divine ground or spark of being. The presence of the *sirr* within is
the closely guarded secret of Allah. It is the one part of the human
being that cannot be tainted or affected. It remains pure regardless
of the thoughts or actions of the individual. The sense of reason is
able to discriminate or choose between outer and inner reality. If
the *qalb* (heart) is turned towards the *nafs* (ego) it collects the
impurities of the lower self that is orientated towards desire for the
objects of the senses. This clouding of the *qalb* casts a veil over the
higher self. Jalal al-Din Rumi (d. 1273) referred to this process by
using the analogy of a mirror. He said:

> Love desires that this secret should be revealed,
> For if a mirror reflects not, of what use is it?
> Knowest thou why thy mirror reflects not?

Because the rust has not been scoured from its face.
If it were purified from all rust and defilement.
It would reflect the shining Sun of God. (Whinfield 1979: 3)

The object of all Sufi disciplines is to turn the *qalb* in a God-ward direction away from the *nafs* and, filtered through the *ruh* and *sirr*, discover the Unity of Allah both within and without His creation. This process of purification that gradually leads to self-illumination is known as the *tariqa*. In order to follow the *tariqa* it is essential to be guided by one who has already purified his or herself and lives in the guidance of Allah rather than the tyranny of the *nafs*. Discipleship under a qualified *sheikh* or *pir* (spiritual master) is central to the Sufi way. In the process of following the *tariqa* and removing the self from the centre of one's life to be replaced by Allah, three elements are required—*maqamat, ahwal* and *tamkin*. *Maqamat* refers to stages through which the *murid* (disciple) is guided by the *sheikh* utilising a series of selective spiritual disciplines. These stages can be achieved by the diligence and effort of the *murid*. *Ahwal* refers to states of being which are provided by the grace of Allah as gifts along the path. *Tamkin* refers to the achievement or the point of arrival at the cessation of self. This state of cessation is known as *fana fi'l-Haqq* or union with the ultimate reality of being and begs comparison with the state of *samadhi* experienced by *yogis*. However, this is not an end in itself since after *fana* the Sufi enters *baqa* or existence in God. This provision of a precise method or discipline under the guidance of an accomplished master would have also provided a link between Sufism and Hinduism.

It is important to recognise that the path of the Sufi is essentially experiential. The lovers of Allah seek deep intimacy and communion with their Lord. Such an experience has always defeated the power of human language. It is expected that Sufis will describe their experience in different ways but the essence of their discovery remains the same. Their paths rest on the deep conviction that when the individual self is lost, Allah remains as the universal Self and the eternal ground of existence. Once the process of purification is complete, the heart is able to directly communicate with its creator in a glorious experience of illumination and ecstasy.

During the eleventh and twelfth centuries many prominent Sufis were beginning to systematise both the Sufi path and its beliefs and practices. The twelfth century, in particular, is the time of the major growth of the *tariqas* as large and disciplined orders that spread throughout Muslim territory. The *tariqas* developed as brotherhoods of mystics each with its own *sheikh* who taught a way unique to his own realisation of closeness to Allah. The main differences were concerned with the methods or practices that were taught to enable inner purification to take place. The *khalifas* or appointed representatives of the *sheikhs* spread their teachings far and wide and established successful centres themselves. On the death of the original *sheikh*, the result was often an increasingly complex network of branches within the overall *tariqa*.

As this complex network of brotherhoods spread around the Muslim world, intermingling and strengthening each other, the main characteristics of the *tariqas* formulated themselves to the pattern that they still bear today. A group of disciples would gather around the inspiration and leadership of a *sheikh* or *pir*, demonstrating their allegiance to him through the ritual *bai'at* (oath of allegiance). He would then guide them along the path through practices tailored to their individual requirements and through a communal *dhikr* or method for the remembrance of Allah that would form the main method for self-purification. It is the differences in the method of *dhikr* that essentially differentiated the *tariqa*, whereas the practices given to individual *murids* differentiated the *sheikhs*. At this time all the great *tariqas* that still command the allegiance of millions of Muslims came into prominence such as the Naqshbandiya, Qadiriya, Rif'aiya, Shadhiliya, Mevleviya, Tijaniya, Chishtiya and Alawiya. Sufism had arrived in India as early as the tenth century but certainly by the twelfth, three major *tariqas* had been established—the Chishtiya, the Suhrawardiya and the Firdawsiya. In addition to the orders with their fixed disciplines and lineages of masters, there were also wandering individual ascetics known as *qalandars* or *fakirs*, who, in practice, would have been indistinguishable for the majority of rural people from the wandering ascetics of Hinduism, the *sadhus*.

When the *sheikhs* died the focus of their followers turned to the grave that would, in turn, develop as an important shrine centre and the focus of the continuing development of the *tariqa*. It was believed that the power to intercede and perform miracles was now contained within the tomb of the saint as he was in some way still alive awaiting Judgement Day. His power was also contained in his bloodline and it was usually his immediate remaining family who would take over the religious functions and administration of the shrine. The proliferation of shrines of deceased saints brought a new dynamic into Muslim belief and practices as millions of rural adherents of the faith concentrated their devotional practices and petitions around the tombs.

The development of a fully fledged theosophy of sainthood, both living and in the tomb, was a contentious issue for many more orthodox Muslims, especially among the ranks of the *ulema*. There was considerable criticism of the need to submit to the authority of charismatic men who claimed a special relationship to Allah through ecstasy. Some believed that Islam was being subverted through vicarious holiness originating in dependence on holy men, pilgrimage to their shrines, adoration of their relics and total commitment of physical and mental resources to their service (Nicholson 1989: 123–24). But the most bitter criticism of the orthodox was reserved for some Sufis who began to proclaim that the intimate relationship with Allah that is enjoyed by the *wali* (friend of God) excludes the requirement of obedience to the outer laws of Islam. Some suggested that obedience to the exoteric laws and requirements of Islam was only a duty during the early stages of spiritual development. It was inevitable that a dichotomy between the experience of those who claimed direct inner access to the divine and therefore felt themselves to be completely surrendered to the divine will and those who dutifully followed the external requirements of the *shari'a* would develop. Niffari claimed that the inner knowers of truth only had to follow the outer requirements of Islam if they were in accordance with their vision of reality (Nicholson 1989: 22). Some Sufis began to suggest that the outer requirements of Islam contained in the Revelation were only for the masses but were not binding on the spiritually elect.

If such sentiments are followed through to their ultimate logical conclusion, Sufism can be perceived as a form of universal mysticism completely disconnected from its Islamic roots and thus able to supply a kindred spirit to the universalists arising out of *bhakti*, especially the North Indian Sants. However, it should be pointed out that most Sufis have been equally critical of those who have departed from obedience to the *shari'a*. The vast majority of the *tariqas* teach that inner development is not possible without the exoteric demands of Islam contained in the final revelation to humankind from Allah delivered to and fully manifested in the behaviour of Muhammad, the final Prophet of God.

Wahdat al-Wujud

Generally, most Sufis in India subscribed to Ibn al-Arabi's formulation of the doctrine of *Wahdat al-Wujud* (Unity of Being) concerning Allah's unity. Not all Indian Sufis followed Ibn al-Arabi's ideas on *Wahdat al-Wujud*. There were those who followed a modified form known as *Wahdat al-Shuhud* (Unity of Appearance). This was first propounded by Ala'u'd-Dawla Simnani (1261–1336) of Iran whose disciples travelled to India. Simnani disagreed that Being and God were the same. He argued that Unity of Being was only a stage on the mystical journey and the final stage reasserted transcendence. Later, in the sixteenth and eighteenth centuries, *Wahdat al-Shuhud* would be adopted by the Naqshbandiya reformers, Sheikh Ahmad Sirhindi (1564–1624) and Shah Wali-ullah (1703–1762), who argued that Muslims had been too influenced by their closeness to Hinduism and needed to purge Islam of accretions brought about by this proximity, and return to a more orthodox position. However, both schools acknowledge the supremacy of divine love.

Orthodox Islam tends to focus on Allah's transcendence and the central doctrine of *tawhid*, the expression of God's oneness and uniqueness as encapsulated in the central formula – *la illaha il'allah* (there is no god but God) – is emphasised as otherness or uniqueness. Sufis, on the other hand, tend to emphasise immanence, concentrating on interpreting the central tenet of Islam as 'there is nothing but God'. This focus on immanence led some Sufis to dance very close to pantheism and monism in their relation with Allah, and in their experience of *fana* (complete loss of self) they were liable to announce a condition of oneness or unity with the divine essence. The most famous of these was al-Hallaj (857–922), known in India as Mansur, the great martyr of Sufism, killed by his fellow Muslims for blasphemy. Al-Hallaj had announced the famous utterance, *ana'l-Haqq* (I am the Truth) and was perceived to have identified himself with God. Al-Hallaj also made an expression of the unity of the lover and the Beloved that was to become so central to Sufi poetic expressions of their relation with the divine.

I am He who I love and He whom I love is I. We are two spirits dwelling in one body. If you see me, you see Him, and if you see Him, you see us both. (Rizvi 1997: 58)

Ibn al-Arabi (1165–1240), a mystic and prolific writer, is the link between eastern and western Sufism. Although born in Spain, he travelled extensively in West Asia, North Africa and Anatolia. His ideas on the unity of Being interpreted *la illaha il'allah* as an expression of the non-existence of any other entity but God rather than a proclamation against idolatry. According to Ibn al-Arabi, God was not only the absolute source of existence but was inseparable from existence. Thus, the Absolute Being manifested itself in every form of existence and to the highest degree in the Perfect Man. Thus to Ibn al-Arabi the One and the many are both forms of the One. Thus the Absolute is the essence or *zat* of existence, and creation is the drama of self-manifestation. Thus, along with all Sufis, Ibn al-Arabi affirmed that, 'he who knows himself, knows his Lord' (Burckhardt 1990: 37). The Supreme Being was hidden behind a veil of His own making and was further concealed by the impurities that covered the mirror of the human heart. The motive for creation was an all-embracing love that wished to know itself by revelation to beings that became aware of its presence and consumed by it in a passionate return of love (Rizvi 1997: 103–09). Ibn al-Arabi described creation in essentially neo-Platonic terms, drawing upon the *Hadith*:

> I was a hidden Treasure, I yearned to be known. That is why I produced creatures, in order to be known in them. (Fakhry 1997: 81)

One more element of Ibn al-Arabi's cosmology needs to be understood as it relates to the Indian context. Ibn al-Arabi stated that the human being was a microcosm of the universe. Just as the cosmos was a giant unity (macrocosm) created at every moment by Allah for the purpose of self-knowledge, so human beings were small universes capable of self-knowledge. The human being had the capacity for becoming the Perfect Man once the mirror of the heart was polished clean of all imperfections and impurities. The Perfect Man was permeated by the Absolute and manifested many of the qualities of the divine names of Allah, thus capable of knowledge of God and creation, and to be Allah's vice-regent on the Earth. Ibn al-Arabi's ideal of the Perfect Man comes very close to the ideal of the Logos and is described as 'the First Epiphany of God' (Rizvi 1997: 107).

The ideal of the Perfect Man was Muhammad, the Seal of the Prophets and the embodiment of sainthood (*awliya*). Although the institution of prophethood had come to an end with Muhammad, as Allah did not need to give another version of divine law to humankind, the Quran having perfected revelation, the state of *wali* (sainthood) would never cease, according to Ibn al'Arabi. Thus the Sufis who had succeeded in losing their egos through inner purification and discovering the already self-existent Unity of Being were also embodiments of the Perfect Man and an aspect of the Absolute.

Ibn al-Arabi believed that the divine is worshipped in all religions, especially where love was the main motive for worship. Love, beyond everything, was Allah's innermost essence. Thus he was able to say:

> My heart has become the receptacle for every form;
> It is a pasture for gazelles and a convent for Christian monks.
> And a temple for idols, and the pilgrim's *Ka'aba*,
> And the tablets of the Torah
> And the book of the Quran.
> I follow the religion of love; whichever way its camels take,
> For this is my religion and my faith. (Rizvi 1997: 108–09)

From the twelfth century, Ibn al-Arabi's ideas became influential in the world of Islam and especially amongst the Sufis. They were taken to India by several prominent Sufis, most notably Abd al-Karim al-Jili (1365–1428) who wrote over thirty books expounding Ibn al-Arabi's philosophy. Another important figure was Fakhru'd-Din Ibrahim (d. 1289), commonly known as 'Iraqi', who lived in Multan for around twenty-five years and had been introduced to the ideas of Ibn al-Arabi whilst travelling in Asia Minor after undergoing pilgrimage to Makkah. Many scholars have debated whether Ibn al-Arabi was pantheist, monist or monotheist. Louis Massignon described Ibn al-Arabi's position as 'existential monism' (Rizvi 1997: 105), but Burckhardt (1963: 23–24) and

Corbin (1969: 209) both dismiss the use of pantheism or monism to describe *Wahdat al-Wujud*. It would not be possible to elaborate on the numerous debates that have taken place amongst Muslims or other scholars and it is unlikely that the millions of converts to Islam in the Indian subcontinent would have discussed the finer philosophical nuances of his theosophy and simply recognised a chord in the teachings of Sufism that echoed the philosophies of their Vedanta and Yoga schools (*darshanas*). This is reinforced by Saiyid Muhammad Ashraf Jahangir Simnani who acknowledged that although most Indian Sufis subscribed to *Wahdat al-Wujud*, they were woefully ignorant of esoteric definitions and the technical terms of the position put forward by Ibn al-Arabi (Rizvi 1997: 268).

Zaehner points out that there are similarities between typical ecstatic utterances of Sufis, such as the following example by Abu Yazid, and the famous phrase of the *Chandogya Upanishad: 'Tat tvam asi'* (That thou art) which suggests that the reality of the *atman* (self) is identical to the reality of *Brahman* (ultimate Being).

> Adorn me with Thy Unity,
> Clothe me with Thy Selfhood,
> And raise me up to Thy Oneness,
> So that when Thy creatures see me
> They will say we have seen Thee
> And Thou art That. (Zaehner 1994: 94)

If the unique understanding of *tawhid* was accessible to an Advaita Vedantic interpretation, then the doctrines concerning union of the lover with the Beloved allowed Sufi teachings access to Hinduism through the far more popular Bhakti (devotional) tradition. Allah is perceived by the Sufis as the Beloved and they see themselves as His lovers longing for union with the divine essence that is only attainable by the heart. Those that achieved the ecstatic state of loss of individual self and were immersed in the bliss of Allah became known as the *awliya* (the friends of Allah). Thousands of Sufis were to write of their experiences of Allah's unity in poetry that used metaphors of sexual love between lover and beloved similar to those used in the *Gita Govinda*, which tell of the love between the Hindu *avatar*, Krishna, and the women who herd cows, the *gopis*.

The key factor here is that both Islamic and Hindu theism were able to interface and even sometimes fuse with each other as well as with the rarer manifestations of monism. By the time of the Mughals, Sufis were well ensconced in the courts of the rulers as well as the hearts of the common people. The Mughal emperor, Akbar (1556–1605), and the eldest son of emperor Shah Jahan, Dara Shikoh (1615–1659), were both followers of Sufis and were integrationist in their approach to India's major religious traditions. In 1657 Dara Shikoh had completed his translation of the Upanishads into Persian and his own introduction to the text indicates that he considered them to echo the teachings of the Quran.

> Every difficulty and every sublime topic that he had desired or thought and had looked for and not found, he obtained from these essences of the most ancient books, and without doubt or suspicion, these books are first of all the heavenly books in point of time, and the source and the fountainhead of the ocean of unity, in conformity with the Holy Quran. (Embree 1988: 473–74)

Dara Shikoh's poetry indicates both the influence of Ibn al-Arabi and the Upanishads.

> Here is the secret of unity, O friend, understand it;
> Nowhere exists anything but God.
> All that you see or know other than Him,
> Verily is separate in name, but in essence one with God.
> Like an ocean is the essence of the Supreme Self,
> Like forms in water are all souls and objects;
> The ocean heaving and stirring within,
> Transform itself into drops, waves and bubbles. (ibid.: 472)

However, although some educated Muslims were beginning to discover Sufism's affinity with the unity of *Brahman* and *atman* as expressed in Shankara's rendering of the Upanishads, the main confluence of Islam and Hinduism was to be with the Bhakti tradition, especially the North Indian *nirguna bhaktas* such as Nanak and Kabir, labelled as the Sant tradition by some scholars such as Hawley, Gold and Juergensmeyer.

The majority of Hindus follow a version of the *bhakti marg* (the path of devotion). There are several ways in which *bhakti* can be defined. Some state its Sanskrit root is *bhanj* (to separate), and that it emphasises the central theme of separation and reunion with the divine as the key characteristic of human life. The Hindu *bhakta* and the Sufi share together the pain of separation and longing for union. Both are recipients of the grace of God given as a loving gift to a servant who remains in constant remembrance of the Lord's Name(s). Both can be absorbed into the divine, in a state where all awareness of individual self is lost, the *bhakta* in the condition of *samadhi* and the Sufi in the state of *fana*. Others claim that the root of *bhakti* is *bhaj* (to worship) and Sandilya in the *Bhakti Sutras* described the condition as 'passionate longing for the Lord from one's whole heart' (Klostermaier 1994: 221–22). The central act of *bhakti* is *prapatti* (self-surrender) that could be likened to Islam (surrender). The central components of *prapatti* are:

i.   the intention of submitting to the Lord
ii. giving up resistance to the Lord
iii. the belief in the protection of the Lord
iv. the prayer that the Lord may save His devotees
v.   the consciousness of complete helplessness and dependence on grace (ibid.: 229)

Muslims began to acknowledge that the Hindus were able to attain mystical experiences similar to their own but still regarded Islam as superior in that it was founded on *shari'a* (Islamic law) as handed down directed from Allah in His final Revelation. Sufis themselves were divided between those who recognised the wisdom of the Hindu scriptures and the similarities between *bhakti marg* and *tasawwuf.* Some were eclectic and although remaining loyal to Islam, found more in common with the Hindu *bhaktas* than the orthodox *ulema* of Islam with their emphasis on the exoteric. Others were more nervous of the contamination resulting from contact with Hindu beliefs and practices, and drew nearer to orthodoxy and closed ranks against Hindu influence.

All Sufis would have had some difficulties with *saguna bhakti* (devotion to form) where worship was directed to an image, especially those believed to be incarnations of God into human form such as the *avatars* of Vishnu. Some may have adopted Ibn al-Arabi's stance that defined idolatry in a narrower sense where the worshipper literally believed the image to be God. He did not consider worshipping through an icon infused with the divine as a representation of God to be idolatry. However, the worship of form would have raised the suspicions of Muslims, but the *nirguna bhaktas* (devotees of the formless) were often perceived as kindred spirits. The medieval North Indian *nirguna bhaktas*, commonly known as Sants, were often familiar with Islamic beliefs and were sympathetic to the Sufi tradition. The common beliefs and practices of the Sants are hard to distinguish from those of the Sufis.

Both share the idea that God is one, all-pervading reality, essentially without form. Both perceive the divine to be immanent in creation and thus capable of being experienced through the human heart/soul. Both practised contemplation or remembrance of the Word or Name(s) of God as the central discipline through which unity with God was achieved. The names were different according to language and culture, may be remembered silently in the heart or chanted by the tongue, but essentially Sufi *dhikr* and the *nam simran* of the Sants performed the same function. The goal of both was continuous remembrance and both speak of a state where the divine takes over and remembers the devotee and effort ceases. The Sants were iconoclasts; they criticised caste, sectarian differences and exterior forms of religion such as sacred languages, scriptures, image worship, fasting, ritual bathing, pilgrimages and asceticism. Sufis were more ambivalent to the external forms of worship as the *shari'a* insisted upon several of the above as essentials of revelation. However, they agreed with the Sants that the externals of religion were of no avail if the esoteric path of the heart had not been discovered. The Sants acknowledged the *guru* as the intermediary between humans and God, and although it is not always clear whether the *guru* is human or some aspect of immanent divinity, tradition always allocates them a human *guru*. The Sufis were equally adamant that a *sheikh* or *pir* was essential in order to progress towards Allah. They would have been suspicious of Hindu claims that the *guru* was an incarnation of the divine made by some Sant traditions, but it is here that Ibn al-Arabi's idea of the Perfect Man could have been used to bridge the divide. The difference between the *guru* or *sheikh* being divine or imbued with divinity can be very fine in practice. Finally, both wrote or sung their poetry and preached their message in the vernacular, reaching the common people of both religions.

It is not surprising that Sufis and Sants began to collect followers from both their communities. There were advantages for Hindus to convert to the religion of their rulers and if a place became a centre of Sufism, then many of the local population might have been converted feeling more at ease with Sufism's spiritual interpretation of Islamic precepts than the orthodoxy of the *ulema*. Others might have more loosely incorporated the Sufi teaching into their own system of-belief already influenced by the Sants and *bhaktas* of northern India. In rural populations, the Muslim saint was often identified with a Hindu mystic or even a deity. The process happened in reverse with Sants such as Guru Nanak (1469–1539) collecting close Muslim followers. The period of the Mughals brought about a number of syncretic movements, most notably Sikhism. New Sufi orders appeared, most notably the Shattariya, the Qadiriya and the Naqshbandiya, although only the first two were influenced by the teachings of Ibn al-Arabi. The Indian Naqshbandiya were from the Central Asian branch that was established in the subcontinent when Babur invaded in 1526. Several of the soldiers were followers of Khwaja 'Ubaidu'llah Ahrar (1404–1490) and other *sheikhs* migrated from Central Asia (Rizvi 1997: 181). The Qadiriya were introduced into India by Mir Nuru'llah bi Shah Khalilu'llah, the grandson of Shah Ni'matu'llah Wali (b. 1330), the founder of the famous Shi'a *tariqa*, the Ni'matullahi (Rizvi 1997: 55). The Shattariya were introduced from Central Asia by Shah Abdu'llah (d. 1485).

The Sufis seemed to be taking the Hindu ideas close to Islam and often the Sufis and the Sants seemed to have more in common with each other than the respective orthodoxies of Brahmin and *alim*. Figures like Bullhe Shah (1680–1752) and Waris Shah (1730–1790) attacked the exoteric paths of both religions, and like Guru Nanak claimed to be neither Hindu nor Muslim. To Bullhe Shah, the path of love overrode the law prescribed by either faith:

Love and Law are struggling: I will settle the doubts of your
  heart, holy sir,
The questions of Law and the answers of Love.
Law says: go to the *mullah* and learn the rules and regulations;
Love says: one letter is enough, close your books and put them
  away.
Law says: perform the five baths and worship in the temple;
Love say: what is this veil for? Let the vision be open.
Law says: go inside the mosque and perform the duty of prayer;
Love says: go to the tavern, read the drinking wine.
Law says: let us go to heaven, we will eat the fruits of heaven;
Love says: we are the keepers and will ourselves distribute the
  fruits.
Law says: faithful one, perform the *hajj*, cross the bridge;
Love says: the *Ka'aba* is the door of the Beloved, from there
  I will not stir.

Law says: we put Shah Mansour to the stake;
Love says: through you he entered the Beloved's door.
The place of Love is the highest heaven, the crown of creation;
Out of love He has created Bullha, humble and of dust. (Embree
1988: 486–87)

It needs to be reiterated that to many Sufis this disregard for
shari'a was anathema and that both the exoteric (*shari'a*) and
esoteric (*tariqa*) dimensions of Islam were essentials. By the time of
Bullhe Shah, the reaction to this kind of eclecticism was already
under way in the hands of Shah Wali-ullah (1703–1762) and his
descendants. Shah Wali-ullah of the Naqshbandi *tariqa* accused
Muslims in the subcontinent of a lack of moral standards that had
led to a decline in Muslim fortunes. He argued that this was due to
contact with Hindus and faulty conversion to Islam by many Sufis. He
accused them of becoming Indians rather than identifying with the
worldwide Muslim *ummah* (community) (Geaves 1996b: 131–33).

Before concluding this essay, it is necessary to explore Sufi piety
and devotion to the Prophet and their *sheikhs*. Although it has been
mentioned in passing, so far the main theme has been the
relationship with Allah, but the love of the Prophet and the *sheikh*
amongst subcontinental Sufis is renowned in the world of Islam.
Muhammad's actions have become the norm for all generations of
pious Muslims and many Sufis attempt to model themselves on his
life right down to fine details of behaviour and even appearance.
This kind of imitation of the Prophet's behaviour, practices, morals,
ethics and appearance is known as *adab*. Members of a spiritual
tariqa are likely to follow the *adab* of their *sheikh*. It is believed that
the *adab* of the *sheikh* will lead to surrender. As the *sheikh* is
believed to be surrendered to the Prophet, so also will the disciple
be led to the next stage of the Prophet's *adab*. The Prophet is
believed to be fully surrendered to Allah and thus the disciple is led
on to the final stage of imitation where he/she is lost in the
consciousness of Allah. The imitation of the Prophet is

accompanied by deep reverence for any relics associated with either his possessions or his physical form, for example, hairs from his beard.

Many Sufis believe that the Prophet preceded his own human existence and is the primordial light that was the first creation of Allah (*nur al-Muhammadiya*) and that creation actually came into existence for the sake of God's ultimate beloved, the final seal of prophethood and the archetype for the *awliya*. This respect for the Prophet is manifested in intercessionary prayers and Sufis along with many devout Muslims will often take the opportunity to increase their love for the Prophet either individually or collectively by praising him or sending blessing to him. There is a vast body of popular poetry and songs (*na't*) that praise Muhammad, and their lyrics are used in Sufi gatherings to increase their love for him. It is believed by Sufis that this demonstration of love for the Prophet will transform the appearance, personality, character and mannerisms of the *murid*. Muhammad also manifests in dreams and vision to transform lives and provide guidance (Geaves 2000: 28–32). For Sufis, life without the spiritual presence of the Prophet in their practices and gatherings would render access to Allah impossible, and Islam would have no inner path and Muslims would be left with only the outer shell.

The transmission of spiritual authority which originates in the Light of the Prophet is believed by Sufis to pass through an authorised *silsila* (chain of authority) passed down through spiritual masters (*sheikhs*) and traceable to Muhammad through either of his two companions, Hazrat Ali or Abu Bakr. These masters are believed to be Allah's friends (*awliya*) and as such they share in the privileges granted to the final messenger of God. They too are alive in the grave and provide a focal point where Muslims can seek intercession to give them hope and solace from the ills and injustices of this world.

The living *sheikh* is no less important to his disciples. It is believed that his power from Allah extends to spiritual insight into an individual's heart and mind (*firasa*), entry into the secrets of God and creation (*kashf*), the ability to perform miracles (*karamat*), and the permission to bless (*baraka*); but above all he is connected spiritually with all the *sheikhs* that form the *silsila* back to the Prophet. For this reason the Light of the Prophet is present in him and he is therefore able to guide his *murids* by first transmitting his spiritual blessings through the initiatory *bai'at*. It is the *sheikh* who will guide the *murid* in his or her personal spiritual discipline. Living *sheikhs* are connected to a cosmic network of *awliya* who are organised into a spiritual hierarchy that is believed to maintain the existence of the physical creation. Such is the awe and devotion of *murids* to their living master that they are liable to perceive him as the *ghaus* or *qutb*, the pinnacle of the saintly hierarchy (Geaves 2000: 35–42).

The Indian subcontinent supports a vast community of past and present saints to this day, and cements the Sufis together into one of the most esteemed devotional traditions of the region. This network of saints extends the influence of Sufi piety into traditional Muslim worship through the countless national, regional and local *mazars* (tomb shrines) that provide an alternative network of sacred places to the mosques, and accommodate the devotional needs of ordinary subcontinent Muslims, both male and female. Some of these, such as the shrines of Muinuddin Chishti (d. 1236) in Ajmer and Data Ganj Bakhsh (d. 1089) attract millions of pilgrims every year, especially on the occasions of their *urs* (death days). The shrines are a sacred space that can be found in most towns and villages that have a strong Muslim presence and which centre around human spirituality embodied in the remains of Muslims who have not only maintained obedience to the outer laws of Islam but whose lives manifested an inner path of proximity of Allah. The power of the saint is not diminished by death and it is this belief that maintains the importance of the shrine and provides the impetus for the manifest devotion of the pilgrims. In addition to this, the Sufi practitioners of the subcontinent maintain the conviction that Allah's essence is the same as the heart's essence and can be reached in a moment of self-shattering ecstasy of unity that breaks the boundaries of normal everyday space and time. To these devout Muslims, every invocation of Allah's name brings the experience of Allah one step closer.

Sufism in the subcontinent remains a vibrant living tradition that has influenced the development of Islam in the region. It remains the dominant force for the expression of Muslim devotion to the Prophet, and for those that chose to go further, the *tariqas* and their network of living *sheikhs* provide the possibility for a life completely focussed on achieving closeness to Allah through the path of *tassawuf.* Sufism has also provided a bridge to certain forms of Hinduism, namely the Bhakti/Sant traditions of northern India where new syncretic traditions were able to provide a means of resistance to perceived injustices, hypocrisies and inequalities that existed in respective orthodoxies. These two traditions together brought a promise of God's salvation to the common people and a vehicle of devotion that was available to all. In the process, these new norms of religion – through poetry and literature written in the vernacular languages – were to produce popular cultural forms which remain embodied in the various regions of India that they influenced.

The Reform Movements

However, although many practitioners of the Sufi *tariqas* have been more tolerant of eclecticism, the Muslim community in India was riven by strong criticisms of all the above religious phenomena. Even in eastern Bengal, where Hindu influences were particularly strong, reaction set in. Kirkpatrick expresses this very succinctly:

In eastern Bengal there was a shift away from the cultural latitudinarianism of the nineteenth century because of the influence of the fundamentalist Wahhabis. The cry of the

Bengali reformers was that Islam is in danger and Muslim piety and practice must be purified from the intrusions of Bengali Hindu customs and culture. (1989: 58)

These criticisms remain very strong in contemporary Muslim communities and are reflected in a number of Muslim reform groups that share with each other the common aim of purifying Islam from cultural accretions associated with Hinduism. These reform movements all insist upon a rigorous application of the *shari'a* and a return to the orthodox tenets of Islam based upon their own interpretation of the Quran and *Sunna* of the Prophet. They are all highly critical of the Sufi *tariqas* and blame them for the apparent corruption of Islamic belief and practice that is perceived to have originated through eclectic or syncretistic contact with Hinduism (Metcalf 1982: 6). However, their origins can be seen in India much earlier than the nineteenth century and the advent of the Wahhabi movement in Arabia.

As early as the sixteenth century, orthodox Muslims had reacted negatively to the compromises of the Mughal emperor Akbar (1556–1603). Akbar's abandonment of *shari'a* law and the apparent establishment of a new religion that placed him above the law was anathema to the orthodox and appalled them. Akbar made the *ulema* sign a decree of infallibility that in effect placed the decisions of the monarch over and above the *shari'a*.

If there be variance of opinion among the *mujjadid* upon the question of religion, and His Majesty, in his penetrating understanding and unerring judgement should incline to one option...and give his decree for the benefit of mankind, and for the due regulation of the world, we do hereby agree that such a decree is binding on us, and on the whole nation. (Titus 1979: 160)

Akbar came to be viewed as an apostate by the orthodox *ulema*, and as a symbol of the corruption and decline of Islam created through its contact with Hinduism. This situation brought to a head the idea that Islam was in danger of being engulfed in an all-embracing sea of Hinduism. Ironically, the criticism of folk practices and popular Sufism was to come from within the ranks of the Sufis themselves. The strongest and most influential voice of protest came from Sheikh Ahmad Sirhindi (d. 1625) of the Naqshbandi *tariqa*. Sirhindi was determined to unite the *ummah* under the rule of the *shari'a*, to destroy the *bida* (innovations) that he saw creeping into Islamic belief and practice, and to persuade Muslims to shun religious contact with the Hindu population (Ikram 1964: 172). Sirhindi attempted to clarify the relationship between Hinduism and Islam. He considered the two religions to be mutually exclusive, with no possibility of integration. He taught that Muslims should avoid unnecessary contact with all unbelievers, and treat Hinduism and its worship of false gods and idols with contempt. He advocated the restoration of the *jizya* tax (tax on non-Muslims) for the Hindu population. Sirhindi also attacked heterodox Sufis who had absorbed ideas from Hinduism, and he sought to close the gap between Sufism and the *shari'a*. This attempt by orthodox Islam to reassert itself became the seed of that Muslim separatism which continued to develop, culminating in the establishment of the separate Muslim state of Pakistan in 1947 (Geaves 1996a).

In spite of his own Sufi affiliation, Sirhindi asserted the prominence of the *shari'a* over the *tariqa*, insisting that Sufis themselves should be exemplary in their obedience to the law (Mujeeb 1966: 246). Simple conformity to the *shari'a* would base the Muslims' faith firmly on revelation rather than on the mystic's intuitional awareness of unity. The heart of Sirhindi's attack on the heterodox forms of Sufism was its openness to pantheistic and monistic ideas, which in turn led to alliances with Hinduism. He considered that education in theology and law should take precedence over Sufi teaching, and that the Prophet and his companions were superior to all the saints of Sufism. The core idea in Sirhindi's plan for revival, central to all later reform movements, was the return of Muslims to perceived standards of the Islam of the Prophet and the *Rashidun* (the first four rightly guided caliphs). Sirhindi's voice of protest against syncretistic movements and eclectic liberal trends was an attempt to protect both Sufism and the Muslim masses from the ideas and morals of Hinduism's pantheistic views. Essentially, Sirhindi saw Hindus as infidels not entitled to their *dhimmi* status; the revival of Islam thus meant the reimposition of *shari'a* and the removal of cultural accretions and innovations arising out of Sufism, Shi'a and, in particular, Hinduism (Haq 1972: 130). True Islam must rest on the Quran and the *Sunna* of the Prophet. Sirhindi's deep awareness of the need for reform, combined with his intense suspicion of innovation and his distrust of any contact with the non-Muslim world, made him the pioneer of Muslim isolationism. Consequently, his assertion of orthodoxy led inevitably to a widening gulf between the Hindu and Muslim communities.

The division between the two communities received fresh impetus with the accession to the throne by Aurangzeb (1658–1707). Theologically conservative and suspicious of mysticism, Aurangzeb gradually introduced policies that were designed to differentiate between Muslims and Hindus. The conservatism of Aurangzeb, however, had disturbed many members of both the Muslim and Hindu nobility. In spite of the increasing tensions between the two faiths, at the beginning of the eighteenth century there was still considerable social amity and mutual understanding. Hindu and Muslim peasants, artisans, craftsmen and merchants worked in close cooperation. Hindu bankers, merchants and money-lenders controlled trade and commerce, and therefore exerted considerable influence in government. On the whole, religion played only a small part in political and official decisions. The non-religious laws of the government maintained control of the administration. The use of Persian as the official language also served as a strong unifying bond between the Hindu and Muslim upper classes.

The war of succession after the death of Aurangzeb inflicted a serious blow to the already stretched resources of the Mughal empire. Neither the weakened Mughals nor the Marathas were able to prevent the gradual influence of the British. The Battle of Plassey in 1757 ended the independence of Bengal. Many Muslims would have felt more comfortable with the Christian British in control than with the native Hindus. They would have felt a closer affinity with the monotheism of Christianity, with which they shared a common religious heritage, than with the perceived polytheism of Hinduism. The Christian British were 'people of the book' and many Muslims may have naively considered that the British had more in common with them than with the Hindus, and thus they would be held in special favour by the new rulers. For others, their sense of nationhood would have united them with Hindus as fellow Indians against a foreign invader.

However, this hope of an alliance between the 'people of the book' did not come to fruition and the decline of Muslim power highlighted a crucial inner tension within Islam; the tension between the ideal and the real. For centuries the pious in India, with their vision of a pure faith and their ideal of Islamic monotheism, had to endure the compromises made by their rulers in order to hold the empire together. As the reformed Sufi orders and the *ulema* seized the initiative, they predictably insisted on a return to the first principles of Islam based firmly on the Quran and the *Hadith*. With the rejection of scholasticism and mysticism, came the call for a pure and uncluttered faith. This intensification of Islamic consciousness assisted the creation of firm lines of demarcation between Muslim and non-Muslim. Many eclectic beliefs and practices tolerated over the centuries were now condemned as not Islamic. The authenticity of Islam was seen in exclusive rather than inclusive terms; compromise was regarded as abomination. Thus the prevailing attitudes were bound to result in antagonism and even conflict.

Shah Wali-ullah (1703–1762), was a *sheikh* of the Naqshbandi *tariqa* and is often described as the greatest Islamic scholar India ever produced. For example, Iqbal affirms Shah Wali-ullah as 'the first great theologian of Islam' (Metcalf 1982: 360). Shah Wali-ullah picked up the major strands of Sirhindi's ideas and developed them into a coherent ideology that was to form the basis of Islamic revival in the subcontinent right through to the present day. Through his inspiration, the religious leadership came to believe that political leaders could no longer hold on to the empire without the motivating force of religion. Like Sirhindi before him, Shah Wali-ullah reiterated that the lack of moral standards that led to the decline of Muslim fortunes was due to contact with Hindus and partially converted Muslims. He accused the Muslims of India of becoming Indians rather than identifying with the larger worldwide *ummah* (Karandikar 1968: 127).

Shah Wali-ullah was especially afraid that Islam, believed by Muslims to be the only religion that had not been corrupted by innovation, was itself in danger of losing its pristine and final revelation (ibid.: 127). This he felt to be the result of Hindu contact that encouraged the admittance into Islam of non-Islamic practices. He insisted that Indian Muslims should see themselves as an integral part of the larger Muslim world (ibid: 128). He saw the intolerable political situation as proof that Indian Muslims had failed to fulfil the requirements of the *shari'a*. It was incomprehensible to him that Islam itself could be at fault. Recommitment was required, and no true Muslim should accept the contemporary decline. He was convinced that a regenerated Islam could again be strong enough to counteract the effects of internal decay and external domination.

Shah Wali-ullah's descendants created a number of reform movements that still remain prominent within the subcontinental Muslim population. They all created strategies of isolation based on communicating the minutiae of strict adherence to the *shari'a* through education and the issuing of *fatwas* (opinion concerning Islamic law issued by an expert on the *shari'a*) (Geaves 1996b: 133–34). These strategies were created to maintain the borders of

Muslim group identity. They also allowed for some control over keeping Muslim life within the bounds of the *shari'a* when there was no Muslim state to enforce the law. The detailed restrictions on daily activity also functioned as a boundary that isolated those Muslims who observed these practices from both Hindu and British India. Furthermore the issuing of *fatwas* confirmed that India was no longer *dar al-Islam*; it was now *dar al-Harb*. When the British entered Delhi, Shah Abdul Aziz, the son of Shah Wali-ullah, issued his famous *fatwa* to this effect (ibid.: 134). The *fatwas* functioned as a recognition that organisation of the state was no longer in Muslim hands.

Conclusion

The success of Sufism in the subcontinent created a unique form of Islam in the locality, providing the possibility of Hindu–Muslim syncretism and various manifestations of eclectic mixing, especially at the popular level of religion. In spite of the success of the reform movements and Muslim communal identities in which factions amongst the *ulema* and other supporters of Muslim nationalism promoted solidarity with the worldwide Muslim community, religious revivalism and the creation of independent Muslim states, Sufism remained the dominant form of Islam in the region and helped maintain Hindu–Muslim unity. Even though both of India's dominant communities have been plagued by communalism, at the time of partition there remained enough Hindu–Muslim unity rallying around a common Indian identity to hold together an independent India with one of the largest Muslim populations in the world. Mushirul Hasan goes as far as to state that the lines of 'cleavage in north India were more sharply drawn between Sunnis and Shi'as than between Hindus and Muslims' (Hasan 2002: 197).

Islam in India is a distinct environment in which there has been considerable interaction with local indigenous traditions. Especially in Bengal and Punjab, local customs and heterodox traditions, blending Hindu and Muslim culture and religion, were assimilated into the wider body of religious practice and belief. Indian Islam has been a contested arena between 'little traditions' firmly rooted in Indian soil and various neo-orthodoxies often developed with political agendas. It is perhaps not surprising that Bengal and Punjab were the last of India's Muslims to sign up to Jinnah's vision of independent Muslim nations, in spite of their proximity to both east and west Pakistan (ibid.). Various commentators from the colonial period have commented on the ability of the two communities to blur the borders between themselves; Hindus celebrating Muharram, Muslims participating in Divali, and the singing of each other's devotional music (ibid.: 41–42).

My own experiences of research in the Indian subcontinent have shown that even in the all-India shrines Muslims, Sikhs and Hindus mix freely together. Furthermore in the village shrines, the local population are rarely concerned with the religion originally practised by the denizen of the tomb or shrine. Their motivations are more pragmatic, being concerned with both the material and spiritual benefits available to them through contact with sanctity (Geaves 1998). The first section of this article has indicated the doctrinal affinity between Sufism and Hinduism. Although it is possible for scholars to analyse the differences between *samadhi* and *fana*, it is highly unlikely that rural people would have discriminated between the subtleties of difference between the varieties of spiritual experience offering union with the Absolute.

Historically, many Sufis had been far more tolerant of Hinduism than the *ulema* of orthodox traditions, and some Sufis had been lax in their practices of the externals of Islam. Consequently, many wandering Sufis would have been content to tolerate the eclectic mixtures of traditions that they discovered in their travels. Carl Ernst demonstrates in his study of Khuldabad Sufis that although the texts indicated an Indianisation of Sufism, in that they utilised local language and imagery appropriate for the expression of their teachings, they were probably not written in that form for the express purpose of dissemination of Islam to non-Muslims. The Chistiya focus on interiorisation rather than the externals of Islam was orientated towards a spiritual elite who comprised the inner circle of a master rather than an audience totally unfamiliar with the essentials of Islam (Ernst 1992: 154–55). However, my point is that the main dissemination of influence would have occurred at the popular level where rural populations came into contact with the charisma and piety of wandering *fakirs* rather than texts written in high languages such as Persian or Arabic.

Even so, the syncretic nature of some Sufi-influenced writings such as those by Dara Shikoh or the mystical poets of Punjab and Bengal would have had their influence on governance. The interactions between Hinduism and Islam which have led to a more tolerant relationship between the two faiths, sometimes producing eclectic interweaving or even syncretist movements, can be analysed under three categories of communication. These can be defined as pragmatic relations, philosophical and religious parallels, and folk traditions. The last two are highly influenced by Sufism in the Indian subcontinent, but it can be argued that the affinity between Hindu and Sufi thought and practice provided the meeting ground for the pragmatic decisions that needed to be made by the Muslim governors of conquered territory; and Sufism's influence on holding together Hindu–Muslim unity at the time of India's struggle for independence remains to be assessed.

It was not only in folk traditions that Sufism helped to provide a Hindu–Muslim compound. In *Ashraf* culture it helped promote a sense of belonging to India that transcended cultural differences and created India as a unique sacred space for Islam. Hasan reminds us that those who migrated to Pakistan agonised on leaving the religious symbols of their faith, the *imambaras* of Lucknow, the shrines of Ajmer and Delhi, and the countless Sufi *dargahs* that formed a spiritual road map of the nation no less than the pilgrimage centres of Hinduism (2002: 212).

References

Ali, Yusef Abdullah. 1405 AH revised edition. *Holy Qur'an.* The Presidency of Islamic Researches, Mushaf Al-Madinah An-Nabiwiyah: King Fahd Holy Quran Printing Complex.

Burckhardt, T. 1963. *An Introduction to Sufi Doctrine.* trans. D.K. Matheson. Lahore.

—. 1990. *An Introduction to Sufism.* Northampton: Aquarian Press.

Corbin, H. 1969. *Creative Imagination in the Sufism of Ibn 'Arabit.* trans. R. Manhem. London.

Embree, A. 1988. *Sources of Indian Tradition,* Vol. 1. Columbia: Columbia University Press.

Ernst, Carl. 1992. *Eternal Garden: Mysticism, History, and Politcs at a South Asian Sufi Centre.* Albany: State University of New York.

Fakhry, Majid. 1997. *A Short Introduction to Islamic Philosophy.* Oxford: Oneworld.

Geaves, R.A. 1996a. India 1857: A Mutiny or a War of Independence? The Muslim Perspective. *Islamic Studies* 35: 1.

—. 1996b. *Sectarian Influences within Islam in Britain.* Monograph Series, Community Religions Project. Leeds: University of Leeds.

—. 1998. The Worship of Baba Balaknath. *International Journal of Punjabi Studies* 5, No. 1 (January–July).

—. 2000. *The Sufis of Britain.* Cardiff: Cardiff Academic Press.

Haq, M. Anwural. 1972. *The Faith Movement of Maulana Muhammad Ilyas.* London: George Allen and Unwin.

Hasan, Mushirul. 2002. *Islam in the Subcontinent.* New Delhi: Manohar.

Ikram, M. 1964. *Muslim Civilisation in India.* New York: Columbia University Press.

Karandikar, M. 1968. *Islam in India's Transition to Modernity.* Bombay: Orient Longman.

Kirkpatrick, Joanna. 1989. The Reflections on Popular Art and Culture in Bangladesh Today: The Persistence of Graven Images. In *Shaping Bengali Worlds, Public and Private,* (ed.) Tony Stewart. South Asia Series Occasional Paper No. 37, Asian Studies Centre. Michigan: Michigan State University.

Klostermaier, Klaus. 1994. *A Survey of Hinduism.* New York: State University of New York.

Lings, Martin. 1995. *What is Sufism.* Cambridge: Islamic Texts Society.

Nicholson, R. 1989. *The Mystics of Islam.* Harmondsworth: Arkana.

Metcalf, B.D. 1982. *Islamic Revival in British India: Deoband 1860–1900.* New Jersey: Princeton University Press.

Mujeeb, M. 1966. *The Indian Muslims.* London: George Allen and Unwin.

Rizvi, Saiyid Athar Abbas. 1997. *A History of Sufism in India*, Vol. 1. New Delhi: Munshiram Manoharlal.

Titus, M. 1979. *Indian Islam: A Religious History of Islam in India.* New Delhi: Munshiram Manoharlal.

Whinfield, E.H. (trans.). 1979. *Masnavi i Ma'navi: The Teachings of Rumi.* London: Octogon Press.

Zaehner, R.C. 1994. *Hindu and Muslim Mysticism.* Oxford: Oneworld.

CHAPTER TEN

Young British Sikhs and Religious Devotion

ELEANOR NESBITT

My mind and body yearn
but my Lover is far away in foreign lands...
Without the Divine One, how can there be sleep or hunger?[1]

Bhakti – in Punjabi *bhagti* – for which one translation is adoration of a personal God (McLeod 1995: 52), finds consummate expression in the *Adi Granth* (the Sikh scriptures, honoured by the title of *Guru Granth Sahib*). This poetry of intense love is the theme of Nikky Singh's rendering of selected passages from the scriptures which she has entitled 'The Name of My Beloved' (1995). The relation of the Gurus' *bhakti* (and of the God for whom they yearn) with North India's Bhakti tradition, and with the conceptualisation of God in the *bhaktas/bhagats*, who are in part represented in the *Adi Granth*, has been discussed by Sikh scholars, who point to shared insights while arguing for distinctive emphases (Neki 1995: 335–38; Singh 1961).

Concentrating instead on the contemporary Sikh diaspora in the United Kingdom, this essay takes a more ethnographic than theological, historical or textual approach to Sikh devotion, and looks at the ways in which young British Sikhs are nurtured in this devotion and give expression to it. However, with a view to exploring this complex of devotional behaviour in a historical and cultural context, the Sikh practice to which they are heir is examined in the light of wider North Indian cultural tradition.

Another context for the fieldwork among young Sikhs in Coventry is religious education in the U.K. (or, more specifically, in England and Wales). Here community (state-funded) primary and secondary schools provide statutory religious education that is multi-faith and non-confessional. Sikhism is one of the 'principal religious traditions in Great Britain' which must be 'tak[en] account of' by the local committees which design religious education syllabi (U.K. Government 1988). This essay therefore concludes with some challenges to the representation of Sikh experience in religious education that are posed by the data. It should be explained that, to an even greater extent than in the religious studies syllabi of higher education, the schools' religious education curriculum both assumes and reinforces an understanding that Sikhism and Hinduism are discrete faith traditions. Also pertinent to this concluding discussion is the fact that pupils are expected to learn from the religions which they study, as well as to learn about them, and that the schools' provision for pupils' 'spiritual development' is one focus of schools' statutory inspections.

The Research

Focussing on evidence of *bhakti* in the religious nurturing and experience of eight- to thirteen-year-old Sikh children in Coventry, this paper draws on data from an ethnographic study at the University of Warwick in 1991 of 'the religious lives of Sikh children' (Nesbitt 2000; Jackson 1997). This is supplemented by reports of more recent, smaller scale studies of Sikh children's experience of their faith in Coventry, Leeds and London (see Albans 1999; Davies 1997; Lall 1999).

The children's expressions of devotion, which were evident during participant observation in local gurudwaras and homes, are their physical participation in worship through respectful posture and gesture as well as through speech and singing. The transcripts of semi-structured interviews yielded their commentary on this involvement, which includes their verbal articulation of respect for certain individuals and for articles associated with Sikh religious practice.

Children's Expression of Devotion

Unless the *Guru Granth Sahib* (volume of scripture) is installed in the house, Sikh children's expression of devotion at home is most clearly directed towards religious pictures. These most often, but far from exclusively, depict Guru Nanak and Guru Gobind Singh. In the gurudwara the children show their respect for the enthroned volume of the scriptures. My preliminary exploration of Sikh children's religious devotion will also consider their expressed love for Babas (living spiritual masters) and will ask how their understanding of 'God' relates to these devotional foci, before questioning whether devotion/*bhakti* is in fact an appropriate term for their religious behaviour.

'Photos'

Thanks to religious pictures, including trade calendars, visual images abound in most Sikh homes (see Swain 1976; Mcleod 1991). These show the Sikhs' Gurus, the Harimandir Sahib (Golden Temple in Amritsar) and, in some cases, Babas and Mataji (the Goddess). I have elsewhere noted the prominence and frequency – by comparison with local English homes – of religious pictures in Punjabi homes (Nesbitt 1993). The pictures on the walls of the Sikh families who participated in the 1991 study conformed to Dosanjh's observation in Nottingham a generation earlier that non-Sikh pictures were few, and that the Sikh pictures were preponderantly of Guru Nanak and Guru Gobind Singh (Dosanjh n.d.). The iconography in Sikh children's homes exemplified visual anthropologists' Collier and Collier's suggestion (1986: 45) that 'the "look" of a home reflects who people are and the way they cope with the problems of life'. Indeed the pictures in these homes, while not constituting a more elaborate shrine (*mandir*) as in Hindu homes, nonetheless provided a focus for the physical expression of religious devotion, not simply an assertion of cultural heritage or religious allegiance.

To give particular examples, two children spoke of daily (morning or evening) seeing their mothers light an incense stick and circle it in front of 'the photos of every god'. (Like their parents, they referred to these pictures as 'photos'.) Lall has noted that such images influence children's devotion and that many 'liked to pray in front of them' (Lall 1999: 33). Similarly, from his study of six- to eight-year-olds in Coventry, Albans quotes from an interview (1999: 3, 6) with twin sisters in which he asked what they did or said in front of the pictures of Guru Gobind Singh and Guru Nanak in their house:

A. We pray. We put out hands together. When we finish we bow our heads.
Q. Do you light anything?
A. My mum lights it and she prays and we go and put scarves on our heads and then we pray…in the mornings, after we've had a wash.

Likewise Ranvir (aged seven) reported that:

When I wake up in the morning I always first do my praise [prayers] to God in front of his photo.

This physical 'photo' may also become a mental image (Lall 1999: 34). So, not surprisingly, Gates found, when he was researching young children's images of God, that almost all the Sikh children drew a bearded, turbaned man (Gates 1976) and Lall quotes from her interview (1999: 16) with a Sikh girl who would look at (Radhasoami)[2] Guru's picture when she was depressed:

The image is always in your mind....If you really believe in someone, then you don't need a photo.

Guru Granth Sahib

In addition to demonstrating, or at least being accustomed to witnessing, expressions of devotion focussed upon 'photos', all the young people knew the need to show respect to the *Guru Granth Sahib* in accepted traditional ways. For this, 'worship' was the word that one twelve-year-old girl used when trying to distinguish Sikhs from Muslims and Hindus:

> We don't worship monuments, like I think it's in Hindu, when they have I think it's a monkey dressed in robes....They have statues in the house and worship them and have photos...[Muslims] don't worship people—Guru, Guru Nanak and all that. They worship, they pray Allah, but Sikhism, we worship a book in a way, *Guru Granth Sahib*.

From infancy, on being brought into the gurudwara, the Sikh children had been taken to press their forehead on the floor in front of the scriptures (the obeisance known as *mattha tekna*). They learned to remove their footwear and to cover their heads before entering the *Guru Granth Sahib's* presence. Moreover they knew that respect ruled out certain postures:

> I can't stick my legs out in front of them because that's bad luck...like we sit in assembly, we just have to cross our legs. (Ten-year-old boy)

If their family had hosted the *Guru Granth Sahib* at home, usually for a special occasion such as a birthday or to bless a new house, the children knew that it must be installed where no one would walk above it (i.e. by walking across an upstairs room), 'or sleep directly on top of the *Maharaj*' (twelve-year-old girl 1991). Here *Maharaj* is the family's respectful term for the *Guru Granth*

Sahib; some others referred to it as the *bir* (volume). The room would be especially cleaned, a sheet would be spread over the carpet and a cloth suspended above the cushions on which the volume would lie. The children knew that the scriptures must be covered with a canopy and attended when open by someone waving the mark of its authority, the *chauri* (made from silky white yak or horse-tail hair), over it. Hence a nine-year-old girl's description:

> I think it's the Guru's hair from the beard and they wave it around....The person that's reading it sometimes waves it.

Children whose family had temporarily installed the scriptures at home in this way knew that the family would also welcome and provide food for the many visitors, of whom most would come to celebrate the *bhog*, the climax of the complete reading of the scriptures. Only vegetarian food could be prepared or served while the *Guru Granth Sahib* was in their house, and for this period the girls would wear Punjabi suits rather than western-style clothes. On arrival (usually by car) and departure from the house, the volume would be carried, appropriately wrapped in its cloths, on someone's head and someone else would sprinkle water on the floor in front of it. To quote the twelve-year-old again:

> It's like when *Maharaj* is coming through the door they splash it so...the person who's walking through the door is walking over clean *pharsh*, floor.

Children recognised the requirement for cleanliness in the presence of the scriptures and for having a bath before reading from them.

They spoke too of the respectful manner in which the volume is laid to rest for the night.

> And then they do Babaji, put Babaji to sleep and then they take Babaji upstairs....On top [i.e. above the door] there's Babaji's *sarup* [form i.e. picture]. It's got a bed and there's Babaji's chair,

Babaji's cushion things, Babaji's *sarup*—like Guru Gobind Singh. (Ten-year-old girl)

This detailed expression of devotion to the *Guru Granth Sahib* as the Guru's physical presence will be contextualised in Sikh tradition and North Indian devotional idiom below.

Babas

To return to the ten-year-old's words, her use of the honorific 'Babaji' applies to not only the *Guru Granth Sahib*, but also to the living Sant (or Baba), Baba Ajit Singh, whom her family revered, and to the tenth Guru, Gobind Singh. Such apparently encompassing usage indicates, as I have argued elsewhere (see Nesbitt 2000: 182–96), that for some Sikhs (including children) these three – i.e. living master, scriptures and historical Gurus – are identified as being one in the intensity of their followers' devotion. So, with reference to Baba Mihan Singh, a Sant in the Nanaksar succession (see Nesbitt 1985: 67–79), a ten-year-old girl explained:

We've got a person like we've got a God to us that we always appreciate and we actually do pray to him.

Indeed, by their translation of Babaji as 'God' and the tenor of their remarks about their family's chosen Sant, the children betrayed their own devotion. As already mentioned, the 'photos of gods' included pictures of living Gurus and Babas. Among these are Ajit Singh, in succession from Vadbagh Singh (see McLeod 1991: 132), Mihan Singh (ibid.), as well as Namdhari and Radhasoami masters, and (in Lall's research) the 'Guru' of Sachkhand Nanak Dham.[3]

'God'

Together with the young people's observation and observance of devotional practices focussed, outwardly at least, upon 'photos' of Gurus and Babas and upon the scriptural volume, the *Guru Granth Sahib*, there were their frequent references to 'God'. They spoke of believing in God, praying to God, loving God, respecting and listening to God, and thanking God, as well as of God forgiving people, helping them, speaking 'in your mind', 'com[ing] into me' and being powerful. On the basis of these ways of talking about God it would be easy to assume that God is other than or beyond the devotional pictures, the physical volume of scripture and the living holy men – and that these are symbols or icons, pointers to or channels of the divine – loci of sacramental exchange between human experience and 'ultimate reality'. However, as I argue elsewhere (Nesbitt 2000: 182–96), the children most often used 'God', often in the plural, as a synonym for 'Guru' (including *Guru Granth Sahib*) and 'Babaji', which itself was used to denote the ten Gurus, subsequent spiritual masters (if their families believed in these) and the scriptures. For the young Sikhs there appeared to be no tension between 'God' as a rendering of '*oankar*' (see many published translations of the *mul mantar*, the opening passage of the *Guru Granth Sahib*) or of '*Vahiguru*' and the use of 'God' for 'Babaji'.[4] Similarly to young British Hindus' usage, slippage from singular to plural (God/gods) was unproblematic for many of the young Sikhs (see Nesbitt 2001b). Rather than pointing to a lack of clarity about the focus of their and their families' devotion, it is perhaps more fruitful to ponder the convergence in this one English word 'God', as currently used, of European theology on the one hand and Hindu/Indic *darshan* on the other—in *darshan*'s dual sense of glimpsing the divine in many forms and of non-exclusive philosophical perspectives.

Devotion or Magic?

Enquiry into Sikh children's devotion raises not only the question of their understanding of God in this context, but also whether devotion/*bhakti* is an appropriate term to apply to ritual activity which they frequently reported in starkly instrumental terms. In many cases, when they reported acts of 'devotion', what came across was the children's perception of these as bringing 'good luck'. In fact the devotional act was performed in the spirit of either a petitionary prayer or a 'magical' invocation. For example a twelve-year-old described the annual *path* (reading of the entire scripture) in her home in the following terms:

> *Maharaj*—Guru Granth Sahib—it comes to our house for a week or so. Every year—Christmas holiday to New Year—we have it in...to bring good things into the coming year.

Another reported the protective power of the scriptures' presence in the house:

> Some people have them [i.e. the *Guru Granth Sahib*, referred to with the plural that shows respect in Punjabi] because they want to keep illness out of their house, to kill illness. My mum was ill and we had *akhand path* (uninterrupted reading). After that she was quite fine and now she's all right.

So too, in similar vein, children explained that they had gone to the gurudwara to pray for a baby sister or for good GCSE results. ('You put your money down [i.e. in front of the scriptures] and you stand up and say something—what you want to come true.') Children told me how before setting out on a journey their families would perform *Ardas* (the congregational petitionary prayer for which all stand), ending with the request 'God keep us safe' (nine-year-old girl 1991). The nine-year-old girl also affirmed:

> Miss, I think the *Ardas* is magic, because our car once stopped.... My grandfather did it [*Ardas*], then the car started...Our doctor said, 'Your dad's not going to get better until six weeks,' and my brother done the *Ardas* and my dad got better in just one week....So all our family thanked God and we went to the temple.

Longitudinal study, asking the same young people to reflect on the *Ardas* and prayer in general when they are adults, might reveal whether this motivation and expectation persist, or whether on this basis a mature understanding of *bhakti* develops.

We now turn to further consideration of the mutually reinforcing ways in which devotional activity is nurtured in young Sikhs, both informally and formally.

Children's Nurture in Devotion

Informal Nurture

Lall (1999: 40) rightly stresses the informality of most Sikh children's 'learning about the faith, done at the child's own pace, largely without formal input'. So too, in this chapter, their experience at home is outlined before paying attention to the more formal induction that some children receive, e.g. in the gurudwara's classes. The impact of relatives' example comes across clearly from the interviews. Children spoke of a parent, grandparent, aunt or uncle at home lighting an incense stick in front of the 'photos', 'praying' and 'doing *path*' (by reading or reciting scriptural passages, especially – in the morning – by listening to a tape-recording of *Japji Sahib*) and drinking holy water (*amrit*), sprinkling it or giving some of it to them to drink (Nesbitt 2000: 197–216). Parents' conversation about these practices entered children's consciousness. So, in speaking of *nam simran* (remembrance of the divine name), one thirteen-year-old boy informed me:

> If you do *nam simran* a lot you can see God. My mum was telling me once, she never used to do *path* or anything, then once in her mind she saw a light flashed…she saw sort of God picture.

Children also learned from experience in the gurudwara or (if the scriptures were being read in their house) in their homes that religious activity involved *seva* (service), in particular the preparing, serving and sharing of vegetarian food (*langar*) no less than listening to and reciting the Guru's words.

Amrit and Commitment

From living with their elders, children also become aware that individuals' lives differ in their degree of devotion, in the sense of commitment to Sikh principles and practices, that they display. Some of the young Coventrian Sikhs mentioned that their parents or some other relative had, at some point, assumed a more marked commitment. They recognised that this entailed their adopting a strictly vegetarian diet and being visually conspicuous as a 'proper Sikh' who would never allow hair to be removed from any part of their body (Nesbitt 2000: 217–41). The decisive act in this transformation' was *amrit chhakana*, i.e. receiving the sweetened water of initiation of recommitment to Khalsa discipline in a ceremony modelled on what is believed to have occurred in Anandpur in 1699 when Guru Gobind Singh initiated the first five Khalsa Sikhs.

Formal Nurture: Language and Music

In order to read the scriptures one needs to know Gurumukhi, the script used for modern Punjabi as well as for the 'sacred language of the Sikhs' (Shackle 1983). Parents enroll children in classes which, often using primers published in India, aim to make children literate in their 'mother tongue'. However only a minority proceed to even the standard of GCSE examination (intended primarily for sixteen-year-olds). In any case, the everyday Punjabi of the home differs in both structure and vocabulary from the *sant bhasha* (vernacular of North Indian Bhakti poets) of the *Guru Granth Sahib*. While children identify strongly with being and speaking Punjabi, in practice few attain to an understanding of the Gurus' poetry (Nesbitt and Jackson 1994: 49–67) and many can do little more than spell out simple words.

Given the centrality of *kirtan* (hymn singing) to Sikh devotion it is not surprising that, in addition to Punjabi tuition, concerned Sikhs organise *kirtan* classes for young Sikhs, teaching boys to play the *tabla* and girls to sing *shabads* and play the *vaja* (harmonium).

Davies found, during her fieldwork in a gurudwara in Leeds, that the young Sikhs concerned were motivated to play 'on stage', i.e. in front of the *sangat* during public worship (Davies 1997: 2). She also noted the importance of playing to their sense of identity as Sikhs and to their commitment to Sikhism (ibid.: 1). More difficult to identify and report is the way in which the individual's *bhakti* can develop through participating in *kirtan*. Gopinder Kaur played the *vaja* and sang in a *jatha* as a teenager and her words then (Babraa 1989: 19), which are reminiscent of Nikky-Guninder Singh's (1995: 7), communicate something of the interiorising of devotion when she had been 'learning kirtan for about two years':

> So, how does kirtan differ from singing any other song? The words you sing are from the *Guru Granth Sahib*. They should be sung in an attitude of prayer and meditation, so that there is something beyond the pleasing melody. Firstly, as the sangat sings, the vibrations coming from within us and around us have a physical effect on the body...kirtan can be soothing, refreshing and uplifting. It leaves us in a state of peace and turns our minds directly and completely to God. Kirtan is therefore a way to experience God.

Furthermore, the fact that many classes are held in a gurudwara environment, with Sikhs entering and showing their respect to the *Guru Granth Sahib*, also contributes to a cumulative nurturing in religious devotion (Davies 1997: 5).

It is noteworthy that in general this teaching of *shabad* does not involve translating into English (the language in which most of the children have a greater proficiency than Punjabi), even though the language of Gurbani (the Gurus' utterance embodied in scripture) differs from the Punjabi that they hear at home or encounter in their Punjabi classes. When asked about the 'meaning' of a *shabad*, they replied in very general terms or translated into English the opening two or three words. This was not surprising as little or no explanation of the words was offered in classes that I observed. In any case, a word-to-word English rendering would be difficult and even the gist of the Guru's poetry is challenging for teachers to convey in English. In fact this type of cerebral understanding was not regarded as a priority by Sikh teachers, and this is consistent with an understanding of *bhakti* as a matter of the heart, or of the whole person, rather than of just the head:

> We deliberately don't tell the meaning. Guru Nanak said that *shabad* is Guru; my thinking is *chela* [disciple]. People were illiterate. The Guru locked knowledge up in the *Guru Granth Sahib*. *Kirtan* opens it out like a wallet file. It's not a matter of head knowledge but *bhakti*. (Sikh teacher, interview 1991)

Albans recorded a conversation in which seven-year-old Jasbir distinguishes *shabads* from 'film songs' by explaining: 'These are to pray to God so he loves you more inside your heart' (1999: 10). Evidently detailed verbal commentary is not necessary for young children to respond to the inwardness and devotion of *shabad*.

Contemporary Sikh Devotion in the Context of the Gurus' Teaching

Nam Simran

The Sikh *bhakti*, into which these children are being nurtured, formally and informally, is articulated in Sikh preaching as the twin practices of *nam simran* and *seva*—inadequately translated as remembering the Name (i.e. of God) and service.

Nam is not merely the name of God but God's essential nature. Sikhs may recite divine names (*Satnam, Vahiguru* i.e. 'Whose Name is truth', 'Wonderful Guru') – this is *japna* or repetition – and also read the Gurbani or they may sing and listen to *kirtan*. The sacred hymns of the Gurbani are *shabad* (*sabda* or Divine Word). Through deliberately saturating themselves in this divine expression of truth, devotees 'unite with the Beloved who is far away, the Beloved who is deep within' (Singh 1995: 7–8). They may indeed become *jivanmuktas*, those who have been blessed during this life with *mukti* (liberation from rebirths). In this process the *sadhsangat* (congregation of righteous people) is a vital factor, influencing its members to be Gurmukh, spiritually oriented towards the Guru, rather than towards ego and waywardness (*man*). The *shabads* themselves are moving articulations of *bhakti*, 'the individual's longing to experience the Transcendent Reality' (ibid.: 1).

Seva

Nikky Singh goes on to say that this 'cleansing through love and devotion' is 'the starting-point of Sikh ethics' as expressed in the community meal (*langar*) and deed of love and service (*seva*) (11). *Seva* is voluntary service, lovingly rendered to others, and in practice refers most often to helping out in the gurudwara, for example, by serving the *langar* or looking after devotees' footwear. This *bhakti* is not one of detachment from the world or asceticism. The Gurus emphasised *grihasthi* (living as a householder with family responsibilities) as the preferred state, rather than endorsing the hierarchy of *ashramas* (stages of life in the Hindu schema for at least high-caste males), which peak in *sanyas* (renunciation). As Darshan Singh emphasises (1968: 74) on the basis of quotations from scripture (*Maru* M1 and *Sukhmani* M5), the Gurus' insight was that even to be an itinerant Hindu monk, a hero (*jodh*), celibate (*jati*) or *sanyasi* was of no use, because without *seva* no one could reap the fruits of his or her asceticism. Sikhs are exhorted to be not only *sant* (a spiritual individual) but also *sipahi* (soldier), ready for at least metaphorical combat. According to tradition Guru Gobind Singh praised his follower, Bhai Ghahnaiya, for distributing water to those who had fallen in the battlefield—this was true *seva* (McLeod 1995: 66). The twin emphases on preparedness for service, both as a host – and as a helper in a time of danger – and also as a fighter, are encapsulated in the Sikh slogan *deg teg fateh* (victory to the cauldron and the sword). Here the *deg*, a large cooking utensil, refers to the *seva* of *Guru ka langar* (provision of free food for the congregation) while the sword (*teg*) ideally frees from injustice and oppression. It must be remembered that, according to a strong strand in Sikh theological exposition, the Gurus were one in their inspiration. In other words this *bhakti* of the *sant-sipahi* is a consistent expression of the exhortation attributed to Guru Nanak some 200 years earlier:

Nam japo, kirt karo, vand chhako.
(Repeat the Name, work and share your earnings with others.)

While this applies to the whole of a Sikh's life, it is the gurudwara which serves as a laboratory for *bhakti*. A gurudwara (gateway of the Guru) is any place where the Guru as *Guru Granth Sahib* is installed, although in practice the term is applied specifically to public places of worship with the twin institutions of *pangat* and *sangat*, the serving of food to all as *langar* and the congregation focussed upon the *Guru Granth Sahib*. Today, with electronic amplification of the proceedings in the congregational hall, the *langar* hall is often as resonant with the word of the Guru as the congregational hall itself. For not only the *path* (reading), but also the content of the *kirtan* and the basis of the *katha* (sermon) vocalise the Gurus' word as embodied in the *Guru Granth Sahib*. And we now turn to the establishment of the *Guru Granth Sahib* as focus for devotion.

Guru Granth Sahib

The young Sikhs' reverence to the *Guru Granth Sahib* needs to be understood in the light of the injunction:

Guru manio granth
Guru granth ji manio.
(Acknowledge as Guru the *Granth*
Acknowledge the *Granth* as Guru.) (McLeod 1976: 66)

These lines are recited daily by Sikhs at the conclusion of the congregational prayer of petition, the *Ardas*. According to Sikh tradition, Guru Gobind Singh issued this exhortation prior to his death in 1708, so invalidating the claims of any aspiring follower to be his successor as Guru. In fact, the words '*guru manio granth*' first appear in the *rahitnama* (code of discipline) attributed to Prahilad Singh (ibid.: 36, 4).[5]

McLeod effectively conveys the loving devotion evident wherever the scriptures have been installed. 'The volume is greeted with affectionate reverence because for the Sikhs of today it is the Guru' (ibid.: 64). This means that not only does the content of the scriptures provide spiritual sustenance for readers and hearers but that also the volume is physically and imposingly present and central for acts of worship. Marriages are solemnised in its presence as well as requiring the recitation and singing of the *lavan*, four stanzas of Guru Ram Das's *Suhi Chhant 2* (*Adi Granth* 773–74). So, too, in order to bless a house or a new enterprise, the scriptures are installed and ceremonially read, either for forty-eight hours continuously (*akhand path*) or at intervals over a longer period (*sahaj path*).

Moreover, it is this requirement of honouring the *Guru Granth Sahib* in the same manner as the human Gurus were honoured which results (as is evident from the descriptions above of young Sikhs' religious nurture) in the volume being installed upon a *palki* (palanquin, i.e. special stand) or *manji* (small bed), on which it is shaded by a *chanani* (canopy) and fanned with a *chauri* (*chanwar*, made of yak- or horse-tail hair mounted in a handle). These were in origin the traditional ways of paying due respect to princes and other dignitaries in the hot climate of India.

The exhortation quoted above carries on by affirming that the *Granth* is '*paragat guran ki deh*' (the manifest body of the Masters) (McLeod 1976: 66). All this accords with the Guru's words according to the probably late eighteenth century *Prashan-uttar* that is traditionally attributed to Nand Lal (McLeod 1989: 53):

This [the *Granth*] you must accept as an actual part of me, treating its letters as the hairs of my body.

It is this regard for the scriptures as the Gurus' own body that results in the detail of devotion. For example, the place to which the scriptures are transferred for the night is often a room with a bed, as per the ten-year-old's description quoted earlier. On this it is ceremonially laid, after being carried, carefully wrapped, from its daytime position in procession on its attendant's head. What is more, in India the *Guru Granth Sahib* would be carried at night to a cooler room in the gurudwara during summer, in winter bed coverings are also adjusted to take account of climate. Indarjit Singh (1985: 24–29), however, sounds a note of protest at such practices:

> When the tenth Guru said, 'Consider the *Granth Sahib* to be the future Guru', he was clearly referring to the teaching, not to the physical paper and ink. He was referring to the contents, not the container. In building increasingly lavish 'rest rooms' for the Guru Granth Sahib in many of our Gurdwaras, are we not failing to distinguish between legitimate reverence and superstitious deification?

The detail and scale of devotion to the *Guru Granth Sahib* which can result from Sikhs' understanding of the *Granth* as body is perhaps most conspicuously exemplified in the conventions observed in gurudwaras of the Nanaksar sub-tradition, of which there is one in Coventry (Nesbitt 1985). This gurudwara was attended by some of the young Coventrians who were interviewed. In Nanaksar gurudwaras such as this the scriptures are installed on a full-scale bed with bedcover-sized *rumalas* (not the usual spare metre or so of cloth). A toothbrush is provided in the *sachkhand* (literally, realm of truth, the *Guru Granth Sahib's* overnight accommodation). Moreover food is offered daily before the scriptures, and at this time a curtain is drawn so that the Guru is spared the indignity of worshippers' stares while tasting the food (Doabia 1981).

Contemporary Sikh Devotion in the Context of North Indian Culture

Nanaksar and Babas

Nanaksar gurudwaras (in India, Britain and Canada) have been set up by followers of a line of spiritual masters (Sants) often referred to as 'Babaji' who are regarded as successors to Nand Singh (c. 1869–1943). Nand Singh himself would sit in meditation in *bhore* (holes in the ground) which ensured that he was lower than the *Guru Granth Sahib*, and so powerful was his faith in the Guru that, before the eyes of the artist Bhagat Singh, Guru Nanak manifested himself from the volume of scripture.[6] It was Nand Singh's disciple, Ishar Singh (b. 1916) who enjoined and justified the scale of devotion to the *Guru Granth Sahib* outlined above (Singh 1978). Their successors are publicly honoured and – privately by some individuals at least – mentioned as on a par with, if not actually being Guru Nanak reborn.

This particular example of Nanaksar-style devotion provides an illustration of a key dynamic – the Sant/Baba factor encountered in children's experience as reported above – in the devotion of many Sikhs. The evident devotion of one individual to the Guru inspires others to gather round him and in following his devotional teaching to express their devotion towards him. Integral to this devotion is the use of a title of loving respect (usually 'Babaji') rather than his names. For such charismatic (but many concerned Sikhs would say schismatic) personalities the generic term is *sant*. From this entourage emerge one (or more) successors, also distinguished by their manifest devotion to the Guru and to the Sant—and competing claims are made by their respective supporters.

Referring principally to the U.K. Sikh diaspora, Tatla (1992) relates how a Sant's followers will set up a gurudwara where he is unconstrained by the administration that is characteristic of the more numerous committee-run gurudwaras. With reference to religious devotion, Tatla is right to record that Sant gurudwaras

> have also become, in some measure, models of religious worship. By a strong emphasis on *nam simran* and hymn singing and a strict code of religious routine throughout the week, these new gurdwaras have set a new standard and pattern for others to emulate.

Certainly observation in Conventry suggests that many Sikhs gravitate to these 'Sant gurudwaras' to worship because of the spiritual atmosphere there which they distinguish from the preoccupations of some committee-run gurudwaras with internal and external politics.

For contemporary Sikhs the role of Sant is a divisive and contentious issue. While it is unproblematic for the Sant to demonstrate devotion to the Guru and to inspire and guide others in this respect, this easily shades into the Sant evoking and (willingly) receiving devotion. LaBrack points out the tension between 'personal worship of the Sant found so universally in Hinduism' and the 'orthodox Sikh' conviction that 'such veneration is due only to the Sikh Gurus and the *Guru Granth Sahib*' (1987).

This dilemma is also spelt out by Tatla with reference to the distinguished Indian freedom fighter and Sikh exemplar, Bhai Randhir Singh, who himself analysed the status of Sant in Sikhism in his *Sant Pad Nirnay*. As Tatla comments, Bhai Randhir Singh's followers, the Akhand Kirtani Jatha, take seriously his teaching that 'all praise must be to *Guru Granth Sahib* and God and there is absolutely no need for any respect for a living sant' but are themselves criticised for paying glowing tributes to Bhai Randhir Singh 'just like a sant' (353–54).

As LaBrack makes clear, from a Hindu perspective, by comparison, the role of living guides is generally unproblematic. Moreover, whether they are styled *bhagvan, swami, guru* or *baba* is not of ultimate concern. There will be differences of opinion between the disciples and the detractors of particular individuals, but there is widespread agreement that a living teacher can bring others closer to union with God (whether understood in personal or impersonal terms) and, indeed, that such a teacher may be indispensable. In this context, in one American Shaivite commentator's words, '*Bhakti* may be directed toward God, Gods or one's spiritual preceptor' (Satguru Sivaya Subramuniyaswami 1993: 693). Thus, on the subject of *bhakti* in Sikhism, Subramuniyaswami states:

> The highest goal can be realised only by God's grace, and this is obtained exclusively by following the *satguru* (or nowadays a *sant* or saint, since there are no living Gurus) and by repeating the holy names of the Lord guided by the *Adi Granth*, the scripture and sole repository of spiritual authority. (ibid.: 543)

This view does, however, contain an inherent contradiction between the advice to follow a saint and the central Sikh understanding that the *Adi Granth* is the 'sole repository of spiritual authority'. But, as LaBrack observes (1987: 268), in practice among the Sant's followers

> there is the same stress on affective worship that is at the core of all bhakti and which is easily expressed through the ragas and *banis* that are an integral part of every Sikh service.

Clearly, both the bodily idiom of Sikhs' veneration of the *Guru Granth Sahib*, in which young diaspora Sikhs are being nurtured, and the emergence of Sant traditions which impact on the nurture of many, are consistent with more general Indic (or 'Hindu') expressions of *bhakti* and can best be understood in this wider context. To take just one example, the Nanaksar practice of curtaining the *Guru Granth Sahib* from onlookers' gaze when food is offered to it, is unmistakably cognate with Hindu practice of drawing a curtain between the *murti* (image of the deity) and those present in the *mandir* (Hindu temple) when food (referred to as *bhog*) is offered to the deity. Moreover, when Ishar Singh, Nand Singh's successor, assured his followers that offering food to the *Guru Granth Sahib* was not idolatrous (unless they believed that the scriptures were simply paper and ink) he adduced instances from the lives of the *bhagats* (the pre-Nanak saints represented in the Sikh scriptures). For, he pointed out, it was through the *bhagat's* faith that the Lord had appeared in physical form from the images worshipped respectively by Dhanna and Namdev with true devotion (Nesbitt 1985: 71).[7]

Sikh Devotion, 'Hindu' Matrix and Religious Education

Clearly, the ethnographic study of young U.K. Sikhs in Coventry discloses Sikh devotion as continuous, as I explore elsewhere (see Nesbitt 1997a: 289–305) with more widespread North Indian practice. This is true whether one look at modes of reverence for the volume of scripture or at the role of Sants. The Coventry picture fits Geaves's account of unbounded, interacting traditions (Geaves 1998: 20–31), and Ballard's understanding of 'popular religion in Punjab' (2003). It certainly challenges uncritical reification and essentialisation of faith traditions (Jackson 1997).

It fits less comfortably with the paradigm of discrete 'world religions' which underpin syllabi and publications for religious education.[8] This paradigm, however, is completely in line with Sikh scholars' emphasis on the distinctness of Sikhism from Hindu tradition. Their conviction of distinctness must be respected as a defining aspect of identity and as a core belief for many Sikhs, and it is the basis of much Sikh theological discourse.

Reiterated in Sikh theologians' exegesis is the view that the Gurus marked a new beginning. So too with *bhakti*:

> *Bhakti* for them [the Gurus] is not a code of formalities and rituals, but an inward disposition. Though it is evolved through

the antecedent tradition of *Bhakti*, yet their concept of *Bhakti* is entirely original and is the product of the prevalent conditions in the country. They have adopted the traditional sense of *Bhakti* and gave it new meanings (Singh 1968: 208).

Moreover, concerned Sikhs are likely to challenge any educationist's or scholar's decision to include in their syllabus the role of Sants in contemporary Sikh devotion on the grounds that this legitimates individuals who jeopardise the Sikh *panth* both doctrinally and politically. To quote Gurbaksh Singh:

> [T]here are many new Sants claiming to be Sikhs but making their own disciples and giving them separate instructions...Sikhs have to watch them, reject them and disassociate from them.[9]

This analysis of the doctrinal and political threat posed by Sants is continuous with deep-seated suspicions and anger that led to a decade of violence including the murder of Nirankari Baba Gurbachan Singh in 1980 in Amritsar and of Maharaj Darshan Das in 1987 in Southall. That Sants are not simply the victims of (others') politics but also engage actively in politics, is evident from the Sant-centred politics of Punjab, from Sant Fateh Singh in the 1960s onwards (Tatla 1992).

Whereas higher education students can engage with the issues raised by the influence of Sants on many British Sikhs' spirituality, their inclusion in the school curriculum is more problematic. However, with reference to teachers' concern for their pupils' (including Sikh pupils') pastoral care and spiritual development, Lall rightly draws attention to the fact that:

> the reality of religious belief and practice for Sikh pupils in our schools is less precisely defined and very much more complex than most teachers have realised....If we are to meet children in the reality of their faith we will need to listen to them. There is a risk in making spirituality the heart of our RE lessons. (48)

This spirituality will draw upon Sikh scriptures and history primarily through the mediation of communicators (who may include relatives and Babas or those inspired by them) who stir their imaginations, hold their attention and motivate their engagement with the tradition of Sikh devotion.

Less controversial than this chapter's acknowledgement of the part played by succession of Sants in focussing young Sikhs' devotion is the centrality of the *Guru Granth Sahib* and the emphasis on *nam simran/japna* and on *seva*. Curricula for religious education and for religious studies which major on the five Ks of Khalsa Sikhism in their representation of Sikh tradition may fail to convey the yearning for the divine which pervades Gurbani. A religious education syllabus that introduces pupils to the poetic imagery of the *Guru Granth Sahib* in translation, and to the aesthetic beauty of *shabad kirtan*, can assist Sikh pupils in articulating in English something of their Gurus' inspiration as they encounter expressions of *bhakti* and – in whatever way – make them their own. It could well contribute to the spiritual development of pupils generally.

The Coventry study underlines the value of ethnographic research for reducing the gap between contemporary Sikh religious experience – nurtured as it is in the home, in the gurudwara and in *kirtan* classes – and the representation of religions in education. This study of young Coventry Sikhs' *bhakti* illuminates vital continuities between religious traditions in South Asia and twenty-first century diaspora youth.[10]

Notes

1. From Guru Nanak's *Bara Maha* (*Tukhari Chhant Mahalla* 1) as translated by Nikky-Guninder Kaur Singh (1995): 156.
2. For Radhasoami see Juergensmeyer 1987: 265–80.
3. For the Namdhari movement see e.g. Grewal (1990: 142–44).

Sachkhand Nanak Dham is a controversial movement whose Guru, Darshan Das, was killed in Southall in 1987.

4. The opening statement of Japji Sahib (and so of the Sikh scriptures) is '*ik oan kar*', usually translated as 'there is one God', but it has different historical and theological connotations. Thus from a Hindu perspective, which is rejected by many Sikhs, '*oan kar*' is the 'mystical' *om* syllable, and Nikky Singh's rendering (note 1 above) as 'One Reality' suggests a monistic rather than monotheistic concept. *Vahiguru* (also translated as God) originally meant 'praise to the Guru!' in the *janam sakhis* and later stories of Guru Nanak.

5. As a 'critical historian' McLeod points out that in fact the words, in the form quoted above, are of eighteenth century composition and that '*granth*' (volume) had replaced an earlier version exhorting Sikhs to regard the *panth* (Sikh community) as Guru. See McLeod 1976: 66.

6. Variants of this picture, in which Guru Nanak sits cross-legged, showing that the upturned sole of one foot is marked with the *padam* that usually signifies an incarnation of Vishnu, appear in Nanaksar gurudwaras and in Bowker (1997: 78–79).

7. The hymns of Dhanna (Rajasthani born c. 1415) and Namdev, a Maharashtrian Bhakti poet (1270–1350), together with the compositions of fellow *bhagats*, including Kabir and Ravidas, were included in the *Granth* by the fifth Guru, Arjan Dev, in 1604. Their inclusion made explicit the continuity between the Bhakti tradition and the insights of Guru Nanak and his successors, and means that these verses (the *bhagat bani*) are sung and heard by Sikhs as (in practice) integral to Gurbani. Miraculous account of their devotion enrich the fund of *sakhis* (traditional stories) recounted in gurudwaras during *kathas* (discourses).

8. See School Curriculum and Assessment Authority (SCAA) (1994a) and SCAA (1994b). For example, SCAA (1994a: 54) speaks of 'distinctive Sikh principles'.

9. As quoted in Lall (1999: 47) from a publication available from the Sikh Missionary Society, U.K.

10. The delicate relationship between religious education curricula and ethnography is explored in (Nesbitt 1997b: 98–110) and in (Nesbitt 2001a: 137–58).

References

Albans, Phillip. 1999. A Field Study of Faith, Nurtive in Young Sikh Children. M.A. essay, University of Warwick.

Babraa, Davinder K. 1989. *Religions through Festivals*. London: Longman.

Ballard, R. 2003. Challenging paradigms of Popular Religion in Punjab. www.art.man.ac/CASAS/presentations/teaching/teaching-files/frame.htm.

Bowker, John (ed.). 1997. *World Religions*. London: Dorling Kindersley.

Collier, J. and M. Collier. 1986. *Visual Anthropology: Photography as a Research Method*. Albuquerque: University of New Mexico Press.

Davies, Sarah. 1997. Children's Perceptions of the Transmission of Sikh Culture/Religion that Takes Place through Religious Music Classes. *Sikh Bulletin* 14.

Doabia, H.S. 1981. *Life Story of Baba Nand Singh Ji of Kaleran (Nanaksar)*. Amritsar: Singh Brothers.

Dosanjh, J.S. n.d. A Comparative Study of Punjabi and English Child Rearing Practices with Special Reference to Lower Juniors (7–9 years). Ph.D. diss., University of Nottingham.

Gates, Brian. 1976. The Language of Life and Death: Religion in the Developing World of Children and Young People. Ph.D. diss., University of Lancaster.

Geaves, Ron. 1998. The Borders Between Religions: The Challenge of the World Religions Approach to Religious Education. *British Journal of Religious Education* 21, no. 1: 20–31.

Grewal, J.S. 1990. *The New Cambridge History of India: The Sikhs of Punjab*. Cambridge: Cambridge University Press.

Jackson, Robert. 1997. *Religious Education: An Interpretive Approach*. London: Hodder.

Juergensmeyer, Mark. 1987. The Radhasoami Revival of the Sant Tradition. In *The Sants: Studies in a Devotional Tradition in India*, (eds.) Karine Schomer and W. Hew McLeod, 329–55. New Delhi: Motilal Banarsidass.

LaBrack, Bruce. 1987. Sants and the Sant Tradition in the Context of Overseas Sikh Communities. In *The Sants: Studies in a Devotional Tradition in India*, (eds.) Karine Schomer and W.H. McLeod, 265–80. New Delhi: Motilal Banarsidass.

Lall, Surinder. 1999. *'I Know who God is': A Study of Sikh Children's Spirituality within various Expressions of Sikhism*. Oxford: Farmington Institute for Christian Studies.

McLeod, W. Hew. 1976. *The Evolution of the Sikh Community*. Oxford: Clarendon.

—. 1989. *Who is a Sikh?* Oxford: Oxford University Press.

—. 1991. *Popular Sikh Art*. New Delhi: Oxford University Press.

—. 1995. *Historical Dictionary of Sufism*. Lanham: Scarecrow.

Neki, J.S. 1995. Bhakti and Sufism. In *The Encyclopaedia of Sikhism*, (ed.) Harbans Singh, 335–38. Vol. 1 A–D. Patiala: Punjabi University.

Nesbitt, Eleanor. 1985. The Nanaksar Movement. *Religion* 15: 67–69.

—. 1993. Transmission of Christian Tradition in an Ethnically Diverse Society. In *Religion and Ethnicity: Minorities and Social Change in the Metropolis*, (ed.) Rohit Barot, 156–69. Kampen: Kok Pharos.

—. 1997a. The Body in Sikh Tradition. In *Religion and the Body*, (ed.) Sarah Coakley, 289–305. Cambridge: Cambridge University Press.

—. 1997b. Bridging the Gap between Young People's Experience of their Religious Tradition at Home and at School: The Contribution of Ethnographic Research. *British Journal of Religious Education* 20: 98–110.

—. 2000. *The Religious Lives of Sikh Children: A Coventry Based Story*. Leeds: Community Religions Project, University of Leeds.

—. 2001a. Representing Faith Traditions in Religious Education: An Ethnographic Perspective. In L.J. Francis, J. Astley and M. Robbins (eds.). *The Fourth R for the Third Millennium: Education in Religion and Values for the Global Future*, 137–58. Dublin: Veritas Publications.

—. 2001b. What Young British Hindus Believe: Some Issues for the Researcher and the R.E. Teacher. In *Towards Religious Competence: Diversity as a Challenge for Education in Europe*, (ed.) H.G. Heimbrock, C. Scheilke and P. Schreiner, 150–62. Munster: Lit-verlag.

— and Robert Jackson. 1994. Aspects of Cultural Transmission in a Diaspora Sikh Society. *The Journal of Sikh Studies* 18 (1): 49–67.

— and Gopinder Kaur. 1999. *Guru Nanak*. Norwich: Religious and Moral Education Press.

Satguru Sivaya Subramuniya Swami. 1993. *Dancing with Siva: Hinduism's Contemporary Catechism*. Concord, California: Himalayan Academy.

School Curriculum and Assessment Authority (SCAA). 1994a. *Model Syllabuses for Religious Education*. Model 1. *Living Faiths Today*. London: SCAA.

—. 1994b. Model 2. *Questions and Teachings*. London: SCAA.

Shackle, Christopher. 1983. *The Sacred Language of the Sikhs*. London: School of Oriental and African Studies.

Singh, Balbir. 1978. *Pragat Guran Ki Deh*. Part I. Jagraon: Balbir Singh.

Singh, Darshan. 1968. *Indian Bhakti Tradition and Sikh Gurus*. Chandigarh: Punjab Publishers.

Singh, Indarjit. 1985. Sikhism: A Philosophy for Today. *The Sikh Messenger* (Autumn): 24–29.

Singh, I.P. 1961. Religion in Daleke, a Sikh Village. In *Aspects of Religion in Indian Society*, (ed.) L.P. Vidyarthi, 191–219. Meerut: Kedarnath Ram Nath.

Singh, Nikky-Guninder Kaur. 1995. *The Name of My Beloved*. London: Harper.

Swain, James B. 1976. Towards a Study of the Religious Dimension of Popular Art in Batala. In *Popular Religion in the Punjab Today*, (ed.) John C.B. Webster, 127–38. New Delhi: ISPCK.

Tatla, Darshan Singh. 1992. Nurturing the Faithful: The Role of the Sant among Britain's Sikhs. *Religion* 22, no. 4: 349–74.

UK Government. 1988. *Education Reform Act*. London: HMSO.

CHAPTER ELEVEN

The Religion of Music

JAMEELA SIDDIQI

The history of music began for me one evening in 1989, when Ustad Nusrat Fateh Ali Khan, (shortly before he was to become a world phenomenon) sang *qawwali* – the music of South Asian Sufis – at a small, private recital in London. Not only did that single recital result in a mind-blowing and transformational experience but, thereafter, every other kind of music I heard spoke to me with renewed meaning. Perhaps I was finally obeying the Sufi dictum of listening with the heart rather than the ears?

That recital also led me to attempt to learn more about the classical music of North India, something that has been, and continues to be, a subject of extensive study both in India and elsewhere. Most of my knowledge in this field is experiential rather than theoretical. And in this essay I do not attempt a scholarly analysis of this great and ancient musical tradition. I began asking questions to as many musicians as I met and then reverted to some written materials as a way of supplementing my understanding. Unable to sing or play an instrument and never having had a single music lesson in my life, I found myself writing about and interpreting music in a way that provided me with an ever-curious audience. Many of my listeners and readers felt excluded from the inner mysteries of Indian classical music and I discovered an ability to capture some of these nebulous concepts in a language that spoke to them. No doubt, in so doing, I learned more. And, it is basically this journey of enchanted discovery that formed the core of my musical presentation at the DHIIR Conference in Cambridge, 2000, on which this chapter is based.

It is perhaps surprising that every civilisation has developed some form of music – independently of others – starting with the human voice and culminating in manufactured instruments. Since musical notes were first produced by the human throat, the Indian sage Bharata, in his *Natya Shastra*, the most definitive work on the arts and music of ancient India, has emphasised the paramount importance of vocal music. The highest and purest type of music could only be that which based itself on the human voice. The voice works on the principle of one note at a time and, over the centuries, India has retained this principle, privileging melody over harmony. From this one principle, it has evolved into a highly complicated and sophisticated system of modal music.

Although different musical traditions eventually influenced one another to a greater or lesser extent, it is a source of never-ending amazement to realise that parallel civilisations heard and distinguished, roughly, the same seven notes (or twelve tones) of music but used them in different ways to produce melody. Yet, different cultures have produced vastly different melodies using the same musical notes, and 'foreign' music is almost always considered strange. But this 'strangeness' does not apply to rhythm. Rhythm contains a universality that is linked to the human heartbeat itself, and seems to cut across linguistic and cultural boundaries. Mystic sages, and most notably the Sufi teacher and musician, Hazrat Inayat Khan (1882–1927), have stated that rhythm appeals to the baser nature of human beings while melody resonates with the more refined aspects of the human soul (Khan 1991). Musicologists still argue about whether the rhythmic element of music grew out of the physical activity of work or whether it was the result of leisure pastimes such as dance. But whatever its secular associations, in most cultures music is closely associated with religious ritual.

Religion is a living reality for the masses of the Indian subcontinent in a way that it has not been in western industrialised

society for a very long time. In India, religion does not just amount
to faith and belief but consists of the observance of elaborate rituals
to reaffirm that faith. The most mundane human tasks and
situations carry a serious religious significance.

No religious ceremony is complete without music, which is
believed to be of divine origin and it is widely thought – in all
religious traditions – that something as beautiful and ethereal as the
sound of music (the sound of Creation itself) could not have
originated from humans. It can only have been a gift from God.
Its technique can be learned and taught by mere mortals, but its
substance can only ever remain with the divine.

While music plays an important part in Indian devotional rituals,
the different religious traditions of India have inherited the same
classical music tradition. The same *ragas* and *talas* (melodic scales
or structures and rhythm cycles) are sung by Sikhs, Hindus and
Muslims, not only in secular contexts but also as functional,
religious music. Indeed, much of North Indian classical music as
we know it today, is a result of the gradual synthesis between Indian
Hindu and Persian Muslim musical traditions. These have evolved
into a distinct form and one that is easily distinguishable from
southern India's ancient music, now known as Carnatic (or South
Indian) music where we find far less evidence of such mixing.

While devotional music, whether of the Hindus, Sikhs or
Muslims is highly ritualised, even secular musicians – that is, those
who perform outside the temple and on western-style concert stages
– evoke the name of God before they start to play or sing. In the
words of Hazrat Inayat Khan, who was the first person to bring
Indian classical music to the West: 'I am His flute and He plays
me whenever He chooses.' Khan frequently narrates a fascinating
Sufi legend about music:

> When God first made a statue of clay (the human body) and
> ordered the soul, which had always existed, to enter that body
> of clay, the soul protested that its nature was to fly about freely,

and not to be constrained by a body. God then ordered the angels to play their music. As they did so, the soul became ecstatic and then realised that to savour this ecstasy to the fullest it would do well to enter the body. Although living inside the human body brought limitations, it also offered certain compensations such as the acquisition of the five senses, thus enabling a greater appreciation of music, with all the emotional sensitivity of a human being as opposed to the calm detachment of soul. So, it is said, it was music that enabled the soul to overcome its reservations at being imprisoned, because this imprisonment, for all its drawbacks brought one major joy—the enhanced ability to savour music. (Khan 1991)

Although this is a Sufi legend forging the inseparability of humankind, music and the Supreme Being, according to ancient Hindu belief, music was not only the property of the gods but served as actual proof of their being. Sound itself was said to be of two kinds: *ahata nada* (audible or struck sound) and *anahata nada* (inaudible or unstruck sound). The aim of mystics and *yogis* through the ages has been to somehow capture the magic of this inaudible sound and to be able to hear it continuously while still living on an earthly plane so as to attain complete *moksha* (or liberation of the soul). In some verses of the Upanishads where the Supreme Being is said to be manifested in and symbolised by the sun, its rays are referred to as the 'seven white horses' corresponding to the seven musical notes. When the sun sets, its rays are no longer seen but go on being heard as music. In tying the seven notes of music to the daily journey of the sun, various theories emerged which appropriated particular melodies for particular times of day or night. It is interesting to note that most religious traditions have prayers or rituals for sunrise as well as sunset. Classical *ragas* are allocated particular times in relation to the position of the sun as seen from earth. The most magical times are deemed to be around twilight (dawn and dusk), and the *ragas* attributed to this sector of the day invariably consist of certain minor notes, generally the second and/or the sixth. These *ragas* are called the *sandhi-prakash ragas*—in which we experience a 'mixing of light'. In musical terms, this signifies an alertness that is triggered by the magical hours of twilight and dusk resulting in an altered and heightened state of consciousness. *Ragas* consisting of these notes, (e.g. Bhairav or Marwa) are not only particular favourites in the Hindu devotional tradition, but are also sung by Muslims and Sikhs in praise of God. Music and song are the principal forms of expression of human sentiment. Devotional religion, which appeals primarily to the emotional sphere of human consciousness, finds its foremost and fullest manifestation in music. Musical activity, therefore, represents the vital and most essential component of the divine service in any tradition of devotional religion.

The whole concept of melody is thought to have emerged as part of a religious rite, more specifically, a sacrificial rite of the ancient Vedic era. When the Aryans first came into India, their culture was introduced through the four Vedas, collections of sacred verses said to have been conceived by the sages through divine inspiration. These verses were strictly prescribed to be chanted in three distinct pitches, or tones of voice—*udaata*, *anudaata* and *svarita*, which roughly translate as 'regular', 'lower' and 'medium'. The *svarita* or medium pitch is the one that connects the regular and lower pitches. Many different patterns of chanting emerged depending on the ritual being performed, and it was believed that the wrong intonation would definitely ruin the benefits of chanting as the gods would be displeased and the sacrifice rendered null and void. In time, these three tones or vocal pitches gave rise to permutations and total combinations that led to rudimentary forms of melody. Later forms—*jatigans*, *samagans*, *ragas* and *raginis* as we know them today, emerged from a long process of evolution. Somewhere along the line a distinction was made between the music of the gods (*margi sangeet*)—that which was sung or played to please the deities; and the music of the people (*desi sangeet*)—that which was linked to particular cycles of life, death, work and celebratory rituals. The latter formed the embryonic phase of what we now know as 'folk music'. (The word 'folk', however, is hardly sufficient to define such a vast and varied body of music that is said to come from the 'soil' as opposed to music which was specifically reserved for use in worship.) While religious or temple music emphasises correct intonation and melody, folk music is generally distinguished by its rhythms, which play a far more important part than melody, since this kind of music is rooted in physical human activity. Folk music is often said to be the music of the land, not least because of its associations with an agrarian way of life. Along with that, it takes a 'cradle-to-grave' approach with songs for birth and songs for death, and everything else in between.

There is a misguided tendency among purists to view classical music as though it were an unchanging cultural monolith, untainted by outside influences. North Indian music, as we know it today, is a synthesis of Hindu–Muslim (Persian) traditions, and even South Indian Music (at first thought to be less influenced by other musics) is now very much in a give-and-take situation with its northern counterpart.

The growth and expansion of the Mughal empire also saw Indian temple music coming into the Muslim courts where it underwent further development to please royal ears. Many innovations were made. Older forms such as *dhrupad* (an ancient, austere style of singing devoid of all ornamentation) was further perfected. Further down the centuries entirely new genres of singing such as *khayal* (a more ornate or romantic style of *raga* rendition) and *thumri* (lyrical, light classical song) were developed. But, during the early Sultanate period, the most enduring contribution and indeed one that gave rise to a completely new music that we now know as North Indian classical music, took root with the arrival of the Arab–Persian mystics or Sufis, during the twelfth and thirteenth centuries. Sufis are Islamic mystics who reject orthodox ritual and dogma in preference for complete surrender and unconditional loving devotion to the One God. In this they share a resonance with the Hindu Bhakti idea. Sufi disciples are trained by a master to overcome the urges of the short-sighted ego (or *nafs*) and to realise the wider purpose of one's existence by serving and loving all of God's creatures. Although they are mystics from within the Islamic tradition, Sufis believe that no one single religion can lay claims to exclusivity over divine truth, and that it is the same God who has revealed this truth to different cultures and civilisations in whichever way it was best understood. The Chishtiya Sufi order goes a step further and considers music to be a most effective language for uncovering the whole mystery of life on earth and *qawwali* remains the single most important religious ritual of Indian (and Pakistani) Sufis. Among all kinds of music, song (or vocal music) occupies the leading position—first because it needs only the human voice to be produced; and second, because song is the only type of music in which God can be praised verbally.

The Indian term that describes the aesthetic or emotional experience is *rasa* (literally 'juice' or any kind of liquid) which implies a flow. *Rasa* is thus the connecting flow between the human and the divine, and it is *rasa* that enables humans to relish the divine. In its original context, it was related to ancient Indian theatre and the dramatic arts where it refers to the sentiments displayed (or 'emoted') by an actor in a drama.

Rasa is a chief component of Bhakti music, and song is a verbal manifestation of *rasa*. Music is the principal vehicle of emotional expression and the primary element to set the flow of *rasa* in motion. Wherever music is practised with sincere devotion and love for God, its positive powers can unfold and become fully effective. Devotional religion makes consequent use of the bliss-giving qualities of music, and it is song that brings humans forward on the way towards their ultimate aim. This point was made most emphatically by the *qawwal*, Ustad Nusrat Fateh Ali Khan in an interview:

The aim of Qawwali is to reduce the distance between Creator and created. When I sing, if even one person in a thousand feels closer to God, then my work is done.[1]

In the South Asian Bhakti tradition, song is regarded as the principal way of divine worship. Singing for God, or *to* God, evokes a spiritual oneness with the beloved divinity—the ultimate quest in any religious tradition in which the human being relates to God on a personal level. When religious feelings become embodied in song, the positive effects of music can unfold in their entirety. Singing in praise of God awakens the singer's consciousness of the divine being and makes him or her (as well as listeners) sensitive to the divine message. Song establishes a direct contact between the divine and human spheres. This relationship can really only function interactively. The necessity to re-establish the relationship between human and God, time and again, accounts for the continuity of song and for the persisting relevance of music in the religion of *bhakti*.

Keeping in mind the vital importance of song, of the vocalised glorification of God, in the tradition of devotional religion, it appears logical that the Indian Bhakti movement was initiated and advanced by mystic poet-singers rather than theoreticians.

(The Indian Sufi element incorporates this unique *bhakti* flavour which is totally absent from the musical traditions of other parts of the Muslim world. Although West Asian and North African music can be spiritually exalting, the music of the Indian Sufis carries an unmistakable element of purely *bhakti* ecstasy.)

In *bhakti*, the relationship between Creator and created is all-pervasive and the human being achieves many more avenues for closeness to God. It is by no means a one-sided or rigid contact in that it is not based on reverential fear. God is not treated as an otherworldly phenomenon but one who is very much part of *this* world. The analogy of human love, with all its sensuality and even eroticism, is often the poetic idiom through which this highly personalised God is addressed. Many of the medieval Bhakti poets composed their verses to sing them as part of the daily ritual service—whether in temples or in the streets.

Attention to the deity throughout the day is an immediate expression of the intimacy in the relationship between human and divine. People relate to God on various levels, and the way in which this relationship is perceived finds its manifestation in the way in which worship is performed. God may be venerated as one's master (or *guru*), respected as one's friend, loved as one's child or adored as one's lover. Worship is not out of a sense of duty or a fear of the consequences of not remembering God, but more as a means of constantly evoking and maintaining an intimate bond. The essence of *bhakti* is that the ritual acts of worship are performed with sincere devotion and not as a mechanical activity. For the Sufi, as for the person experiencing *bhakti*, the ultimate quest is for spiritual union with Allah/God.

When the Sufis arrived they were so completely enraptured by ancient temple music and so enamoured of the old Hindi dialects of North India, that they incorporated these elements into their own Arab–Persian tradition, and *qawwali*, as we now know it in North India, was born. Even so, *qawwali* hardly resembles modern-day Persian or Arabic music and is most definitely a semi-classical offshoot of Indian music, distinguished from mainstream classical styles by its powerful rhythms, hand clapping and a chorus of male voices. Most vitally, *qawwali* carries· an unmistakable element of *bhakti* which lends it a particular brand of ecstasy that is not found in Sufi music outside of India. (I should qualify that North African, Persian and other Arabic Sufi music can be very exalting and spiritually uplifting, but *qawwali* is unique in that it contains the flavour of *bhakti* borrowed from Hindu devotional tradition.)

Qawwali's chief architect was the poet-musician-mystic Amir Khusrau of Delhi (1253–1325), a brilliant and multifaceted genius of his time and a leading disciple of one of the greatest Indian Sufi masters, Hazrat Nizamuddin Awliya (1242–1325) of Delhi. It is an ancient Khusrau composition that is generally acknowledged as the world's first *qawwali*:

> *Man kun toh Maula*
> *Fah Ali un Maula.*
> If you accept me as your Master
> Then Ali, too, is your Master.

The lyrics are in the narrative voice of the Prophet Muhammed and allude to the high regard He had for his son-in-law, the fourth *caliph*, Hazrat Ali. Hazrat Ali is often considered the first real Sufi in terms of his relentless striving at becoming a better human being. There are numerous *qawwali* song texts in praise of Ali, collectively known as *Manaqibat-e-Ali* the idea being that whereas the Prophet was a naturally perfected human being, Ali, like most ordinary mortals, had to work hard to achieve (spiritual) perfection.

Khusrau composed verses in Farsi (Persian) as well as Braj Bhasha (old literary Hindi) with equal fluency. While the Prophet and Hazrat Ali formed the main subjects of his Persian poems, Khusrau's Hindi verse made free use of the Radha–Krishna love story. The poetic metaphor of Radha's broken water pot and Krishna's mischievous 'now you see me, now you don't' antics became the perfect symbols for the difficulty of attaining knowledge of the divine through an elusive and at times 'mischievous' guide or master:

> *Bahut kathin hai dagar panghat ki*
> *Kaise ke bhar laaon madwa se matki.*
> The way to the river isn't easy
> How do I fill my pot with nectar [sweet water]?

The tough path leading to the water is a metaphor for the difficulties awaiting the disciple on the spiritual path. Just as Radha fears that Krishna might lie in wait, ready to break her pot at the first opportunity, so the spiritual disciple must remain alert to all the treacheries that await the seeker on this path. The water source

itself, represents knowledge of God and one's capacity for this
knowledge depends on the size of this 'pot'—if it hasn't been
smashed by unseen forces, that is. In other Hindi poems, Khusrau
uses the poetic convention of *shringar rasa* (the erotic sentiment,
which is often expressed through the image of *vasakasajja*—the
woman who adorns herself to meet her beloved). One of his most
enduring poems on this theme is still a great favourite at *qawwali*
recitals.[2] While spiritual seekers use it to remember the
all-important underlying message of facing one's gods (and demons)
in a final moment of reckoning, the song is also enormously
popular with the spiritually uninitiated who can relate to it as an
erotic song of seduction. Such dual meaning is persistent in all of
Khusrau's Hindi verse:

Apni chhab banayke
Main to pi ke paas gayi.
Jab chhab dekhi pihu ki
Main apni bhool gayi.
Chaap tilak sab chheeni re mose naina milayke.
Prem bhati ka madwa pilayke
Matwari kar deeni re mose naina milayake.
Khusrau Nijaam [Nizamuddin Awliya] ke bal bal jaiye
Mohe suhagan keeni re mose naina milayke.

I made up my face
And went to see my Beloved
But as I looked upon him
I forgot all about my own appearance.
Our eyes met, and all my finery, my decorum came to nothing.
He fed me the nectar of love
And I became drunk when our eyes met.
Khusrau sacrifices everything for Nizam
He made me a married woman, when our eyes met.

The image is that of a besotted young woman who has
painstakingly worked on her appearance for a meeting with her

beloved, but when she comes face to face, all her make-up is smudged, her fine clothes crushed and her jewellery redundant in the ecstasy of union. The imagery is enormously powerful and erotic alluding to the dishevelment that is inevitable during lovemaking. In Sufi terms, the essential underlying message is that however much we adorn ourselves, when we finally stand before our Creator, we stand naked. The rest of the poem refers to Khusrau's relationship with his master, Nizamuddin Awliya, and their spiritual intimacy is, typically, couched in the language of sexual intimacy. The verses follow the classical Hindi poetic idiom of a smitten female lover and a male beloved and the song is in the persona of the female. (In Urdu or Persian poetry this would be reversed—the pining lover, male, and the uncaring, somewhat affected and coquettish beloved, always female.)

Numerous light classical and folk songs (particularly the *thumri, hori, kajri* and *sawan* of Uttar Pradesh) have been incorporated into the *qawwali* repertoire so that the beloved can be read both ways—human or divine. For instance, Amir Khusrau's famous:[3]

> *Ghar nari, ganwari, kahe so kahe*
> *Main Nijam [Nizam] se naina lagae aayi re.*
> Let the illiterate woman [next door] say what she wants to say
> My eyes have entangled with the eyes of Nizam.

The 'entangling' of eyes, is a favourite Hindi (Braj Bhasha) poetic metaphor alluding to the 'meeting' of eyes and the first such meeting resulting in what is known in the West as 'love at first sight'.

Qawwali still falls outside the practices of orthodox Islam and may only be performed at the *dargahs* (or tombs) of Sufi saints and masters. Where orthodox Islam was concerned, music was recognised as a powerful and possibly corrupting influence, and its very power became its undoing. Further, when powerful mystical poetry was combined with music the result was so intoxicating that the clergy took it upon itself to ban music altogether. Mystic musicians became adept at deliberately garbling the 'message' and turning it into nonsense syllables such as 'da ra dir re ta na na dhim', etc. which can easily pass off as 'meaningless' rhythmic beats for the uninitiated. This song form, known as *tarana* survives to this day and forms an essential part of North Indian Sufi music. But *tarana* is not the only musical form to employ such covert tactics. There is considerable evidence that more modern musicians, although not necessarily threatened with religious persecution, nevertheless had a variety of reasons (mainly political) for obscuring the meaning of some of their songs. And, this deliberate 'garbling' is by no means restricted to eastern traditions of music. A notable case in point is Elvis Presley whose musical roots came from Blues and Gospel, and who often reinterpreted other people's songs adding newer layers of meaning and sometimes pretended to forget the words using the opportunity to lapse into staccato (Nazareth 1997: 50, 55, 64).

Although music can offer a distinct spiritual experience, the dividing line between such an experience and pure emotionalism or entertainment is very fine. The Islamic clergy soon recognised that they could not harness the power of music and so decided it was best outlawed. As a result, to this day, there can be no musical recitals in a mosque. All the same, it was the sound of human-made instruments that was outlawed, and not the human voice itself which still recites the *azaan* (the Islamic call to prayer) rhythmically and melodically. An Afghani musician and exile, reacting to the former Taliban government's outlawing of music said:

> They ban the pipes and drums and strings. But just let them ban the birds from singing! Don't they know that the birds sing because Allah makes them sing?

Be that as it may, many an orthodox Muslim leader would argue: 'Allah might well make them sing. But it's Satan who makes them dance…'

Although it is never performed in a mosque, *qawwali*, performed within the context of a *mehfil-e-sama'a* (or assembly of listeners for spiritual purposes) can only be executed with the strictest of rules and procedures for listeners and performers alike. Such a *sama'a* can never take place without being presided over by a *sheikh* (or Sufi master) and listeners are instructed to arrive in a state of *wudhu* (ritual ablution as performed before a Muslim prayer). They are seated according to the *sheikh's* instructions, the most senior listener being placed on the right of the *sheikh*. Needless to say, seniority is not determined by age but by spiritual stations attained. Although an entranced listener may rise up in a spontaneous dance, applause is forbidden at all times and one may only show appreciation by saying *Subhan Allah* (Allah be praised) or some similar phrase, the idea being that however talented an individual may be, it is ultimately God who deserves praise. Similarly, when a listener is particularly moved by a melodic phrase or a poetic verse, he gets up to make an offering of a small amount of money and this is presented to the senior listener who must then hand it to the musicians. The listener must only use his right hand and the money, known as *nazar* (from *nazrana* meaning gift) should be given as a spontaneous, not calculated gesture. The amount of money is irrelevant as it is supposed to signify the offering of the listener's head in a symbolic, sacrificial gesture of 'laying one's head down' in appreciation of a particular line – or even word – of poetry. The modern-day concert-hall practice of listeners showering *qawwals* (performers of *qawwali*) with heaps of dollars and pounds and sometimes even throwing in the car keys and the wife's jewellery, is both vulgar and demeaning and a far cry from the original purpose of *nazar*.

In a *sama'a*, the entire *qawwali* recital takes place in the purest of surroundings, the object being to raise the level of spiritual awareness in singers and listeners alike. It is for this reason that a group of *qawwals* can never sit on a western-style stage or podium. Purists argue that it is vital for musicians and listeners to sit at the same level, on the floor, with every vibration of sound enhancing spiritual awareness in the listener's whole being (Siddiqi 2000: 203).

The late *qawwal*, Ustad Nusrat Fateh Ali Khan (1948–97) who was almost single-handedly responsible for the popularisation of *qawwali* in the West, told me in his last interview that as the duty of a *qawwal* (performer of *qawwali*) is to reduce the distance between the Creator and created, even if one person in a thousand can feel closer to his Creator, then his job is done.[4] Ironically, Nusrat's fame as a *qawwal* in the western world rocketed at almost exactly the same time as Islam was being demonised in the media in the aftermath of the Rushdie affair.[5] It would appear that audiences (who by and large didn't speak or understand any of the languages in which Nusrat was singing) basically reacted to the pounding rhythms of *qawwali*, while its essential lyrical message of the Islamic mystic's quest was of no consequence. When I asked Nusrat about this in 1997, he said:

> Whether they speak the language or not, Allah's message is such that it bypasses the *aql* (intellect) and goes straight to the heart.[6]

Pakistani mystic singer Abida Parveen explained this in a BBC World Service interview:

> What you hear is not even a small fraction of what I actually feel. And it is that depth of *feeling* that communicates itself to listeners.[7]

While the rules governing the ritual of *sama'a* are so stringent about purity and cleanliness of body and spirit, a visit to a Sufi shrine to listen to *qawwali* can, at first, appear to be an anomaly. The uninitiated visitor to the tomb of Hazrat Nizamuddin Awliya in Delhi can become too easily waylaid by the distractions that are a permanent feature of India's prime Sufi spots. Noise, dirt, chaos, confusion, hustlers, black-market-currency dealers rubbing shoulders – quite literally – with the great, good and rich, as well as the poor and homeless of Delhi. The approach to the main tomb is by means of long, winding tunnels, lined with stalls selling baskets of rose petals, rose water and embroidered pieces of cloth which are purchased by pilgrims as offerings for the tomb. Late at night, these same tunnels are lined with hundreds of sleeping bodies, their ragged shawls and blankets providing a thin veil between their emaciated limbs and the harsh Delhi winter. As one gets closer to the entrance, the tunnels seemed to get more and more narrow, and full to the brim with numerous 'shoe-minders' who operate a stunningly efficient system amidst the mayhem, ensuring the safe-keeping and return of hundreds of thousands of pairs of shoes. By the time this congested tunnel life is traversed and a reasonable shoe-keeping rate negotiated, the faint-hearted or claustrophobic may well feel an uncontrollable urge to turn back and run, but somewhere in the near distance, the strains of an ancient Khusrau composition would entice one to stay:

> *Khusrau rayn suhaag ki,*
> *Main jagi pi ke sang*
> *Tan mora, man pihu ka, dou bhaye ek rang...*
> O Khusrau, this wedding night
> I spent awake with my Beloved
> My body, his soul, enmeshed as one...

The *qawwal* has a religious duty to perform. His is a family business handed down through the generations and his duty is clearly spelled out to him. Like other musicians he too needs a thorough grounding in the basic rules of North Indian classical music but he also has to commit to memory numerous mystical poems in Persian as well as old Hindi, the two main languages of *qawwali*. A *qawwal's* ability to produce literally thousands of verses from memory alone, is of paramount importance. *Qawwali*, although sung from a pre-set composition for the main song and refrain, is completely open to improvisation for the practice of *girah* (literally a knot, meaning here, additional verses) inserted on an extempore basis where the inserted verse enhances the meaning of the original song. Individual *qawwals* are often distinguished by their ability to surprise and delight listeners with an appropriate *girah*, giving that particular performance an added uniqueness.

At the Sufi *dargah* of Nizamuddin Awliya, the birthplace of *qawwali*, the Nizami family has held the position of 'Qawwal Bachche' – literally the offspring of the original *qawwals* as trained by Amir Khusrau – for nearly seven hundred years. The Qawwal Bachche are not to be confused with the Sajjadanashin, or the actual blood descendants of Nizamuddin. Although he never married, Nizamuddin had a married sister whose descendants are now the 'minders' of the shrine with the Qawwal Bachche serving as resident musicians.

Attached to the main courtyard of the *dargah* at Nizamuddin is a small mud hut with a corrugated tin roof. The *teykhana*, or cellar, of this hut – once kitchen of the *khaniqah* (shrine) – now serves as a small sitting room. In its heyday, this kitchen turned out meals for infinite numbers of people. Tens of thousands still line up for food daily, and it is said that despite the fact that the shrine cooks have no idea of numbers, there is always enough for everyone, nor is there any wastage of food. The *qawwals* say this phenomenon of abundance or *barqat* is the result of Nizamuddin's blessing. Apart from providing a focal point for Sufi music, and a place for food and temporary shelter for the poor, the Sufi *dargah* acts like a magnet for supplicants: the sick pray for magic cures, the childless for children, pining lovers for success in love, students for success in exams...

In 1997, the oldest Nizami was Mahmood Nizami, then said to be ninety-six. I asked him to verify the history of *qawwali*, particularly with regard to Amir Khusrau who is cited by many scholars but nobody seems to agree on the details of his life.

'What do I want with books written by western-educated professors?'. Mahmood Nizami snapped at me. 'I choose to believe what has been handed down by my elders,' he added.

He then proceeded to tell me his version of the story of *qawwali*. It is a plausible story, passed down through the generations but absolutely unverified by historical documentation:

A teenaged Amir Khusrau is said to have turned up at the home of Nizamuddin on hearing about the great Master. He is met in the outer courtyard by a senior disciple who, of course, has instructions not to allow the upstart poet to come in. Khusrau says he has a question for the Master. He poses the question in the form of a riddle, making the first line of a couplet, and asks the disciple to relay this to the Master. He adds the condition that the answer should come back in a form that solves the riddle *and* completes the couplet, and then only then, would he accept the greatness of the Master.

Nizamuddin, who is not used to being addressed in this way, surprises his disciples when he decides to rise to the challenge, and promptly, sends the answer through the same disciple—solving the original riddle and completing the couplet.

Khusrau is said to have been completely overwhelmed by the Master's brilliance and from that moment is desirous of becoming a disciple. But it is another eight years before the Master formally initiates him.

During those eight years of waiting and hoping, Khusrau continues to turn up at the Master's almost every day, only to be repeatedly denied an audience with Nizamuddin. He proceeds to send elaborate verse messages pleading with the Master to accept him into discipleship.

The original disciple who carried the message from Khusrau to Nizamuddin, carried several such messages over the years. In time, these Persian verses became more elaborate and eventually they came to be sung. That messenger became the Master's 'official' singer and gradually other disciples joined in the chorus. Khusrau himself would compose the tunes and instruct the 'messengers' on how to sing his verses for the Master. His brilliance as a poet and as a musician finally began to take form through the process of sending messages to Nizamuddin. The musical form that emerged from these messages came to be known as *qawwali* (as we hear it today) and its performers, *qawwals*. The Qawwal Bachche are the direct descendants of those singers who were originally trained by Khusrau to sing his verse-messages for the Master.

In time the repertoire swelled and increased to include the Master's poetry, sayings from the *Hadith* (or traditions of the Prophet), as well as poems in medieval Hindi (or Braj Bhasha) which was the main regional North Indian language at that time. The high point of these compositions is called *rang* (literally means 'colour'). Khusrau composed *rang* to celebrate his long-awaited acceptance into discipleship. Almost every modern-day *sama'a*, or *qawwali* recital, still ends with *rang*. The poem, which suggests a contagious, joyful exuberance is testimony to Khusrau's unbounded ecstasy at being initiated by the Master. Seven hundred years on, it still has the power to move sensitive listeners to joyful tears:

> *Mohe apne hi rang mein rang de*
> *Mohe rang basanti rang de*
> *Joh tu maange rang ki rangayi*
> *Mora joban girhvi rakh le.*
> Dye me in your colour, O Beloved Master
> Dye me the colour of spring
> And if you want payment
> Then I pawn my youth to you.

Qawwali is essentially a family business and only males may sing or participate as accompanying musicians or hand-clappers. Daughters and daughters-in-law do, of course, exist and reside at *dargahs*, but are seldom seen by outsiders. Many still follow the practice of *purdah* or veiling and are largely confined to the home and the kitchen where they raise the children, and turn out sumptuous meals for their musically gifted husbands, brothers and sons, and the hundreds of admirers who follow them everywhere. But the twentieth century has seen a radical departure from tradition at least in the case of one phenomenal female mystic singer: Abida Parveen, of Sindh, Pakistan. But Abida is not, technically speaking, attached to an actual Sufi *dargah*. The many *dargahs* and Sufi shrines of Pakistan have simply accepted her as one of their very own in a radical departure from a tradition that dictates that women remain out of the public eye. She is probably the first Muslim woman to have carved out such a unique niche for herself—an internationally renowned female singer of devotional music. Her repertoire is based largely on Sindhi, Seraiki (eastern Punjab) and Punjabi Sufi poetry, and the mystic poets who wrote these verses drew freely from the folk-story tradition of legendary love tragedies, that of Laila–Majnun, Shirin–Farhad, Sohni–Mahival and Heer–Ranjha. In a culture that thrives on these love stories, yet totally rejects the concept of romantic love in its reality, all these legends are easily transformed into powerful allegories of the mystical quest. Although her songs are similar to *qawwali*—at least in poetic content and sentiment, her song-style is known as *kafi*, and is largely based on the mystical verses of the Sufi saints of Sindh. Shah Abdul Latif (1690–1752) wrote his verses (known as the *rissalo* and popularly called 'The Way of Shah Abdul Latif') to be sung in particular classical melodies. The verses of Waris Shah, the Punjabi poet of *Heer* (based on the story of the doomed legendary lovers Heer–Ranjha) are also sung in specifically prescribed *ragas*, as detailed by the poet-musicologist himself. The verses are still sung by faithful *fakirs* at the tomb every single night. Unlike *qawwali*, which relies heavily on a chorus of male voices as well as heavy clapping for rhythm, *kafi* is primarily a solo genre with a poetic metre of its own. It shares certain traits with the *ghazal* form, but unlike the *ghazal* which can also be read, *kafi* is designed really *only* to be sung, and many authors clearly specify the melody which singers should use. These melodies are drawn from the vast repertoire of North Indian classical music which consists of over 500 set melodic structures (*ragas*) with their own stringent and ancient musical rules, as well as specified and prescribed times of day and night when these *ragas* may be performed.

Abida Parveen's songs include outstanding verses not only from Shah Abdul Latif but from all the prominent mystic poets of the region, and since these verses were written to be sung and memorised, she is seen to be doing much towards keeping the tradition alive. The poetry of Shah Hussain (d. 1593), Sultan Bahu (whose *taqhallus* or distinguishing poetic signature was to finish every verse with the Sufi word '*Hu*'), Bullhe Shah (1758) and Sachal Sarmast (d. 1823)—all figure prominently in her repertoire.

One of her best loved songs is the mesmerising rendition *Yaar di gharoli* ('The Friend's water pot') by Sarmast which she uniquely blends with Shah Hussain's *Ghoom Charakra* ('Turn, spinning wheel, turn!'). The mixing of two different poetic metaphors re-emphasises and enhances the message of both poets. Both poems are centred on ordinary household tasks of the medieval period. In the first song, she sings:

> I have filled my Friend's water pot, and now I fear no one except the One God.

The poem goes on to depict the plight of the clay water-pot drawing a poignant likeness to the striving disciple on the spiritual path:

> I was first beaten and shaken, then kneaded like the potter's clay
> Then I was put on to the wheel as the fire of separation engulfed me
> The fire blazed away, and my life was consumed in You.

In *Ghoom Charakra* the scenario is that of a young woman, mesmerised by the repetitive sounds of the spinning wheel:

> The wheel cries 'Lord, Lord!'
> And the yarn says 'You Are!'
> And Hussain the fakir says
> 'Lord, You are all.'

But Abida Parveen's best known and most popular song in the West is *Dumadum Mast Qallander*, also known as *Jhul-e-lal*. It is in the Seraiki language and its subject is Usman Marwandi, popularly called Lal Shahbaz Qallandar. *Jhul-e-lal* is an additional term of endearment meaning 'the living ruby' (the precious one), and is one of the many names given to this mysterious Sufi saint who arrived in the lower Indus Valley from his home in Marwand in Azerbaijan during the thirteenth century. He died in 1274 and is buried in a beautiful tomb in Sewan Sharif. The words of the song refer to *mast Qallandar* (the God intoxicated dervish) and the tune is set to the hypnotic rhythm of the *'dhamal'* dance which has been performed in front of his tomb for hundreds of years after the sunset prayer (*maghreb*).

Abida Parveen says she was drawn to mystics and to the music of the shrine *fakirs* at a very young age. Her father, Ustad Ghulam Haider, a gifted classical musician and teacher who also became her *murshid* (guide), noticed her talents very early on and concentrated all his energies on training and grooming her as a singer. In fact, when she was still only five years old, he nominated *her* as his musical successor, over and above his male descendants. She also trained with one of the greatest classical singers of all time, Ustad Salamat Ali Khan who now lives in Lahore, Pakistan. In doing this, she was already making a radical departure from tradition, a tradition that dictates that girls from 'good homes' do not sing or dance. That kind of thing is left to the courtesans.

Abida Parveen, herself, has no problem in treating any venue, however sanitised or smart, as an underground Sufi cell adjacent to a shrine. It is obvious to any onlooker that she is on some deep mystical quest of her own. She throws herself into the music wholeheartedly – swaying freely – hands stretched upwards, her index fingers pointing heavenwards to emphasise the oneness of God. I asked her how, given the limitations of language, Europeans as well as younger generation Indians and Pakistanis, and people of all nationalities could become so overpowered with her songs.

'The truth doesn't need to be told. It can only be experienced. Remember, I'm not performing. He is singing through me. It is His song, and it sings by itself.'

'So are you very close to Him when you sing?' I ask.

'I am always close to Him, whether singing or not,' she replies. (Siddiqi 2001: 10)[8]

Sacred scriptures prescribed to be sung in specific *ragas* is also a feature of *shabad kirtan*, the focal point of Sikh religious practice. *Shabad kirtan* consists of sacred verses designed to be sung in particular *ragas*. The verses sing the praises of the Formless One and are recited continuously at the holiest Sikh shrine, the Harmandir Sahib at Amritsar. The singers need rigorous training in classical music as the *ragas* have to be correctly delineated. The songs are set to fixed *talas* (or rhythm cycles) to provide a full spiritual experience of the carefully measured verse. Guru Arjan Dev, the fifth Guru of the Sikhs, is credited with compiling the verses known as *Guru Granth Sahib*, set to thirty-one different *ragas* of the North Indian classical music tradition. For this reason, *shabad kirtan* shared certain musical characteristics with *dhrupad*, *khayal* and even *qawwali*.[9]

In the Hindu tradition, music was a well-established part of the temple ritual. However, orthodox Hinduism was challenged by devotional music that took root outside the temple – in the streets and the bazaars – composed by mystic poets of the Bhakti movement. Bhakti (which roughly translated as 'loving devotion') was a protest movement of the medieval period, that ran parallel to the flowering and development of Sufi musical traditions, with both systems actively feeding off each other. Like the basic Sufi message of love, Bhakti too highlighted love between the Creator and created, over and above the rigidity of scriptures that only the learned could read and interpret. In the Hindu devotional tradition itself there are two main modes of worship. The *saguna* approach is based on devotion to a deity with a physical form, while the *nirguna* approach considers God to be beyond the limitations of physical form. The Bhakti movement, emphasised *viraha* (separation) from the Beloved. This kind of separation was said to heighten the suffering of the lover (or devotee) who senses his or her separation from an unseen Beloved (God) and can only hope to ease that pain through realising the presence of God in his/her own heart and in everything else.

Some of the most beautiful love poetry in the world comes from the leading lights of the Bhakti movement: the *Gita Govinda* of Jayadeva and the *bhajans* (Hindu devotional hymns) of Tulsidas, Surdas, Kabir and Mirabai are popular to this day. The popularity of the Bhakti poets also played a vital part in the development of regional vernaculars, posing a serious challenge to the language of the scriptures, Sanskrit, which had hitherto been the sole sacred language of the land. Many *bhajans* emphasise the importance of realising God – seen and unseen – in every aspect of life. The lyrics often stress the importance of the *guru* (like the Sufi Master) and emphasise that only a true *guru* can show the way to God. Kabir, for instance, often uses 'God' and '*guru*' as interchangeable terms, but also distinguishes between them by sometimes placing *guru* higher than God. He say:

> *Guru Govind dohu kharde*
> *Kin ke lagoon paaye*
> *Balihari Gurudev ki*
> *Govind diyo bataye.*
> If God and Guru both stand before me
> At whose feet should I fall?
> I choose the Guru
> Because he has led me to God.

This idea is completely consistent with the Sufi message of unconditional surrender to the Master, and with Sufi and Bhakti saint-poets both sharing the same classical music tradition, it was simply a matter of time before poetic idioms began to be shared as

well. In the verses of Kabir, for instance, all traditions seemed to
gel into one. Little wonder then that all three main religions of
India, to this day, eagerly claim him as their very own.

The idea of complete and unquestioning devotion to the *guru*
(or Master) is also central to the traditional system of classical music
training. Although this devotion usually relates to one's spiritual
guide, it is equally reserved for the music teacher (more often than
not one's own father or uncle, or another male relative). The
tradition of the *guru–shishya parampara* (teacher–disciple etiquette)
is common to musicians all over India, regardless of religion, region
or even musical form. It is an almost perfect reflection of the
spiritual guide and pupil relationship. Often, one's music teacher is
also a teacher of life. Although now often replaced by western-style
music academies and colleges, the traditional *gharana* system of
training in classical music is still considered the purest and best.
Gharana literally means family and learning music from one's
musical predecessors is considered the only way to maintain musical
purity and stylistic integrity. Different *gharanas* have their own
features and styles. These features range from highly complex
musical and technical rules to the simple matter of how to sit, or
how to hold the instrument. The pupil learns by imitating the
teacher—an ideal solution in the absence of musical notation.
Traditionally, pupils who were not related by blood were still
expected to move into the teacher's family house and perform
various mundane tasks like cleaning, washing or fetching water.
This was in lieu of payment to the teacher for imparting his musical
knowledge. The entire system rested on complete subservience to
the *guru* or teacher to the extent of not even speaking in his
presence. This traditional *gharana* system of training, obviously, not
only had to change in India but with so many European and
American students becoming interested in Indian music, newer
methods of teaching had to evolve for societies where respect and
deference to seniority do not come naturally. Much however
remains relatively unchanged—for instance, the unquestioning

devotion to the *guru*, the voluntarily and lovingly performed acts of service to him/her, the oral transmitting of knowledge and so on. But enough has changed for the Sufi teacher and musician Hazrat Inayat Khan to note wryly in his biography: 'In the West, there are no disciples; only teachers' (De Jong-Keesing 1974).

Perhaps the most astounding thing in all the different traditions of devotional music in India is that the religious vocabulary of the poetic idiom is easily interchangeable with Muslim Sufis freely citing the Radha–Krishna story while there are numerous pleas to Sufi masters in some *bhajans*.[10] Some of the most evocative verses celebrating the love of Lord Krishna and his consort Radha are still part of the classical *qawwali* repertoire.[11] In classical vocal music itself, the best *Ganesh stutis* (songs in praise of Lord Ganesh) are still sung by the many great Khans of Hindustani vocal music. Many of these Muslim maestros have Hindu disciples who begin their lessons with the single word *Bismillah* (in the name of Allah), while Muslim disciples of Hindu maestros are taught breath control with the mantra *Om*. The Dagar family of *dhrupad* singers, Muslims, still begin every recital with the invocation *Om* and say that singing *dhrupad* is their main religious ritual.

Parallel to the Sufi–Bhakti traditions and to some extent feeding off them, a form of devotional music also emerged in Bengal—the music of the Bauls.[12] Its esoteric content is similar to Sufi and Bhakti songs but its musical content is derived from the enormously rich folk tradition of Bengal with a lilting, distinctive sound of its own. Their name is derived from the Sanskrit root word *baul* (meaning 'mad') and the Bauls are essentially wandering minstrels who can be either Hindu or Muslim. The essential underlying message of their music is the same—unconditional love and surrender to God. The music of the Bauls is devotional music par excellence. The Bauls show a very self-conscious attitude in their relationship with God, treating this relationship as intensely personal and rejecting any form of organised religion and scriptural authority. Only the emotional aspect is of relevance, for God cannot be reached through knowledge obtained from the study of scriptures without the emotional bond being tied. In order to establish emotional contact with the 'man of the heart', Bauls resort to the most simple and natural vehicle—song through which they verbalise all their experiences on the way towards their ultimate aim. Thoughtful contemplation on universal principles is combined with the articulation of momentary emotional states, with the expression of pain as long as the desired union is yet to come, but always with the omnipresent sentiment of boundless, limitless devotion and love. The language of Baul songs is rich in symbolism and the songs are arranged in such a way as to guarantee that the meaningful words are delivered with full effectiveness. Words of particular significance for their poetic content are given special musical emphasis; such words are often maintained on stretched melodic phrases ascending to very high registers. Sometimes these philosophical statements are hidden in poetic pictures, at other times they are in plain and straightforward language. The unsteadiness of the spiritual path, time and again described and lamented in Baul poetry, is reflected in the musical structure of the songs which is characterised by frequent alteration of sections in free rhythm and strictly metricised parts. The melodic material is drawn from the rich tradition of Bengali folk music. While the Bauls reject all organised religion and ritual they too follow a 'discipline' which has been termed *ultisadhana* (literally 'topsy-turvy devotion') believing that life on earth is a mere bridge through which one passes to the other side. The love of God is seen as the only lasting commodity in an otherwise transitory existence and in keeping with the Sufi–Bhakti legacy, the longing for divine union is conveyed through vivid images and metaphors of romantic human love. The poet-musician Rabindranath Tagore was very inspired by the Bauls and some of his verses were written specifically for them. But the Bauls are not healers or soothsayers attempting to comfort ailing hearts with music. On the contrary, their aim is to goad and provoke, to charm and tease, and to inspire their audiences as much with pleasant contemplation as with the necessary task of facing their own inner demons. Thus Bauls are not only feared, but often actively despised in areas where the masses are driven by religious dogma and ritual piety. They arouse extreme emotions wherever they go, from outright hostility and condemnation to unrestrained joy and fervour. A Bengali proverb asserts that 'the sound of a Baul's lute sets off a mad wind which drives everybody crazy', and true enough, some are driven mad with joy while others are driven mad with hatred and outrage.

Baul music is particularly captivating in that it combines the best spiritual elements of Sufi and Bhakti traditions with the musical traditions of Bengali folk, notably *bhatiyali* (or the songs of the boatmen) whose energetic rhythms of lapping water make an ideal backdrop for the Baul's 'crazy' love. Using the metaphor of the hazardous water journey (life), the Baul often implores the boatman (the *guru* or Master) to row him across safely to the other side (passing from the earthly plane to the heavenly one). In a region where water is one of the main forms of transport, the Bengali peasant knows his temperamental rivers only too well. He is born beside them, lives by them, and in death his ashes flow down their turbulent currents.

But the Baul who was the original *fakir* and wandering ministrel now performs to packed concert halls in Paris and in London, in much the same the same way that the resident Sufi tomb musician, the *qawwal*, does. Both have lucrative recording contracts and feed an unending demand for their music created by an affluent diaspora as well as native populations in the western world. The fact that most European and North American *qawwali* fans had been raised in a secular tradition seems to have made no difference to their enjoyment of this music.

The term 'World Music' was coined in 1987 as a blanket description for non-western popular music, initially in response to the increasing interest in African popular music forms. Western popular culture discovered Africa in the 1980s, the way India and the Orient had been discovered during the previous two hundred years. 'World Music' became a commercial definition for making 'foreign' music rather than a description of a particular music. The only prerequisite was that it sported certain 'ethnic' elements to make it fit into popular western culture. *Qawwali* seemed particularly well suited for this new category of extremely marketable, profitable 'World Music' because it sounds strangely familiar (just as the sitar, in the 1960s, had sounded vaguely like an electric guitar to pop musicians and their fans). The words may be unintelligible to non-Hindi/Persian/Urdu/Punjabi speakers but the syncopated rhythm set up by the hand clapping is so close in feel to the ubiquitous rock 'back-beat' that western audiences immediately feel at home. In time, two kinds of *qawwalis* emerged: that which was performed for the benefit of the masses and the 'real thing' which was reserved for aficionados who were prepared to take the trouble to brave the heat and dust of real Sufi shrines. In a similar process, *bhajans* too were more and more 'showcased' into expertly engineered, high-quality recordings and concert performances; but the real thing, nevertheless, went from strength to strength within its original temple context. Even so, an ever-growing number of discs emerged from 'new age' labels marketing these Bhakti songs as an ideal accompaniment for *yoga* and meditation taught in largely western institutions. That they did so without diluting the essential *bhakti* element of the music is a tribute to the sensitivity of (some) record producers as well as their recording artistes.[13]

While every religion in the world has a musical culture of its own, the Indian subcontinent is unique in that however widely differing in belief and ritual, all the religions share the same musical and poetic tradition. More important, two of the best and most enduring things to have come out India – the North Indian classical music tradition and the Urdu language – came about as a result of Hindu–Muslim encounters. In this respect at least an Indian Muslim, if he is being honest, will admit that he shares more common ground with an Indian Hindu or Sikh than he does with say, a Syrian or Egyptian Muslim. But relatively recent political events often make it difficult for warring sides to acknowledge any kind of cultural sharing, whatever its historical validity. The present climate of Hindu–Muslim tensions, both in India and abroad, precludes any understanding of this fact and in any study of classical North Indian music, each side is generally reluctant to acknowledge the contribution of the other. It is equally sad to see orthodox Wahhabi[14] trends in mainstream Islam dismissing *qawwali* as heresy inherited from the Hindu tradition, as it is to see extreme sectarian elements within the Hindu tradition recklessly undermining Muslim contribution to North Indian languages and music. Some of these extreme elements have attempted to rewrite Indian history so that the period of Muslim ascendancy is shown to amount to nothing more than widespread debauchery and senseless bloodshed. British imperial interests were at times well served in perpetuating the myth of a 'golden age' of Hindu culture which was said to have been ruthlessly ransacked by invading Muslim armies. Similarly, post-independence Islam, particularly in Pakistan, was one that sought to rediscover a mythical Arabian past rejecting its Indian roots as a hangover from 'Hinduisation'. It is a sad fact that when lands are partitioned on grounds of religious differences it is very tempting for both severed parts, already ruptured by political events, to also actively destroy any semblance of cultural homogeneity.

As something of a romantic idealist, I have a cherished dream: just as India's devotional music grew out of a tradition of give-and-take between Hindus and Muslims, I hope and pray that this same music, now so celebrated all over the world, will once again serve to bring different religions closer. It grew out of their closeness and it should, now, become the main cementing factor in achieving a renewed understanding and respect for each other's religious beliefs. As the late *qawwal* 'Munshi' Raziuddin Ahmed of Karachi said, 'You can call Him what you like. He remains One!'[15]

Notes

1. In an Urdu interview with the author at Lahore, Pakistan, for *Songs of the Sufi Mystic*, Programme 3, BBC World Service Series, March 1997.

2. Various excellent renditions on the *qawwali* exist on different recordings. Try Nusrat Fateh Ali Khan's *Traditional Sufi Qawwalis: Live in London 1989*. Volume 2, track 3; NAVRAS NRCD 0017, *Greatest Hits of Sabri Brothers*. Vol. 2, track 5; Serengeti Sirocco SIR CD-046.

3. Ibid.

4. Interview, March 1997. See Note 1.

5. In 1989, when Salman Rushdie's *Satanic Verses* was published, orthodox Muslims all over the world, and particularly in Britain took it as a direct insult against their faith. Iran's leader Ayatollah Khomeini pronounced a *fatwa* (or death sentence) against the author. The incident led to much negative publicity for Islam as an intolerant faith. Ironically, 1989 was the very year in which the West embraced *qawwali*! See also Farrell 1997.

6. Interview, March 1997. See Note 1.

7. In an interview with the author for 'Every Woman', BBC Radio and World Service, August 2001.

8. For examples of Abida Parveen's music try *Songs of the Mystics*, NAVRAS NRCD 5505/6 (2-disc set) and *Chants Soufis du Pakistan*, Inedit W 260003.

9. For examples of *shabad kirtan*, listen to *Gavo Sachi Bani*, Shabads by Singh Bandhu, NAVRAS NRCD 3507.

10. One bhajan of Tulsidas popularised by Pandit Bhimsen Joshi is *Raghuvar tum ko meri laaj...Tum to garib navaaj* ('Gharib Nawaaj' was a term of endearment for the Sufi master Khwaja Moinuddin Chishti).

11. *Hori khele Kanhayi, dekhi tori chaturai,*
    Sees mukut, hathan pichkari
    More angan hori khelan ayo.
    Bar-jori nahi re Kanhayi,
    Paniya bhari gagri mori giraayi.
    And a host of such short, lilting compositions use the Radha–Krishna story in a Sufi context. The best of these are recorded by the late 'Munshi' Raziuddin Ahmad of Karachi and his cousin, Manzoor

Niyazi, both descended from the *qawwals* of the shrine of Nizamuddin Awliya of Delhi.

12. Se Purna Das Baul, *Bauls of Bengal*, Cramworld EF A 641-2 and Baul Bishwa, *Sixth Sense*, (with CD Rom track) 3001822.

13. A good example of this is *Divinity* SONA RUPA, srcd 026, Music composed and arranged by Ashit Desai (instrumental only).

14. Although the term Wahhabi refers specifically to the brand of Islam practised in Saudi Arabia, nowadays it has become a sort of psycho-social phenomenon which transcends national boundaries and represents Islam as a militant and fundamentalist force devoid of any non-Arab cultural content. It has become particularly powerful among Pakistani Muslims living in Britain, perhaps more so than in Pakistan itself.

15. *Songs of the Sufi Mystics*, Programme 3, BBC World Service, 1997.

References

De Jong-Keesing. 1974. *Inayat Khan: A Biography*. The Hague: East-West Publications.

Farrell, G. 1997. *Indian Music and the West*. Oxford: Oxford University Press.

Khan, Inayat. 1991. Prologue to *A Sufi Message of Spiritual Liberty*, Vol. 2. *The Mysticism of Sound and Music*. Dorset: Element.

Nazareth, Peter. 1997. Elvis as Anthology. In *Search of Elvis*, (ed.) Vernon Chadwick. Colorado: Westview Press.

Siddiqi, Jameela. 2000. Pakistan/North India Qawwali/Folk: Songs of Praise. In *The Rough Guide to World Music*, Vol. 2. Harmondsworth: Penguin.

———. 2001. 'Interview with Abida Parveen'. In Sufi 51 (Autumn). London and New York: Khaniqaqhi Nimatullahi Publications.

Thielemann, S. 1999. *The Music of South Asia*. New Delhi: APH Publishing Corporation.

CHAPTER TWELVE

Dying the Good Death:
The Transfigurative Power of Bhakti

GRAHAM M. SCHWEIG

Introductory Remarks

A certain irony surrounds my contribution to the present volume that directly bears upon its content. Tamal Krishna Goswami, the scholar from whom this piece was originally solicited, has now himself become a significant part of the focus for this chapter's topic. For not only did he live his life in *bhakti* and for *bhakti*, but very recently, he died in *bhakti*, unable to complete his work on this subject.[1] Since I had known Goswami as a friend and colleague for many years, I consider it a privilege to present this chapter's theme, which he was so intent on writing. Although I make no pretence to write what he would have written, I have retained the words of his original chapter title in his honour. Tamal Krishna Goswami's desire was to explore death and dying within the *bhakti* practice, particularly as viewed by the Chaitanyite Vaishnava tradition and its modern manifestation as the worldwide Krishna movement, known as the International Society for Krishna Consciousness (ISKCON), the tradition out of which he came and was himself a leading member.

It will be clear from the words that are to follow, Goswami's interests in this topic have guided me in my own discussion of the theme, as I draw primarily from both traditional and modern Chaitanyite sources.[2] I will examine two fundamental questions that arise when reviewing the theme of death in relation to *bhakti*. The first question that Goswami was inevitably to address in his presentation, is the process of dying within *bhakti* as compared with death in the greater pan-Hindu context. How conceptions of death in *bhakti* differentiate sharply from, and yet, at least partially, share similarities with the wider Hindu context is problematic. This interesting question raises the second deeper one: the extent to which human effort and volition are involved in *bhakti;* the extent to which divine grace and supreme will influence *bhakti;* and the power that each has at the time of death and in one's salvation. To address these questions, I will begin by examining Goswami's interest in the present topic, and then move to some prominent scholars' observations.

A Bhakta's Encounters with Death

Tamal Krishna Goswami, who was western born, became formally initiated into the practice and way of life of a *bhakta*, or devotee, in the Chaitanyite Vaishnava tradition, as a very young man in the late 1960s. Just a few years later, he accepted the vow of *sanyasa* (the renunciation vows of a monk) and, as a leading and intimate disciple of A.C. Bhaktivedanta Swami Prabhupada (founder-teacher of the Krishna movement), took on hundreds of his own disciples around the world after the departure of his *guru*. Naturally, the longer he lived his life of devotion, the more he encountered *bhaktas* dear to him facing the end of their earthly lives.

It was specifically the deaths, however, of two persons that inspired Goswami to address the theme of death in his own scholarly and devotional work.[3] As a disciple, Goswami experienced his own *guru's* departure, and as a *guru* Goswami experienced his own disciple's departure. The former represents the traditional as well as *bhakti* model in many respects, and the latter represents a transformation of the traditional ideal. To appreciate these two significant encounters with death in the life of Goswami, some brief biographical background is required.

Goswami was intimately involved in taking care of his *guru* during his final months of progressing towards death. Being very moved by his *guru's* passing away (in 1977) at the age of eighty-two in Vrindavan, India, Goswami recorded the event in the form of a drama entitled *Prabhupada Antya-Lila: The Final Pastimes of Shrila Prabhupada* (1988).[4] The departure of Goswami's *guru* exemplifies the most desirable way for the *bhakta* to leave this world: to die in the holiest of pilgrimage places, surrounded by loving devotees singing the praises of God.[5] In many ways, the death of Goswami's *guru* typifies the pan-Hindu ideal for dying, such as reaching the full term of one's life and choosing to die in a holy city that awards liberation. However, the meaning of his *guru's* death goes deeper than this traditional Hindu perspective. The story of the death of his own disciple revealed a new understanding of the end-of-life process for Goswami.

After his dear disciple, Kirtida dasi, passed away a few years ago in Dallas, Texas, at the age of sixty-one, Tamal Krishna Goswami was inspired to begin writing this very chapter on the nature of death and dying, reflecting upon her example of Vaishnava behaviour during her encounter with the death process.[6] Goswami's project, as I understand it from the few pages of notes that he left, was to understand how *bhakti* practice allows the *bhakta* to die the 'good death', despite external circumstances in which a *bhakta* might find him or herself. According to Goswami, the theme of death for devotees or *bhaktas* outside of India exposes the tensions of traditional practices cast in an urban, western setting. This topic for Goswami is a further development of some of his previous work.[7]

Goswami states his intentions clearly in his rough draft, in the following words:

Using the narrative frame of this special Vaishnavi's final days, this chapter examines the ways in which *bhakti* allows a devotee the means to die the 'good death'.

A conflict is established in Goswami's piece: Kirtida's death was 'self-willed', but it was willed away from the traditional *tirthas* or holy places of India to a western devotional setting. My focus also is on the non-conventional, yet feasible arrangements for death within *bhakti*, and on the unique divine arrangements for the *bhakta*, who is exempt, I will argue, from traditional expectations surrounding the death process, due to the transfigurative power of *bhakti*. I am especially interested in how the procedure for dying in *bhakti*, while projecting an ideal way to die, is not required to conform to traditional demands for dying 'the good death'. For the *bhakta*, even the qualification of 'self-willing' one's death is ultimately not what is valued; rather, it is the will of God or the 'God-willing' of one's death that ultimately constitutes the 'good death'. The very nature of the *bhakti* path is to transform the soul from an intrinsically egocentric orientation to that of an utterly theocentric orientation, and this distinction is what separates *bhakti* from other paths or approaches to liberation.[8]

What Is the 'Good' Death?

Tamal Krishna Goswami's wording for the title of this chapter, interestingly, is not entirely his own. His title both mirrors and contrasts the title of the book, *Dying the Good Death: The Pilgrimage to Die in India's Holy City* (Justice 1997), which focusses its discussion on the more general Hindu process of dying in the holy city of Banaras. Justice's book describes the Hindu ideal for dying, satisfied by a life reaching its natural duration and term into old age, and the bringing of the *rogi* (the dying or sick person) to the holy city of Banaras where, after death, one's soul is guaranteed release (*mukti* or *moksha*) from the endless cycle of birth and death (*samsara*).

According to the pan-Hindu conception, life is a total life-cycle involving four phases or *ashramas*. The first quarter of one's life is spent as a student, preparing to enter the world. The second is the phase of marriage, in which one is very much engaged in the world within a general type of work, or *varna*. These *varnas* are also of four types—the educators of society who are in teaching or priestly occupations; those who assume governing and law-making positions as leaders of society; those engaged in trade and business, and agriculture; and the various types of labourers who support the other three *varnas*. The third phase of life involves the gradual pulling away or retreating from worldly activities that were established in the second phase, into a phase of retirement. These first three *ashramas* of the Hindu life-cycle for people in the West would probably seem quite natural; however, it is the fourth and final phase of renunciation that would most likely challenge the westerner.

The ancient Hindu mind insists that at this stage of life, one must prepare for the journey of death by practising a comprehensive withdrawal from the world in which one has been so involved. At this stage, a man will often leave his wife and family, even his surrounding community, and wander as an ascetic or mendicant, focussing on the ultimate reality to which he expects to return at the time of death. This fourth phase is a kind of preliminary death to death itself, in which a person is to die to the life one has known, for the purpose of practising and fully preparing for the death experience. One will often situate oneself at a place of pilgrimage or in a holy city, where one will abandon society in order to become permanently free from the cycle of birth and death. Indeed, this stage is considered so essential that if it is not successfully pursued, one's death effectively becomes the undesirable preliminary stage of rebirth back into this world to begin the life-cycle all over again, within another human or even subhuman body.

The ultimate goal of much Hindu life and practice is to become eternally free from this birth–death cycle. Human life is intended to be a preparation for the inevitable journey of death; a journey, if not to a lower birth due to the karmic results of sinful actions, then to either a higher birth within this world, or to the perfection of eternal release from it. The last quarter of one's life is an adjustment period designed to help one consciously prepare for dying from the world. For the general Hindu, a 'good' death must meet specific qualifications, i.e. there are certain circumstances to be expected and particular processes to be pursued as departure approaches; there are auspicious and inauspicious deaths, timely and untimely deaths.

Goswami's focus, however, was clearly different as the second part of his title indicates—his focus was to be upon 'the transfigurative power of *bhakti*'. For the *bhakta*, while there is emphasis placed on the end of life, there is much more importance placed on the quality of living throughout one's life, not just in terms of *karma* or 'action', but in terms of developing and fully absorbing oneself in pure devotion to God. Although the *bhakti* process accepts the life-cycle and the hierarchically arranged types of work within the worldly active phases of it, this life structure is only the outer superficial shell for the *bhakta*. The devotee is connected to the world only minimally and secondarily, while remaining primarily absorbed in devotion to God, and the identity of the devotee follows this dual involvement:

> Even while engaged in worldly activities, devotional love can be achieved by hearing and praising the divine attributes of the Beloved Lord.
>
> Upon reaching this fulfillment, worldly activities should not be relinquished—rather, the fruits of such activities should be relinquished, while prescribed practices of devotional love must certainly continue.[9] (*The Bhakti Sutra*, Texts 37, 62)

Therefore, the higher value, the higher identity and the inner life of the *bhakta*—all allow the *bhakta* to be engaged in worldly affairs, to be detached from such affairs, and to be devotionally absorbed, simultaneously. Death is not an isolated incident at the end of one's life for which the *bhakta* is preparing; nor is death any concern whatsoever, once the *bhakta* is absorbed in loving service to the deity, for such devotees claim they have already attained the eternal state of deathlessness.

The devotee, at one level, is dead to the world, since his or her heart is no longer invested in the temporary pleasures and identities of this world. The *bhakta*, however, is also active in the world, all the while deeply fixing the mind and heart on God. *Bhakti*, unlike other paths from which practitioners seek the more self-centred enterprise of escaping from the world of suffering, is self-disinterested and thus, solely theocentrically interested. The *bhakta* is only concerned about loving service to the Lord, no matter where it may take place, in this world or the next. The *Bhakti Sutra* tells us that 'the essential nature of devotional love is immortality' (Text 3); therefore, when *bhakti* or this process of devotional love is cultivated, 'one becomes immortal' (Text 4). Just what is this special transfigurative power of *bhakti*, and how does this power affect the process of dying as a *bhakta*? How much of a divergence is the *bhakti* process of death and dying from that of the wider Hindu tradition?

Bhakti traditions in general experience a disaccord between pan-Hindu principles of *dharma* and their own conceptions of *bhakti dharma*. Specifically, I will argue that the Chaitanyite tradition does not feel obligated to sustain ties with the pan-Hindu process, and puts forward a process that ultimately transcends any of the pan-Hindu requirements. This is possible because the very practice of *bhakti* is both intrinsically the means to liberation and itself constitutes liberation. Death, then, becomes merely a shift in location and does not consist of release or liberation from the world, as the *bhakta* has already been liberated from the world through his or her *seva* (loving service) to God. Furthermore, death can also be seen positively, as an opportunity to become more intimately connected to the deity. Indeed, the *bhakta* may even wish for or desire his or her own death out of a heightened sense of love for God:

For one whose love for God is very deep,
   it is not possible to withstand separation.
Therefore such an intensely loving person
   desires one's own death.[10] (*Chaitanya Charitamrita*, 3.4.62)

Thus, there is within the Chaitanyite vision of death, a distinctly opposing understanding from that of the greater Hindu complex out of which it arose. This tension could be described as death according to *karma* versus death according to *kripa*; i.e. death as a result of one's own actions, intentions and what one has earned (the traditional concept), in contrast to death as a result of attracting the grace of God, a special gift of release from this world back to the divine world (the Chaitanyite concept). Further, I propose that the *bhakti* vision supports a dual perspective of all life events and this would apply to the final event of life as well—a vision which includes the outer world involving external action, *karma*, but only as it exists in relation to the internal world of the devotee, which is governed by grace.

The Good Death and the Bad Death

Conceptions of transmigration and the afterlife are complex within Indic religions. While there is no unifying sense of the afterlife that is shared by all Hindu traditions, the ancient burial rites and practices in India are consistent, implying some basic themes. These funeral rites find their source in Vedic practices and have pervaded village India all the way up to the present. Gavin Flood states that such rites reveal general 'village level' ideas of the afterlife that contrast the model of reincarnation found in brahminical traditions, which I will explore below in the discussion from the Bhagavad Gita. Flood claims that

here the dead. go to an intermediate realm, the 'world of the ghosts' (*preta-loka*) and, once they have a complete body constructed through the *pinda* offerings, go into the realm of the ancestors or fathers (*pitr-loka*). (1996: 207–08)

The deceased have not departed in the total sense of having gone away; rather, they have shifted to a different region from which they are able to receive regularly performed offerings prepared by the living. Klaus Klostermaier also contrasts this village or Vedic model of the afterlife, i.e. the dead joining the realm of venerated ancestors without rebirth, with the variety of sectarian ideas of various heavens and hells to which the dead may go (1994: 189–92).[11]

There are many factors that play a part in understanding the nature of someone's death—the mental state or consciousness of the dying person, the age of the person, the arrangements or circumstances surrounding the death, the manner of the soul's departure through the orifices of the body, the place of the death, etc. Any of these factors are considered auspicious or inauspicious, according to how each meets the expectations of a particular view of the afterlife, as reviewed above. In his work, *Death in Banaras*, Jonathan Parry discusses the Hindu ideal of a 'good death' and a 'bad death' (1994: 158–66). The former term is translated as *akal mrityu* and the latter, *kal mrityu*. There are many elements that constitute a good death. A person ideally should be mentally prepared to depart. One should intentionally and consciously give oneself up to the process of dying, and a person's body should be fit to become a sacrifice by fasting unto death. A good death possesses the elements of predictability, control, proper arrangements, and mental and emotional resignation. If a person can also arrange for dying in a sacred city or by a holy river, surrounded by loved ones or even by saintly persons, at the end of one's natural life-span, then this is considered timely and auspicious.

A departure is considered untimely or inauspicious when there has been no intention of giving up the body. A premature death, i.e. dying before the anticipated life-span of a person has been fulfilled, suicidal death, and dying as a result of a violent act or accident are all considered untimely. Generally speaking, death that has taken a life by force or against one's will is regarded as inauspicious. Parry presents the term *akasmik mrityu* as meaning sudden, abrupt, or accidental death (ibid.: 163). A 'bad death' is one in which no 'control' has been exercised or in which the dying person has not participated in the end-of-life process, voluntarily releasing him or herself into the process, which is considered ideal (ibid.: 162). While Parry relates Madan's thinking that 'a good death is the product of a good life' (ibid.: 161), the question still remains how a good life can undo a bad death if the death has been untimely and inauspicious.

The scriptures of *bhakti*, on the other hand, recognise varying conceptions of the afterlife as representing different strata of the universe to which a soul can go. They also perceive different factors of preparedness and control involved in the dying process, but such factors are secondarily important and when applied, are done so only in the service of *bhakti*. This will be addressed further below. In contrast to the more general Hindu way, which makes definite distinctions between auspicious and inauspicious deaths, timely and untimely deaths, or self-willed and unwilled deaths, the *bhakta* does not concern him or herself with such distinctions. Devotional love of God, or *bhakti*, is the very sustenance of life for the *bhakta*. Death, however it comes, is merely the transition from the physical body and world in which the soul has been located, to another realm in which the soul will continue to be absorbed in loving service to God. While the circumstances of death are not important, they are also not entirely ignored. It will be observed that there are preferences for how one leaves one's mortal coil, but these preferences are only external considerations, albeit devotional.

Loving God as Immortality for the Soul

Key statements found in the verses of the Bhagavad Gita are relevant for the present discussion. The Gita presents death as a change for the eternal soul, as a transferring of the soul from one context to another, and not as annihilation of the soul. The following verse indicates this with an intriguing analogy:

Just as the embodied soul attains childhood,
   youth, or old age while in the body,
So the embodied acquires still another body—
   the wise are not bewildered by this.[12]

The Gita recognises the various naturally occurring alterations of the body throughout the normal life-cycle as a series of deaths throughout one's life, and compares this type of intra-bodily series of transformations or 'deaths' to the inter-bodily changes or deaths from one life to the next. Just as souls are generally not bewildered by these intra-bodily changes within the life-cycle, each transformation constituting a different type of body and each constituting the necessary step toward the next, so the learned soul is not disturbed by the inter-bodily transition from one life to the next.

By positing the externality of the soul, the tragic dimension of life, for the *bhakta*, is virtually eliminated. The soul is not dissolved into nothing at the end of this life; it is an eternal entity that experiences a succession of bodies associated with different births.[13] Krishna, in the Bhagavad Gita, explains just this to Arjuna—that the eternal soul is not worth grieving for, since in any case the soul will live on as it always has:

For one who is born, death is certain,
   and for one who dies, birth is certain.
Therefore, while inescapable in its design,
   you don't deserve to grieve. (Bhagavad Gita 2.27)

Krishna desires to console Arjuna on the battlefield of Kurukshetra where he is about to engage in battle with friends, teachers and relatives, all on the opposing side, by assuring him of the eternal nature of the soul:

There was never a time when I did not exist,
  nor you, nor all these kings,
And never shall there be a time
  when we shall ever cease to be. (ibid. 2.12)

Thus, *bhakti* recognises the soul who either experiences a continual series of births and rebirths in this world, or a permanent life beyond the repetitions of births and deaths in the material world, as a liberated being in the spiritual setting of Krishna's abode. To remain in the cycle of birth and rebirth involves, no doubt, much anxiety and hardship that is meant to move the soul toward an eternal life of no suffering, of pure blissfulness. The goal of much of Hindu religion is to be released from this cycle of *samsara* and to attain *moksha* at the time of death:

There are two passages from this world
  that are thought to be eternal:
  one is light and the other darkness.
By the former one does not return
  to the endless cycle of suffering, and
  by the latter one returns again. (ibid. 8.26)

Krishna claims that the *dharma* of *bhakti* is required for escape from the world of birth and death:

Persons who are without faith
  in this *dharma*, O Arjuna,
  destroyer of the enemy,
Having not attained me,
  are reborn into the cycle
  of the transmigratory path of death.

For those whose intelligence is engaged,
  giving up the results
  born of action (*karma*),
Such wise souls are freed

from the bondage of birth
and they go to the place
that is free from suffering. (ibid. 9.3; 2.51)

The Gita, as the earliest philosophical formulation of *bhakti*, presents not only some of the basic tenets surrounding the theme of death and the afterlife, but a bridging of Hindu folk religious, brahminical and *bhakti* conceptions of the soul and death. The soteriological statement of the following verse demonstrates this synthetic quality of the Gita:

Those who are devoted to the gods, go to the gods;
   those who are devoted to the ancestors, go to the ancestors.
Those who sacrifice for the spirits, go to the spirits;
   but those who sacrifice for me, come to me. (ibid. 9.25)

The *bhakta*, however, is not entirely disinterested in attaining the gods, ancestors or spirits. In the more developed Bhakti formulation this is apparent:

Conversing with one another with choked voices, elated with bodily ripplings of bliss, with tears flowing, these single-minded devotees purify their own families and the whole world.

Their forefathers rejoice, the gods dance, and the world becomes protected by such single-minded devotees. (*Bhakti Sutra* 68, 71)

The *bhakti* traditions establish the deity of Krishna as the ultimate being among all deities, the supremely powerful deity who has the capacity above all other divinities to carry the soul beyond the world of birth and death. The soul cannot reach the ultimate unless it worships the ultimate. When a soul adores a higher deity or departed being, the soul attains what it worships, but only temporarily. Krishna declares the relationship between worship offered directly to him and worship offered indirectly to him through other divinities:

Even those who sacrifice, who are devoted
   to the worship of other divinities, who are filled with faith,
O son of Kunti, they also sacrifice to me,
   though not according to my injunctions.
For I am the enjoyer
   and indeed the master of all sacrifices.
But they do not know this truth about me—
   therefore they fall down. (Bhagavad Gita 9.23–24)

Devotion to the supreme not only allows the soul to attain the Supreme, but to do so permanently, from that point on:

Once having attained me,
   taking birth again in this place
   of suffering and impermanence
Does not occur for great souls,
   because they have achieved.
   the highest perfection. (ibid. 8.15)

Therefore, the *bhakta* desires only the deity of Krishna who establishes himself as the Lord of all sacrifices, the source of all universes, and the dearest friend of all souls:

As the enjoyer of all sacrifices and austerities,
   as the supreme power of all worlds,
As the dear friend of all beings;
   knowing me in these ways, one attains peace. (ibid. 5.29)

Next, I will review how the soul can attain immortality and this eternal residence with God through *bhakti*.

Death Conquered by Absorption in the Supreme

The principle of utter absorption, or *samadhi*, in the devotional love for God is the highest state of consciousness for the *bhakta*.

The Gita prescribes such absorption in order to reach the Supreme at the time of death:

> Be absorbed in thinking of me,
>   be devoted to me,
>   sacrifice everything for me,
>   and bow down to me.
> Truly you will come to me—
>   I promise you this,
>   for you are very dear to me. (Bhagavad Gita 18.65)

In earlier stages of devotion, more concentrated effort is required in order to bring the mind under control:

> Therefore, at all times,
>   you must struggle
>   and remember me.
> With the mind and intelligence
>   fixed upon me,
>   you will surely come to me—
>   of this there is no doubt. (ibid. 8.7)

So emphatic is the Gita regarding this absorption, that one finds the first half of the following verse to be identical with the first half of the verse quoted earlier in this section (18.65):

> Be absorbed in thinking of me,
>   be devoted to me,
>   sacrifice everything for me,
>   and bow down to me,
> You will certainly come to me,
>   having engaged
>   your very self completely
>   in devotion to me. (ibid. 9.34)

It is clear from these verses that being absorbed in *bhakti* leads to union with God. It is also interesting to note that both the cause and result of being so devotionally absorbed is the same—singular and full attention directed to the Supreme. This absorption in *bhakti* is strongly emphasised:

> For devotional love is cultivated by uninterrupted, constant worship of the Beloved.
> The Beloved Lord alone should be lovingly worshipped at all times, with all one's heart, without any other thoughts and concerns.
> Having attained this devotional love, one sees, one hears, one speaks, and one thinks only of the Beloved. (*Bhakti Sutras* 36, 79, 55)

Once obtaining such an elevated state of devotion, the *bhakta* joins the Supreme upon departure from this world:

> Those who know me as the supreme Lord,
>   as well as the supreme being
>   and the Lord of sacrifice,
> They will truly know me
>   even at the time of death,
>   being fully mindful of me.
>
> And at the end of one's time, indeed,
>   having relinquished the body
>   while remembering me,
> One who departs,
>   goes to my state of being—
>   there is no doubt about this (Bhagavad Gita 7.30, 8.5).

Thus, it is the way of life that determines the outcome of death for the *bhakta*, who, unlike the practitioner within the pan-Hindu context, does not consider the cause, time and place of death, and other such externals. Death is conquered by the *bhakta* through complete absorption in the beloved object. At such an advanced stage of devotion, there is no concern for escaping from the world of repeated birth and rebirth, since there is no fear or apprehension of remaining in the world:

> If one receives a vision of Krishna
>   or the grace of Krishna,
> One then gives up the desire for liberation
>   and by worshipping his divine attributes,
>   one attains Krishna's feet.[15] (*Chaitanya Charitamrita* 2.24.127)

For such a soul, there is simply no anxiety about what happens at the time of death. Indeed, there is no self-concern whatsoever— there is only selfless love and service to God, *bhakti*.

Grace of the Deity and Devotee

In *bhakti*, the devotee has already died to the world as a place for selfish interests and enjoyments, through the initiation process given by the spiritual master, or *guru*. While the parents provide for the physical birth of a soul, the *guru* provides for the spiritual second birth. An initiatory ceremony is held for the young male teen, as one of the several *samskaras* or rites of passage in pan-Hindu practice, which constitutes a furtherance of this life-cycle system of birth and rebirth. Far more important for the *bhakta*, however, is the initiation into the eternal life practices of *bhakti*, awarded by the *guru* or spiritual preceptor coming from within the *parampara* (succession of teachers originating with the supreme *guru* himself, the Lord), who becomes accessible to the *bhakta* through divine grace:

> The grace of great souls can be achieved only by the grace of the Beloved.
>
> For there is no difference between the grace of the Beloved and the grace of these great souls. (*Bhakti Sutras* 40, 41)

The significance of the general principle of the *bhakta* receiving the blessings of saintly devotees cannot be over-emphasised, since this

is perceived as the key factor in attaining an eternal life of devotion
within this life:

> Primarily, however, devotional love is cultivated by the
> grace of great souls, or by a fraction of the grace of the
> Beloved Lord.
>
> Connection with great souls is difficult to attain, yet its effects
> are incomprehensible and infallible.
>
> One therefore must strive for connection with great souls—
> one must strive only for the grace of great souls. (ibid. 38, 39,
> 42)

The grace of God and the grace of the *guru* are stressed
repeatedly by the tradition. This powerful element of grace is
eloquently described in verses like the following, praising the *guru:*

> By the grace of *guru* comes the grace of God—
>   without the grace of *guru* one certainly
>   does not achieve the means to success.
> Contemplating and praising my glorious master
>   during the three propitious moments of the day,
>   I worship the lotus feet of such a *guru.*[16] (*Gurvashtakam* verse 8)

So potent is contact with the saintly devotee or *guru* that it can
award all liberation:

> Contact with a saintly devotee,
>   contact with a saintly devotee!
>   It is thus stated in all scriptures—
> Just one moment of contact
>   with a saintly devotee
>   grants all perfection. (*Chaitanya Charitamrita* 2:22:54)

The relationship of *guru* to the Lord is explained by the following
words:

The *guru*, an abundant rain cloud
     drawing from an ocean of divine qualities,
     pours down rains of compassion
Upon the raging fire of endless suffering,
     delivering afflicted people of this world—
     I worship the lotus feet of such a *guru*. (*Gurvashtakam* verse 1)

This verse offers a vivid metaphor of a 'raging fire' of suffering that only a rain cloud can put out. No human effort can put out a raging forest fire; only by arrangements of natural higher powers that are mightier than our own is it possible. The *guru*, then, draws from the divine realm and delivers souls. That is the grace of the *guru*, according to this tradition.

Indeed, this grace of God and great souls empowers the *bhakta* in his or her devotion. It is a constituent part of the relationship with God in *bhakti*. One submits oneself in loving devotion to God and in turn God saves such a devoted soul from suffering, both having established an indissoluble eternal connection:

As all souls submit themselves to me,
     accordingly, I reciprocate
     lovingly with them.
In every way,
     humans follow my path,
     O son of Pritha. (Bhagavad Gita 4.11).

This reciprocal relationship in *bhakti* is observable in this famous verse from the Gita:

Completely giving up
     all purposes, *dharmas*,
     please accept me
     as your only shelter.
I shall cause you
     to be freed from all sin.
     Please do not grieve anymore. (ibid. 18.66)

In this verse, Krishna emphatically urges an unconditional loving surrender of the *bhakta*, involving the abandonment of all *dharmas*, or purposes, even though *dharma* is promoted throughout much of the Gita. The only true *dharma*, after all, is the shelter of Krishna, and this exclusive shelter is possible by complete renunciation of the world and its various purposes—that death itself demands of every soul. Now, therefore, I shall turn to the relationship between death and renunciation.

Death as Renunciation

After one receives the blessings of great devotees and is initiated into the practices of *bhakti* by the *guru*, this world suddenly becomes the arena for actions that are essentially non-different from those performed in the eternal abode of Krishna himself. Thus one has already died to this world while still existing within it. Moreover, the high level of absorption in *bhakti* is not thought to be an impediment to this minimal worldly involvement, since any such involvement is but part of one's devotional offering and sacrifice in *bhakti*:

> One need not worry about the failures of this world, having surrendered unto the Beloved one's very self, worldly duties, and obligations prescribed in the revealed scriptures. (*Bhakti Sutras* 61)

For the *bhakta* who has developed egalitarian vision, the various identities and concerns of worldly achievements are simply of no interest:[17]

> Among these devotees, there are no distinctions based on social class, education, beauty, family status, wealth, livelihood and the rest. (ibid. 72)

Importantly, *bhakti* does not subscribe to ascetical austerities for the sake of achieving spiritual powers or wisdom, nor does *bhakti* subscribe to extreme levels of withdrawal from society normally associated with other more stoic types of renunciation. Rather, the renunciation of *bhakti* arises naturally, out of love. The *Bhakti Sutra* of Narada distinguishes between the love of *bhakti* and lust:

> Devotional love does not arise out of lust, since its intrinsic nature is that of renunciation. (ibid. 7)

Indeed, renunciation in *bhakti* is the result of loving God; the *bhakta* is simply disinterested in and detached from anything else, save and except the beloved Lord:

> In this renunciation, there is exclusive dedication to the Beloved and indifference towards all that opposed to devotional love.
> Exclusivity in devotional love entails giving up all other refuge and types of dependence. (ibid. 9, 10)

The *Bhakti Sutra* goes on to describe how the *bhakta* renounces or 'transcends' this world by serving saintly devotees and relinquishing connections with worldly persons:

> Who can transcend? Who can rise above the illusion of this world? One who gives up unfavourable connections, who instead serves those filled with deep devotional feeling, and who gives up self-centredness....One who lives in a solitary place, who uproots all attachment to mundane society, who becomes freed from the three underlying forces of nature, and who gives up desire for materialistic acquisition and security.[18] (ibid. 46, 47)

The result of such transcendence is that not only does the *bhakta* attain liberation, but the entire world also benefits:

> One who renounces all worldly activities and their rewards, and thereby becomes free from the dualities of this world.
> One who renounces even the injunctions of the revealed scriptures and attains pure, uninterrupted affection for the Beloved.

Indeed, such a person transcends all duality and helps the rest of the world to transcend. (ibid. 48–50)

Thus, renunciation is a natural by-product of absorption in *bhakti*, as the total life focus for the devotee becomes devotional love that is 'cultivated uninterrupted, constant worship of the Beloved' (ibid. 36). Now we shall turn to a particular story from the *Bhagavata* that poignantly illustrates how a soul may choose a path of renunciation that constitutes a form of death to this world, in order to give oneself fully to the process of *bhakti*.

The *Bhagavata's* Question on Death

All the stories, philosophical discourses and the exquisite poetry of the famous *Bhagavata* text are presented to address the question of how to prepare for death. The ultimate and authorial first voice of the work is understood to be that of Vyasa, the compiler of the Vedas. The work opens by introducing the voice of the general narrator, the sage Suta, as he addresses all the sages who are gathered in the Naimisha forest to hear him speak the outer narrative shell of the *Bhagavata* text. Within the concluding chapter of the first of twelve books, Suta narrates the story – which I will summarise here – in which the predominant narrative voice one hears throughout the *Bhagavata*, that of Shukadeva, is engaged.[19]

One day, a great king by the name Parikshit was hunting in the forest. After a while he became fatigued and began to search for a source of water. The king then came across an exalted sage by the name of Shameeka in his hermitage, appearing to be absorbed in deep meditation. The king requested water from the sage. He received no response due to the sage being in a meditative trance. The king felt resentful and angry, that he was not being formally received the way a king should be. Thus, on his way out of the hermitage, the king picked up a dead snake lying nearby with his bow and angrily placed it on the shoulder of the sage.

Meanwhile, Shringi, the powerful young Brahmin son of the sage, heard how the king had insulted his father. Shringi became infuriated, knowing that his father was virtually the king's master in the *dharmic* order of things, and therefore deserved to be treated respectfully. In anger, Shringi cursed the king: he would die of the poisonous bite of a snake-bird within seven days.

Shringi then returned to the hermitage of his father, crying out of grief. The crying awakened his father from his meditation. The father noticed the dead snake around his neck and casually threw it aside, asking his son why he was crying. On learning what had happened, the father lamented his immature son's having cursed the king for such a minor offence. Indeed, he felt that his son had committed a greatly sinful act by cursing the most highly regarded man in the kingdom; after all, the king was to be honoured and respected as the supreme Lord himself. The sage declared that he and his son would be held responsible for a multitude of sins that would result from the cursing to death of one who was known to be such a exalted *bhakta*, indeed a *rajarshi*, a 'saintly king'. The sage then prayed to the Lord to pardon his sinful son for acting so foolishly.

On his way back to the palace, the king was remorseful and felt that he deserved to be punished for committing the sin of not offering respect to the sage, who after all, was from the superior priestly order. In the mood of repentance, deeply regretting his act, when the king learned of the news of the curse, he accepted it as good news, since it would inspire his renunciation from the world. The king, having thus turned over the kingdom to his own son, sat down to mediate on the bank of the river Ganga. He knew that for one who is destined to die, taking shelter of such a holy river is advisable (*Bhagavata Purana* 1.19.6), and he decided to fast until death while meditating on Krishna.[20]

Soon, many sages arrived where the king was seated, now a place of pilgrimage. The king greeted these renowned personalities, requesting of them, 'Let the snake-bird bite me at once. I only desire that all of you continue reciting the glorious divine acts of Lord Vishnu' (ibid. 1.19.15). The king then inquired from the sages, 'What is the duty of one who is about to die?' (ibid. 1.19.24). Just then the saintly son of Vyasa, known as Shuka appeared, who was only sixteen years old and strikingly beautiful. The king offered praise to the youthful sage upon his arrival and made the following request:

> Therefore I am inquiring from you,
>   the greatest teacher of all yogis,
>   about ultimate perfection.
> In this world,
>   what should every person do
>   who is about to die?
>
> What therefore should a person hear,
>   what should a person speak,
>   what should be pérformed
>   by such persons, O Master?
> What should be remembered
>   or what should be worshipped?
> Please explain what should be done
>   or what should not be done. (ibid. 1.19.37–38)

The second book of the *Bhagavata* begins with words of praise for the king from the sage Shuka. The sage praised the king because he saw the king as a great devotee asking the most important question. One response to the king's question is, 'What use are so many years of life to a careless man if they are wasted in ignorance? It is better to have a short duration of life in this world if one utilises it for attaining life's perfection' (ibid. 2.1.12).

The *Bhagavata*, a Sanskrit text of 335 chapters, is comprised of stories illustrating the philosophy of *bhakti* along with philosophical discourse, and is considered by the Chaitanyite school to be a response to this essential question of what one is to do to prepare for death. Of the twelve books forming the *Bhagavata*, the most important is the tenth and longest book (comprised of ninety chapters), especially the earlier chapters famed for the stories of Krishna's childhood *lilas*, or 'divine revelation dramas'. Among these, the story of the Rasa Lila, 'the *lila* of the wondrous circle dance of divine love,'[21] is the most honoured and worshipped episode of all. It is to this story that we shall now briefly turn, because it poetically expresses how love in *bhakti* conquers death, and further, it is viewed by Chaitanyites to be the highest meditation.

Death as Deepest Attraction to God

The early teachers of the Chaitanyite school of Vaishnavism, including Chaitanya himself, regard the personal intimate deity of Krishna, the beautiful blueish cowherd boy who plays the flute, as the ultimate deity of the godhead.[22] Krishna's *madhurya lilas* (*lilas* of sweetness) as a child and young boy in the idyllic setting of Vraja, are utterly adored by *bhaktas*.[23] The supreme Lord's eternally occurring intimate *lilas* consist of his playing the part of a mischievous child with his parents in the morning, frolicking around in the fields of Vraja with cows and his cowherd friends in the afternoon, and engaging in sweet amorous play with the cowherd girls in the evening. The cowherd maidens, known as the Vraja *gopikas* or simply the *gopis*, the heroines of the Rasa Lila story, are recognised by the tradition as the paradigmatic example of *bhakti*.[24] This five-chapter story that appears approximately one-third of the way through the ninety chapters of the tenth book, is understood as the 'the essence of all *lilas*' or the 'crown jewel of all *lilas*'.[25] It is believed that the Rasa Lila story is the ultimate vision of God and of devotion to the deity on which the *bhakta* is to meditate throughout one's life and certainly, therefore, at the time of death.

Aspects of the Rasa Lila story symbolise the transfigurative power of *bhakti*, for the relationship of the *bhakta* to the world and to death is a subtle but prominent theme in the story line. The *gopis'* departure from their homes represents death in this story, i.e. a shift from one body to another, the former being composed of material elements and the latter being of immortal spiritual essence. It also represents a threshold into an eternal blissful world of love, and removal from the temporary physical world of suffering. Let us observe this 'death' for the *gopis* as it begins to occur when they react to hearing Krishna's divine flute music, at the beginning of the Rasa Lila story:

> Seeing lotus flowers bloom
>   and the perfect circle of the moon,
> Beaming like the face of Ramá,
>   reddish as fresh saffron *kumkuma*,
> Seeing the forest coloured
>   by the moon's gentle rays,
> He began to make sweet music,
>   melting the hearts of
> fair maidens with beautiful eyes.[26] (*Bhagavata Purana* 10.29.4)

The *gopis* are so moved by their Beloved's alluring flute music, that they suddenly abandon their everyday lives, and hasten to join Krishna. In the next several verses, their passionate devotion and irresistible attraction is evident:

> Upon hearing that sweet music,
>   their passion for him swelling,
> The young women of Vraja whose
>   minds were captured by Krishna,
> Unaware of one another,
>   ran off towards the place
> Where their Beloved was waiting,
>   with their earrings swinging wildly.[27]

Some left abruptly
  while milking the cow—
  due to excitement
  the milking had ceased.
Some left the milk
  as it boiled over,
  others departed
  with cakes on the hearth.

Some suddenly stopped
  dressing themselves,
  others no longer
  fed children their milk.
Some left their husbands
  without being served,
  others while eating
  abandoned their meals.

Some were massaging
  their bodies with oils,
  or cleansing themselves,
  others applying ointment to their eyes;
Their garments
  and ornaments in utter disarray,
  they hastened
  to be with Krishna.

Their husbands,
  fathers, brothers—
  all relatives endeavoured
  to detain them.
Since their hearts
  had been stolen by Govinda (Krishna),
  they who were entranced
  did not turn back.[28]

Those *gopis* who could not abandon their everyday lives by physically or externally departing, were also successful in giving up their lives through the internal yogic means of deep and devotional inner contemplation:

Some Gopis,
  unable to leave,
  had gone inside their homes.
With closed eyes,
  fully absorbed in love,
  they meditated upon Krishna.

The intense burning
  of unbearable separation
  from their dearest Beloved
  disrupted all inauspiciousness.
Due to the joy
  of embracing Achyuta (Krishna)
  attained through meditation,
  even their worldly happiness was lost.[29]

To enter this world of their Lord, either externally or internally, the bodies of the *gopis* were abandoned, effectively constituting a kind of death. This death represents a release of these souls to the eternal realm of God, born of their passionate love for Krishna:

Though he is the supreme Soul,
  still they knew him
  intimately as their lover.
They relinquished their bodies
  composed of material elements,
  and any worldly bondage
  was instantly destroyed. (*Bhagavata Purana* 10.29.4–11)

Death can be compared to the *gopis'* departure from their homes, which suddenly disrupted, in fact ceased vital *dharmic* activities, such as feeding infants, serving husbands their meals, milking cows, etc. The *gopis*, the ideal *bhaktas*, 'deserted their bodies composed of material elements' and arrived in the forest, one must infer, in bodies more suitable for meeting their Beloved. The tradition understands this new body for each of the *gopis* as the spiritual, perfected body, *siddha-deha*, i.e. the body that a *bhakta* ultimately develops during the course of pursuing the process of *bhakti*.[30] It is in such a spiritual body that complete absorption becomes possible:

> Within the mind of one whose
>   own body is spiritually perfect,
> One contemplates day and night
>   the service of Krishna in Vraja.
> (*Chaitanya Charitamrita* 2:22:157)

It is important to note that the development of a spiritual body does not preclude the possibility of maintaining a physical body. In other words, it is possible, according to the tradition, to remain in this world while living in a spiritual body. This is illustrated in the Rasa Lila story by the *gopis* who, at the end of the episode, return to their homes.

For the Chaitanyites, meditation on the loving example of the *gopis* in the Rasa Lila enables the devotee to take on a spiritual form in which one is able to be intensely absorbed in devotion:

> One who hears or one who recites (the Rasa Lila)
>   the benefit for such a person is
> Full absorption in love,
>   serving (the Lord) day and night.

> What can be said of the benefit for such a person?
>   It is simply impossible to convey.
> Such a person is eternally perfect,
>   and such a person acquires a perfect body. (ibid. 3.5.49–50)

Furthermore, the result of hearing or describing the Rasa Lila is that one is purified of the disease of the heart:

> This is the divine play of Vishnu
>   with the fair maidens of Vraja.
> One who is filled with faith,
>   who hears or describes this play,
> Having regained the highest
>   devotion for the Beloved Lord,
> Has lust, the disease of the heart,
>   quickly removed without delay;
>   such a person is peaceful and wise.

Such a soul then becomes qualified to go to Krishna's highest heaven to perform loving service to God along with other perfected souls, such as the *gopis*.

Love as Stronger than Death

If there is one principle of *bhakti* that describes its very foundation, it would be this: it is love at its highest level, in its unremitting, purest state. It is utterly devotional desire to please the deity that lifts the *bhakta* from this world, even while still living in it:

> Not wealth, nor followers, nor romance,
>   nor meritorious results do I desire,
>   O Lord of the universe.
> Please bestow upon me, birth after birth,
>   selfless devotional love unto you,
>   the beloved supreme Lord.[31] (*Chaitanya Charitamrita* 3:20:29)

In this verse, allegedly written by Chaitanya himself, it is clear that the *bhakta* who experiences such an elevated state of devotion, is completely disinterested in worldly achievements of all kinds. Furthermore, the *bhakta* is not concerned with a good or bad death, or with escaping *samsara*, since he or she is absorbed in devotional love that overpowers death. In the biblical 'Song of Songs' (8.4), it is stated that 'love is as strong as death'. In *bhakti*, however, it is clear that love is indeed stronger than death, as it carries the soul beyond the death event, even prior to death in the embodied state.

The development of the *bhakti* doctrine reveals a trend towards more and more reliance upon God's will and divine grace for the results or achievements in *bhakti*. While the Gita attempts to break away from *karma* or human effort in salvation, later developments in *bhakti* rely upon grace to an even greater degree, as demonstrated in the *Bhakti Sutra* of Narada and the Chaitanyite sources. This doctrinal trend toward divine grace does not necessarily reduce human responsibility; rather, it acknowledges that the *bhakta* is ultimately and utterly dependent on a gracious and compassionate deity for salvation. Although devotees certainly must strive to serve and love God, depending upon results arising from the human will is antithetical to the *bhakti* process. Indeed, without the grace of God and saintly devotees, no progress can be made.

Krishna reciprocates the love of his devotee, who is instructed to seek contact with saintly devotees and give up worldly connections, etc. It is reassuring for the *bhakta* to know that any involvement in *bhakti* practices, no matter how minimal, is understood as having inestimable value and power for attracting God's grace. In spite of such inconceivable grace, the *bhakta* who has not yet developed full faith in the salvific power of the *bhakti* process, may still exhibit some preoccupation for what is 'auspicious' and 'inauspicious' in regard to death—residual thinking from the pan-Hindu religion. Such concepts can be imposed upon the pure practice of *bhakti*, as can be observed in the following words eulogising the passing on of Tamal Krishna Goswami:

> The car toppled in the region of Phuliyagrama, a sacred area associated with the great saint Haridasa Thakura...

...The car accident occurred on the holy disappearance day of both Gaura-kishora Dasa Babaji and Rasikananda Prabhu, two important spiritual masters in the line of Lord Chaitanya, and it was around 5:00 a.m., and auspicious time of day. It was as if the Lord Himself had orchestrated a suitable place and time for his servant to pass from this world. 'Dying the Good Death' would be TKG's final project while in his bodily form. Though he hadn't finished writing it, he had clearly achieved it.[32]

Clearly, devotees of the Chaitanyite Vaishnava path, then, may have a tendency to look for 'auspicious' signs that surround the circumstances or occurrences of a particular death, perhaps due to their own need for comfort or divine assurance. It surely must have comforted all who loved Goswami to know that just before he departed from this world, he had been in a joyful gathering of many of his dearest devotional colleagues from all over the world, who had assembled for two weeks in the holy city of Mayapura, West Bengal. The funerary rites were promptly and lovingly performed by and among the same colleagues in the beautiful setting of a grand temple.

The danger exists, however, in eclipsing the transfigurative power of *bhakti* by unnecessarily falling back into pan-Hindu attitudes towards the good death, involving *karma* or action-determined outcomes. From the surface, Goswami's death can easily appear to be less than ideal; after all, his departure happened ostensibly as the result of an automobile accident; he had not lived out the full term of his natural life, as he was in his mid fifties; and, he was on the verge of completing his doctoral degree at Cambridge University. All of these factors, however, both positive and negative, are simply irrelevant from the Vaishnava perspective. The words of Goswami's own *guru* confirm this point:

However, for the pure devotee in Krishna consciousness, there is no fear of returning, whether he leaves the body at an auspicious or inauspicious moment, by accident or arrangement. (Prabhupada 1989: 441)

Furthermore, Bhaktivedanta Swami Prabhupada emphasises that the devotee is perfectly content to leave all arrangements for dying in the hands of his or her beloved Lord:

The unalloyed devotees of the Supreme Lord, who are totally surrendered souls, do not care when they leave their bodies or by what method. They leave everything in Krishna's hand and so easily and happily return to Godhead. (ibid. 440)

It is clear to those of us who knew Tamal Krishna Goswami, that he had already died to this world long ago, for he was a *bhakta:* someone who was deeply involved with the divine world of his Lord, yet moved about in this world to connect with the hearts of others. He had taken the vow of renunciation, but this too is external to the meditation of the *bhakta* who, as we have seen, has developed an internalised state of consciousness and absorption within the innermost devotional heart. He was engaged in meditating on the names of God from the earliest hours of the morning throughout the day, engrossed in loving service to his *guru*, to the saintly devotees and to God, and absorbed in the worship of the temple. He left behind a large community of loving devotees who will continue to bathe in the inspiration of his example of loving surrender to the *bhakti* process, for generations to come. He also made a significant contribution to theological scholarship in the doctoral dissertation he had just completed for Cambridge University. In spite of all that a *bhakta* leaves behind, there is nothing more painful in this world for those with whom such a devotee shares affection than the bereavement of the loss of a saintly person:

Chaitanya inquires,
  'What is the most miserable
  type of suffering among all types of suffering?'

Ramananda responds,
    'Separation from the devotee of Krishna—
    beyond this, I know of no greater suffering'.
    (*Chaitanya Charitamrita* 2.8.248)

My concluding thought is simply this: I am hopeful that we are now in a better position to ask the question, did Goswami die 'the good death'? Goswami's death was neither a 'death' in the normal sense, nor was it 'good' or 'bad', since his death went beyond these considerations to a realm of pure love and grace. Although the deep sense of loss is felt among so many, the element of tragedy does not apply here. Rather, the triumph of *bhakti* about which we have been speaking is the essential point. And it is this triumph of *bhakti* and its transfigurative power in which the devotee lives. Indeed, it is this triumph that is found in Krishna's loving promise to all *bhaktas* in the Bhagavad Gita (6.30):

One who sees me everywhere,
    and sees all things in me,
To such a person I am never lost,
    and such a person is never lost to me.

Notes

1. The term *bhakti* refers to the religious practices and experiences of devotional love in Indian traditions. Traditions within the Hindu religious complex that emphasise *bhakti* as their the primary or sole mode of salvation either relegate the other approaches of action, knowledge or yogic discipline as secondary processes, or reject these entirely in favour of devotion. For a historical and etymological analysis of the word *bhakti*, see Dhavamony (1971), and for the tradition's synthesis of the doctrinal and philosophical dimensions of *bhakti*, see my forthcoming (a) book, *The Bhakti Sutra: Concise Teachings of Narada on Devotional Love* [probable title], in Translations from the Asian Classics Series, forthcoming from Columbia University Press, New York. Moreover, the first traditional philosophical formulation

of *bhakti* can be found in the classic sacred text of India, the Bhagavad Gita.

2. Many scholars refer to the *bhakti* tradition that arose in Bengal in the sixteenth century with the appearance of the great *bhakti* ecstatic and revivalist, Krishna Chaitanya, by the name Bengal or Gaudiya Vaishnavism. These names, however, indicate the place from which the tradition arose rather than its founder, which I feel is a problem, since Bengal Vaishnavism is not limited to Bengal, but spread south to the state of Orissa and northwest to Uttar Pradesh and Rajasthan. In order to maintain consistency with the other major Vaishnava traditions that are named after their founders, and to avoid geographical inaccuracy, I have chosen to name this Vaishnava tradition after Chaitanya.

3. For an analysis and general treatment of the teachings of Goswami's *guru*, A.C. Bhaktivedanta Swami Prabhupada, on *karma*, death, and dying, see Baird (1986).

4. For the marvellous and comprehensive biographical account of Bhaktivedanta Swami Prabhupada, see Satsvarupadasa Goswami, *Srila Prabhupada-lilamrta*, volumes 1–6 (1980–83); see especially the chapter, 'The Final Lesson', volume 6, which narrates the events of the end of his life.

5. Vrindavan is the holiest place of pilgrimage for devotees of Vishnu, or Vaishnavas, who particularly focus upon the divine ultimate manifestation of the personal deity of Krishna. This rural village is known as the place of Krishna's birth and also the place where his divine acts or dramas, *lilas*, were re-enacted on this earth several millennia ago.

6. For the description of Kirtida's passing, see Sarvabhaumadasa (2002: 24–30). Tamal Krishna Goswami had asked his disciple to write an account for the Krishna movement's bimonthly magazine in her honour.

7. On the tensions of traditional Hindu practices in urban, western settings, see Tamal Krishna Goswami (1999).

8. The paths of *karma* (action), *jnana* (knowledge), and *yoga* (mental and physical discipline) all focus on some type of achievement for the self in its desire for liberation. On the other hand, India's religion of the heart – *bhakti* ('devotional love of God') – does not concern itself ultimately with liberation, but with fulfilling what it is that pleases God. This difference is discussed in some detail in *The Bhakti Sutra* text, particularly *sutra* texts 25–33.

9. All translations presented in this chapter from the text of *The Bhakti Sutra* of Narada are mine.

10. All translations presented in this chapter from this text are mine. For an English translation along with the original Bengali and Sanskrit text, see Krsnadasa Kaviraja Gosvami, *Sri Caitanya-caritamrta* (9 vols.), translated by A.C. Bhaktivedanta Swami Prabhupada. For an academic treatment and English translation of the text, see Edward C. Dimock, Jr., *Caitanya Caritamrta of Krsnadasa: A Translation and Commentary* (1999). Note that Dimock's English translation utilises a different numbering system for the verses than the first mentioned above. My translation here conforms to the numbering system of the first publication.

There are other verses in which death is considered a positive thing for devotion. See *Caitanya Caritamrta* 3.11.96 and 3.14.53. This desire for death on the part of the *bhakta* is clearly not suicidal; quite the contrary, it is out of ecstatic rapture that such a desire would arise.

11. For a very good overview of the ways devotional India agrees upon conceptions of *karma*, religious dying, and death, see Klostermaier (1986). Klostermaier attempts to observe arrangements on these themes among devotional Bhakti religion in India, including the views of various Vaishnava sects (e.g. like those established by Ramanuja, Madhva, Chaitanya et al.) and even more generally with devotionalists not associated with these Vaishnava sects.

12. Bhagavad Gita 2.13. All translations presented in this chapter from the text of the Bhagavad Gita are mine.

13. J.A.B. van Buitenen makes some fascinating observations about Indian classical drama that are germane to this discussion. The Indian classical theatre reveals much about the general world view of the Hindu towards death, which is foundational for understanding the *bhakti* attitudes towards death. Van Buitenen points out that it is significant to note the element of the 'tragic' is missing within Indian classical drama. In his chapter on 'The Classical Drama', in *The Literatures of India: An Introduction* (1974), he states the following: 'It is out of this *dharma*-oriented world view that the absence of tragedy in the Indian classical theatre can be explained. The playwright does not pit his character against a force that is bent on his defeat; he places him in a facsimile of the *dharmic* society and sets him on his way....It takes for granted the constant presence of other characters who likewise have their conscious places in life.

What conflict ensues is essentially *minor* conflict, adventitious to the proper order of things, and ultimately resolvable according to this proper order' (86). Earlier, van Buitenen states that the untragical character of Indian life and thought is due not only to its doctrine of transmigration, but due to a realistic sense of how death and life are intimately connected: 'Its governing doctrine that each individual has a continuing series of lives, with conditions in each one changing as a result of activities in previous ones, makes any single life merely an episode in the longer chain. No single life makes ultimate sense in itself, but the chain of lives does; and this chain, in turn, is contrasted to a higher condition of release from it all, to a reality outside it. Yet it is not entirely out of such high thought that the untragical character of the Indian drama is to be explained, but also out of a more direct view of life' (82–83).

14. Note how both the forefathers and the gods are satisfied by *bhakti*.

15. This verse clearly demonstrates the Chaitanyite disinterestedness in liberation, expressing the selflessness of love in *bhakti*. This later view contrasts with the earlier *bhakti* of the Bhagavad Gita in which the devotee desires liberation. For a description of the Chaitanyite vision of the Bhagavad Gita and this text's relationship to Chaitanyite *bhakti*, see my 'The Essential Meaning of the *Bhagavad Gita: According to Chaitanya Vaishnavism*' (2001).

16. Translations of *Gurvashtakam* are mine.

17. For a more in-depth discussion on the relation of this world to the world of the *bhakta* and the dual identity with the world and devotion, see Schweig 2002.

18. Note the expression here in the second *sutra* text: 'one who lives in a solitary place'. This phrase indicates a solitary state within society, not away from society, and thus does not represent the extreme stoicism found in other traditions within the Hindu complex. Again, the *bhakta* does not reject the world, but works within it in protective and disciplined ways.

19. The story that I am about to summarise here can be found in the *Bhagavata Purana* 1:19. Many translations of the *Bhagavata Purana* are available. The Bhaktivedanta Book Trust edition (20 vols.) has both Sanskrit text and transliteration, along with its translation and commentary in English, drawn from traditional commentarial sources, in addition to the original comments by A.C. Bhaktivedanta Swami Prabhupada.

20. All translations presented in this chapter from the text of the *Bhagavata Purana* are mine.

21. I am presenting an introduction to this famous story, as well as my translation of it along with critical notes, in my forthcoming (b) book tentatively titled, *Dance of Divine Love: The Rasa Lila of Krishna from the Bhagavata Purana*. My discussions and translations in this chapter related to this story are drawn from this book.

22. The Chaitanyite Vaishnava theology contrasts the commonly held view that Krishna comes from Vishnu. Chaitanyite theology holds that Vishnu comes from Krishna, despite the list of ten *avatars* ('divine descents of God') given in the *Bhagavata* and other places, which includes Krishna. For understanding the Chaitanyite school's thinking on this theological issue, see Schweig (Forthcoming (b)).

23. The ultimate aspect of the godhead and the highest form of the deity is this most intimate manifestation (*madhurya* or 'sweetness' aspect of the godhead) of Krishna, who plays a flute, and wears a peacock feather in his hair. It is from this most intimate form of Krishna that the powerful and majestic cosmic form (*aishvarya*, or 'supremely powerful' dimension of the deity) of Krishna as Vishnu is said to manifest; thus the ultimate form of the deity of Krishna is the most intimate. For a general treatment of Krishna's manifestations of *aishvarya* and *madhurya*, see Kinsley (1975).

24. In the *Bhakti Sutra* the only exemplars of *bhakti* presented, whose devotion is emphasised in this famous *sutra* text, are the *gopis*. See *The Bhakti Sutra* texts 20–24.

25. Several Vaishnava schools regard the Rasa Lila passage of the *Bhagavata Purana* as the highest expression of *bhakti*—Chaitanya, Vallabha and Radhavallabha schools.

26. Ramá is the Goddess Lakshmi, consort of Vishnu (Krishna's cosmic persona with a four-armed form). *Kumkuma* is vermillion, a brilliant deep reddish coloured powder. 'Fair maidens with beautiful eyes' refers to the cowherd heroines of the story, known as the *gopis*.

27. Vraja is the beautiful village of and surrounding rural area in central northern India, considered a divine manifestation of the highest spiritual heaven in this world. The name Krishna means 'the dark-complexioned one', or 'the divinely attractive one'. Krishna is the primary name of the beloved Lord, who is both supremely powerful and supremely intimate.

28. Govinda is a name for Krishna, meaning 'one who tends the cows'.

29. Achyuta is a name for Krishna, meaning 'the infallible one'.
30. The process of *bhakti* has two general phases. The first is *vaidhi bhakti* 'devotional love in the various forms of discipline'. *Raganuga bhakti* – devotional love following the *raga bhaktas*, or pure spontaneous associates of the Lord – is the second phase during which a spiritual body is said to develop. For a thorough treatment of *raganuga bhakti*, see Haberman (1988).
31. This is the fourth of the eight verses, known as the *Shikshashtakam*, believed to be the only known writing of Chaitanya himself. All eight verses are presented in the last section of this text.
32. See also Satyarajadasa's eloquent biographical eulogy for Goswami (2002: 19).

References

Baird, Robert D. 1986. Swami Bhaktivedanta: Karma, Rebirth and the Personal God. In *Karma and Rebirth: Post-Classical Developments*, (ed.) Ronald W. Neufeldt, 277–97. Albany: SUNY Press.

Dhavamony, Mariasusai. 1971. *Love of God According to Saiva Siddhanta: A Study in the Mysticism and Theology of Saivism*. Oxford: Oxford University Press.

Dimock, Edward C. (Jr.). 1999. *Caitanya Caritamrta of Krsnadasa: A Translation and Commentary*. Cambridge: Harvard University Press.

Flood, Gavin. 1996. *An Introduction to Hinduism*. Cambridge: Cambridge University Press.

Gosvami, Krsnadasa Kaviraja. 1957. *Sri Sri Caitanya Caritamrta*. With Amrta Pravaha-Bhasya. Commentary by Bhaktivinoda Thakura. Calcutta: Gaudiya Mission.

—. 1975–1996. *Sri Caitanya–Caritamrta*. Vols. 1–9 Trans. A.C. Bhaktivedanta Swami Prabhupada. Los Angeles: The Bhaktivedanta Book Trust.

Goswami, Satsvarupadasa. 1980–83. *Srila Prabhupada lilamrta*. Vols. 1–6. Los Angeles: The Bhaktivedanta Book Trust.

Goswami, Tamal Krishna. 1999. Being Hindu in North America: The Experience of a Western Convert. In *Religious Conversion: Contemporary Practices and Controversies*, (ed.) Christopher Lamb and M. Darrol Bryant, 278–86. London: Cassell.

Haberman, David L. 1988. *Acting as a Way of Salvation: A Study of Raganuga Bhakti Sadhana.* New York: Oxford University Press.

Justice, Christopher. 1997. *Dying the Good Death: The Pilgrimage to Die in India's Holy City.* Albany: SUNY Press.

Kinsley, David R. 1975. *The Sword and the Flute.* Berkeley: University of California Press.

Klostermaier, Klaus K. 1986. Contemporary Conceptions of Karma and Rebirth: Among North Indian Vaisnavas. In *Karma and Rebirth: Post Classical Developments,* (ed.) Ronald W. Neufeldt, 83–108. Albany: SUNY Press.

—. 1994. *A Survey of Hinduism.* 2nd edn. Albany: SUNY Press.

Parry, Jonathan. 1994. *Death in Banaras.* Cambridge: Cambridge University Press.

Prabhupada, Bhaktivedanta Swami. 1989. *Bhagwad Gita as it is.* Los Angeles: The Bhakti Vedanta Book Trust.

Sarvabhaumadasa. 2002. Where to Die? Is Vrindavana the Only Choice for Devotees of Lord Krishna? *Back to Godhead* (Jan–Feb): 24–30.

Satyarajadasa. 2002. You Can Know a Tree by its Fruits. In *Back to Godhead Magazine* (July/August): 19.

Schweig, Graham M. 2001. The Essential Meaning of the *Bhagvad Gita* According to Caitanya Vaishnavism. *Journal of Vaishnava Studies* 9, No. 2 (Spring).

—. 2002. Humility and Passion: A Caitanyite Vaishnava Ethics of Devotion. In *Journal of Religious Ethics* 30 (Fall).

—. 2004. Krishna: The Intimate Deity. In *The Hare Krishna Movement: The Post-Charismatic Fate of a Religious Transplant,* (eds.) Edwin F. Bryant and Maria Ekstiand. New York: Columbia University Press.

—. Forthcoming (a). *The Bhakti Sutra: Concise Teachings of Narada on Devotional Love* (tentative title). Translations from the Asian Classics series. New York: Columbia University Press.

—. Forthcoming (b). *Dance of Divine Love: The Rasa Lila of Krishna from the Bhagvata Purana* (tentative title). Princeton: Princeton University Press.

Van Buitenen, J.A.B. 1974. The Classical Drama. In *The Literatures of India: An Introduction,* (eds.) Edward C. Dimock et. al. Chicago: University of Chicago Press.

Vishvanatha Chakravartin: *Gurvashtakam.*

Notes on Contributors

John Brockington is Professor of Sanskrit in the School of Asian Studies (of which he was the first head) at the University of Edinburgh. He is the author of numerous articles for various journals, and the books, *The Sacred Thread: Hinduism in its Continuity and Diversity* (1981); *Righteous Rama* (1984); *Hinduism and Christianity* (1992); and *The Sanskrit Epics* (1998). His special area of research is the Sanskrit epics, and he is a member (previously Convenor) of the 'Ritual and Devotion' Research Group of DHIIR, as well as a member of its Advisory Council. He is also Secretary General of the International Association of Sanskrit Studies.

Winand Callewaert is Professor of Sanskrit and Hinduism at the Katholieke University Leuven, Belgium. He has been studying and working in India since 1965, holding degrees in Hindi, Sanskrit and Philosophy from Ranchi, Pune and Varanasi, and a Ph.D. and D.Lit. from Leuven. Besides numerous research articles he has published 19 books in English and Hindi, and 14 in Dutch. His most recent works include: *The Life and Works of Raidas* (with P. Friedlander) (1992); *The Sarvangi of Gopal Das* (1993); *According to Tradition: Hagiographical Writing in India* (with Rupert Snell, in *Khoj, A Series of Modern South Asian Studies* 5, eds. Monika Horstmann and Ali S. Asani, 1994); *Gods and Temples in South India* (1994); *Shri Guru Granth Sahib* (1996); *Ramcaritmanas* Word-index, (with Philip Lutgendorf) (1997); *Descriptive Bibliography of Allama Muhammad Iqbal* (with Dieter Taillieu and

Francis Laleman) (1999); *The Hagiographies of Anantadas*; *Banaras: Vision of a Living Ancient Tradition* (with Robert Schilder) (2000); *The Millennium Kabir-Vani* 1 (with Swapna Sharma and Dieter Taillieu) (2000). For the last eight years he has been working on a 5-volume dictionary (into modern Hindi and English) for *bhakti* literature.

Kate Crosby is lecturer in Buddhist Studies at the School of Oriental and African Studies, University of London, where she lectures on South and Southeastern Asian Buddhism and Pali in the Department for the Study of Religions. She is also co-director of Pali and Buddhist literature on the capacity building programme at the Buddhist Institute, Phnom Penh. She is author of a number of publications on Pali literature and Theravada Buddhist practice, including on so-called 'Tantric Theravada', i.e. the *yogavacara* meditation practices of Sri Lanka and Southeast Asia. Her particular research interests are medieval Pali language and literature. She is currently completely two monographs in this area, while recipient of an AHRB research leave award, one on Sri Lanka and Cambodian liturgical texts for meditation rituals, the other on the *Mahaparinibbanasutta* and its subsequent ramifications in Theravada practice. She also collaborates on Sanskrit Buddhist literature with Andrew Skilton. Their work includes a study and translation of Santideva's *Bodhicaryavatara* (1996), developed further in her recent Numata lectures in Buddhist Studies at McGill University.

Peter Flügel currently chairs the Centre of Jaina Studies in the Department of the Study of Religions at the School of Oriental and African Studies, University of London. By training he is a social anthropologist and specialises in the study of the contemporary Jaina mendicant traditions. Currently he is working on death rituals and the cult of relic *stupas* amongst contemporary Jains, and on Jaina law. He is the author of a number of research articles and of *Asceticism and Devotion: The Ritual System of the Terapanth*

Svetambara Jains (forthcoming); and, with G. Houtman, is co-editor of *Asceticism and Power in the Asian Context* (forthcoming). He is editor of the new Jaina Studies Series published by Routledge Curzon.

Ron Geaves is Professor of Religious Studies at Chester College. His main interest is the adaptation of subcontinent religious traditions in diaspora, but he has a long-standing personal and academic contact with a number of Sufis from several *tariqas* around the Muslim world. He has recently co-edited *Islam and the West post 9/11* (2004); and written *Aspects of Islam* (2005). He is the author of *The Sufis of Britain: An Exploration of Muslim Identity* (2000). Other recent publications include contributed chapters 'Sufism in Britain: Islamic Mysticism or Reinforcement of Cultural Identity', in *Islam in the Contemporary World*, ed. Theodore Gabriel (2000); 'The Haqqani Naqshbandis: A Case Study of Apocalyptic Millennialism within Islam', in *Faith in the Millenium* (2001); and 'Religion and Ethnicity: Community Formation in British Alevi Community', in *NUMEN* 50 (2003).

Anna S. King is Senior Lecturer in the Centre for Theology and Religious Studies, University College Winchester. She trained as a social anthropologist at the Institute of Social and Cultural Anthropology, Oxford University. Her research interests have focussed on the sacred city of Hardwar in North India and the Kumbha Mela. Her recent articles include 'ISKCON: A Society in Transition', in *Contemporary Spiritualities: Social and Religious Contexts*, ed. C. & J. Erricker (2001); 'The Guru-Disciple Relationship', in the *Journal of Vaishnava Studies* (2003); 'Dalit-Theology: A Theology of Outrage', in *Festschrift for Klans Klostermaier*, eds. W. Dupre, P. van der Velde et al. (in press). She is Convenor of the Oxford Spalding Symposium on Indian Religions, and editor of its forthcoming papers. She is also Chair of the 'Ritual and Devotion' Research Group of the DHIIR.

Julia Leslie was Reader in Hindu Studies, and Founder and Chair of the Centre for Gender and Religions Research in the Department of the Study of Religions at the School of Oriental and African Studies, University of London. As well as articles on classical Hinduism, law, gender, and Indian religions and culture, and a novel, her publications include: *The Perfect Wife: The Orthodox Hindu Woman According to the Stridharmapaddhati of Tryambakayajvan* (1989); *Roles and Rituals for Hindu Women,* ed. (1991, 1992); *Rules and Remedies in Classical Indian Law,* ed. (1991); *Myth and Mythmaking: Continuous Evolution in the Indian Tradition,* ed. (1996); and *Invented Identities: The Interplay of Gender, Religion and Politics in India* (co-editor with Mary McGee) (2001). Her most recent monograph, *Authority and Meaning in Indian Religions: Hinduism and the Case of Valmiki* (2003), is a study of the way in which myth and narrative have been used to construct scriptural authority and contemporary religious meaning, with particular reference to the Valmikis, an ex-'untouchable' religious community found in both Britain and India today. Before Julia died she was working on two further monographs. *The Pandit at Work* is a study of how an eighteenth-century scholar used the Sanskrit Ramayana to teach *dharma* at the court of a south Indian Hindu king. *Suicide and Self-Harm in India* brings together early Sanskrit narratives and urgent issues relating to contemporary Indian society in an attempt to illuminate both.

Eleanor Nesbitt is Reader in Religions and Education in the Institute of Education, University of Warwick, and has conducted ethnographic studies of religious nurture in Christian, Hindu and Sikh communities. Her publications include *Intercultural Education: Ethnographic and Religious Approaches* (2004); *Interfaith Pilgrims: Living Truths and Truthful Living* (2003); *The Religious Lives of Sikh Children: A Coventry Based Study* (2000); and *Hindu Children in Britain* (with Robert Jackson) (1993). Her book (written with Gopinder Kaur) *Guru Nanak* (1999) won the Shap Award for 2000.

Paula Richman is Irvin E. Houck Professor in the Humanities and Chair of the Department of Religion at Oberlin College in the United States. She has written widely in the areas of the Ramayana tradition in South Asia and Tamil religious literature. Some of her recent publications include *Extraordinary Child: Poems from a South Indian Devotional Genre* (1997); and 'Epic and State: Contesting Interpretations of the *Ramayana*' in *Public Culture* (1997). She also edited and contributed to *Many Ramayanas: The Diversity of a Narrative Tradition* (1991); and *Questioning Ramayanas, A South Asian Tradition* (2001). Her most recent publications include 'Why Can't a Shudra Perform Asceticism? Shambuka in Three Modern South Indian Plays', in *Ramayana Revisited*, ed. M. Bose (2004); and 'Shifting Terrain: Rama and Odysseus Meet in London', in *Journal of Vaishnava Studies* (2004). At present she is completing a study of retellings of *Ramkatha* in Tamil, in Madras, from 1929–1973, as well as a study of Ramayana performances in the United Kingdom, titled 'Ramayanas Abroad'.

Graham M. Schweig is Associate Professor of Religious Studies and Director of the Indic Studies Program at Christopher Newport University, near Virginia Beach in the United States. He did his graduate studies in Sanskrit and Indian studies at the University of Chicago and Harvard University, and he earned his doctorate in Comparative Religion from Harvard. He has contributed many articles for professional journals and encyclopaedias and various chapters of books, and he is a senior editor for the *Journal of Vaishnava Studies* and a series editor for Deepak Heritage Books. His forthcoming books present English translations and scholarly treatments of *bhakti* Sanskrit texts such as *Dance of Divine Love: The Rasa Lila of Krishna from the Bhagavata Purana* (2005); *Song of the Beloved Lord: Bhagavad Gita* (2005); and *The Bhakti*

Sutra: Concise Teachings of Narada on the Nature of Devotional Love (2006).

Jameela Siddiqi was born in Kenya of Indian parents and came to Britain as a refugee from Uganda in 1972. She studied English, History and Politics at Makerere University, Kampala and at the London School of Economics, and has worked as a television producer and broadcaster since 1976. She is a Sony Gold Award winner for her series *Songs of the Sufi Mystics* on BBC World Service Radio (1997) and was presenter of the highly acclaimed Radio 3 series *Nights of the Goddess*, featuring music from the Indian city of Mumbai. She has written extensively on classical Indian music, and has translated Urdu and Hindi poetry for a number of publications.

Index